HEALTH PROMOTION
for Persons with INTELLECTUAL and DEVELOPMENTAL DISABILITIES

HEALTH PROMOTION
for Persons with INTELLECTUAL and DEVELOPMENTAL DISABILITIES

The State of Scientific Evidence

Wendy M. Nehring
RN, PhD, FAAN, FAAMR, Editor

SPONSORS:
Agency for Healthcare Research and Quality
American Association on Mental Retardation
Centers for Disease Control and Prevention
Special Olympics International, Inc.

AMERICAN ASSOCIATION ON MENTAL RETARDATION
Washington, D.C.

Published by
American Association on Mental Retardation
444 North Capitol Street, NW, Suite 846
Washington, DC 20001-1512
www.aamr.org

The points of view herein are those of the authors and do not necessarily represent the official policy or opinion of the American Association on Mental Retardation. Publication does not imply endorsement by the editor, the association, or its individual members.

Library of Congress Cataloging-in-Publication Data

Health promotion for persons with intellectual/developmental disabilities : the state of scientific evidence / Wendy M. Nehring, editor ; sponsors, Agency for Healthcare Research and Quality ... [et al.].
     p. ; cm.
  Includes bibliographical references and index.
  ISBN 0-940898-91-8 (pbk. : alk. paper)
1. Health promotion—Congresses.
2. People with mental disabilities—Services for—Congresses. 3. People with mental disabilities—Research—Congresses.
[DNLM: 1. Disabled Persons—rehabilitation—Congresses. 2. Health Promotion—Congresses. 3. Health Services—Congresses. WB 320 H434 2005] I. Nehring, Wendy M., 1957- II. United States. Agency for Healthcare Research and Quality.

RA427.8.H4975 2005
362.2—dc22

2005021785

Additional Information that is required:
This publication was supported, in part, by the Department of Health and Human Services, Agency for Healthcare Research and Quality, Grant Number 1 R13 HS014731 and the Public Health Service, Centers for Disease Control and Prevention Grant Number C13/CCU323624-01. Its contents are solely the responsibility of the authors and do not necessarily represent the official views of the Agency for Healthcare Research or the Centers for Disease Control and Prevention.

Additional support was provided by Special Olympics International, Incorporated, 1133 19th Street, NW, Washington, DC 200236

To Neil, Pat, and Monica,

my cousins, my family—I love you!

and

To the researchers whose research findings

have and will positively impact all persons

with intellectual and developmental disabilities

to promote their optimal health

CONTENTS

CONTRIBUTORS

WENDY M. NEHRING, PhD, RN, FAAN,
FAAMR, Editor
Associate Dean for Academic Affairs,
Director of the Graduate Programs, and
Associate Professor
Rutgers, The State University of New Jersey
College of Nursing
Newark, NJ

LYNDA ANDERSON, MPH, MA
Doctoral Candidate
University of Minnesota
St. Paul, MN

DONNA BAINBRIDGE, PT, EdD, ATC
Director, Wellness Club
Rural Institute on Disabilities
University of Montana
Missoula, MT

LINDA BANDINI, PhD, RD
Associate Professor of Nutrition
Eunice Kennedy Shriver Center
University of Massachusetts Medical School
Waltham, MA
and
Boston University
Department of Health Sciences
Boston, MA

BETSEY A. BENSON, PhD, FAAMR
Nisonger Center
Ohio State University
Columbus, OH

STEPHEN B. CORBIN, DDS, MPH
Dean Special Olympics University
Special Olympics International
Washington, DC

JOSE F. CORDERO, MD, MPH
Assistant Surgeon General and Director
National Center on Birth Defects
and Developmental Disabilities
Center for Disease Control and Prevention
Department of Health and Human Resources
Atlanta, GA

DAVID L. COULTER, MD, FAAMR
Assistant Professor of Neurology
Harvard Medical School
Children's Hospital
Boston, MA

ROBERT DOLJANAC, PhD
Research Associate
Research and Training Center on
Community Living
University of Minnesota
Minneapolis, MN

CHRISTOPHER C. DRAHEIM, PhD
School of Kinesiology
University of Minnesota
Minneapolis, MN

JULIANA HUEREÑA
Assistant to Ms. Moore
Governor's Council Development Disabilities
Phoenix, AZ

S. BLYTHE HISS, MS
Research Assistant
Institute on Disability and Human Development
University of Illinois at Chicago
Chicago, IL

KATHLEEN HUMPHRIES, PhD
Research Associate
Rural Institute on Disabilities
University of Montana
Missoula, MT

EDWARD A. HURVITZ, MD
Associate Professor
Pediatric Physical Medicine and Rehabilitation
University of Michigan Health Systems
Ann Arbor, MI

SHERYL A. LARSON, PhD, FAAMR
Institute on Community Integration
University of Minnesota
Minneapolis, MN

MAUREEN A. LEFTON-GREIF, PhD, CCC/SLP
Johns Hopkins Children's Center
Baltimore, MD

PAULA M. MINIHAN, PhD, MPH
Assistant Professor of Family Medicine
and Community Health
Tufts University School of Medicine
Boston, MA

TERESA L. MOORE
Statewide Self-Advocacy Coalition
Project Manager
Governor's Council on Developmental
Disabilities
Phoenix, AZ

RUTH NORTHWAY, PhD, MSc, RNLD, ENB 805,
Cert Ed(FE)
Professor, Learning Disability Nursing
Unit for Development in Intellectual
Disabilities
School of Care Sciences
University of Glamorgan
Pontypridd, Wales

JAMES H. RIMMER, PhD
Director, National Center on Physical Activity
and Disability
Institute on Disability and Human Development
University of Illinois at Chicago
Chicago, IL

TOM SEEKINS, PhD
Director, Rural Institute on Disabilities
A Center for Excellence in Disability Education,
Research, and Services
University of Montana
Missoula, MT

JUSTINE JOAN SHEPPARD, PhD, CCC, BRS-S
Speech and Language Pathology and Audiology
Teachers College of Columbia University
New York, NY

RICHARD SOBSEY, PhD
Director, JP Das Developmental Disabilities
Centre
University of Alberta
Edmonton AB, Canada

MEG ANN TRACI, PhD
Director, Montana Disability and Health
Program
Rural Institute on Disabilities
University of Montana
Missoula, MT

SHERYL WHITE-SCOTT, MD, FACP, FAAMR
Director, St. Charles Developmental
Disabilities Program, SVCMC
Assistant Professor of Medicine, NYMC
Sister Thea Bowman
Brooklyn, NY

ACKNOWLEDGMENTS

The American Association on Mental Retardation (AAMR) is pleased to present *Health Promotion for Persons with Intellectual Developmental Disabilities: The State of Scientific Evidence.* Promoting good health and preventing primary, secondary and tertiary disabilities have long been priorities of our Association. We recognize that the quality of life experienced by individuals with intellectual and related developmental disabilities is often dependent on the availability of credible health information and accessibility to community health services offered by well-trained clinicians and practitioners. Accordingly, we strongly support moving swiftly ahead with a national health agenda for individuals with intellectual disabilities that includes disseminating research-based knowledge in understandable language, providing evidence-based health services in concert with individual needs and preferences, and advancing progressive health policy at all levels of government.

The challenges faced by individuals with disabilities in securing health care, as well as recommendations for change, were clearly presented in reports issued earlier this decade including the *Health Status of People with Mental Retardation* commissioned by Special Olympics Inc. and the 2002 Surgeon General's Report: *Closing the Gap: A National Blueprint to Improve the Health of Persons with Mental Retardation.* This AAMR book makes another major contribution to the expanding health care dialogue by clearly articulating the current depth and breadth of health science promotion research, while underscoring the need for more high quality information.

We are deeply indebted to Wendy M. Nehring for leading this effort and for stepping forward to serve as Editor of this essential research book. AAMR also wishes to express sincere appreciation to the many knowledgeable and outstanding contributors whose work reflects the current state-of-the-art and who have made a unique contribution to our field by establishing the baseline for health promotion research. Thank you Christopher Draheim, Linda Bandini, Joan Sheppard, Maureen Lefton-Grief, David Coulter, Betsey Benson, James Rimmer, Blythe Hiss, Sheryl Larson, Lynda Anderson, Robert Doljanac, Sheryl White-Scott, Richard Sobsey, Ruth Northway, Edward Hurvitz, Paula Minihan, Tom Seekins, Meg Ann Traci, Donna Bainbridge, Kathleen Humphries, Juliana Huerena, and Teresa Moore. Thank you one and all!

Health Promotion for Persons with Intellectual Developmental Disabilities: The State of Scientific Evidence and the preceding 2004 National Conference that led to this publication were made possible through the generous support of the Department of Health and Human Services (HHS), Public Health Service, Centers for Disease Control, National Center for Birth Defects and Developmental Disabilities; HHS the Agency for Healthcare Research and Quality; and Special Olympics International. We are deeply appreciative of their support and for the participation of Jose F. Cordero, Vincent A. Campbell, Edward M. Brann, Timothy Shriver, Stephen B. Corbin, and Courtney Pasterfield in this initiative. Your moral and financial support was invaluable. Thank you!

Knowledge is power and this book supports our collective power by providing us with credible information about what we know, what we do not know, and what we must do to promote good health among our constituency with intellectual disabilities. Our AAMR vision calls for a world where everyone will have optimal physical, mental, emotional, social, environmental, and spiritual well-being. AAMR is deeply committed to advancing that vision along in partnership with individuals with intellectual disabilities and the entire disability network. Working together we will achieve a better quality of life for all.

M. Doreen Croser
AAMR Executive Director

PREFACE

The members of the Health Promotion and Prevention Committee of the American Association of Mental Retardation (AAMR) determined in 2003 that a national conference was needed to address the state of the science regarding specific health promotion topics in persons with intellectual and developmental disabilities (I/DD). We are grateful for the ongoing work and support of the agencies that helped to fund this conference: Agency for Healthcare Research & Quality, Centers for Disease Control and Prevention, and Special Olympics, International. Individuals who also assisted to make this possible are Denise Dougherty of the Agency for Healthcare Research & Quality; Jose Cordero, Vince Campbell, and Ed Brann of the Centers for Disease Control and Prevention, National Center for Birth Defects and Developmental Disabilities; and Tim Shriver, Stephen Corbin, and Courtney Pasterfield of Special Olympics International. It is anticipated that the synthesized findings presented in this book of proceedings will influence health care practice, knowledge of current research, and public policy.

Purpose and Background for the National Conference and These Proceedings

Recent publications and conferences of national and international interest have stressed the need for research on interventions and solutions for eliminating the health disparities that exist for persons with I/DD. For the past decade, experts in the field of I/DD have identified the health concerns of people with I/DD and discussed the need for primary and secondary prevention, and for health promotion (cf., Horwitz, Kerker, Owens, & Zigler, 2000; Pope & Tarlov, 1991; U.S. Public Health Service, 2002). Specifically, experts in the field have strongly asserted the need for medical and dental school curricula to include content on primary conditions leading to I/DD, secondary conditions, and the outcomes of treatment of these conditions over time.

No comprehensive review and analysis exists, however, of the current literature and scientific evidence on health promotion issues as they relate to people with I/DD for researchers, educators, and clinicians to base curriculum or interventions. While standards of practice and federal practice guidelines (see *www.guideline.gov*) are available for the general population in this country, their applicability to persons with I/DD is largely untested. Among the over 1500 practice guidelines disseminated by the National Guideline Clearinghouse, only 4 are identified with the search word "mental retardation." The Cochrane Reviews (2005) lists no new and updated topics that concern persons with I/DD. In review of all of the titles in their review, there are 39 reviews specific to persons with I/DD, most having to do with the efficacy of medications. This lack of attention to the population of persons with I/DD is in sharp contrast to the research emphases of the U.S. Preventive Services Task Force that authored the *Guide to Clinical Preventive Services* (2nd ed., 1996), which provides periodic systematic scientific evidence reviews and recommendations for practice and ratings on a variety of preventive services topics (*www.preventiveservices.ahrq.gov*):

1. Identify effective and practice primary care interventions for modifying personal health practices of patients, especially around issues such as diet, exercise, alcohol, and drug use, and risky sexual behavior.

2. Clarify the optimal periodicity for certain screening tests and counseling interventions.

3. Identify practical ways to allow patients to share decision-making about preventive care, especially for services of possible but uncertain benefit.

4. Examine the most sensitive and efficient ways to identify high-risk groups who may need different services than the average population.

5. Expand the use of decision-analysis and cost-effectiveness analysis to help identify optimal use of clinical preventive services (Atkins & DiGuiseppi, 1998, p. 335).

Among the recommendations are screening for low-risk pregnancies for Down syndrome and the use of folic acid in multivitamins for women who are planning a pregnancy, or who are of childbearing age, to prevent neural tube defects. Current recommendations for dealing with habits that affect health such as smoking, alcohol and drug use, sleep, nutrition, physical activity, and obesity are **not** addressed for persons with I/DD.

Recent interest in the health care needs of persons with mental retardation by Special Olympics, Inc. led to congressional hearings that prompted the Surgeon General's conference on health disparities in this population in 2001 (Special Olympics, Inc., 2000). In its publication, *Promoting Health for Individuals with Mental Retardation—A Critical Journey Barely Begun* (2001), Special Olympics applauded the federal government for including a chapter on persons with disabilities in their publication, *Healthy People 2010,* but emphasized that there is very little current evidence to form the foundation for many of the health objectives for this population. The Special Olympics report concludes that while evidence of the prevalence of many chronic diseases and conditions may be similar to the general population, the adverse impacts can be greater, and symptoms can be more frequent and more severe, and can occur at an earlier age, as in Down syndrome. The report also asserts that including people with I/DD in research studies on health promotion and disease prevention can assist them to have better health, a longer life, and an improved quality of life. This assertion echoes that made 12 years ago by Pope and Tarov (1991): "Additional study is needed of the relationship between chronic disease, disability, and aging in terms of health promotion, quality of life, and access to services. Such study should include issues related to age-related disability, as well as aging with a disability (p. 208).

The Surgeon General's report, *Closing the Gap* (2002), reaffirmed these needs in making a critical set of goals:

1. Integrate health promotion into community environments of people with mental retardation.

2. Increase knowledge and understanding of health and mental retardation, ensuring that knowledge is made practical and easy to use.

3. Improve the quality of health care for people with mental retardation.

4. Train health care providers in the care of adults and children with mental retardation.

5. Ensure that health care financing produces good health outcomes for adults and children with mental retardation.

6. Increase sources of health care services for adults, adolescents, and children with mental retardation, ensuring that health care is easily accessible for them.

Among the action steps for goals 2 and 3 are (a) to develop a national research agenda that identifies gaps in existing scientific knowledge related to health and mental retardation, including methodologic challenges, priorities, feasibility, and timetables for achieving priority research; and (b) to identify, adapt, and develop standards of care for use in monitoring and improving the quality of care for individuals with mental retardation.

In January 2003, the Arc of the United States facilitated an invitational conference of national experts in I/DD to identify national goals, the state of knowledge, and a research agenda for persons with I/DD. One topical area was health. Members of this group discussed that "disability-specific health care guidelines and standards exist for a number of specific conditions, such as Down syndrome and Fragile X, but health and health services for persons with intellectual and developmental disabilities are rarely assessed according to established protocols" (p. 22).

The Institute of Medicine (1995) recommended six criteria for the development of practice guidelines: (a) prevalence, (b) morbidity and mortality estimates, (c) costs of treatment, (d) differences in practice among primary care providers, (e) potential to improve health outcomes, and (f) potential to reduce cost. Current or future evidence distinguishing persons with I/DD from the general population can be incorporated into federal and organizational guidelines that address the entire population and guide practice.

For these reasons, the members of the Health Promotion and Prevention Committee of the American Association on Mental Retardation (AAMR) convened a national conference on June 1, 2004, preceding the annual meeting of AAMR, to address the state of the scientific evidence concerning health promotion topics as they relate to the population of persons with I/DD. We expected that this initial effort would address the absence of critical health promotion and prevention information and begin to inform research initiatives, policy, clinical practice, and health care outcomes.

Planning for the National Conference, Including Conference Topics

In preparation for the conference, a total of 14 topics were identified by the Health Promotion and Prevention Committee of AAMR: hypertension, obesity and overweight/nutrition, respiratory disorders in adults and children, epilepsy, mental health, physical activity and mobility, access to health care, reproductive health, safety/injury and violence, case management/care coordination, alternative and complementary medicine, tobacco use/substance abuse, health risk assessment tools, and conceptual health promotion models. The topics were identified after a discussion of leading health indicators as identified by *Healthy People 2010* (2000) and a list of priority areas for improvement in the quality of health care as identified by the Committee on Identifying Priority Areas for Quality Improvement of the Institute of Medicine (Adams & Corrigan, 2003). After topics were identified, the Committee determined the experts for each of these topics based on a record of publications and/or presentations, and each was asked to participate as a speaker at the conference and as writer of a chapter in this book of proceedings. Teresa Moore, a nationally recognized self-advocate, was invited to provide a response to the conference topic presentations.

Next, a meeting was held with representatives from federal agencies whose interests include persons with I/DD at the offices of the American Association on Mental Retardation. These federal representatives provided valuable advice on how to proceed with this conference idea.

Plans were then made for a preconference planning meeting and funding was secured. An information specialist was hired to identify all relevant research articles for each topic from any available source. The following databases were searched: Medline, CINAHL, SocioFile, Health Star, PsychInfo, Pharmaceutical Abstracts, Web Science, Academic Search Premiere, Ingenta, and GPO Access. The following search terms were used besides the topic: *mental retardation, developmental disabilities,* and *Down syndrome.* Other terms, such as *cerebral palsy* were used when appropriate. The information specialist reported that her findings revealed many case studies, surveys, and small sample research studies, with an absence of randomized control group studies. For example, in Chapter 7 "Access to Health Care," a preponderance of survey research publications were found that included a variety of subjects from service providers to state agency administrators. Few studies used chart reviews, checklists, or health assessments and specifically, interacted with persons with

I/DD and sought their opinions. A special thanks is extended to Joann Donatiello, who served as our information specialist.

On November 7–8, 2003, the speakers, members of the Health Promotion and Prevention Committee, and other invited guests met in Washington, DC to discuss the information on each topic, the format for presentation and book chapter, and the final format for the June 2004 conference. One issue that arose was the use of definitions. It was determined that the American Association on Mental Retardation definition of mental retardation (Luckasson et al., 2002) and the federal definition of developmental disabilities (Developmental Disabilities Assistance and Bill of Rights Act Amendments, 2000) would be used. The speakers received their packet of articles obtained by the information specialist at this meeting. Presenters were allowed to do further searches if they chose for the preparation of their presentations and papers. This preconference planning meeting was funded by the Centers for Disease Control and Prevention.

Methodology for Obtaining and Analyzing the Scientific Evidence

A review of the literature found a number of systems for the analysis of scientific evidence with and without the outcome of practice guidelines (Agency for Health Care Policy and Research, 1997; Bero & Rennie, 1995 [Cochrane Collaboration]; Butler & Campbell, 2000 [American Academy for Cerebral Palsy and Developmental Medicine, AACPDM]; Institute of Medicine, 1995; West et al., 2002). For the most part, their methodologies are similar and for the purposes of this conference the following format was used for the presentations as well as for the chapters in this book of proceedings:

1. A list of key questions was determined from the available evidence.

2. The evidence will be described in detail including: (a) how the literature search was completed (e.g., what sources and search engines were reviewed); (b) the range of dates of the evidence; (c) key words used in the searches; (d) commercial Web sites searched (e.g., Dr. Koop, WebMD, ReutersHealth, Intellihealth, Medscape, NewsPage, and/or professional organizations); and (e) inclusion and exclusion criteria. The inclusion criteria are applied to determine the number of original pieces of evidence.

3. The findings will be presented in tables to include the following information as applicable: (a) study information (author[s], year); (b) research design; (c) levels of evidence (see Table A); (d) population studied; (e) total number of subjects; (f) ages of subjects; (g) dimension of disability; (h) intervention; (i) control group intervention if different; (j) treatment duration; (k) number of subjects in treatment group; (l) number of subjects in control group; (m) outcome of interest; (n) measures used; (o) results; (p) clinical importance; (q) statistics; (r) type of adverse effects; and (s) number of cases to experience each type of adverse effect (these variables are adapted from the protocol used by the AACPDM, 2000).

TABLE A *Levels of Evidence*

LEVEL	NONEMPIRICAL	GROUP RESEARCH	OUTCOMES RESEARCH	SINGLE SUBJECT RESEARCH
I		Randomized controlled trial All or none case series		N-of-1 randomized controlled trial
II		Nonrandomized controlled trial Prospective cohort study with concurrent control group	Analytic survey	ABABA design Alternating treatments Multiple baseline across subjects
III		Case-control study Cohort study with historical control group		ABA design
IV		Case series and registries without control group		AB design
V	Case report Anecdote Expert opinion Theory based on physiology; bench, animal research Common sense/ first principles			

Source: Butler & Campbell, 2000.

4. Conclusions will be provided by the author(s) based on the evidence.

5. Finally, future research and practice recommendations will be presented.

The National Conference on the State of Scientific Evidence

The national conference was held as a preconference to the annual meeting of AAMR. There were 125 people in attendance. The agenda for the conference followed the World Health Organization's international classification of impairments (see Appendix). Time was allowed for questions and comments from the audience. References from the presentations were posted on the AAMR Web site after the conference based on attendee requests.

During the annual meeting on June 2, 2004, Dr. Nehring and members of the Health Promotion and Prevention Committee led a plenary session during the AAMR national conference to disseminate findings or the preconference to professionals, direct support staff, students, family members, and self-advocates who attended the national meeting.

Priorities for Action

The presenters and authors of these chapters found varying amounts of research evidence depending on the topic. Concerning adequacy of the research findings, chapters on physiologic issues (e.g., physical activity, epilepsy, mental health) found the highest degree of research evidence available. Yet overall, the research on health promotion topics concerning individuals with I/DD consists mainly of descriptive and case studies. This initial effort clearly presents the need and public visibility for well-designed research studies with adequate sample sizes to produce findings that form the foundation for evidence-based health care practice and consequent health care policy that includes the consideration of health care needs of persons with I/DD in planning and implementing standardized health care (e.g., *Guide to Clinical Preventive Services* by the U.S. Preventive Services Task Force). Seekins, et al., in Chapter 13 on secondary conditions risk appraisal in adults with I/DD, discussed the current knowledge base concerning the assessment of health risk and secondary conditions. Increased research in this area is also warranted for best practice concerning health promotion for individuals with I/DD of all ages. It is anticipated that AAMR will continue to hold future conferences and publish proceedings that describe the state of the scientific evidence concerning health promotion topics as they pertain to the optimal health of persons with I/DD.

Wendy M. Nehring, RN, PhD, FAAN, FAAMR
Editor

REFERENCES

Adams, K., & Corrigan, J. M. (2003). *Priority areas for national action: Transforming health care quality.* Washington, DC: National Academies Press.

Agency for Health Care Policy and Research. (1997). *Clinical practice guidelines in practice and education* (AHCPR Pub. No. 97-R077). Washington, DC: Author.

Agency for Health Care Policy and Research. (2003). *National guideline clearinghouse.* Retrieved October 19, 2003 from *http://www.guidelines.gov.*

Arc of the United States. (2003). *Keeping the promises. Findings and recommendations: January 2003 invitational conference. National goals, state of knowledge, and research agenda for persons with intellectual and developmental disabilities.* Washington, DC: Author.

Atkins, D., & DiGuiseppi, C. G. (1998). Broadening the evidence base for evidence-based guidelines: A research agenda based on the work of the U. S. Preventive Services Task Force. *American Journal of Preventive Medicine, 14,* 335–344.

Bero, L., & Rennie, D. (1995). The Cochrane Collaboration: Preparing, maintaining, and disseminating systematic reviews of the effects of health care. *Journal of the American Medical Association, 274,* 1935–1938.

Butler, C., & Campbell, S. (2000). Evidence of the effects of intrathecal baclofen for Spastic and dystonic cerebral palsy. *Developmental Medicine & Child Neurology, 42,* 634–645.

Cochrane Collaboration. (2004). *Abstracts of new and updated Cochrane reviews.* Retrieved April 15, 2005 from *http://www.cochrane.org.*

Developmental Disabilities Assistance and Bill of Rights Act Amendments of 2000, P. L. No. 106-402, 114 Stat. 1677 (2000).

Horwitz, S. M., Kerker, B. D., Owens, P. L., & Zigler, E. (2000). *The health status and needs of individuals with mental retardation.* Retrieved March 30, 2001 from *http://www.specialolympics.org.*

Institute of Medicine. (1995). *Setting priorities for clinical practice guidelines.* Washington, DC: National Academies Press.

Luckasson, R., Borthwick-Duffy, S., Buntinx, W. H. E., Coulter, D. L., Craig, E. M., Reeve, A., et al. (2002). *Mental retardation: Definition, classification, and systems of support.* Washington, DC: American Association on Mental Retardation.

Pope, A. M., & Tarov, A. R. (Eds.). (1991). *Disability in America: Toward a national agenda for prevention.* Washington, DC: National Academies Press.

Satcher, D. (2000). *Statement of David Satcher, M.D., Ph.D., Surgeon General, U.S. Public Health Service, Department of Health and Human Services on the special hearing on promoting health for people with mental retardation before the U.S. Senate Committee on Appropriations.* Retrieved March 30, 2001 from *http://www.specialolympics.org.*

Special Olympics, Inc. (2001). *Promoting health for individuals with mental retardation—A critical journey barely begun.* Retrieved March 30, 2001 from *http://www.specialolympics.org.*

U.S. Department of Health and Human Services. (2000). *Healthy people 2010: Understanding and improving health* (2nd ed.). Washington, DC: U.S. Government Printing Office.

U.S. Preventive Services Task Force. (1996). *Guide to clinical prevention services* (2nd ed.). Washington, DC: U.S. Department of Health and Human Services, Public Health Service, Agency for Health Care Policy and Research, AHCPR Publication No. OM97-0001.

U.S. Public Health Service. (2002). *Closing the gap: A national blueprint for improving the health of individuals with mental retardation. Report of the Surgeon General's conference on health disparities and mental retardation.* Washington, DC: Author.

West, S., King, V., Carey, T. S., Lohr, K. N., McKoy, N., & Sutton, S. F. (2002). *Systems to rate the strength of scientific evidence.* Evidence Report/Technology Assessment No. 47 (Prepared by the Research Triangle Institute-University of North Carolina Evidence-Based Practice Center under Contract No. 290-97-0011). AHRQ Publication No. 02-E016. Rockville, MD: AHRQ.

World Health Organization (1997). *ICIDH-2: International classification of impairments, activities and participation.* Geneva, Switzerland: WHO.

FOREWORD

CLOSING THE GAP ON INTELLECTUAL DISABILITIES

I am honored to be here with you today and would like to thank the AAMR for hosting this conference. We at the Centers for Diseases Control and Prevention (CDC) and at the National Center on Birth Defects and Developmental Disabilities (NCBDDD) are proud to partner with you in this important meeting.

NCBDDD was created by Congress in the Children Health Act of 2000 to focus attention on birth defects and developmental disabilities and has brought more attention to these issues within CDC, public health agencies, among our partners, the general public, and even globally. Today, I want to share with you how CDC is addressing the issues associated with intellectual disabilities.

One of the most important activities of NCBDDD has been to partner with the National Institute of Child Health and Human Development in assisting former Surgeon General David Satcher develop the landmark report, *Closing the Gap: A national blueprint to improve the health of persons with mental retardation.* This report highlighted the importance of developing a national research agenda that identifies gaps in our scientific understanding of health issues facing people with intellectual disabilities, and their families; and improving the quality of health care for individuals with intellectual disabilities. This conference is a big step toward meeting the challenges of the Surgeon General's report. The research being shared at this conference will help stimulate additional studies, and provide valuable data that can be used by scientists and health care providers in closing the gap. By expanding and refining the data, we hope to develop and adapt standards that will help address disparities in this field.

When we look at the progress that was made during the 20ᵗʰ century addressing the prevention of intellectual disabilities and improving the health of people living with intellectual disabilities, we can conclude that tremendous progress was made, particularly in the last half of the century. As a result, we must also address the consequences of that tremendous success. In the 1950s we began to recognize that newborn screening could effectively lead to prevention of mental retardation caused by phenylketonuria, or PKU. As a result, now there are thousands of individuals living with PKU, without intellectual disability. A consequence of that success is that about 3,000 adult females are in their reproductive years, and need to have optimal control of their PKU before becoming pregnant, so to prevent the serious teratogenic effects of high phenylalanine in utero. Access to medical foods low in phenylalanine is a continual challenge as well as providing health care for adults with PKU whether they have an intellectual disability or not.

Down Syndrome is another success story. In the 1960's the median age of death for children with Down Syndrome was about 1 year. By 1997, it had risen to 49 years. However, there is a significant health disparity by race and ethnicity. White children with Down Syndrome reached a median age of death at 50 years. On the other hand, for Blacks with Down syndrome, that age was only 25 years. And for the other groups—mostly Hispanics—it was only 11 years. We must find ways to continue increasing life expectancy for people with Down Syndrome. We have already ruled out obvious potential reasons such as differences in congenital heart disease, or associated causes of death. So the reason or reasons for the disparities is still unknown, but we are actively conducting research to explain this health disparity.

Tracking developmental disabilities over time is essential in measuring progress. At CDC we are committed to monitoring and tracking developmental disabilities such as, cognitive disability, cerebral palsy, autism, and others. The Metropolitan Atlanta Developmental Disabilities Surveillance Program (MADDSP) has been monitoring the occurrence of selected developmental disabilities, including intellectual disability, since 1991. This program helps provide a framework to initiate special studies of children who have certain developmental disabilities, find their causes, and identify ways to prevent complications of their underlying conditions. Because we have MADDSP, it is possible to report the average annual prevalence of mental retardation among children 3–10 years of age in the Atlanta Metro region. During the period from 1991 to 1994, it was 9.7 per 1,000. Nearly one of every 100 children 3 to 10 years old had mental retardation.

Racially, there is a great discrepancy in people with intellectual disabilities. Using data from the annual report to Congress on implementation of the Individuals with Disabilities Education Act (IDEA) as reported by all 50 states and the District of Columbia, of students ages 6–21, Asian/Pacific Islanders had the lowest percentage enrolled in special education for mental retardation: 0.4%. Hispanics ranked next at 0.5%, Whites at 0.8%, Native Americans at 1.0% and Blacks at 2.1%.

So racial disparity is an issue, but knowing what is appropriate and adequate health care for individuals with developmental disabilities is another major issue. The late Dr. Pierre Decouflé reported that among children identified as having 1 of the 5 major developmental disabilities (mental retardation, cerebral palsy, hearing impairment, vision impairment, or epilepsy), 16.7% had two or more of the developmental disabilities. Among children with mental retardation, 22.3% had two or more developmental disabilities. Thus, cognitive disability is often seen with other conditions, and all must be addressed and managed accordingly.

CDC is committed to providing continued financial support and technical assistance for the development and expansion of this research. Of course, we want to follow up by using this important data for research, prevention, and intervention activities. These are our ultimate goals—prevention and intervention.

All of you here today are important partners in achieving these goals, and CDC is committed to supporting you. We all know that there is a lot of work to do. It is one of my primary goals to enhance our partnerships so that we can work together and eliminate duplication of efforts. After all, it is through our combined, sustained efforts, and documented effectiveness, that we will truly succeed in improving the health and lives of people with intellectual disabilities and their families.

Thank you for the vital role that you play in this endeavor. We want you to be successful. We realize that this is a difficult mission. We know the benefits of the work, and we are redoubling our efforts to meet our common goals. Together we can strive to promote health and well-being among all.

José F. Cordero, MD, MPH
Assistant Surgeon General and Director,
National Center on Birth Defects and Developmental Disabilities,
Centers for Disease Control and Prevention,
Department of Health and Human Services,
Atlanta, Georgia 30333
jcordero@cdc.gov

INTRODUCTION

I had the good fortune to work in the Federal Office of Disease Prevention and Health Promotion in the late 1980s—it was a heady time. The target date for the first set of Health Objectives for the Nation was at hand and there was a ground swell of enthusiasm from all sectors about the *Healthy People 2000* objectives. Clearly, health promotion had come of age on a grand scale in America, for most people. It would take another decade before explicit health objectives would be enunciated for people with disabilities in *Healthy People 2010*. Yet, intellectual disability was barely mentioned with no specific objectives other than primary prevention.

We are now into the 21st century and people with intellectual disability have waited long enough. They are living longer, in many cases better, than in previous decades, and they and their families expect more. While there was a time when envisioning people with intellectual disability as having concerns and goals for their personal health was a remote concept, that time has faded.

Recent efforts by the U.S. Centers for Disease Control and Prevention, National Institute of Child Health and Human Development, Surgeon General David Satcher, and the American Association on Mental Retardation have focused attention on the unmet needs for disease prevention and health promotion for people with intellectual disabilities specifically. It is now time for the nation as a whole and, especially our public and private leaders in science and public health, to get serious about pursuing such an agenda.

I congratulate the American Association on Mental Retardation for undertaking their theme conference in 2004 on health promotion for people with intellectual disability. The broad review of the state of science across disease, condition, and risk categories is a logical step in the forward march to support people with intellectual disabilities in achieving the highest possible level of personal health and having a voice in determining it.

Special Olympics is pleased that it could help support the development of the scientific materials for the conference and publication and that we had an opportunity to participate in a meaningful way. We look forward to using these materials to advance the health of our athletes and to leveraging relationships with organizations and individuals to help bring about healthier lives for all people with intellectual disability.

Stephen B. Corbin, DDS, MPH
Dean, Special Olympics University

1

HYPERTENSION

Christopher C. Draheim, PhD

The Seventh Report of the Joint National Committee on Prevention, Detection, Evaluation, and Treatment of High Blood Pressure (JNC-7), supported by the National Heart, Lung, and Blood Institute National High Blood Pressure Education Program, outlined the importance of preventing and treating hypertension as well as the associated health conditions caused by hypertension (Chobanian et al., 2003). This chapter summarizes the findings of the JNC-7 report as a lead-in to the findings on hypertension and health promotion for persons with intellectual and developmental disabilities (I/DD). The JNC-7 report focuses on important areas of health promotion, termed "lifestyle modifications," as initial treatment and prevention strategies for hypertension. The recommendations outlined by the JNC-7 are used to guide the direction of the health promotion strategies described in this chapter that are aimed at reducing or controlling hypertension for persons with I/DD. The JNC-7 also includes recommendations for medication therapies to reduce and control blood pressure; however, this chapter focuses only on lifestyle modifications.

Hypertension is one of the most prevalent diseases in the United States, affecting more than 50 million people in this country. Hypertension leads to cardiovascular disease (CVD) and kidney disease over time and is in fact one of the most important risk factors for CVD. Even starting at levels considered to be relatively healthy (115/75), each incremental increase of 20 mm Hg of systolic blood pressure or 10 mm Hg of diastolic blood pressure doubles the risk of CVD. Because of the strong relationship of blood pressure to CVD and other health conditions, the JNC-7 has developed a new "Prehypertension" category, starting at the relatively low pressures.

Prehypertension is defined as a systolic blood pressure between 120 and 139 mm Hg or a diastolic blood pressure between 80 and 90 mm Hg. The new category of Prehypertension classifies persons with blood pressures previously considered "normal" as having an increased risk for hypertension and associated health conditions and indicates that they should initiate lifestyle modifications to decrease the risk of developing hypertension. The Prehypertension category also signals physicians and health care providers to the need for increased education on strategies to reduce blood pressure to prevent hypertension.

Although hypertension is strongly associated with increasing age, common causes of hypertension include sleep apnea, chronic kidney or renovascular disease, various endocrine disorders, chronic steroid therapy, coarctation of the aorta, excess sodium intake, use of medications, and excess alcohol intake (Chobanian et al., 2003). In some cases, hypertension is genetically linked, but it is also associated with physical inactivity and excess body weight. It is often preventable through lifestyle modifications and treatable through use of medications.

The main benefit of lowering blood pressure includes the risk reduction of CVD events. Lowering blood pressure to recommended levels can reduce the risk for stroke by up to 40% to 55%, the risk for myocardial infarction by up to 20% to 25%, and the risk for heart failure by more than 50% (Chobanian et al., 2003). Reducing elevated blood pressure has also been associated with reduced mortality rates. Even small reductions in blood pressure have been shown to decrease the overall risk for associated health conditions.

The Seventh Report of the Joint National Committee on Prevention, Detection, Evaluation, and Treatment of High Blood Pressure (JNC-7) includes an algorithm for the treatment of hypertension. The first step in treatment of elevated blood pressure is lifestyle modification. The recommendations include weight reduction, adopting the "Dietary Approaches to Stop Hypertension" (DASH) eating plan, dietary sodium reduction, increasing physical activity levels, and reducing alcohol consumption. A short description of each of the recommended lifestyle modifications follows, together with information on typical reductions in blood pressure associated with each (Chobanian et al., 2003).

The recommended body weight is a body mass index (BMI) between 18 and 25 (BMI is a ratio of body weight in kilograms to height in meters squared). Reductions in weight were associated with varying reductions in blood pressure but are often associated with a 5–20 mm Hg reduction in systolic blood pressure per 10 kg (22 lbs.) of weight loss. The DASH eating plan includes increasing fruit and vegetable intake, using low-fat dairy products, lowering total and saturated fat consumption, reducing intake of sweets and foods with a high sugar content, and reducing red meat consumption. Adopting the DASH eating plan was associated with an 8–14 mm Hg reduction in systolic blood pressure. The recommended dietary sodium intake is less than 2.4 g of sodium per day (6 g of sodium chloride per day) and was associated with a 2–8 mm Hg reduction in systolic blood pressure. The recommended exercise is 30 minutes of aerobic physical activity almost daily. Engaging in the recommended physical activity levels was associated with a 4–9 mm Hg reduction in systolic blood pressure. The recommended consumption of alcohol is two or fewer drinks per day (one drink or less per day for smaller people) and was associated with a 2–4 mm Hg reduction in systolic blood pressure. Adopting the lifestyle modifications is also a recommended preventative strategy for persons with an elevated risk for developing hypertension and may reduce the likelihood of hypertension development for all persons. The JNC-7 algorithm for treating hypertension suggests the use of medications to control blood pressure if the lifestyle modifications are not successful. The algorithm lists the recommended medications for different levels of hypertension; however, the medication issues are beyond the scope of this chapter. Medication use should be discussed with one's physician.

Information about the prevalence of hypertension and typical or average blood pressures for persons with I/DD generally has been lacking and is an understudied area of research. The benefits of lifestyle modifications in preventing and reducing hypertension were even less studied in the I/DD population. The sections that follow summarize available research reports related to blood pressure and hypertension in persons with I/DD.

Research Questions

A number of research questions were identified to frame the literature search, including: (1) Is there a high prevalence of hypertension in persons with I/DD? (2) If so, who has the greatest risk for (or greatest prevalence of) hypertension? (3) What are the recommended health promotion strategies to prevent or treat hypertension and what are the nonpharmacological treatments for hypertension? (4) Is there evidence that supports the recommended treatments for persons with I/DD? and (5) What is the evidence of these recommendations in persons with I/DD?

Methods

The process of locating research included searches of common terms for elevated blood pressure, including hypertension, blood pressure, systolic blood pressure, diastolic blood pressure, and ambulatory blood pressure, along with searches on lifestyle modifications for treating hypertension, which include physical activity, exercise, dietary intake, nutrition, weight, weight loss, and body fat. In addition, the following search terms were explored as well: mental retardation, developmental disabilities, intellectual disabilities, learning disabilities, cognitive disabilities, Down syndrome, Prader-Willi syndrome, and Williams syndrome. The following databases were searched: Medline, CINAHL, SocioFile, Health Star, PsychInfo, Pharmaceutical Abstracts, Web Science, Academic Search Premiere, Ingenta, and GPO Access. Because studies concerned specifically with hypertension/blood pressure in persons with I/DD and prevention of hypertension and health promotion in persons with I/DD were not found, all studies that were located were included.

Results

The results of the literature search are presented in two parts. The first discusses research reporting the prevalence of hypertension and mean blood pressures for persons with I/DD. The second part discusses research related to the benefits of lifestyle modifications in reducing blood pressure. The search of the literature resulted in the identification of three syndromes—Down syndrome, Williams-Beuren syndrome, and Prader-Willi syndrome—associated with unique blood pressure differences compared to values in individuals with and without I/DD. Research related to blood pressure for each of these syndromes is discussed separately in the first part.

PREVALENCE OF HYPERTENSION IN PERSONS WITH I/DD

The reported prevalence of hypertension in persons with I/DD varied greatly among studies, ranging from 0% to 41%. Differences in the prevalence of hypertension among countries and among different etiologies of I/DD were reported. Some of these may be attributable to differences in definitions of hypertension among the studies or to the absence of a definition of hypertension in a particular study. Similarly, some of the differences could be attributed to differences in the populations sampled and to differing sampling techniques. Small sample sizes were common for many studies as well. It appears that the goal of most of the reports was not to estimate specifically a larger population's hypertension prevalence; however, because of the lack of larger reports these smaller studies are discussed as well. The prevalence of reported hypertension in persons with mental retardation (MR) and details of the samples are presented in Table 1-1.

The prevalence of hypertension in the United States is approximately 29% of the adult population (Hajjar & Kotchen, 2003). Three studies reported the prevalence of hypertension in samples of persons with I/DD from the United States. One of the larger reports indicated that 25% of adults (18–65 years of age) with mild to moderate MR had hypertension (Draheim, Williams, & McCubbin, 2002); however, the sample included a higher proportion of persons with Down syndrome (approximately 50%) than what is typically seen in the general population or for the population of persons with I/DD. Further analysis of the data indicated that the prevalence of persons without Down syndrome with hypertension is greater than 41%. Kapell et al. (1998) reported a study in which 22% to 24% of 147 adults (45–74 years of age) with mild to profound MR without Down syndrome had hypertension. The criteria for hypertension used by Draheim et al. and Kapell et al. was a resting systolic blood pressure greater than or equal to 140 mm Hg or a resting diastolic blood pressure greater than or equal to 90 mm Hg. McDermott, Platt, and Krishnaswami (1997) reported that only 10% of 366 adults (19–64 years of age) with mild to profound MR had hypertension compared to 41% of a non-MR Medicaid control and 15% of another insured non-MR control group. The definition of hypertension was not listed in the report, making it difficult to evaluate or to compare to other reports on hypertension in persons with or without I/DD. In general, U.S. studies reporting the prevalence of hypertension that included persons with mild to profound MR had lower prevalence rates (10% to 23%) than those reporting the prevalence among persons with mild to moderate MR (25% to 41%). Previous research on health conditions indicated that persons with mild to moderate MR had more health conditions than persons with severe to profound MR (Rimmer, Braddock, & Fujiura, 1993; Rimmer, Braddock, & Marks, 1995).

TABLE 1-1 *Prevalence of Hypertension in Persons with Intellectual and Developmental Disabilities (I/DD)*

REFERENCE	SAMPLE SIZE	GENDER AND AGE, YRS	SAMPLE DESCRIPTION	PREVALENCE OF HYPERTENSION (%)	DEFINITION OF HYPERTENSION
Persons with mental retardation (MR)					
United States					
Draheim et al., 2002b (re-analysis)	145	Men and women, 18–65	MR/DS, mild to moderate	25	≥ 140/90 mm Hg SBP/DBP
	70	Men and women, 18–65	MR, mild to moderate	41	≥ 140/90 mm Hg SBP/DBP
Kapell et al. 1998	147	Men and women, 45–74	MR, mild to profound	23	≥ 140/90 mm Hg SBP/DBP
McDermott et al.,1997	366	Men and women, 40 ± 11	MR, mild to profound	10	Not defined
Non-United States					
Beange et al., 1995 (Australia)	98	Men, 20–49	MR/DS, mild to profound	12	≥ 95 mm Hg DBP or meds
	104	Women, 20–49		9–10	
Cooper, 1998 (England)	134	Men and women 65+	MR, all	12	Not defined
	73	Men and women 20–64	MR, all	1	Not defined
Barr et al., 1999 (Ireland)	297	Men and women, 19+	MR (learning disability)	18	Not defined
Persons with Down syndrome (DS)					
United States					
Draheim et al., 2002b	75	Men and women, 18–65	DS, mild to moderate	9	≥ 140/90 mm Hg SBP/DBP
Kapell et al., 1998	128	Men and women, 45–74	DS, mild to profound	3	≥ 140/90 mm Hg SBP/DBP
Braunschweig et al., 2004	48	Men and women, 40 ± 11	DS, mild to moderate	13	> 130/80 mm Hg SBP/DBP
Non-United States					
Van Allen et al., 1999 (Canada)	18	Men and women, 30–43	DS, severe to profound	0	Not defined
	20	Men and women, 47–68		0	Not defined
Barr et al., 1999 (Ireland)	76	Men and women, 19+	DS (learning disability)	13	Not defined
Persons with Williams-Beuren syndrome (WBS)					
Broder et al., 1999 (U.S.)	20	Boys and girls, 11–44	WBS	40	≥ 135/85 MABP
Persons with Prader-Willi syndrome (PWS)					
Butler et al., 2002 (U.K.)	106	Boys and girls, 0–46	PWS, mild to profound	7	Not defined

DBP, Diastolic blood pressure; MABP, mean ambulatory blood pressure; SBP, systolic blood pressure

Three studies reported the prevalence of hypertension in samples of persons with MR from countries outside the United States. Beange, McElduff, and Baker (1995) reported that in Australia, the prevalence of hypertension of 9% to 12% of 202 persons with mild to profound I/DD was similar to that in the general population. The definition of hypertension used by Beange et al. was a diastolic blood pressure greater than or equal to 95 mm Hg or current treatment with antihypertensive medications. In a study in the United Kingdom, Cooper (1998) reported that the prevalence of hypertension in 207 persons with all levels of I/DD was 1% to 12%. Hypertension was associated with increasing age, as older participants were more likely than those in younger age groups to have elevated blood pressure. In an Irish study, Barr, Gilgunn, Kane, and Moore (1999) reported that 17% of 373 persons with I/DD had hypertension. The Barr et al. (1999) report did not include a description of the levels of MR, but likely included persons with mild to profound MR. A definition of hypertension was not provided in either the Cooper (1998) or the Barr et al. (1999) report, making the prevalence of hypertension difficult to evaluate or to compare to other reports on hypertension among persons with or without I/DD in the United States or other countries.

Although the reported prevalence of hypertension varied among the U.S. and the non-U.S reports, it appears that the prevalence of hypertension may be greater in the United States as compared to other countries. The greater prevalence of hypertension in the United States could be due to differences in samples or to the high prevalence of obesity and overweight of adults with MR in the United States as compared to other countries (Frey & Rimmer, 1995). The differences in prevalence could also be the result of some studies including all levels of MR (mild to profound) versus the less severe levels of MR (mild to moderate).

Prevalence of Hypertension in Persons with Down Syndrome

In general, persons with Down syndrome (DS) have lower blood pressure than persons with or without MR. In one study, unlike blood pressure in adults with MR without DS, mean blood pressure values for 75 men and women with DS residing in community settings were extremely low (only 108.9 ± 10.8 mm Hg for systolic blood pressure and 73.0 ± 10.5 mm Hg for diastolic blood pressure) (Draheim, McCubbin, & Williams, 2002a). In general, persons with DS were reported to have a systolic blood pressure approximately 13–20 mm Hg lower than that of others with I/DD and a diastolic blood pressure approximately 6–20 mm Hg lower than that of others with I/DD (Draheim, McCubbin, & Williams, 2002; Morrison et al., 1996). The mean blood pressures and details of the samples for persons with MR with and without DS are presented in Table 1-2.

The reported prevalence of hypertension in persons with DS also varied among studies and countries but was consistently reported to be lower than in others with I/DD. In a U.S. study, Braunschweig et al. (2004) reported that 13% of 48 adults with DS had hypertension. This was a small study and the definition of hypertension used in the report was a systolic blood pressure of at least 130 mm Hg or a diastolic blood pressure of at least 85 mm Hg. The definition of hypertension used by Braunschweig et al. (2004) yields a less conservative estimate of systolic hypertension and a more

TABLE 1-2 *Mean Systolic and Diastolic Blood Pressures in Persons with Intellectual and Developmental Disabilities (IIDD)*

REFERENCE	SAMPLE SIZE	SAMPLE GENDER AND AGE	SAMPLE DESCRIPTION	BLOOD PRESSURE M ± (SD) MM HG
Persons with mental retardation (MR)				
Draheim et al., 2002a (United States)	30	Women, 18–65	MR, mild to moderate	123 ± 16 Systolic, 84 ± 13 Diastolic
	40	Men, 18–65		127 ± 13 Systolic, 87 ± 12 Diastolic
Morrison et al., 1996 (Scotland)	21	Women	MR	132 ± 4 Systolic, 85 ± 3 Diastolic
	39	Men		130 ± 3 Systolic, 85 ± 2 Diastolic
Persons with Down syndrome (DS)				
Draheim et al., 2002a (United States)	41	Women, 18–65	DS, mild to moderate	107 ± 12 Systolic, 73 ± 11 Diastolic
	34	Men, 18–65		111 ± 14 Systolic, 73 ± 10 Diastolic
Braunschweig et al., 2004 (United States)	48	Men and women	DS, mild to moderate	106 ± 17 Systolic, 68 ± 11 Diastolic
Morrison et al., 1996 (Scotland)	17	Women	DS	109 ± 4 Systolic, 68 ± 2 Diastolic
	27	Women		105 ± 3 Systolic, 64 ± 2 Diastolic
	35	Men		110 ± 3 Systolic, 66 ± 2 Diastolic
	35	Men		113 ± 3 Systolic, 65 ± 2 Diastolic
Persons with Williams-Beuren syndrome (WBS)				
Giordano et al., 2001 (Italy)	17	Boys and girls, 14 ± 4	WBS	114 ± 11 Systolic, 69 ± 11 Diastolic
Salaymeh et al., 2001 (United States)	13	Boys and girls, 3–12	WBS	125 ± 12 Systolic

conservative diastolic hypertension than 140/90 mm Hg cutoff points. It is not known why these cutoff points were used to define hypertension. The prevalence of hypertension in 128 persons with DS was reported to be much lower (2% to 9%) in another study of adults with DS from the United States (Kapell et al., 1998).

Two reports indicated the prevalence of hypertension among persons with DS residing in countries outside the United States. Barr et al. (1999) reported that the prevalence of persons with DS was only 13% as compared to the 18% reported for others with MR without DS. Van Allen, Fung, and Jurenka (1999) reported that 0% of their sample of 38 persons with DS had hypertension. The prevalence of reported hypertension of persons with DS and details of the samples are presented in Table 1-1.

Prevalence of Hypertension in Persons with Williams-Beuren Syndrome

In Italy, both resting and ambulatory blood pressures of persons with Williams-Beuren syndrome (WBS) have consistently been reported to be higher than in others with and without MR (Giordano et al., 2001). Hypertension also develops at a younger age in persons with WBS than in others with and without MR. This autosomal dominant disorder is a result of mutations in the *elastin* gene and clinical signs also include supravalvular aortic stenosis, multiple peripheral pulmonary arterial stenosis, infantile hypercalcemia, and mental retardation among others. Salaymeh and Banerjee (2001) reported that mean systolic blood pressures of children with WBS were 24 mm Hg higher and mean diastolic blood pressures were 9 mm Hg higher than in other children without I/DD. The prevalence of hypertension in children with WBS is very high, with reports indicating 40% to 68% of children with WBS in the United States have hypertension (Broder et al., 1999). The prevalence of reported hypertension of persons with WBS and details of the samples are presented in Table 1-1.

Prevalence of Hypertension in Persons with Prader-Willi Syndrome

The prevalence of hypertension may be lower for persons with Prader-Willi syndrome (PWS) compared with others with and without MR. The prevalence of hypertension for persons with PWS was reported for both adults and children in an English study (Butler et al., 2002). In this study, 6% to 13% of adults were reported to have hypertension and no children were reported to have hypertension. The definition of hypertension in this report was a resting systolic blood pressure greater than or equal to 140 mm Hg or a resting diastolic blood pressure greater than or equal to 90 mm Hg. The prevalence of reported hypertension of persons with PWS and details of the samples are presented in Table 1-1.

Lifestyle Modification and Hypertension Research in Persons with I/DD

Research on the recommended JNC-7 lifestyle modifications of persons with I/DD was also lacking. Most of the research discussed in the following is related to the recommended areas of lifestyle modifications for reducing blood pressure; however, none of the research was specifically designed to modify blood pressure. Research involving persons with I/DD and the areas of the recommended lifestyle modifications is reviewed. Because the lifestyle modifications are also recommended for the prevention of hypertension, each of the sections includes a brief review of current studies reporting the percentage of persons with I/DD participating in the recommended lifestyle modifications. Because the number of reports specifically considering persons with DS, WBS, and PWS is low, all reports are presented together without separating studies involving persons with these syndromes.

OVERWEIGHT

The researchers indicate that the prevalence of overweight and obesity for adults with I/DD is at least as high as in the general population and likely higher (see Chapter 2). Rimmer et al. (1993) reported that adults with mild to moderate MR and those residing in community settings had the highest rates of obesity, with more than 70% of the women overweight. Similarly, Draheim et al. (2002a) reported that 69% of adults with mild to moderate MR residing in community settings were overweight, which is higher than the latest U.S. reports of approximately 65% of the population being overweight. Further analysis of the Draheim et al. (2002a) report indicates that the same sample of adults with MR are more likely to be obese (44.1% vs. 31% of the U.S. population) and to be severely obese compared to the general population (8.3% vs. 5% U.S. population) (Flegal, Carroll, Ogden, & Johnson, 2002).

The elevated rates of overweight and obesity for persons with I/DD are important issues on their own, primarily because of the morbidity associated with overweight and obesity. In the general population, much research has demonstrated the important association between weight loss or weight control and blood pressure reduction; however, only two cross-sectional studies reported an association between body weight (or percentage body fat) and blood pressure in persons with I/DD. Morrison et al. (1996) reported a strong positive correlation between body weight and both systolic blood pressure and diastolic blood pressure in men but not women with I/DD. Draheim et al. (2002a) examined the relationship between overweight and hypertension and abdominal obesity and hypertension. Persons with I/DD who were overweight were three to four times more likely to have hypertension and persons with I/DD with abdominal obesity were three to nine times more likely to have hypertension than those who were not overweight or without abdominal obesity (Draheim et al., 2002a). No longitudinal studies designed to reduce blood pressure using weight loss techniques were found. The references of reports researching the relationship of overweight and obesity to hypertension in persons with I/DD and details of the samples are presented in Table 1-3.

ADOPTING THE DASH DIET

No reports were found that evaluated the DASH diet and blood pressure reduction in persons with I/DD. Dietary cross-sectional research involving persons with I/DD indicate that unhealthy diets are prevalent and supports a relationship between diet and hypertension. Draheim et al. (2002a) reported that only 7.6% of adults with

TABLE 1-3 *Lifestyle Modifications and Hypertension Research for Persons with Intellectual and Developmental Disabilities (I/DD)*

REFERENCE	SAMPLE SIZE	SAMPLE GENDER AND AGE	SAMPLE DESCRIPTION	STUDY DESIGN	FINDINGS
Weight loss Draheim et al., 2002b	145	Men and women, 18–65	MR/DS, mild to moderate	Cross-sectional/ comparative	Overweight participants three to four times more likely to have hypertension. Participants with abdominal obesity three to nine times more likely to have hypertension.
Morrison et al., 1996	70 44	Men Women	DS	Cross-sectional/ comparative	Weight correlated to SBP ($r = .50$), BMI correlated to SBP ($r = .62$), BMI correlated to DBP ($r = .43$), No significant correlations for women.
Adopting DASH diet Draheim et al., 2002b	145	Men and women, 18–65	MR/DS, mild to moderate	Cross-sectional/ comparative	Participants w/high-fat diet three times more likely to have hypertension. No association between fruit and vegetable intake and hypertension.
Dietary sodium reduction No reports located					
Physical activity Draheim et al., 2002b	145	Men and women, 18–65	MR/DS, mild to moderate	Cross-sectional/ comparative	Active participants not less likely to have hypertension.
Draheim et al., 2003	145	Men and women, 18–65	MR/DS, mild to moderate	Cross-sectional/ comparative	Active participants in Sp. Olymp had lower SBP (8 mm Hg) and lower DBP (3–7 mm Hg).
Moderation of alcohol No reports located					

BMI, Body mass index; DBP, diastolic blood pressure; DS, Down syndrome; , MR, mental retardation; SBP, systolic blood pressure; Sp. Olymp, Special Olympics

10

mild to moderate I/DD residing in community settings had a dietary fat intake within recommended levels (less than 30% total intake), and only 36.6% of the participants consumed the recommended fruit and vegetable intake (more than five servings per day). Researchers reported that the dietary intake of individuals with MR who resided in group homes was less adequate than that of residents of larger institutional settings (Mercer & Ekvall, 1992). Another study that evaluated eight food menus indicated that group home diets were high in total energy (2570 kcal/day), fat (42% of daily kilocalories), and sugar (24% of daily kilocalories) (Lindeman, 1991). The results of these three studies do support that persons residing in group homes likely consume a high-energy, high-fat diet. Draheim et al. (2002a) reported that adults with I/DD who consumed high-fat diets were three times more likely to have hypertension than adults who consumed low-fat diets; however, no association between fruit and vegetable intake and hypertension was reported. The references of reports researching the relationship of dietary intake to hypertension in persons with I/DD and details of the samples are presented in Table 1-3.

REDUCING DIETARY SODIUM INTAKE

No studies were found that investigated the relationship between dietary sodium intake and hypertension in persons with I/DD.

PHYSICAL ACTIVITY

The relationship between physical activity and health is discussed in Chapter 6; however, reports on the overall activity levels of persons with I/DD and the relationships between activity and hypertension are briefly included here. Two large studies investigating physical activity of adults with MR have reported that adults with MR were less active than adults without MR (Beange et al., 1995) and that adults with MR residing in group homes were less active than adults residing in institutional settings (Rimmer et al., 1995). In adults with I/DD residing in community settings the overall prevalence for no physical activity and physical activity less than three times per week (10.5% and 51.3%, respectively) for men with MR (Draheim, Williams, & McCubbin, 2002b) are similar to those reported for U.S. men without MR (13% and 48%, respectively) (Crespo, Keteyian, Heath, & Sempos, 1996). Also, the overall prevalence rates for no physical activity and physical activity less than three times per week (14.9% and 47.3%, respectively) for women with MR residing in community settings (Draheim et al., 2002b) are similar to those reported for U.S. women without MR (23% and 57%, respectively) (Crespo et al., 1996). Even more interesting is the extremely low prevalence of men (1.3%) and women (1.4%) participating in regular vigorous physical activity. Other estimates of physical activity indicate that only 21.1% of the women and 21.5% of the men with MR accumulated the recommended 10,000 steps per day (Stanish & Draheim, 2005) and only 17.5% of the participants reported at least five sessions of moderate to vigorous physical activity per week totaling 30 minutes per session (Stanish & Draheim, in press). Beange et al. (1995) reported that 72% to 75% of persons with I/DD did not participate in vigorous exercise as compared to 49% to 65% of persons without I/DD.

Only two cross-sectional studies were found that investigated the relationship between hypertension and physical activity. Draheim, Williams, & McCubbin (2003) reported that adults who were physically active and who participated in Special Olympics weekly had significantly lower systolic and diastolic blood pressure than others who were not physically active or who did not participate in Special Olympics. Draheim et al. (2002a) reported no relationship between persons reporting five or more sessions of physical activity per week and hypertension. The lack of a significant relationship could be due to the crude estimates of physical activity levels or to the fact that the relationship tested was between physical activity and hypertension without separating systolic and diastolic blood pressure. More research is needed in this area. The references of reports researching the relationship of physical activity to hypertension of persons with I/DD and details of the samples are presented in Table 1-3.

MODERATION OF ALCOHOL CONSUMPTION

No studies were found that investigated the relationship between alcohol consumption and hypertension in persons with I/DD. Rimmer et al. (1995) reported a small amount of alcohol consumption for person with I/DD as compared to persons without I/DD and Beange et al. (1995) in Australia reported that a considerably smaller percentage of persons with I/DD (only 25%) consumed alcohol compared to the general population (87%). Alcohol consumption may not be a major concern for most individuals with I/DD; however, decreasing alcohol consumption for persons with hypertension should be considered an option for persons with I/DD who consume alcohol.

Conclusions

Although there were only a few reports of the prevalence of hypertension and many of the reports were flawed in determining population prevalence rates, hypertension rates for persons with I/DD appear to be similar to and may be higher than in the general population. Persons with DS appear to have lower blood pressures and a lower prevalence of hypertension compared to others with I/DD. Children with WBS appear to have a greater prevalence of hypertension than others with I/DD. Persons with PWS may have a slightly lower prevalence of hypertension than others with I/DD, although only one report was found that supported this finding. In general, in the United States, persons with mild to moderate I/DD without DS may have a higher prevalence of hypertension than the general population. It also appears that persons with mild to moderate I/DD may be more likely to have hypertension than others with severe to profound I/DD, as the prevalence rates reported in studies that included persons with severe to profound I/DD were lower than rates for samples that included only persons with mild to moderate I/DD (see Table 1-1).

Very few studies were found that reported the relationship between lifestyle modifications and hypertension. Although the evidence for health promotion of hypertension in persons with I/DD is severely lacking, the evidence found supports the JNC-7 recommendations for lifestyle modifications of decreasing body weight, dietary interventions, and increasing physical activity for persons with I/DD. Two studies indicated a strong relationship between body weight and hypertension/ blood pressure in persons with I/DD and persons with DS. No studies were found that specifically investigated the relationship between the DASH diet and hypertension in persons with I/DD. One study reported a strong positive relationship between low-fat diets and hypertension. Two studies investigating the relationship of hypertension and blood pressure in persons with I/DD reported different findings, one supporting the benefits of physical activity and one reporting no relationship. No studies were found that investigated relationships among dietary sodium intake and blood pressure or moderation of alcohol and blood pressure. No longitudinal or experimental studies were found that investigated the relationships between lifestyle modifications and hypertension.

The only type of design implemented in the studies was a cross-sectional/ comparative design. Unfortunately, this type of study design can only support causation and not show cause-and-effect relationships between the behaviors and hypertension. Results from cross-sectional study designs are often difficult to evaluate and are often open to different interpretations depending on the amount of other plausible influences of reported relationships. Cross-sectional designs are also flawed by the lack of a timeframe linking the behaviors (lifestyle modifications) with the outcome or disease (hypertension). Future research should utilize experimental designs developed to evaluate interventions specifically designed to reduce blood pressure.

The varied samples and varied definitions of hypertension used among the studies make comparisons very difficult. Many studies used a convenience sample or volunteers to estimate the prevalence of hypertension. Samples may not have included representative proportions of different ages, genders, races, and levels of I/DD. Also, some studies included a very small sample. The small sample sizes and differences in sampling techniques make it difficult to determine the accuracy of the prevalence of hypertension and to compare the prevalence of hypertension among persons with and without I/DD. Different definitions of hypertension were used across studies, and some studies reported no definition. The differing definitions of hypertension also make it difficult to determine the accuracy of the prevalence of hypertension and to compare the prevalence of hypertension among persons with and without I/DD.

It is recommended that the JNC-7 guidelines be used for the prevention and treatment of hypertension for person with I/DD. Programs should focus on the education of individuals with I/DD and health care providers regarding the importance of controlling blood pressure and adopting the recommended lifestyle modifications to prevent and help treat hypertension. Prevention and treatment of hypertension should be implemented for persons who are at risk for hypertension and for those with the newly developed prehypertension blood pressure levels. It is likely that persons with I/DD will face the same challenges of managing hypertension as does the general population. Future research should focus on developing realistic and effective programs using lifestyle modifications specifically designed for reducing blood pressure. Once these programs are shown effective for reducing hypertension in persons with I/DD they can also be used for prevention of hypertension for those who are at risk. Additional research should focus on developing effective motivational strategies specifically designed to assist persons with I/DD in adhering to the lifestyle modifications.

Although this chapter did not focus on medication use for the treatment of hypertension, it is recommended that the medication guidelines of the JNC-7 be used for the prevention and treatment of hypertension for person with I/DD. Physicians and health care providers should be aware of the high prevalence of medication use in persons with I/DD. Additional attention should be given to possible interaction effects of multiple medication use, which is often seen in persons with I/DD.

REFERENCES

Barr, O., Gilgunn, J., Kane, T., & Moore, G. (1999). Health screening for people with learning disabilities by a community learning disability nursing service in Northern Ireland. *Journal of Advanced Nursing, 29,* 1482–1491.

Beange, H, McElduff, A., & Baker, W. (1995). Medical disorders of adults with mental retardation: A population study. *American Journal on Mental Retardation, 99,* 595–604.

Braunschweig, C., Gomez, S., Sheean, P., Tomey, K., Rimmer, J., & Heller, T. (2004). Nutritional status and risk factors for chronic disease in urban-dwelling adults with Down syndrome. *American Journal on Mental Retardation, 109,* 186–193.

Broder, K., Reinhardt, E., Ahern, J., Lifton, R., Tamborlane, W., & Pober, B. (1999). Elevated ambulatory blood pressure in 20 subjects with Williams syndrome. *American Journal of Medical Genetics, 83,* 356–360.

Butler, J. V., Whittington, J. E., Holland, A. J., Boer, H., Clarke, D., & Webb, T. (2002). Prevalence of, and risk factors for, physical ill-health in people with Prader-Willi syndrome: A population-based study. *Developmental Medicine and Child Neurology, 44,* 248–255.

Chobanian, A. V., Bakris, G. L., Black, H. R., Cushman, W. C., Green, L. A., Izzo, J. L. Jr., et al. (2003). Seventh report of the Joint National Committee on Prevention, Detection, Evaluation, and Treatment of High Blood Pressure: The JNC-7 report. *Journal of the American Medical Association, 289,* 2560–2572.

Cooper, S. A. (1998). Clinical study of the effects of age on the physical health of adults with mental retardation. *American Journal of Mental Retardation, 1998,* 582–589.

Crespo, C. J., Keteyian, S. J., Heath, G. W., & Sempos, C. T. (1996). Leisure-time physical activity among US adults. *Archives of Internal Medicine, 156,* 93–98.

Draheim, C. C., McCubbin, J. A., & Williams, D. P. (2002a). Differences in cardiovascular disease risk between non-diabetic adults with Down syndrome and mental retardation. *American Journal of Mental Retardation, 107,* 201–211.

Draheim, C. C., Williams, D. P., & McCubbin, J. A. (2002b). Physical activity, dietary intake, and the insulin resistance syndrome in non-diabetic adults with mental retardation. *American Journal of Mental Retardation, 107,* 361–375.

Draheim, C. C., Williams, D. P., & McCubbin, J. A. (2002c). Prevalence of physical inactivity and recommended physical activity in adults with mental retardation residing in community settings. *Mental Retardation, 40,* 436–444.

Draheim, C. C., Williams, D. P., & McCubbin, J. A. (2003). Cardiovascular disease risk factor differences between Special Olympians and Non-Special Olympians. *Adapted Physical Activity Quarterly, 20,* 118–134.

Flegal, K. M., Carroll, M. D., Ogden, C. L., & Johnson, C. L. (2002). Prevalence and trends in obesity among US adults, 1999-2000. *Journal of the American Medical Association, 288,* 1723–1727.

Frey, B., & Rimmer, J. (1995). Comparison of body composition between German and American adults with mental retardation. *Medicine and Science in Sport and Medicine, 27,* 1439–1443.

Giordano, U., Turchetta, A., Giannotti, A., Digilio, M. C., Virgilii, F., & Calzolari, A. (2001). Exercise testing and 24-hour ambulatory blood pressure monitoring in children with Williams syndrome. *Pediatric Cardiology, 22,* 509–511.

Hajjar, I., & Kotchen, T. A. (2003). Trends in prevalence, awareness, treatment, and control of hypertension in the United States, 1988–2000. *Journal of the American Medical Association, 290,* 199–206.

Kappell, D., Nightingale, B., Rodriguez, A., Lee, J., Zigman, W., & Schupf, N. (1998). Prevalence of chronic medical conditions in adults with mental retardation: Comparison with the general population. *Mental Retardation, 36,* 269–279.

Lindeman, A. K. (1991). Resident manager's nutrition concerns for staff and residents of group homes for mentally retarded adults. *Research and Professional Briefs, 91,* 602–604.

McDermott, S., Platt, T., & Krishnaswami, S. (1997). Are individuals with mental retardation at high risk for chronic disease? *Family Medicine, 29,* 429–434.

Mercer, K., & Ekvall, S. (1992). Comparing the diets of adults with mental retardation who live in intermediate care facilities and in group homes. *Journal of the American Dietetic Association, 92,* 356–358.

Morrison, R., McGrath, A., Davidson, G., Brown, J., Murray G., & Lever, A. (1996). Low blood pressure in Down syndrome: A link to Alzheimer's Disease. *Hypertension, 28,* 569–575.

Rimmer, J. H., Braddock, D., & Fujiura, G. (1993). Prevalence of obesity in adults with mental retardation: Implication for health promotion and disease prevention. *Mental Retardation, 31,* 105–110.

Rimmer, J. H., Braddock, D., & Marks, B. (1995). Health characteristics and behaviors of adults with mental retardation residing in three living arrangements. *Research in Developmental Disabilities, 16,* 489–499.

Salaymeh, K. J., & Banerjee, A. (2001). Evaluation of arterial stiffness in children with Williams syndrome: Does it play a role in evolving hypertension? *American Heart Journal, 142,* 549–555.

Stanish, H. I., & Draheim, C. C. (2005). Assessment of walking activity using a pedometer and survey in adults with mental retardation. *Adapted Physical Activity Quarterly, 22* (2), 136–145.

Stanish, H. I., & Draheim, C. C. (in press-b). Walking habits of adults with mental retardation. *Mental Retardation.*

Van Allen, M. I., Fung, J., & Jurenka, S. B. (1999). Health care concerns and guidelines for adults with Down syndrome. *American Journal of Medical Genetics, 89,* 100–110.

2

OBESITY

Linda Bandini, PhD, RD

T he incidence of obesity in the general population in the United States has
increased during the past 20 years. The most recent data for 2001–2002 indicate that the prevalence of overweight and obesity combined is 65.7% and
the prevalence of obesity is 30.6% in the general adult population (Hedley et al.,
2004). Despite these statistics, there is limited information on the prevalence of
obesity in persons with mental retardation (MR) or on the risk factors associated
with the development of obesity in this population. This chapter reviews the current
information on the incidence of obesity in persons with MR including individuals
with Down syndrome, Prader-Willi syndrome, and spina bifida.

Background

Obesity is broadly defined as an excess of body fat. In general, establishing the
prevalence of obesity in a population will depend in part on the criteria used to
identify the condition. To determine its prevalence across multiple studies, a uniform definition of obesity is needed. Laboratory methods used to measure body fat
are not available in clinical or field settings. Therefore, measurements that are
highly correlated with body fat are used to identify obesity in these settings. Body
mass index, commonly referred to as BMI, is defined as weight in kilograms divided
by the square of height in meters (wt/ht^2) and has been shown to be highly correlated with body fatness in the general population. The World Health Organization
(WHO, 1998) and the National Institutes of Health (NIH, 1998) established common
criteria based on BMI to identify persons who are overweight and obese. An individual

with a BMI of 25–29.9 is considered overweight and one with a BMI greater than or equal to 30 is considered obese. Prior to 1997, there were no uniform criteria for the identification of obesity.

Many of the studies reported here were conducted prior to the establishment of these guidelines for the identification of obesity. Thus, different investigators used different criteria for the assessment of obesity. In the studies reviewed in this chapter, three measures were commonly used to identify obesity: (1) BMI, (2) subcutaneous skinfold thickness, and (3) relative weight.

Many early studies used BMI to identify individuals who were obese. However, the BMI cutoff point to identify obesity in the United States has changed since 1985. In the 1985 guidelines, derived from a National Institutes of Health (NIH) Consensus Conference, obesity was defined as a BMI greater than 27.3 for females and greater than 27.8 for males (NIH, 1985). Thus, earlier studies using the lower 1985 criteria would have found a higher prevalence of obesity than those using the cutoff point of greater than or equal to 30 for obesity.

Skinfold thickness measures subcutaneous body fat. The assumption is that subcutaneous fat correlates well with total body fat. Published equations have been developed to calculate body fat from measures of multiple skinfolds (Durnin & Wormersley, 1974; Jackson, Pollack, & Ward, 1980). Most equations use at least three or four skinfolds, are gender specific, and differ in the choice of skinfolds to measure. For example, some equations use biceps, triceps, subscapular and suprailiac folds to determine percentage body fatness (Durnin & Wormsley, 1974) while others use triceps, suprailiac, and thigh folds (Jackson, Pollack, & Ward, 1980). Furthermore, no criteria have been developed that establish the body fat percentage associated with obesity. Another limitation in the use of skinfold thickness to identify obesity in this population is that the equations to determine body fat were derived from a population of persons without disabilities. Alterations in body composition have been observed in persons with intellectual and developmental disabilities (I/DD) (Luke, Roizen, Sutton, & Schoeller, 1994; Schoeller, Levitsky, Bandini, Dietz, & Walczak, 1988; Shepherd, Roberts, Golding, Thomas, & Shepherd, 1991). For example, it has been reported that children with Down syndrome have less fat-free mass than typically developing children (Luke et al., 1994). Thus, it is questionable whether equations derived to determine body fatness from skinfold thickness measures in the general population are applicable for persons with MR.

Relative weight was frequently used in the 1980s to identify overweight. Relative weight is a percentage of weight above a reference standard. The standard for relative weight often differed among studies, especially when measured in countries other than the United States.

In children, BMI changes with age as a result of growth and these changes are gender specific. In the United States, children with a BMI greater than or equal to the 95th percentile for age and gender are considered overweight whereas children with a BMI greater than or equal to the 85th percentile are considered at risk for overweight. In the United States, these are referenced against the 2000 Centers for Disease Control and Prevention (CDC) growth reference (National Center for Health Statistics, 2000). Outside of the United States, the International Obesity Task Force cutoff points identify children who are obese as those with a BMI greater than or equal to the 95th percentile (Cole, Bellizzi, Flegal, & Dietz, 2000). While the terminology describing the cutoff points differs, the actual values are the same. However, since the reference populations differ, the estimates they provide are not comparable. Because these classifications are relatively new, most of the studies that reported on children with MR used criteria based on relative weight or skinfold thickness.

Research Questions

The research questions addressed in this chapter are:

1. What is the prevalence of obesity in persons with mental retardation?

2. What factors are associated with obesity in persons with mental retardation?

3. What is the prevalence of obesity in persons with Down syndrome (DS), Prader-Willi syndrome (PWS), and spina bifida?

4. What are the factors associated with obesity in persons with DS?

Methods

An information specialist searched Medline, CINAHL, SocioFile, Health Star, Psych-Info, Pharmaceutical Abstracts, Web Science, Academic Search Premiere, Ingenta, and GPO Access to identify all relevant articles based on search terms used for obesity and the population under study. In addition, references cited within articles were also reviewed. The studies reported herein span a period of 22 years, with 28 of 31 (90%) studies conducted from 1990 to 2004. All research articles identified by the searches in this time span were reviewed. Over this period of time, the prevalence of obesity in the general population in the United States and worldwide increased substantially (WHO, 1998). Half of the studies reported here came from countries other than the United States. Risk factors associated with obesity such as living arrangement, diet, and activity may differ among countries.

Results

ORGANIZATION OF THE EVIDENCE

The tables presented summarize data on the prevalence of obesity in persons with MR (Table 2-1), DS (Table 2-3), PWS (Table 2-5), and spina bifida (Table 2-6). DS, PWS, and spina bifida are three developmental disabilities associated with obesity. Each table is discussed separately. In addition, the MR and Down syndrome supplementary tables (Table 2-2 and 2-4) summarize studies that examined factors associated with obesity, that is, age, gender, severity of retardation, and living arrangement. Finally, Table 2-7 summarizes the results of two national surveys in the United States that assessed the prevalence of overweight in children with MR.

The strength of the information provided in each study was rated according to level of evidence. All of the studies reviewed were community- or institution-based samples and therefore are not representative of the general population of persons with MR. Cross-sectional studies with a control group or a reference group with more than 25 people were assigned a level of evidence of IV. Cross-sectional studies with no reference group or those with fewer than 25 subjects were assigned a level of evidence of V. Cross-sectional studies that included statistical analyses of differences between comparison groups were assigned a level of evidence of III. No randomized control trials or controlled trials were found.

TABLES OF EVIDENCE

The first table summarizes studies reported in the literature on the prevalence of overweight and obesity in children and adults with MR (Table 2-1). Fourteen studies were conducted, 11 of these between 1991 and 2004. All of these studies are descriptive. Because they are not representative of the general population of persons with MR, the ability to make valid comparisons of the prevalence estimates from these samples with those obtained from nationally representative data sets is limited. Of the fourteen studies cited, seven were conducted in the United States; one each in Norway, Ireland, and Finland; and two in the United Kingdom and Japan. Not all the studies reported overall prevalence data, but among those that did, the prevalence of obesity among persons with MR ranged from 10% to 58%.

Table 2-2 provides data examining the prevalence of obesity in persons with MR in relation to age, gender, living situation, and severity of retardation. All of these studies were cross-sectional and the level of evidence ranged from III to IV. Twelve studies examined at least one of the factors—age, gender, living situation, or severity of retardation. Two of the studies examined the relationship of obesity to secondary conditions.

Of the three studies that examined age as a factor in weight in adults, all found the prevalence of overweight to increase with age (Fox & Rotatori, 1982; Lea, 1999; Marshall, McConkey, & Moore, 2003). In two of the three studies of children, the prevalence of overweight was greater in adolescents than in school-age children (Suzuki et al., 1991; Takeuchi, 1994). Seven studies compared the prevalence of obesity among males and females with MR. Of these, two reported no significant difference (Lea, 1999; Marshall, McConkey, & Moore, 2003), four reported a higher prevalence in females than in males (Fox & Rotatori,1982; Rimmer, Braddock, & Fujiura, 1993; Suzuki et al., 1991; Takeuchi, 1994), and one reported higher relative weights in males than in females (Emery, Watson, Watson, Thompson, & Biderman, 1985). Three studies examined the relationship of living situation to prevalence of overweight. Two of the three studies found an increase in the prevalence of obesity in persons living at home compared to those with MR living in a group home or institutional setting (Emery et al., 1985; Rimmer et al., 1993), whereas the third study found no significant differences associated with living arrangement (Marshall et al., 2003). Severity of retardation and its relationship to obesity was assessed in six studies. Of these, five found a higher prevalence of obesity, higher mean BMI, or greater percentage of fat in those with mild to moderate MR than in individuals with severe to profound MR (Emery et al., 1985; Hove, 2004; Kelly, Rimmer, & Ness,

1986; Rimmer et al., 1993; Simila & Niskanen, 1991), and one reported no significant differences associated with severity of MR (Marshall et al., 2003).

Only two studies reported on secondary conditions associated with obesity. One study found a significant relationship between obesity and hypertension (Marshall et al., 2003), and the other reported an increased risk for hyperinsulinemia, high triglyceride levels, and hypertension with obesity (Draheim, Williams, & McCubbin, 2002) (see Chapter 1).

Table 2-3 summarizes the studies reported in the literature for persons with DS. Five studies were conducted between 1992 and 2004. The level of evidence ranged from IV to V. All of the studies examined cross-sectional data of nonrepresentative samples to determine the prevalence of obesity. Three of the studies were conducted in the United States and two were conducted in the United Kingdom. The prevalence of overweight ranged from 18% to 56%, and the prevalence of obesity ranged from 25% to 70% among the males and females with DS in these five studies.

Table 2-4 provides data examining the prevalence of obesity in persons with DS in relation to age, gender, living situation, and severity of retardation. All of the studies were cross sectional and the level of evidence was III. Three studies examined the relationship between age and obesity. Two out of three found a trend toward a lower BMI with age (Prasher, 1995; Rubin, Rimmer, Chicoine, Braddock, & McGuire, 1998) while the third found no correlation between age with obesity (Fujiura et al., 1997). Of the four studies that compared the prevalence among males and females, one study reported males to have a higher BMI (Prasher, 1995), two reported females to have a higher BMI (Braunschweig et al., 2004; Rubin et al., 1998), and the fourth did not find gender to be a significant factor (Fujiura, Fitzsimons, & Marks, 1997). Both studies that looked at the relationship of BMI with living situation found a higher BMI in those living at home compared to those living in an institution (Prasher, 1995; Rubin et al., 1998). No significant differences were observed in the study that looked at the relationship between severity of MR and obesity (Prasher, 1995).

One study (Fujiura et al., 1997) examined whether other factors in addition to gender, age, diet, and activity predicted weight status in persons with DS. The researchers found that social opportunity and friendship variables accounted for 21% of the variance, although diet, physical activity, gender, and age were not significant predictors of overweight.

Only one study examined the relationship of BMI with total cholesterol, high-density lipoprotein (HDL) cholesterol, low-density lipoprotein (LDL) cholesterol, or triglyceride levels (Braunschweig et al., 2004). They found a significant correlation of BMI with blood glucose, but not with total cholesterol, HDL cholesterol, LDL cholesterol, or triglycerides in persons with DS.

Table 2-5 provides data on body composition from five studies (three on children, two on adults) in persons with PWS. These studies were all cross sectional and the level of evidence ranged from IV to V. In the three studies reported in children (Brambilla, Bosio, Manzoni, Pietrobelli, & Beccaria, 1997; Schoeller et al., 1988; van Mil et al., 2001), percentage body fat was not significantly different from that of obese controls; however, fat-free mass was lower in children with PWS. In one of the

TABLE 2-1 *Prevalence of Overweight and Obesity in Persons with Mental Retardation*

STUDY INFORMATION	RESEARCH DESIGN/ LEVEL OF EVIDENCE	POPULATION STUDIED	TOTAL NUMBER OF SUBJECTS	AGES OF SUBJECTS, YRS ($X \pm$ S.D.)	SETTING (HOME/FAMILY, CONGREGATE, INSTITUTION)	MEASURES USED/ CRITERIA FOR OVERWEIGHT (OW) AND OBESITY	OUTCOME RESULTS
Bell & Bhate, 1992	Cross-sectional. Reference data (no statistical comparisons done with reference data) Level IV	MR England	$N = 125$ Men ($N = 71$) Women ($N = 54$)	Women: 20–53 Men: 20–68	Family, social services hostel, or supervised flatlets	Ht., Wt. Criteria: BMI 25–30: OW BMI > 30: Obese Adult British reference group: OW: 34% men, 24% women Obese: 6% men, 8% women	37% men OW 13% men obese 31% women OW 31% women obese
Draheim et al., 2002	Cross-sectional Level V	MR USA (51.7% DS)	$N = 145$	18–65	Residents in community setting: independent (4.1%); semi-independent (33.8%) Group home (45.5%) Family (16.6%)	Ht., Wt. Criteria: BMI = 25: OW Blood pressure Lipid profile Fasting insulin	69% OW
Emery et al., 1985	Cross-sectional. Reference group Level IV	MR USA	$N = 217$ Men ($N = 110$) Women ($N = 107$)	30.9 ± 9.0 Range: 18–74	Home or group home	Ht., Wt. Normative data from Metropolitan Life Insurance Co. (1959), National Health Survey (Abraham et al., 1979)	Significantly higher actual weight than normal for women but not men; for both men and women actual weight > IBW

Study	Design / Level	Country / Population	Age	Sample	Setting	Measures / Criteria	Results
Fox & Rotatori, 1982	Cross-sectional Level V	MR USA	18–77	$N = 1152$ Men ($N = 646$) Women ($N = 506$)	Public institutions, private institutions, sheltered workshop, semi-residential, not specified for others	Ht, Wt. Criteria: Obesity: Relative weight (Wt./Ht.) > 120% (Fogarty Center tables; Bray, 1979)	Obesity: Men: 15.6% Women: 25.1%
Harris et al., 2003	Cross-sectional. Reference data (no statistical comparisons done with reference data) Level IV	Special Olympic athletes who participated in 1999 Summer and 2001 Winter World Special Olympics Games	9–11 ($N = 11$) 12–17 ($N = 528$) 18–19 ($N = 243$) 20–39 ($N = 869$) >40 ($N = 98$)	$N = 1749$ US Athletes ($N = 562$) International athletes ($N = 1187$) Men ($N = 63\%$) Women ($N = 37\%$)	N/A	Ht, Wt. Criteria: At risk for overweight for children US BMI 85th–95th percentile range, OW 95th–100th percentile BMI adults: OW: 25–29.9 Obese: ≥30 Reference group: NHANES III	BMI Children and adolescents: 22% vs. 9% non-U.S. 85th–95th percentile 23% vs. 5% non-US 95th–100th percentile BMI adults: 33% OW vs. 24% non-U.S. 32% obese U.S. vs. 7% non-U.S.
Hove, 2004	Cross-sectional. Reference data (no statistical comparisons done with reference data) Level IV	MR Norway	Adults	$N = 282$ Men ($N = 143$) Women ($N = 131$)	N/A	Questionnaire sent to health professionals Ht, Wt. Criteria: BMI 25–29.9: OW BMI >30: Obese	34.8% OW 19% obese Prevalence > in DS group than those without DS

(continued)

TABLE 2-1 *Continued*

STUDY INFORMATION	RESEARCH DESIGN/ LEVEL OF EVIDENCE	POPULATION STUDIED	TOTAL NUMBER OF SUBJECTS	AGES OF SUBJECTS, YRS (X ± S.D.)	SETTING (HOME/FAMILY, CONGREGATION, INSTITUTION)	MEASURES USED/ CRITERIA FOR OVERWEIGHT (OW) AND OBESITY	OUTCOME RESULTS
Kelly et al., 1986	Cross-sectional. Reference data (no statistical comparisons done with reference data) Level IV	MR USA	N = 553 Men (N = 343) Women (N = 210)	Range: 18–40	Institution	Skinfolds Men: chest, abdomen, thigh; Women: triceps, thigh, suprailiac Criteria for obesity For men: > 20%BF For women: > 30%BF	45.2% men obese 50.5% women obese
Lea, 1999	Cross-sectional. Reference data (no statistical comparisons done with reference data) Level IV	Learning disability (MR) UK	N = 273 Men (N = 157) Women (N = 116)	20–85+	Residential facility	Ht, Wt. Criteria: BMI = 25.1–29.9: OW BMI ≥ 30: Obese Reference: East Surrey Health Promotion Unit, 1994 Women: OW, 22%; obese, 6% Men: OW, 35%; obese, 6%	Men: 20.4% OW, 10.2% obese Women: 17.5% OW, 16.7% obese

Study	Design/Level	Population/Country	N	Age	Setting	Measures	Results
Marshall et al., 2003	Cross-sectional. Reference data (no statistical comparisons done with reference data) Level IV	Intellectual disability (MR) Ireland	N = 407 54% Men 46% Women	X = 31 Range: 10–68	Residential (N = 21%) Family (N = 79%)	Ht, Wt. Criteria: BMI > 25: OW BMI > 30: Obese Note: used adult standards for children British Reference Population Obese: 21% Women 17% Men Blood pressure high, SBP > 140	27.0% OW 31.5% obese
Murphy et al., 1992	Cross-sectional. Reference group (non-MR subjects from same hospital) Level IV	USA, included: persons with MR, learning disabilities, attention deficit, hyperactivity disorder, autism, cerebral palsy, and PWS	N = 223 MR (N = 110) Non-MR (N = 107) Unknown (N = 6)	6.2 ± 4.2 Men (N = 161) Women (N = 61)	N/A	Ht, Wt. from medical record BMI; age-corrected BMI	NSD between BMI for children with and without MR
Rimmer et al., 1993	Cross-sectional. Reference data (no statistical comparisons done with reference data) Level IV	MR USA	N = 364	36.8 ± 11.2	Institution (N = 103) ICF/MR (N = 94) Group home (N = 44) Family (N = 123)	Skinfolds Men: biceps, triceps, suprailiac, and subscapular Women: triceps, suprailiac, and thigh	Obesity Men: 27.5 % Women: 58.8 % Setting: Institution: 16.5% ICF/MR: 50.5%

(continued)

TABLE 2-1 *Continued*

STUDY INFORMATION	RESEARCH DESIGN/ LEVEL OF EVIDENCE	POPULATION STUDIED	TOTAL NUMBER OF SUBJECTS	AGES OF SUBJECTS, YRS (X ± S.D.)	SETTING (HOME/FAMILY, CONGREGATION, INSTITUTION)	MEASURES USED/ CRITERIA FOR OVERWEIGHT (OW) AND OBESITY	OUTCOME RESULTS
						Criteria: Obesity > 25% BF for men > 30% BF for women (Buskirk, 1987) Reference: NCHS (1973) Obese: 19% Men 28% Women	Group home: 40.9% Family: 55.3%
Simila & Niskanen, 1991	Cross-sectional (no statistical comparisons done with reference group) Level IV	1966 birth cohort of Finns with MR	MR $N = 112$	MR: 20 Control: 20–29	N/A	Ht., Wt. Criteria: BMI 25–29.9: OW BMI $\geq$ 30: Obese Reference: Finnish demographic survey of 1966–1972 $N = 57{,}000$ (Heliovaara and Aromaa, 1988)	33% OW 9.8% obese

26

Reference	Design	Population	N	Age		Notes	Obesity/severe obesity
Takeuchi, 1994	Cross-sectional. Reference group Level IV	MR Japan: children from 240 special schools for mental retardation (organic MR, DS, autism, epilepsy, PWS and others)	N = 20,031	6–11 Males (N = 4381) Females (N = 2181)	N/A	"Standard weight" based on gender, age, and height	Obesity/severe obesity
							Elementary boys: 10.3%/2.0% Elementary girls: 12.4%/2.5%
				12–14 Boys (N = 3928) Girls (N = 2056)		Criteria: > 120% obese > 150% severely obese > 200% hyperobese	Junior high boys: 11.3/2.8% Junior high girls: 17.2/3.9%
				15–17 Boys (N = 4706) Girls (N = 7016)		Reference: Annual Report by the Japanese Ministry of Education (1989)	Senior high boys: 11.5/2.7 Senior high girls: 14.1/2.8%
							In comparison to boys without MR in junior high level, prevalence of obesity higher than in girls without MR. No comparative data on senior high available.

% BF, Percentage body fat; BMI, body mass index; DS, Down syndrome; Ht., height; IBW, ideal body weight; ICF, intermediate care facility; MR, mental retardation; OW, overweight; PWS, Prader-Willi syndrome; Wt., weight N/A, Not available

TABLE 2-2 *Factors Associated with Obesity for Persons with Mental Retardation: Age, Gender, Severity of Retardation, and Living Arrangements*

STUDY	RESEARCH DESIGN/ LEVEL OF EVIDENCE	AGE	GENDER	LIVING ARRANGEMENT	SEVERITY OF MR	CO-MORBIDITY
Draheim et al., 2002	Cross-sectional Level IV	N/A	N/A	N/A	N/A	OW significantly increased risk for hyperinsulinemia, high triglycerides, hypertension
Emery et al., 1985	Cross-sectional Level III	NSD	Significantly greater than normal weight for males than for females	Greater in group home than at family home	NSD	N/A
Fox & Rotatori, 1982	Cross-sectional Level III	Prevalence increases with age	Significantly greater in females than in males	No	Significantly greater in mild/ moderate than severe MR	N/A
Harris et al., 2003	Cross-sectional Level III	N/A	N/A	N/A	N/A	N/A
Hove, 2004	Cross-sectional Level III	N/A	N/A	N/A	Incidence of mild/ moderate is greater than severe MR	N/A
Kelly et al., 1986	Cross-sectional Level III	N/A	Unclear	N/A	% BF is greater in mild/severe than in profound MR.	N/A
Lea, 1999	Cross-sectional Level III	Increases with age	NSD	N/A	N/A	N/A

Study	Design					Significant relationship between obesity and HTN
Marshall et al., 2003	Cross-sectional Level III	Increases with age	NSD	NSD	NSD	N/A
Rimmer et al., 1993	Cross-sectional Level III	N/A	Prevalence greater in females than in males	Greater prevalence in family home than in institution	Greater prevalence in mild/moderate than severe MR	N/A
Simila & Niskanen, 1991	Cross-sectional Level III	N/A	N/A	N/A	Mean BMI significantly higher in mild vs. severe MR	N/A
Suzuki et al., 1991	Cross-sectional Level III	Mean %BF greater in 14–19 yo	Significantly greater in males than in females	N/A	N/A	N/A
Takeuchi, 1994	Cross-sectional Level III	Increases with age	Prevalence greater in females than in males	N/A	N/A	N/A

% BF, Percentage body fat; HTN, hypertension; MR, mental retardation
N/A , Not available; NSD, not significantly different

TABLE 2-3 *Prevalence of Obesity in Persons with Down Syndrome*

STUDY INFORMATION	RESEARCH DESIGN/ LEVEL OF EVIDENCE	POPULATION STUDIED	TOTAL NUMBER OF SUBJECTS	AGES OF SUBJECTS, YRS ($X \pm S.D.$)	SETTING (HOME/FAMILY, CONGREGATION, INSTITUTION)	MEASURES USED/ CRITERIA FOR OW AND OBESITY	OUTCOME RESULTS
Bell & Bhate, 1992	Cross-sectional. Reference group (no statistical comparisons done with reference group) Level IV	England DS	$N = 58$ Men ($N = 34$) Women ($N = 24$)	Women: 20–53 Men: 20–68	Family, social services hostel, or supervised flatlets	Ht, Wt. Criteria: BMI 25–30: OW BMI > 30: Obese Adult British reference group: OW: 34% men, 24% women Obese: 6% men, 8% women	38% men OW 32% men obese 54% women OW 42% women obese
Braunschweig et al., 2004	Cross-sectional. No reference group Level V	USA	$N = 48$ Men ($N = 27$) Women ($N = 21$)	Men: 39.1 ± 5.9 Women: 40.1 ± 7.4	Day or residential group home	Ht, Wt. Criteria: BMI 25–29.9: OW BMI > 30: Obese	18.8% OW 70.8% obese
Fujiura et al., 1997	Cross-sectional No reference group Level V	USA	$N = 49$ Men ($N = 28$) Women ($N = 21$)	Women: 37.1 ± 10.4 Men: 25.2 ± 6.5	Home and residential facilities	Ht, Wt. Criteria: OW based on MLI, 1983; Obese: > 125% men > 130% women	25% men obese 42.9% women obese

Author, year	Design	Country	Sample	Age	Setting	Measure / Criteria	Results
Prasher, 1995	Cross-sectional. Reference group Level IV	England	$N = 239$ Men ($N = 102$) Women ($N = 137$)	42.2 ± 12.5 Range: 16–76	Family, supervised community or hospital	Ht, Wt. Criteria: BMI 25–30: OW BMI > 30: Obese General population: Obese: 6% women 8% men	31% men OW 48% men obese 22% women OW 47% women obese
Rubin et al., 1998	Cross-sectional. Reference group (no statistical tests done for comparison with reference group) Level IV	USA	$N = 283$ Men ($N = 146$) Women ($N = 137$)	Men: 35.4 ± 10.7 Women: 8.7 ± 10.6 Range: 15–69	Family ($N = 126$) Group home ($N = 157$)	Ht, Wt. Criteria: OW = BMI > 27.3 women and 28.3 for men Reference group: CDC, 1997 Prevalence of OW in US: 33% men and 36% women	45% men OW 56% women OW BMI in DS significantly greater than reference group

% BF, Percentage body fat; BMI, body mass index; DS, Down syndrome; Ht, height; MLI, Metropolitan Life Insurance; OW, overweight; Wt, weight

TABLE 2-4 *Factors Associated with Obesity for Persons with Down Syndrome: Age, Gender, Level of Retardation and Living Arrangements*

STUDY	LEVEL OF EVIDENCE	AGE	GENDER	LIVING ARRANGEMENT	SEVERITY OF MR	CO-MORBIDITY
Braunschweig et al., 2004	Cross-sectional Level III	N/A	N/A	N/A	N/A	Yes*
Fujiura et al., 1997	Cross-sectional Level III	NSD	NSD	N/A	N/A	N/A
Prasher, 1995	Cross-sectional Level III	Trend to lower BMI w/age (no statistics given)	Men were significantly heavier	BMI significantly greater in family than community homes or hospital	NSD	N/A
Rubin et al., 1998	Cross-sectional Level III	Trend for BMI to increase to age 30 then decline (no statistics given)	Significantly greater mean BMI in females than in males	BMI levels significantly greater in family setting than group home	N/A	N/A

*No significant relationship of BMI with total cholesterol, HDL, LDL, or TG, triglyceride levels
Significance seen only with glucose
N/A, Not available; NSD, not significantly different

studies in adults, visceral fat was found to be lower in adults with PWS than in obese controls (Goldstone et al., 2001).

Table 2-6 presents data on six studies of children and adults with spina bifida. Each of the findings was expressed differently. These studies were all cross-sectional and the level of evidence ranged from IV to V. Van den Berg-Emons, Bussmann, Meyerink, Roebroeck, and Stam (2003) reported 29% of persons with spina bifida were obese. Fiore et al. (1998) reported 40% of subjects to be overweight. Energy intake in 75% of the overweight persons was less than or equal to 100% of the Recommended Daily Allowance (RDA) for energy. Polito et al. (1995) reported the BMI z-score to be significantly higher in children with spina bifida than in controls, and subscapular but not tricep skinfold z-scores to be significantly greater than in controls. Mita et al. (1993) reported 58% of children older than 6 years of age had an abnormally high percentage of body fat and were obese. Shepherd et al. (1991) reported a greater percentage of body fat in those with high lesions but not in those with lower lesions. Bandini, Schoeller, Fukagawa, Wykes, and Dietz (1991) reported the mean percentage body fat to be 37.7% in males and 46.4% in females with spina bifida.

The final table (Table 2-7) provides the results from two large nationally representative surveys that were used to compare the prevalence of overweight in children with MR to those without MR. The National Health and Nutrition Examination Survey-II (NHANES II) data were collected from 1976 to 1980 (National Center for Health Statistics, 1987) and the NHANES III data were collected from 1988 to 1994 (National Center for Health Statistics and Centers for Disease Control and Prevention, 1996). In the NHANES II, only 20 persons were identified with MR and only 26 persons were identified with MR in the NHANES III. The small numbers of persons identified with MR are lower than the estimated prevalence (Larson et al., 2000). The prevalence of overweight among MR children did not differ from that in children without MR in both studies (Bandini, Curtin, Tybor, Hamad, & Must, 2003; Murphy et al., 1992). The level of evidence in these studies was rated as IV.

Discussion

The data presented suggest that overweight is a significant problem in persons with MR. However, because the samples are not representative, it is not clear whether the prevalence of overweight and obesity is different from that in the general population. The prevalence of obesity in the general population has also increased significantly over the last 20 years. As a result of these secular trends in obesity, the prevalence of obesity in persons with MR in earlier studies cannot be compared to that in the general population today. Likewise, because of variable criteria used to define obesity in the studies, an overall prevalence of obesity for this population cannot be determined. Furthermore, it is not clear if the classification of MR was consistent among populations. For example, some studies that identify subjects with MR for their sample often include people with disabilities who do not have MR. There is a lack of data on co-morbidity associated with overweight and obesity in persons with MR and other developmental disorders. There are virtually no data on the factors associated with the development of obesity such as diet and physical activity.

TABLE 2-5 *Prevalence of Overweight and Obesity in Persons with Prader-Willi Syndrome*

STUDY INFORMATION	RESEARCH DESIGN/ LEVEL OF EVIDENCE	POPULATION STUDIED	TOTAL NUMBER OF SUBJECTS	AGES OF SUBJECTS, YRS ($X \pm$ S.D.)	SETTING (HOME/FAMILY, CONGREGATION, INSTITUTION)	MEASURES USED	OUTCOME RESULTS
Brambilla et al., 1997	Cross-sectional Level IV	Italy	$N = 81$ PWS ($N = 27$) Boys ($N = 15$) Girls ($N = 12$) Age- and sex-matched control subjects; obese ($N = 27$), non-obese ($N = 27$)	PWS 14.2 ± 5.1; Control obese 13.7 ± 4.1; control non-obese 13.7 ± 4.1	N/A	Ht. Wt., body composition by DEXA (% BF); regional adiposity by DEXA	BMI in PWS NSD than obese controls but greater than normal controls (27.1 ± 6.6 vs. 29.7 ± 5.4 vs. 18.7 ± 2.7; no comparisons made on BMI z-score; % BF greater in PWS than in obese controls or normal weight controls, 47.4% ± 7.2 vs. 41.9% ± 9.9 vs. 20.6% ± 9.4. Arm and leg % fat was significantly higher in PWS than in obese controls or normal weight controls.
Goldstone et al., 2001	Cross-sectional Level IV	UK	$N = 57$ PWS ($N = 13$) Control ($N = 44$) Obese: $N = 14$ Non-obese: $N = 30$	PWS 27 ± 7 Control non-obese: 31 ± 8; Obese: 36 ± 10	N/A	Visceral fat by MRI scan	Visceral fat volume was lower in PWS than in obese controls; after adjustment for age and adiposity PWS subjects had reduced insulin resistance in comparison to obese controls
Hoybye et al., 2002	Cross-sectional Level V	Sweden	$N = 19$ Men ($N = 10$) Women ($N = 9$)	$X = 25$ 17–37	Group home ($N = 8$) Parental home ($N = 9$) Alone ($N = 2$)	Ht. Wt. Criteria: BMI 25–30: OW BMI > 30: Obese % BF by DEXA	100% obese women 10% OW men 60% obese; men 52.9% BF; women 44.3% BF, men

Schoeller et al, 1988	Cross-sectional Level V	USA	Study 1: N = 20 PWS (N = 10) Obese control (N = 10) Study 2: N = 6	Study 1: PWS: 16 ± 4 Control: 15 ± 3 Range: 8–24 Study 2: 24 ± 4	Home	Study 1 % BF Study 2 %BF	Study 1: % BF PWS: 45 ± 6% Obese control = 48 ± 7% Study 2: % BF PWS: 35 ± 6% No significant difference in % BF in obese control vs. PWS. FFM lower in PWS.
van Mil et al, 2001	Cross-sectional Level V	The Netherlands	N = 34 PWS (N = 17) Boys, 7 Girls, 10 Non-PWS (N = 17) Boys, 7 Girls, 10 Subjects matched for gender and bone age	PWS: 11.9 ± 3.4 7.5–19.8 Obese control: 11.3 ± 2.6 6.3–15.3	N/A	Ht., Wt., body composition (fat-free mass and fat mass) by isotopic dilution and dual-energy X-ray absorptiometry DEXA	Fat-free mass lower in PWS; fat mass and BMI were not significantly different among PWS and controls. No comparisons made on BMI z-score

% BF, Percentage body fat; BMI, body mass index; DEXA, dual-energy x-ray absorptiometry; Ht., height; OW, overweight; PWS, Prader-Willi syndrome; Wt., weight

TABLE 2-6 Prevalence of Overweight in Persons with Spina Bifida

STUDY INFORMATION	RESEARCH DESIGN	POPULATION STUDIED	TOTAL NUMBER OF SUBJECTS	AGES OF SUBJECTS, (X ± S.D.)	SETTING (HOME/FAMILY, CONGREGATION, INSTITUTION)	MEASURES USED	OUTCOME RESULTS
Bandini et al., 1991	Cross-sectional Level V	USA	N = 16 Boys (N = 5) Girls (N = 11)	Boys 17.8 ± 1.1 yrs Girls 16.8 ± 2.7 yrs Range: 13–24	Home and residential school	Ht, Wt. Total body water	Female BMI: 29.0 ± 3.9 Male BMI: 25.8 ± 8.7 Female % BF: 46.4 ± 6.1 Male % BF: 32.7 ± 10.2
Fiore et al., 1998	Cross-sectional Level IV	Italy	N = 100 Boys (N = 54) Girls (N = 46)	6 mos–19 yrs	N/A	BMI Criteria: BMI > 95th percentile	40% OW although energy intake of 75% of OW subjects was < RDA
Mita et al., 1993	Cross-sectional Level IV	Japan	N = 164 SB (N = 35) Control (N = 129)	Spina bifida 2.8–16.5 yrs Control 4–16.9 yrs	N/A	Skinfolds (right mid-triceps and subscapular) Criteria: %BF > 2 SD Obese	58% children > 5 years obese.
Polito et al., 1995	Cross-sectional Level V	Italy	N = 32 Boys (N = 14) Girls (N = 18)	2.3–12.7 yrs	N/A	BMI z-score and skinfold thickness	BMI z-score sig greater for subjects with MMC than control 1.7 ± vs. 0.7 ± 1.05). SSSF z-score 1.32 ± vs. 0.32 ± 0.17; TSF NSD

Study	Design/Level	Country	Sample	Age		Methods	Findings
Shepherd et al., 1991	Cross-sectional Level IV	USA	$N = 59$ Boys ($N = 27$) Girls ($N = 32$)	0.3–29 yrs	N/A	Total body potassium, total body water to measure body composition. Reference data (Durnin and Wormelsy, 1974; Fomon et al., 1982)	% BF was sig. > in those with high and mid-lesions but not in those with low lesions when compared to that expected age and gender.
van den Berg-Emons et al., 2003	Cross-sectional. Reference data (no statistical comparisons done) Level V	The Netherlands	$N = 14$ Men ($N = 8$) Women ($N = 6$)	18 ± 4 yrs	N/A	% BF from skinfolds, biceps, triceps, subscapular, and suprailiac. Eq of Durnin Rahaman (1967) age 14–15 yrs eq. Durnin Wormelsy (1974) in older subjects. Criteria: > 25% males > 32% females. Fitness—aerobic test. Physical activity—activity monitor	29% obese. Prevalence higher than in Dutch population (10% (Seidell, 2000). Inverse correlation between % BF and fitness ($r = -0.58$). No correlation between physical activity and %BF

% BF, Percentage body fat; BMI, body mass index; Ht., height; OW, overweight; Wt., weight N/A, Not available

TABLE 2-7 *Prevalence of Overweight and Obesity in Children with Mental Retardation in Large National Surveys*

STUDY INFORMATION	RESEARCH DESIGN/ LEVEL OF EVIDENCE	POPULATION STUDIED	TOTAL NUMBER OF SUBJECTS	AGES OF SUBJECTS, YRS ($X \pm$ S.D.)	MEASURES USED	OUTCOME RESULTS
Bandini et al., 2003	Cross-sectional Survey Level IV	NHANES III	$N = 5811$ 24 with MR	6–17	BMI z-score (CDC 2000)	NSD in prevalence of over-weight in children with and without MR
Murphy et al., 1992	Cross-sectional Survey Level IV	NHANES II Included: Persons with MR, learning disabilities, attention deficit, hyper-activity disorder, autism, cerebral palsy and PWS	$N = 4039$ 20 with MR	5.7 ± 3.8 Boys: 48% Girls: 52%	BMI, age-corrected BMI, subscapular/triceps skinfold ratio	NSD between BMI for children with and without MR or between ratio of skinfolds

% BF, Percentage body fat; BMI, body mass index; Ht., height; OW, overweight; PWS, Prader-Willi syndrome; Wt., weight NSD, No significant differences

Although limited, the studies on prevalence of obesity in persons with DS, PWS, and spina bifida consistently show a high prevalence of obesity in these populations. Thus, it can be concluded that current studies on the prevalence of obesity in persons with MR and developmental disorders are limited but suggest that obesity is a significant health problem in this population.

Future Research

The following areas need to be included in future research:

➤ More representative studies are needed to assess prevalence of obesity as well as the factors associated with obesity in persons with MR and other related I/DD.

➤ Studies are needed to develop criteria for identifying overweight and obesity in persons with alterations in body composition.

➤ Studies are needed to determine disease risk for persons with MR and other related I/DD who are overweight and obese and to determine if disease risk differs for persons with mental retardation and/or I/DD compared with individuals without MR.

ACKNOWLEDGMENTS

The author gratefully acknowledges Xena Grossman for her help in the preparation of this manuscript.

REFERENCES

Abraham, S., Johnson, C. L., & Najjar, M. R. (1979). *Weight by height and sex for adults 18-74 years, United States, 1971-74. Vital and health statistics: Series II, Data from the National Health Survey; No. 298* (DHEW Publication No. [PHS] 79-1656). Hyattsville, MD: U.S. Department of Health, Education, and Welfare.

Bandini, L. G., Curtin, C., Tybor, D. J., Hamad, C., & Must, A. (2003). Prevalence of overweight among children with mental retardation based on nationally representative surveys. *Obesity Research, 11* (Suppl), A120.

Bandini, L. G., Schoeller, D. A., Fukagawa, N. K., Wykes, L. J., & Dietz, W. H. (1991). Body composition and energy expenditure in adolescents with cerebral palsy or myelodysplasia. *Pediatric Research. 29* (1),70–77.

Bell, A. J., & Bhate, M. S. (1992). Prevalence of overweight and obesity in Down syndrome and other mentally handicapped adults living in the community. *Journal of Intellectual Disability Research. 36*, 359–364.

Brambilla, P., Bosio, L., Manzoni, P., Pietrobelli, A., & Beccaria, L. (1997). Peculiar body composition in patients with Prader-Labhart-Willi syndrome. *American Journal of Clinical Nutrition, 65*, 1369–1374.

Braunschweig, C. L., Gomez, S., Sheean. P., Tomey, K. M., Rimmer, J. H., & Heller, T. A. (2004). Nutritional status and risk factors for chronic disease in urban-dwelling adults with Down syndrome. *American Journal of Mental Retardation, 109*, 186–193.

Bray, G. E. (Ed). (1979). *Obesity in America* (National Institutes of Health Publication No 79-359). Washington, DC: U.S. Department of Health, Education, and Welfare.

Brozek, J., Grande, F., Anderson, J. T., & Keys, A. (1963). Densitometric analysis of body composition: Revision of some quantitative assumptions. *Annals of the New York Academy of Sciences, 110,* 113–140.

Buskirk, E. R. (1987). Obesity. In J.S. Skinner (Ed.). *Exercise testing and exercise prescription for special cases* (pp. 149–174). Philadelphia: Lea and Febiger.

Cole, T. J., Bellizzi, M. C., Flegal, K. M., & Dietz, W. H. (2000). Establishing a standard definition for child overweight and obesity: International survey. *British Medical Journal, 320,* 1240–1243.

Draheim, C. C., Williams, D. P., & McCubbin, J. A. (2002). Physical activity, dietary intake, and the insulin resistance syndrome in nondiabetic adults with mental retardation. *American Journal on Mental Retardation, 107,* 361–375.

Durnin, J. V. G. A., & Womersley, J. (1974). Body fat assessed from total body density and its estimation from skinfold thickness measurements on 481 men and women aged from 16 to 72 years. *British Journal of Nutrition, 32,* 77–97.

East Surrey Health Promotion Unit. (1994). *Surrey lifestyle survey 1993.* East Surrey, England: East Surrey Health Authority.

Emery, C. L., Watson, J. L., Watson, P. J., Thompson, D. M., & Biderman, M. D. (1985). Variables related to body-weight status of mentally retarded adults. *American Journal of Mental Deficiency, 90,* 34–39.

Fiore, P., Picco, P., Castagnola, E., Palmieri, A., Levato, L., Gremmo, M., et al. (1998). Nutritional survey of children and adolescents with myelomeningocele (MMC): Overweight associated with reduced energy intake. *European Journal of Pediatric Surgery, 8* (Suppl. I), 34–36.

Fomon, S. J., Haschkle, F., Ziegler, E. E., & Nelson, S. E. (1982). Body composition of reference children from birth to age 10 years. *American Journal of Clinical Nutrition, 35,* 1169–1175.

Fox, R., & Rotatori, A. F. (1982). Prevalence of obesity among mentally retarded adults. *American Journal of Mental Deficiency, 87,* 228–230.

Fujiura, G. T., Fitzsimons, N., & Marks, B. (1997). Predictors of BMI among adults with Down syndrome: The social context of health promotion. *Research in Developmental Disabilities, 18,* 261–274.

Goldstone, A. P., Thomas, E. L., Brynes, A. E., Bell, J. D., Frost, G., Saeed, N., et al. (2001). Visceral adipose tissue and metabolic complications of obesity are reduced in Prader-Willi syndrome female adults: Evidence for novel influences on body fat distribution. *The Journal of Clinical Endocrinology & Metabolism, 86,* 4330–4338.

Harris, N., Rosenberg, A., Jangda, S., O'Brien, K., & Gallagher, M. L. (2003). Prevalence of obesity in international Special Olympic athletes as determined by body mass index. *Journal of the American Dietetic Association 103,* 235–237.

Hedley, A. A., Ogden, C. L., Johnson, C. L., Carroll, M. D., Curtin, L. R., & Flegal, K. M. (2004). Prevalence of overweight and obesity among US children and adolescents, and adults, 1999-2002. *Journal of the American Medical Association, 291,* 2847–2850.

Heliovaara, M., & Aromaa, A. (1988). Height, weight, and obesity of Finnish adults. Publications of the Social Insurance Institutions, Finland ML:19.

Hove, O. (2004). Weight survey on adult persons with mental retardation living in the community. *Research in Developmental Disabilities, 25,* 9–17.

Hoybye, C., Hilding, A., Jacobsson, H., & Thoren, M. (2002). Metabolic profile and body composition in adults with Prader-Willi syndrome and severe obesity. *Journal of Clinical Endocrinology & Metabolism, 87,* 3590–3597.

Jackson, S. A., Pollack, M. L., & Ward, A. (1980). Generalized equations for predicting body density in women. *Medicine and Science in Sports and Exercise, 12,* 175–182.

Kelly, L. E., Rimmer, J. H., & Ness, R. A. (1986). Obesity levels in institutionalized mentally retarded adults. *Adaptive Physical Activity Quarterly, 3,* 167–176.

Larson, S., Lakin, C., Anderson, L. A., Kwak, N., Lee, J. H., & Anderson, D. A. (2000). *Prevalence of mental retardation and/or developmental disabilities: Analysis of the 1994/1995 HNIS-D*. Minneapolis: Research and Training Center on Community Living, Institute on Community Integration, University of Minnesota.

Lea, A. (1999). Assessment of body mass index for the residents of a long-stay institution for people with learning disability. *Journal of Human Nutrition and Dietetics, 12,* 141–149.

Luke, A., Roizen, N. J., Sutton, M., & Schoeller, D. A. (1994). Energy expenditure in children with Down syndrome: Correcting metabolic rate for movement. *Journal of Pediatrics, 125,* 829–838.

Marshall, D., McConkey, R., & Moore, G. (2003). Obesity in people with intellectual disabilities: The impact of nurse-led health screenings and health promotion activities. *Journal of Advanced Nursing, 41,* 147–153.

Metropolitan Life Insurance Company. (1959). New weight standards for males and females. *Statistical Bulletin, 40,* 2–3.

Ministry of Education. (1989). *The annual report of School Health Examination Survey 1988.* Tokyo: The Japanese Government Printing Office.

Mita, K., Akataki, K., Itoh, K., Yoshihiro, O., Ishida, N., & Takashi, O. (1993). Assessment of obesity of children with spina bifida. *Developmental Medicine & Child Neurology, 35,* 305–311.

Murphy, C. M., Allison, D. B., Babbitt, R. L., & Patterson, H. L. (1992). Adiposity in children: Is mental retardation a critical variable? *International Journal of Obesity, 16,* 633–638.

Nagamine, S. (1975). Evaluation of body fatness by skinfold. In K. Asahina, & R. Shigiya (Eds.). *Physiological adaptability and nutritional status of the Japanese: Growth, work capacity and nutrition of Japanese* (pp. 16–20). Tokyo: University of Tokyo Press.

National Center for Health Statistics. (1973). *Plan and operation of the Health and Nutrition Examination Survey for United States, 1971–1973* (NIH Publication NO. 73-1310). Washington, DC: US Government Printing Office.

National Center for Health Statistics. (1987). Obese and overweight adults in the US. *Vital and Health Statistics., Series 11* (230), 3–4.

National Center for Health Statistics. (2000). *CDC growth charts 2000: United States.* Bethesda, MD: U.S. Department of Health and Human Services.

National Center for Health Statistics and Centers for Disease Control and Prevention. (1996). *Third national Health and Nutrition Examination Survey, 1988–94: Plan and operations procedures manuals* (CD-ROM). Hyattsville: Authors.

National Institutes of Health. (1998). Clinical guidelines on the identification, evaluation, and treatment of overweight and obesity in adults: The evidence report. Obesity Research, 6 (Suppl 2), 51S–209S.

National Institutes of Health. (1985). Consensus development conference statement. Health implications of obesity. *Annals of Internal Medicine, 103,* 981–1077.

Polito, C., Delgaizo, F., Del Gaizo, D., Manso, G., Stabile, D., & Del Gado, R. D. (1995). Children with myelomeningocele have shorter stature, greater body weight, and lower bone mineral content than healthy children. *Nutrition Research, 15,* 1605–1611.

Prasher, V. P. (1995). Overweight and obesity amongst Down's syndrome adults. *Journal of Intellectual Disability Research, 39,* 437–441.

Rimmer, J. H., Braddock, D., & Fujiura, G. (1993). Prevalence of obesity in adults with mental retardation: Implications for health promotion and disease prevention. *Mental Retardation, 31,* 105–110.

Rubin, S. S., Rimmer, J. H., Chicoine, B., Braddock, D., & McGuire, D. E. (1998). Overweight prevalence in persons with Down Syndrome. *Mental Retardation, 36,* 175–181.

Schoeller, D. A., Levitsky, L. L., Bandini, L. G., Dietz, W. H., & Walczak, A. (1988). Energy expenditure and body composition in Prader-Willi syndrome. *Metabolism, 37,* 115–120.

Seidell, J. C. (2000). Obesity, insulin resistance and diabetes—a worldwide epidemic. *British Journal of Nutrition, 83* (Suppl. 1), S5–S8.

Shepherd, K., Roberts, D. W., Golding, S., Thomas, B. J., & Shepherd, R. W. (1991). Body composition in myelomeningocele. *American Journal of Clinical Nutrition, 53,* 1–6.

Simila, S., & Niskanen, P. (1991). Underweight and overweight cases among the mentally retarded. *Journal of Mental Deficiencies Research, 35,* 160–164.

Suzuki, M., Saitoh, S., Tasaki, Y., Shimomura, Y., Makishima, R., & Hosoya, N. (1991). Nutritional status and daily physical activity of handicapped students in Tokyo metropolitan schools for deaf, blind, mentally retarded and physically handicapped individuals. *American Journal of Clinical Nutrition, 54,* 1101–1011.

Takeuchi, E. (1994). Incidence of obesity among school children with mental retardation in Japan. *American Journal of Mental Retardation, 99,* 283–288.

van den Berg-Emons, H. J., Bussmann, J. B., Meyerink, H. J., Roebroeck, M. E., & Stam, H. J. (2003). Body fat, fitness and level of everyday physical activity in adolescents and young adults with meningomyelocele. *Journal of Rehabilitation Medicine, 35,* 271–275.

van Mil, E. G., Westerterp, K. R., Gerver, W. M., Van Marken Lichtenbelt, W. D., Kester, A. D., & Saris, W. H. M. (2001). Body composition in Prader-Willi syndrome compared with nonsyndromal obesity: Relationship to physical activity and growth hormone function. *Journal of Pediatrics, 139,* 708–714.

World Health Organization (1998). *Obesity: Preventing and managing the global epidemic.Report of a WHO consultation, 3-5 June 1997.* Geneva, Switzerland: Author.

3

SWALLOWING DYSFUNCTION/DYSPHAGIA IN ADULTS AND CHILDREN

Maureen A. Lefton-Greif, PhD, CCC/SLP, and Justine Joan Sheppard, PhD, CCC

Disruptions in feeding and swallowing[1] are common in individuals with intellectual and developmental disabilities (I/DD) (Field, Garland, & Williams, 2003; Reilly, Skuse, & Poblete, 1996; Schwarz, Corredor, Fisher-Medina, Cohen, & Rabinowitz, 2001; Sullivan et al., 2000). These problems may result in health and social challenges for individuals with I/DD and their caregivers by compromising the control of oral secretions during daily activities and the ingestion of foods, liquids, and oral medications. Deficiencies in swallowing that are not adequately managed may result in degradation of nutrition, hydration, respiratory status, and overall well-being. Conversely, imbalances or deficits in these health domains may increase the risk for feeding and swallowing problems. Following a brief review of normal swallowing, this chapter focuses on the nature and prevalence of swallowing disorders in this population, provides a review of the evidence base for interventions for these problems, and discusses the implications for health promotion initiatives and directions for future research.

---

[1]In this chapter, the term "feeding" refers to the gathering, preparation, and delivery of food, liquid, or medications to the mouth. Swallowing is considered as a component of the feeding process.

NORMAL SWALLOWING AND DYSPHAGIA

Swallowing or deglutition refers to the process of moving ingested materials (e.g., saliva, liquid, food, or medication) from the mouth into the stomach. For discussion purposes, the act of swallowing is divided into three partially overlapping phases—the *oral, pharyngeal,* and *esophageal* phases of swallowing (Miller, 1982). During the *oral* phase, food is processed into a "swallow-ready ball" (bolus) and then transported to the back of the mouth. Skills required for bolus formation are dependent on the consistency of food. For example, foods that require chewing (e.g., a piece of steak) are processed differently than foods that are ready to swallow on entering the mouth (e.g., ice cream). After a bolus is formed, it is transported to the pharynx. The *pharyngeal* phase is comprised of a series of integrated and complex motor events that direct and propel the bolus through the pharynx and into the esophagus, while preventing misdirection of the bolus into the airway. This phase of swallowing is closely coordinated with breathing. The transit of the bolus through the esophagus into the stomach is referred to as the esophageal phase of swallowing. Once the bolus is in the stomach, the lower part of the esophagus helps prevent gastric contents from "refluxing" or flowing backward into the esophagus. The sphincter between the esophagus and the pharynx functions similarly to prevent esophageal contents from refluxing into the pharynx.

Dysphagia (swallowing dysfunction) and related feeding disorders may result from disruptions in neuromuscular control, anatomic abnormalities of the aerodigestive tract, or systemic conditions (e.g., gastrointestinal, cardiopulmonary, or metabolic disease). Dysphagia may involve any or all phases of swallowing. The extent of the structural or neurologic abnormality and the ability of an individual to compensate for the disorder determine the magnitude of the dysfunction and its impact on that individual's health. For example, the consequences of swallowing dysfunction with concomitant aspiration are less likely to be tolerated by individuals with poor nutritional status and diminished pulmonary reserve (e.g., secondary to deformities of the chest wall or spine) than by persons who are well nourished and without respiratory problems (Toder, 2000).

Disturbances in any or all of the phases of swallowing may affect the adequacy of nutrition or hydration, or compromise an individual's pulmonary function or overall well-being. In individuals with I/DD, oral phase problems may result in drooling, limited food options (e.g., solid foods are avoided because of chewing difficulty), and prolonged mealtimes. Pharyngeal phase deficits may result in an increased risk for aspiration of saliva or liquid or solid food into the airway. Furthermore, the failure to cough in response to aspiration (i.e., "silent aspiration") is common in individuals with I/DD who aspirate (Arvedson, Rogers, Buck, Smart, & Msall, 1994; Loughlin & Lefton-Greif, 1994; Seddon & Khan, 2003; Toder, 2000). The risk of pulmonary infection is increased when an individual does not have an effective cough response after foreign materials enter the airway. In individuals with I/DD, oral and pharyngeal phase deficiencies are associated with an elevated risk for choking. Esophageal phase dysfunction may be associated with the formation of strictures or present as regurgitation or feeding refusal with subsequent nutritional compromise. It is noteworthy that the same symptoms may result from problems involving different phases of swallowing.

PREVALENCE AND HISTORY OF DYSPHAGIA

There is a high prevalence of dysphagia in persons with I/DD. Reilly et al. (1996) estimated that 80% to 95% of individuals with I/DD are expected to have swallowing and feeding problems at some time in their lives. The onset of dysphagia is variable. Problems may emerge in infancy, during the development of mature swallowing and eating skills, in association with exacerbations of existing conditions, with adult-onset medical disorders, or with aging (Burklow, Phelps, Schultz, McConnell, & Rudolph, 1998; Field et al., 2003; Rogers et al., 1994; Sullivan et al., 2000; Waterman, Koltai, Downey, & Cacace, 1992). Dysphagia in children may persist and become a chronic condition or it may resolve. Swallowing disability in I/DD is associated most often with maxillofacial, neurologic, orthopedic, psychiatric, pulmonary, and gastrointestinal impairments (Rubin & Crocker, 1989). Side effects from medications may compromise swallowing function, especially in the presence of preexisting dysphagia. Promoting good health in individuals with I/DD with respect to swallowing function includes:

➤ Preventing problems by establishing appropriate conditions for participating safely and effectively in swallowing activities and for acquiring mature swallowing skills

➤ Developing systems for early identification of dysphagia

➤ Establishing multidisciplinary teams for the assessment of signs, symptoms, and contributing factors associated with an individual's specific disabilities

➤ Developing systems for monitoring and treating the dysphagia and the associated risks for nutritional, respiratory, pulmonary, and gastroesophageal consequences of the disorder

➤ Providing resources and services for reassessment and long-term management of chronic dysphagia and its consequences

Research Questions

The following research questions are addressed in this chapter:

1. What categories of feeding and swallowing interventions were reported for individuals with I/DD?

2. What evidence supports the reported interventions?

Methods

We reviewed the research literature for evidence delineating feeding and swallowing disorders and associated health risks in children and adults with I/DD and for management of these risks. The purposes of this review were to identify the existing interventions and determine the evidence supporting their use. A systematic literature search was conducted by using the electronic data bases Medline, CINAHL, SocioFile, Health Star, PsychInfo, Pharmaceutical Abstracts, Web science, Academic Search Premiere, Ingenta, GPO Access, and PubMed with a time period restricted to the 10 years between 1994 and 2004; however, a selective review of literature published from 1984 to 1993 supplemented the primary search. The search strategy paired the key search terms *dysphagia, deglutition, swallowing, drooling, choking, failure to thrive, food refusal,* and *feeding disorders* with key search terms that delineate I/DD. These key terms included *developmental delay, developmental disability, intellectual disability, mental retardation, cerebral palsy,* and *Down syndrome.* All experimental articles were included. Foreign language material, review articles, and articles limited to expert opinion alone were excluded. General categories identified included prevalence and characteristics of dysphagia, swallowing pathophysiology, assessment, management, and combinations of the aforesaid. For the purposes of this chapter, management includes prevention, identification, evaluation, interventions and therapeutic treatments, and daily care.

Results

The results of our search are presented with reference to the research question.

1. What categories of feeding and swallowing interventions were reported for individuals with I/DD?

Interventions focused on seven general feeding or swallowing related areas: mealtime behaviors (e.g., eating, food refusal, rumination), consequences of feeding and swallowing problems (e.g., pulmonary sequalea secondary to aspiration), nutrition, tube feeding, oral hygiene (i.e., teeth brushing), drooling, and caregiver attributes (see Table 3-1). Specific interventions included the development of individualized care plans (e.g., oral hygiene); the impact of dysphagia therapies on swallowing dysfunction (e.g., positioning, alterations in dietary textures, oral motor exercises); the effect of behavioral therapies on negative mealtime behaviors (e.g., rumination or limited food intake); the utility of oral appliances, acupuncture, medical therapies, or surgical procedures for control of drooling (e.g., botulinium toxin injection, intraoral feeding appliances, etc.); and the influence of instruction on caregiver adherence.

2. What evidence supports the reported interventions?

The level of evidence supporting interventions for the seven general feeding or swallowing categories was varied. Of the 17 investigations examined, the frequency of those meeting criteria for each level of evidence was 2, 3, 2, 9, and 1 for evidence levels I, II, III, IV, and V, respectively. Table 3-2 illustrates each of the evidence-based interventions, including summaries of research design, the levels of evidence, and characteristics of the populations studied.

Discussion

Overall, the results of the included studies indicate that improvements in health and well-being, as associated with feeding and swallowing behaviors, may be achieved through individualized approaches to management. Individualized care plans resulted in improvements in oral hygiene; however, ongoing, tangible reinforcement was found to be important for maintaining improvement in oral hygiene behaviors. Drooling may be reduced by medical and surgical treatments in some children; however, adverse effects should be considered in patient and treatment selection. Caregiver adherence to mealtime guidelines is variable by setting, type of guideline, and caregiver's perception of the severity of risk. Therapy interventions provided by speech–language pathologists and other allied health professionals may improve acceptance of food and liquid, rate of intake, swallowing efficiency, and pulmonary health and function in some children and adults. Nutrition may be improved with an individualized dietary program provided by a dietician. And, rumination may improve in some individuals when diet is altered. No studies addressed the ingestion of oral medications.

Conclusion and Future Research Directions

There is ample evidence that feeding and swallowing problems exist for children and adults with I/DD (Collins et al., 2003; Field et al., 2003; Fung et al., 2002; Morton, Bonas, Minford, Tarrant, & Ellis, 1997; Munk & Repp, 1994; Samson-Fang, Butler, & O'Donnell, 2003; Schwarz et al., 2001; Strauss, Kastner, Ashwal, & White, 1997; Sullivan et al., 2000, 2002; Tawfik, Dickson, Clarke, & Thomas, 1997). To date, most investigations on swallowing dysfunction have focused on the prevalence of disorders, identification of dysphagia characteristics, and co-morbidities associated with dysphagia in individuals with I/DD. Some studies addressed swallowing function, respiration, nutrition, oral hygiene, drooling, and regurgitation across the variety of diagnoses associated with I/DD (e.g., cerebral palsy and Down syndrome) and others investigated these issues for specific primary diagnoses associated with I/DD (e.g., Rett syndrome alone). For some individuals, it appears that oral hygiene may be improved with the development of individual programs and problematic drooling may be better controlled with some treatment modalities (e.g., surgical, pharmacologic, or appliance). No studies were found that address ingestion of oral medications.

Well-designed clinical trials of different treatment modalities are critical for determining the best practice methods and implementing appropriate programs for service delivery. Despite the frequency of feeding or swallowing related problems in individuals with I/DD, there remains a paucity of information on prevention, risk management, treatment efficacy, and the impact of specific therapies on respiratory, nutritional, and gastroesophageal/gastrointestinal health outcomes. We acknowledge that such research is met with multiple challenges including the heterogeneity of the population even among individuals with the same underlying diagnostic conditions, the variability in the symptomatic presentations of feeding

TABLE 3-1 *Research Studies of Dysphagia and Related Health Promotion Issues in People with I/DD*

STUDY	RESEARCH DESIGN	LEVEL OF EVIDENCE	POPULATION	EXPERIMENTAL GROUP N	CONTROL GROUP N	AGES OF SUBJECTS
Altabet et al., 2003	2 × 2 repeated measures factorial design Two groups	I	Mild–moderate; severe–profound	39	40	22–57 yrs
Bothwell et al., 2002	Case series	IV	Children with cerebral palsy (CP) or other neurologic problems and severe drooling	9	Each subject was own control.	4–17 yrs
Chadwick et al., 2002	Observation Interview Cohort study	III	Caregivers of adults with I/DD	46	NA	NA
Chadwick et al., 2003	Observation Interview Group comparison by treatment setting	II	Adults with I/DD	40	NA	19–74 yrs
Crysdale et al., 2001	Retrospective data base analysis	IV	Neurologically involved patients (including, CP, Down syndrome, DD)	522	Each subject was own control.	Mean age 13.2 yrs
Gisel et al., 2003	Case series	IV	CP with severe motor impairment	3	Each subject was own control.	18–43 mo
Helfrich-Miller et al., 1986	Case series	V	CP	6	Each subject was own control.	10–31 yrs

Study	Design/Purpose	Level	Population	N	Control	Age
Hoch et al., 1995	Use of swallow induction avoidance procedure to establish eating	IV	Severe MR, ADHD; middle ear dysfunction, after liver transplant, normal swallowing	1	Subject was own control.	3.5 yrs
Hogan & Evers, 1997	Group comparisons for change in weight and height	II	Severe DD	32	29	16 and older
Johnson et al., 2004	Case series	IV	Children with CP, drooling, and dysphagia	18, only 6 completed study	Each subject was own control.	4–13 yrs; mean 7 years 10 mos
Johnston & Greene, 1992	Retrospective review of programmatic research—10 yr	II	MR	10	Each subject was own control	Adults
Luiselli, 1994	Case series	IV	Child with multiple developmental disabilities	2	Each subject was own control.	Female 10 yo; Male 7 yo
Mier et al., 2000	Placebo-controlled, double-blind, crossover dose-ranging study	I	Patients with DD associated with multiple etiologies (most with CP) and excessive sialorrhea + adverse effects	39	Each subject was own control.	4.3–19.0 yrs; mean age 10.75 yrs
Savarese et al., 2004	Clinical trial	IV	Persons with CP	21	Each subject was own control.	Children and young adults
Wolber et al., 1987	Single case study ABBA design	III	Severe MR	1	Each subject was own control.	33
Wong et al., 2001	Case series	IV	Severe physical and/or cognitive disability and persistent drooling	10	Each subject was own control.	2–18 yrs; mean age 7.3 yrs

TABLE 3-2 Outcomes for Studies of Dysphagia and Related Health Promotion Issues in People with I/DD

STUDY	OUTCOME OF INTEREST	DIMENSION OF DISABILITY	STATISTICS	TREATMENT DURATION	MEASURES	RESULTS	CLINICAL IMPORTANCE
Altabet et al., 2003	To determine the effectiveness of individualized oral care plans on oral hygiene	Teeth brushing	Two by two repeated measures factorial design; ANOVA; paired t-tests	1 yr	Oral hygiene ratings by dentist of level of plaque formation on teeth	People in treatment group showed significantly greater improvement.	Individualized oral care plans can improve oral hygiene within a one-year period. Training for care staff did not make a difference for the non-treatment group.
Bothwell et al., 2002	To determine the effectiveness of *Botulinum* toxin A injection in the reduction of drooling	Drooling	Descriptive statistics	Pre- and post-injection observations with 16-wk follow-up	Objective changes in frequency and quantity of drooling; Subjective caregiver responses about changes in frequency and severity of drooling, and side effects	Five pts improved following injections; 55% of parents reported therapy was beneficial; one adverse event that was not sustained was reported	Botulinum toxin A may reduce problematic drooling in some children with DD and mental retardation (MR)

Chadwick et al., 2002	To determine adherence of caregivers to individualized guidelines for feeding provided by speech-language pathologists	Caregiving	Fisher's exact t-test; one way ANOVA; Spearman's rank correlation coefficient	Median = 23 mos; R = 4–168 mos 2-day training workshop	Caregiver knowledge of management strategies; behavioral adherence of caregivers to management plan; caregiver understanding of perceived risk of noncompliance	Significance was achieved for more frequent adherence to recommendations for food consistency, equipment and utensils. Adherence was significantly greater than explicit knowledge. Adherence was significantly greater when perceived risk was higher.	Workshop training and SLP supervision is not sufficient for assuring adherence to feeding guidelines
Chadwick et al., 2003	To determine if caregiver adherence to mealtime guidelines differed by management setting	Caregiving	Fisher's Exact t-test; one-way ANOVA; Spearman's rank correlation coefficient	8 mos	Percentage of guidelines followed across settings; differential adherence to guidelines for consistency modification, physical position and posture, equipment and utensil use, and support, prompting and socializing	Caregivers at day centers adhered to guidelines more than other settings. Guidelines were adhered to more consistently for dependent eaters than for independent eaters.	Expectations for adherence to guidelines are highest in day treatment settings and for food consistency and positioning. Extra attention is needed to promote adherence by caregivers assisting self-feeders and by caregivers at home and in residential settings.

(continued)

TABLE 3-2 *Continued*

STUDY	OUTCOME OF INTEREST	DIMENSION OF DISABILITY	STATISTICS	TREATMENT DURATION	MEASURES	RESULTS	CLINICAL IMPORTANCE
Crysdale et al., 2001	To determine the impact of two surgical procedures on drooling in patients (older than 6 yrs) with neurologic impairments (NI), low cognitive levels, and persistent and significant drooling after a minimum of 6 mos of oral motor therapy for profuse drooling	Drooling	t-tests for information obtained from questionnaires.	N/A— surgery and follow-up survey	Mean numerical scores for volitional oral–motor, swallowing and feeding skills.	Similar surgical impact with submandibular duct relocations with sublingual gland excision (SDRSGE) and submandibular duct relocation (SDR); SDRSGE appears to be associated with fewer complications; neither SDRSGE nor SDR eliminates drooling; poorer post-surgical outcomes in children with severe impairments in volitional motor function and profuse drooling.	Patients with NI and profuse drooling may have less postoperative complications with SDRSGE vs. SDR
Gisel et al., 2003	To determine whether pulmonary function would improve 1 yr after the initiation of optimal positioning for feeding, control of GER,	Pulmonary complications associated with aspiration	Descriptive statistics	1 yr following initial studying period	Changes in pulmonary function testing, postural control, GER status, nutritional status, and functional feeding skills	Variable responses with two children showing some improvement in functional residual capacity	Study shows that further research about the associations between dysphagia, GER, and nutrition on pulmonary function are needed

Study	Purpose	Treatment	Statistics	Duration	Outcome measures	Results	Conclusions
	and use of best textures to decrease aspiration as demonstrated on videofluoroscopic swallow study						
Helfrich-Miller et al., 1986	To determine if swallow function improves following the treatment program	Dysphagia therapy	Descriptive statistics	18 mo	Ear-nose-throat examinations and modified bariums swallow studies (MBS) for glottic closure, pharyngeal transit time, amount aspirated, valleculae and pyriform residue, and number of swallows required to clear oropharynx	Improved swallow efficiency seen on MBS follow up. Regression seen in subjects withdrawn from thermal stimulation. Reduced upper respiratory infections and reduced feeding time seen in four of six and three of six subjects, respectively.	A treatment program that includes dietary modifications, feeding strategies, thermal stimulation, and chewing exercises improves swallow function in some cases.
Hoch et al., 1995	To determine if oral feedings can be achieved by treating a child without prior oral feedings because of previous medical conditions	Oral feeding	Descriptive statistics	1 yr	Changes in negative behaviors with oral feeding efforts (e.g., expulsion, gagging) and changes in the volume consumed per meal (grams)	Improved acceptance of foods and liquids, increased speed of swallowing after food presentations, favorable parental responses at discharge from program and 1 year follow up	Individualized plan for increasing the acceptance of oral feeding may be established when a therapeutic plan is specifically designed for children with profound MR and normal swallowing but without early feeding experiences.

(continued)

TABLE 3-2 *Continued*

STUDY	OUTCOME OF INTEREST	DIMENSION OF DISABILITY	STATISTICS	TREATMENT DURATION	MEASURES	RESULTS	CLINICAL IMPORTANCE
Hogan & Evers, 1997	To determine if an individualized, clinical, dietary program would result in weight gain in under-nourished subjects	Nutrition	Parametric statistics	6 mo	Weight for height ratio (z-scores)	Subjects < 5th percentile showed significant weight gain. Limited increase in liquid intake was achieved.	Weight gain can be achieved in individuals with chronically low weight for height given an individualized clinical dietary program, attention to food service delivery issues, and education for care giving staff.
Johnson et al., 2004	To determine the effectiveness of an intraoral appliance (ISMAR) in improving drooling and eating skills	Drooling and eating skills	Effect of bias due to high dropout rate assessed by *t*-tests for normal data, Fisher's exact test for proportions, and Mann-Whitney U were used for non-normal data. Spearman's rho correlations coefficient was used to assess association between eating, drinking, and drooling	18 mo, with six (33%) subjects completing all phases of study	Comparisons between frequency and severity of drooling during each phase of study; comparisons of measures of drooling and feeding skills during all phases of study	Improvement in severity of drooling; no changes in frequency of drooling; improvement in cup drinking	The ISMAR appliance may improve some aspects of drooling and eating; however, the non-compliance rate is high, associated with child refusal fatigue, or illness, poor parental compliance, and problems w. the ISMAR

54

Reference	Purpose	Target	Analysis	Duration	Measures	Results	Conclusions
Johnston & Greene, 1992	To determine if satiation diets decrease rumination	Rumination	Parametric statistics	One to three meals daily for 2 wks or more	Number of post-prandial rumination episodes	Mean rate of ruminating decreased with increasing meal size in subjects with diagnosis of rumination	Once the differential diagnosis of rumination and emesis from other causes is made, trial therapy with satiation diet is warranted
Luiselli, 1994	To achieve consistent oral consumption	Chronic feeding refusal	Descriptive statistics	4–6 mo	Opening mouth and consuming meal within 30 min	Female 10 yo; Male 7 yo	Individualized treatment in naturalistic settings may facilitate consistent oral consumption in children with DD
Mier et al., 2000	To determine safety and efficacy of glycopyrrolate in the treatments of children with DD and sialorrhea	Drooling	Paired two-tailed t-tests and unpaired t-tests	4 mo	Parent and investigators of change in drooling and adverse effects	0.10 mg/kg per dose of Glycopyrrolate is effective in controlling sialorrhea; even at low doses, 20% of children exhibit severe adverse effects sufficient to require discontinuation of medication	Glycopyrrolate is effective in the control of excessive sialorrhea in children with DD; however, 20% of children may have significant adverse responses to treatment
Savarese et al., 2004	To determine the effect of intra-parotid injections Botulinum toxin A on drooling and saliva production	Drooling	Descriptive	2 mo of follow up after single injection	Subjective measures of frequency and severity of drooling (visual scales) and counts of the number of bib changes daily	Botulinum toxin A injections reduced the frequency and severity of drooling, and the number of bib changes daily	Intraparotid injections of botulinum toxin A are efficacious for reducing saliva production in children with CP

55

(continued)

TABLE 3-2 *Continued*

STUDY	OUTCOME OF INTEREST	DIMENSION OF DISABILITY	STATISTICS	TREATMENT DURATION	MEASURES	RESULTS	CLINICAL IMPORTANCE
Wolber et al., 1987	To determine the effectiveness of reinforcement on acquisition of tooth brushing skills	Teeth brushing	*t*-test	85 sessions during 42 days	Number of steps of teeth brushing routine completed	There was significant difference between baseline and tangible reinforcement condition.	Ongoing reinforcement is an important component of an oral hygiene program. Tangible reinforcement is better than social reinforcement. Behaviors extinguish without reinforcement.
Wong et al., 2001	To determine the efficacy of tongue acupuncture (TAC) in the treatment of drooling	Drooling	Comparison of pre- and post-treatment scores analyzed by Wilcoxon matched-paired signed-rank analysis	30 sessions over 6 wks	Changes in the severity and frequency of drooling on Visual Analog scales, semiquantitative observation, and question based scoring system.	Decrease in all three drooling scores. Procedure tolerated without any side effects	TAC may be efficacious as an adjunctive or alternative treatment for patients with drooling problems.

and swallowing related problems, and difficulty in blinding investigators to participants. Nonetheless, the need for evidence-based interventions for prevention and management of the health problems related to swallowing and feeding disorders is critical given the increased survival rates of young children with complex medical conditions, the increased longevity of adults with I/DD, and the deterioration in swallowing function in this population with aging (Altabet, Rogers, Imes, Boatman, & Moncier, 2003; Chadwick, Jolliffe, & Goldbart, 2002, 2003; Helfrich-Miller, Rector, & Straka, 1986; Hogan & Evers, 1997; Johnston & Greene, 1992; Sheppard, 2002; Wolber, Carne, Collins-Montgomery, & Nelson, 1987).

REFERENCES

Altabet, S., Rogers, K., Imes, E., Boatman, I. M., & Moncier, J. (2003). Comprehensive approach toward improving oral hygiene at a state residential facility for people with mental retardation. *Mental Retardation, 41,* 440–445.

Arvedson, J., Rogers, B., Buck, G., Smart, P., & Msall, M. (1994). Silent aspiration prominent in children with dysphagia. *International Journal of Pediatric Otorhinolaryngology, 28,* 173–181.

Bothwell, J. E., Clarke, K., Dooley, J. M., Gordon, K. E., Anderson, R., Wood, E. P., et al. (2002). Botulinum toxin A as a treatment for excessive drooling in children. *Pediatric Neurology, 27,* 18–22.

Burklow, K. A., Phelps, A. N., Schultz, J. R., McConnell, K., & Rudolph, C. (1998). Classifying complex pediatric feeding disorders. *Journal of Gastrointestinal Nutrition, 27,* 143–147.

Chadwick, D. D., Jolliffe, J., & Goldbart, J. (2002). Carer knowledge of dysphagia management strategies. *International Journal of Language and Communication Disorders, 37*(3), 345–357.

Chadwick, D. D., Jolliffe, J., & Goldbart, J. (2003). Adherence to eating and drinking guidelines for adults with intellectual disabilities and dysphagia. *American Journal on Mental Retardation, 108,* 202–211.

Collins, M., Kyle, R., Smith, S., Laverty, A., Roberts, S., & Eaton-Evans, J. (2003). Coping with the usual family diet. *Journal of Learning Disabilities 7,* 137–155.

Crysdale, W. S., Raveh, E., McCann, C., Roske, L., & Kotler, A. (2001). Management of drooling in individuals with neurodisability: A surgical experience. *Developmental Medicine & Child Neurology, 43,* 379–383.

Field, D., Garland, M., & Williams, K. (2003). Correlates of specific childhood feeding problems. *Journal of Paediatric Child Health, 39,* 299–304.

Fung, E. B., Samson-Fang, L., Stallings, V. A., Conaway, M., Liptak, G., Henderson, R. C. et al. (2002). Feeding dysfunction is associated with poor growth and health status in children with cerebral palsy. *Journal of the American Dietetic Association, 102,* 361–373.

Gisel, E. G., Tessier, M. J., Lapierre, G., Seidman, E., Drouin, E., & Filion, G. (2003). Feeding management of children with severe cerebral palsy and eating impairment: An exploratory study. *Physical and Occupational Therapy in Pediatrics, 23,* 19–44.

Helfrich-Miller, K. R., Rector, K. L., & Straka, J. A. (1986). Dysphagia: Its treatment in the profoundly retarded patient with cerebral palsy. *Archives of Physical Medicine and Rehabilitation, 67,* 520–525.

Hoch, T. A., Babbitt, R. L., Coe, D. A., Ducan, A., & Trusty, E. M. (1995). A swallow induction avoidance procedure to establish eating. *Journal of Behavioral Therapy and Experimental Psychiatry, 26,* 41–50

Hogan, S. E., & Evers, S. E. (1997). A nutritional rehabilitation program for persons with severe physical and developmental disabilities. *Journal of the American Dietetic Association, 97,* 162–166.

Johnson, H. M., Reid, S. M., Hazard, C. J., Lucas, J. O., Desai, M., & Reddihough, D. S. (2004). Effectiveness of the Innsbruck Sensorimotor Activator and Regulator in improving saliva control in children with cerebral palsy. *Developmental Medicine & Child Neurology, 46,* 39–45.

Johnston, J. M., & Greene, K. S. (1992). Relation between ruminating and quantity of food consumed. *Mental Retardation, 30*(1), 7–12.

Loughlin, G. M. & Lefton-Greif, M. A. (1994). Dysfunctional swallowing and respiratory disease in children. *Advances in Pediatrics, 41,* 135–162.

Luiselli, J. K. (1994). Oral feeding treatment of children with chronic food refusal and multiple developmental disabilities. *American Journal on Mental Retardation, 98,* 646–655.

Mier, R. J., Bachrach, S. J., Lakin, R. C., Barker, T., Childs, J., & Moran, M. (2000). Treatment of sialorrhea with glycopyrrolate: A double-blind, dose-ranging study. *Archives of Pediatric and Adolescent Medicine, 154,* 1214–1218.

Miller, A. J. (1982). Deglutition. *Physiological Review, 62,* 129–184.

Morton, R. E., Bonas, R., Minford, J., Tarrant, S. C., & Ellis, R. E. (1997). Respiration patterns during feeding in Rett syndrome. *Developmental Medicine & Child Neurology, 39,* 607–613.

Munk, D. D. & Repp, A. C. (1994). Behavioral assessment of feeding problems of individuals with severe disabilities. *Journal of Applied Behavioral Analysis, 27,* 241–250.

Reilly, S., Skuse, D., & Poblete, X. (1996). Prevalence of feeding problems and oral motor dysfunction in children with cerebral palsy: A community survey. *Journal of Pediatrics, 129,* 877–882.

Rogers B., Stratton P., Msall M., Andres M., Champlain M.K., Koerner P., Piazza J. (1994). Long-term morbidity and management strategies of tracheal aspiration in adults with severe developmental disabilities. *American Journal of Mental Retardation, 4,* 490–498.

Rubin, I. L., & Crocker, A. C. (1989). *Developmental disabilities: Delivery of medical care for children and adults.* Philadelphia: Lea & Febiger.

Samson-Fang, L., Butler, C., & O'Donnell, M. (2003). Effects of gastrostomy feeding in children with cerebral palsy: an AACPDM evidence report. *Developmental Medicine & Child Neurology, 45,* 415–426.

Savarese, R., Diamond, M., Elovic, E., & Millis, S. R. (2004). Intraparotid injection of botulinum toxin A as a treatment to control sialorrhea in children with cerebral palsy. *American Journal of Physical and Medical Rehabilitation, 83,* 304–311.

Schwarz, S. M., Corredor, J., Fisher-Medina, J., Cohen, J., & Rabinowitz, S. (2001). Diagnosis and treatment of feeding disorders in children with developmental disabilities. *Pediatrics, 108,* 671–676.

Seddon, P. C. & Khan, Y. (2003). Respiratory problems in children with neurological impairment. *Archives of Diseases in Children, 88,* 75–78.

Sheppard, J. J. (2002). Swallowing and feeding in older people with lifelong disability. *Advances in Speech-Language Pathology, 4,* 119–121.

Strauss, D., Kastner, T., Ashwal, S., & White, J. (1997). Tubefeeding and mortality in children with severe disabilities and mental retardation. *Pediatrics, 99,* 358–362.

Sullivan, P. B., Juszczak, E., Lambert, B. R., Rose, M., Ford-Adams, M. E., & Johnson, A. (2002). Impact of feeding problems on nutritional intake and growth: Oxford Feeding Study II. *Developmental Medicine & Child Neurology, 44,* 461–467.

Sullivan, P. B., Lambert, B., Rose, M., Ford-Adams, M., Johnson, A., & Griffiths, P. (2000). Prevalence and severity of feeding and nutritional problems in children with neurological impairment: Oxford Feeding Study. *Developmental Medicine & Child Neurology, 42,* 674–680.

Tawfik, R., Dickson, A., Clarke, M., & Thomas, A. G. (1997). Caregivers' perceptions following gastrostomy in severely disabled children with feeding problems. *Developmental Medicine & Child Neurology, 39,* 746–751.

Toder, D. S. (2000). Respiratory problems in the adolescent with developmental delay. *Adolescent Medicine, 11,* 617–631.

Waterman, E. T., Koltai, P. J., Downey, J. C., & Cacace, A. T. (1992). Swallowing disorders in a population of children with cerebral palsy. *International Journal of Pediatric Otorhinolaryngology, 24,* 63–71.

Wolber, G., Carne, W., Collins-Montgomery, P., & Nelson, A. (1987). Tangible reinforcement plus social reinforcement versus social reinforcement alone in acquisition of toothbrushing skills. *Mental Retardation, 25,* 275–279.

Wong, V., Sun, J. G., & Wong, W. (2001). Traditional Chinese medicine (tongue acupuncture) in children with drooling problems. *Pediatric Neurology, 25,* 47–54.

4
EPILEPSY

David L. Coulter, MD, FAAMR

Many individuals with intellectual and developmental disabilities (I/DD) have seizures or epilepsy. A *seizure* is defined as an event during which an abnormal electrical discharge occurs in the brain that is accompanied by a simultaneous change in sensation, motor activity, and/or consciousness. Electrical discharges not accompanied by clinical changes are sometimes called electrical or electrographic seizures. Seizure-like behavioral changes not accompanied by electrical discharges are usually considered nonepileptic in origin, or pseudoseizures. Pseudoseizures are fairly common in persons with I/DD. Prolonged video and electroencephalographic monitoring is often used to "capture" behaviors or events that caregivers believe may be epileptic seizures. Several studies of individuals with I/DD have shown that fewer than 50% of such events that are documented through such monitoring meet the definition of a seizure (Donat & Wright, 1990; Holmes, McKeever, & Russman, 1983; Neill & Alvarez, 1986). Demonstrating that these events are not seizures is important because health care providers need not prescribe anticonvulsant medications and can focus instead on identifying the true cause of the target behavior.

Epilepsy is defined as a relatively chronic condition of the brain that predisposes the individual to have seizures, and has already caused two or more seizures. Acute conditions that cause seizures (such as a high fever or low blood sugar level) are not epilepsy. Individuals who have a chronic seizure tendency and have had only one seizure so far are at fairly high risk for recurrent seizures, but technically do not have epilepsy until they have had two or more seizures. The prevalence of epilepsy in the general population is approximately 0.6% to 1.0% but is substantially higher in persons with I/DD. Epilepsy affects approximately 21% of individuals who have I/DD but not cerebral palsy and approximately 50% of individuals who have both I/DD and cerebral palsy (Hauser & Hesdorffer, 1990).

Seizures and epilepsy are generally classified according to the systems of the International League Against Epilepsy (Committee on Classification and Terminology, 1981, 1985), and this classification is used for this review of the scientific evidence. In practice, precise classification is often difficult for persons with I/DD, but should be attempted whenever feasible, because diagnostic precision often results in more effective treatment.

Previous publications have provided an overview of the management of epilepsy in persons with I/DD (Coulter, 1997; Devinsky & Westbrook, 2002). The International Association for the Scientific Study of Intellectual Disability (IASSID) convened a working group to develop clinical guidelines for epilepsy management based on their review of the scientific evidence (IASSID Working Group, 2001). This chapter incorporates and updates those findings and recommendations.

Review Questions

Specifically, this chapter addresses six questions that are derived from research and clinical practice and considers the scientific evidence available to answer those questions. These questions are:

1. Does antiepileptic drug efficacy differ for persons with epilepsy and I/DD compared to persons with epilepsy alone?

2. Do adverse effects of antiepileptic drugs differ for persons with epilepsy and I/DD compared to persons with epilepsy alone?

3. Do persons with epilepsy and I/DD have more mental health problems compared to persons with epilepsy alone?

4. Does adaptive or social functioning differ for persons with epilepsy and I/DD compared to persons with I/DD alone?

5. Does mortality differ for persons with epilepsy and I/DD compared to persons with I/DD alone?

6. Do the types and frequencies of injuries differ for persons with I/DD and epilepsy compared to persons with I/DD alone?

Methods

The literature was reviewed using a number of search terms, including *epilepsy, seizures, mental retardation,* and *intellectual disability.* From the articles identified through this search, publications were selected that addressed the specific questions. Articles were classified as Level I if they were randomized clinical trials, Level II if they were prospective matched cohort studies, Level III if they were prospective case series in which a statistical comparison was made to baseline, and Level IV if they were retrospective case series using mainly descriptive statistics (see Table A in the Preface). A total of 36 studies are reviewed.

Results and Discussion

1. Does antiepileptic drug efficacy differ for persons with epilepsy and developmental disabilities compared to persons with epilepsy alone?

The American Academy of Neurology (AAN) recently published a review of the scientific evidence regarding the use of seven newer antiepileptic drugs for patients with either new-onset epilepsy or treatment-resistant (refractory) epilepsy (French et al., 2004a, b). Drugs reviewed included gabapentin, lamotrigine, topiramate, tiagabine, oxcarbazepine, levetiracetam, and zonisamide. Ten Level I or Level II studies were available for treatment of patients with new-onset epilepsy alone, but no Level I or Level II studies were found for treatment of patients with new-onset epilepsy and I/DD. Lamotrigine, but not gabapentin, was found to be effective for absence seizures. Gabapentin, lamotrigine, topiramate, and oxcarbazepine were found to be effective for tonic–clonic and partial seizures.

Twenty-three Level I studies were found for treatment of patients with refractory epilepsy alone. This reflects the fact that investigational drugs are usually tested first on this population prior to approval by the Food and Drug Administration (FDA). All seven of the new drugs were found to be effective for refractory complex partial seizures in patients with epilepsy alone, which reflects their approval by the FDA for this indication. Topiramate was specifically found to be effective for refractory tonic–clonic seizures, but data to evaluate the other drugs for this indication were insufficient.

Lennox-Gastaut syndrome is a type of epilepsy in which virtually all patients also have I/DD. Seizures in this syndrome are typically resistant or refractory to conventional treatment. In the AAN review (French et al., 2004a, b), Level I studies showed that both lamotrigine and topiramate are effective in this syndrome.

In an updated review of the literature (beyond that contained within the AAN review), no Level I studies, other than those for Lennox-Gastaut syndrome, were found that specifically evaluated the efficacy of antiepileptic drugs for persons with epilepsy and I/DD. Indeed, these patients are usually excluded from clinical trials of investigational drugs for epilepsy. The articles that were identified through this search are summarized in Table 4-1. Level III studies were found suggesting that gabapentin (Crawford, Brown, & Kerr, 2001), nitrazepam (Hosain, Green, Solomon, & Chutorian, 2003), and lamotrigine (Crawford, Brown, & Kerr, 2001; McKee et al., 2003) are effective in this population. Additional Level IV studies (primarily reports of uncontrolled case series) were found suggesting that gabapentin (Mikati et al., 1998), lamotrigine (Buchanan, 1995; Coppola & Pascotto, 1997; Gidal et al., 2000), topiramate (Singh & White-Scott, 2002), oxcarbazepine (Gaily, Granstrom, & Liukkonen, 1998), levetiracetam (Gibson, 2002), zonisamide (Iinuma, Minami, Cho, Kajii, & Tachi, 1998), and vigabatrin (Ylinen, 1998) are effective in this population.

TABLE 4-1 *Studies Examining the Efficacy of Antiepileptic Drugs for Persons with Epilepsy and I/DD*

STUDY AND LEVEL OF EVIDENCE	NUMBER OF SUBJECTS	AGE RANGE (YRS)	DESIGN	ANALYSIS	RESULTS*
Buchanan, 1995 Level III	34	3–26	Retrospective case series of LTG add-on	Compare to baseline, descriptive only	Response = 26 (78%)
Coppola & Pascotto, 1997 Level IV	37	2–22	Retrospective case series of LTG add-on	Compare to baseline, descriptive only	Response = 13 (35%)
Crawford et al., 2001 Level III	GBP-39, LTG-44	15–59	Randomized, open label, parallel group, add-on trial	Compare to baseline; compare groups	GBP: MRSF = 51%; LTG: MRSF = 48.6% (Diff NS)
Gaily et al., 1998 Level IV	40	1–17	Retrospective case series of OXC add-on	Compare to baseline, descriptive only	Response = 19 (48%)
Gibson, 2002 Level IV	6	25–51	Retrospective case series of LEV add-on	Compare to baseline, descriptive only	Response = 6 (100%)
Gidal et al., 2000 Level IV	44	8–59	Retrospective case series of LTG add-on	Compare to baseline, descriptive only	Response = 26 (55%)
Hosain et al., 2003 Level III	14 with LGS	1–8	Prospective, open label, add-on trial of NZP	Compare to baseline	MRSF = 41% ($p = 0.001$)
Iinuma et al., 1998 Level IV	66	1–15	Retrospective case series of ZSM add-on	Compare to baseline, descriptive only	Response = 25 (41%)
McKee et al., 2003 Level III	67	14–54	Prospective, open label, add-on trial of LTG	Compare to baseline	MRSF = 22.5 % ($p = 0.02$)
Mikati et al., 1998 Level IV	26	2–16	Prospective, open label, add-on trial of GBP	Compare to baseline	MRSF = 33% ($p = 0.05$)

TABLE 4-1 *Continued*

STUDY AND LEVEL OF EVIDENCE	NUMBER OF SUBJECTS	AGE RANGE (YRS)	DESIGN	ANALYSIS	RESULTS*
Singh & White-Scott, 2002 Level IV	20	21–57	Prospective, open label, add-on trial of TPM	Compare to baseline, descriptive only	Response = 11 (55%)
Ylinen, 1998 Level IV	36	Not stated	Retrospective case series of VGB add-on	Compare to baseline, descriptive only	Response = 15 (42%)

*Response: Greater than 50% reduction in seizure frequency.
GBP, gabapentin; LEV, levetiracetam; LTG, lamotrigine; MRSF, mean reduction in seizure frequency; NZP, nitrazepam; OXC, oxcarbazepine; TPM, topiramate; VGB, vigabatrin; ZSM, zonisamide.

2. Do adverse effects of antiepileptic drugs differ for persons with epilepsy and I/DD compared to persons with epilepsy alone?

Antiepileptic drugs are generally thought to cause more adverse behavioral effects in patients with I/DD compared to patients with epilepsy alone. Harbord (2000) confirmed this observation in a study of 216 children and adolescents with epilepsy, 67 of whom also had an I/DD. Behavioral side effects occurred with administration of all drugs but were more common with benzodiazepines (14%) and barbiturates (17%). Behavioral side effects occurred in 19 (28%) of those with epilepsy and I/DD, compared to 9 (6%) of those with epilepsy alone. This difference was not accounted for by the amount or type of drug used.

Case studies have documented adverse behavioral effects in patients with epilepsy and I/DD who were taking phenytoin and carbamazepine (Ilvanainen, 1998; Kalachnik, Hanzel, Harder, Bauernfeind, & Engstrom, 1995), as well as most of the newer antiepileptic drugs (Rutecki & Gidal, 2002). Lamotrigine is often thought to produce cognitive or behavioral improvement (McKee, 2003), but behavioral worsening has also been reported (Beran & Gibson, 1998; Ettinger et al., 1998). No well-designed Level I studies were found that carefully analyzed the effects of antiepileptic drugs on behavior in patients with I/DD, or that carefully explored the potential reasons why these effects may be more likely to occur in this population.

Valproate is known to cause carnitine deficiency. Usage of other antiepileptic drugs has also been associated with carnitine deficiency, and the condition seems to be more common in patients with I/DD (Coulter, 1995). No Level I studies have addressed the impact of carnitine deficiency or its treatment in patients with epilepsy and I/DD, however.

3. Do persons with epilepsy and I/DD have more mental health problems compared to persons with epilepsy alone?

Considerable evidence suggests that individuals with I/DD have mental health problems more frequently than the general population (see Chapter 5). A literature review noted that behavioral problems in patients with I/DD and epilepsy may relate more to the etiology of the I/DD than to the epilepsy (Caplan & Austin, 2000). Four Level III case-control studies showed no evidence of increased psychopathology in patients with epilepsy and I/DD compared to those with I/DD alone, whether residing at home (Lewis et al., 2000), in institutional or community settings (Deb, 1997), or in specialized inpatient psychiatric settings (Johnson, Lowengrub, & Lubetsky, 1995; Pary, 1993;). An exception to this may be found in autism, which is known to be associated with epilepsy and I/DD (Steffenburg, Gillberg, & Steffenburg, 1996).

4. Does adaptive or social functioning differ for persons with epilepsy and I/DD compared to persons with I/DD alone?

Several researchers have examined adaptive or social functioning in persons with epilepsy and I/DD and in persons with I/DD alone. Sabaz, Cairns, Lawson, Bleasel, and Bye (2001), in their Level III case-control study, using a health-related quality of life scale, showed that children with refractory seizures were more likely to have psychosocial problems regardless of whether they had an I/DD or not. Limitations in adaptive functioning were also related primarily to the degree of seizure control (Beckung & Uvebrant, 1997; Kurihara, Kumagai, Noda, Watanabe, & Imai, 1998). Movement of individuals with complex epilepsy from an institutional to a community setting with significant supports resulted in an increased level of psychosocial functioning which was associated with improved seizure control (Litzinger, Duvall, & Little, 1993). A Level III case-control study of 353 institutionalized persons with I/DD found that those with epilepsy had significantly less social and adaptive skills compared to those without epilepsy (Matson, Bamburg, Mayville, & Khan, 1999). On the other hand, among 59 adults with Down syndrome who did not have other medical or psychiatric disorders, those with epilepsy scored significantly higher on an adaptive behavior profile for reasons that were unclear (Prasher, 1995). It would be difficult to draw any firm conclusions from these data, but the degree of seizure control may be the most significant variable in determining adaptive or social functioning in this population.

5. Does mortality differ for persons with epilepsy and I/DD compared to persons with I/DD alone?

Forsgren, Edvinsson, Nylstrom, & Blomquist (1996) followed all 1478 persons with I/DD living in a single province in Sweden for 7 years (1985–1992) and analyzed the causes of death in this group during this time. Of the total number of subjects, 296 had epilepsy as well. They found that the standardized mortality ration (SMR) was 1.6 for those with I/DD but no epilepsy and 5.0 for those with I/DD and epilepsy. Mortality increased with increasing seizure frequency, but having a seizure was not the direct cause of death in these subjects.

McKee and Bodfish (2000) obtained similar results when they examined the rates of sudden, unexpected death in 305 residents of a single institution for persons with I/DD, 180 residents also had epilepsy. The rate of sudden, unexpected death was 1.3 per 1000 patient-years for those without epilepsy and 3.6 per 1000 patient-years for those with epilepsy. Increased seizure frequency was significantly correlated with the rate of sudden, unexpected death.

Both of these well-designed studies indicate that mortality is significantly increased when epilepsy is present and seems to correlate with seizure control. Whether or not improving seizure control in this population would decrease mortality has not been studied.

6. Do the types and frequencies of injuries differ for persons with I/DD and epilepsy compared to persons with I/DD alone?

Very little data were found to answer this important question. Clinical experience suggests that seizure-related injuries are a significant problem for patients with epilepsy and I/DD. Much of these data are likely contained within the administrative files of agencies that provide residential and other supports for this population and are not published in the literature or available for public inspection. Jancar and Jancar (1998) reported an increased risk of fractures in patients with epilepsy and I/DD (26%) compared to those with I/DD alone (15%). Several reasons were considered, including associated lack of mobility in the epilepsy group and possible antiepileptic drug–induced osteoporosis.

The dearth of published data on this issue is also frustrating for caregivers who must devise individual strategies to reduce the risk of injuries for patients with epilepsy and I/DD. Prospective studies of interventions to reduce seizure-related injuries are urgently needed.

Clinical Recommendations

The IASSID Working Group on Epilepsy noted the relative paucity of Level I data on treatment of patients with epilepsy and I/DD. Based primarily on extrapolation from studies conducted in populations without I/DD, they provided general recommendations for treatment of patients with different types of seizures (IASSID Working Group, 2001). For patients with generalized tonic–clonic, myoclonic, or absence seizures, they recommended either valproic acid or lamotrigine, with topiramate as an alternative. For patients with Lennox-Gastaut syndrome, they recommended lamotrigine or topiramate, with felbamate as an alternative. For patients with partial seizures, they recommended valproic acid, carbamazepine, or lamotrigine. Oxcarbazepine may be preferable to carbamazepine. As noted previously, the AAN group found that all of the new drugs may be useful as add-on treatment for patients with refractory seizures (French et al., 2004b). These recommendations are not strongly evidence-based but are reasonably based on clinical judgment.

Adverse drug effects may be difficult to detect in patients with I/DD. What appears to be behavioral agitation may be a nonverbal patient's way of indicating discomfort, nausea, dizziness, or some other adverse drug effect. Although the data suggest that antiepileptic drugs may cause more behavioral side effects in this population, the studies reviewed do not explore the possible reasons for this. Clinicians prescribing antiepileptic drugs must be familiar with the common and uncommon adverse effects that may occur with their use in patients with I/DD. In general, it is reasonable to recommend that clinicians choose antiepileptic drugs that are least likely to cause adverse drug effects, and that patients are monitored closely for the possible emergence of subtle or overt adverse drug effects.

Mental health problems may occur in patients with epilepsy and I/DD, but the evidence suggests that having epilepsy is not the cause of these problems. Mental health problems should be identified, investigated, and treated in this population as they would be for other patients with I/DD. Clinicians need to be aware of potential interactions between treatments for mental health problems and treatments for epilepsy, however.

Comprehensive epilepsy management includes assessment of overall social and adaptive functioning. Good seizure control is correlated with higher functioning and possibly also with decreased mortality. Concern about possible injuries and other safety issues is often cited as a factor restricting independence and social inclusion for persons with epilepsy and I/DD. The paucity of data on effective interventions to reduce these risks makes it difficult to provide strong recommendations. In general, clinicians should strive first of all to improve seizure control as much as possible. When seizures are a continuing concern, caregivers should develop an individualized safety plan that anticipates the risks of injuries and implements strategies that reduce these risks. Caregivers should also promote social and adaptive functioning as much as possible without increasing risk.

Research Recommendations

Clearly more research is needed. How applicable are studies in patients with epilepsy alone for patients with epilepsy and I/DD? Can (or should) we extrapolate from these data in treating patients with I/DD? Well-designed randomized clinical trials of antiepileptic drugs in persons with epilepsy and I/DD should be conducted. Comparative studies that evaluate relatively equivalent drugs and treatments would help clinicians select the safest and most effective drug for a specific problem.

Researchers should also address the issue of how best to define a population of individuals with epilepsy and I/DD. Individuals with I/DD vary greatly with regard to genetic, neurologic, and behavioral factors and with regard to their level and pattern of functioning. It may be preferable to study individuals with a specific epileptic syndrome, such as the Lennox-Gastaut syndrome noted earlier. Or it may be useful to study specific genetic conditions causing epilepsy, such as infantile spasms in patients with tuberous sclerosis. Use of more well-defined, homogeneous groups of research subjects would help caregivers to evaluate the applicability of the research results for specific clinical situations.

Research is also needed to address the comparative efficacy of antiepileptic drugs in this population and the cost-effectivenss of the newer drugs for epilepsy (compared to the older drugs) in persons with I/DD. Meta-analyses have suggested that the newer drugs are not necessarily more effective than the older drugs, but they may be safer and cause fewer adverse drug effects. The costs of these adverse effects, and of monitoring for them, should be included in these cost–benefit studies. If a newer drug causes fewer adverse effects and permits improved social and adaptive functioning, this also needs to be considered.

Perhaps the greatest need is for research that demonstrates effective ways to manage risk, reduce seizure-related injuries, and promote social and adaptive functioning for persons with epilepsy and I/DD. This area of research has been virtually neglected so far, yet it has the greatest potential for enhancing the quality of life for these individuals. Designing good studies to address this issue will require some creativity and collaboration between researchers and research groups to ensure reliable and valid results. It is hoped that the next evidence-based review of epilepsy and I/DD will have much more high-quality data on this and other topics that will result in stronger evidence-based recommendations.

REFERENCES

Beckung, E., & Uvebrant, P. (1997). Impairments, disabilities and handicaps in children and adolescents with epilepsy. *Acta Pediatrica, 86,* 254–260.

Beran, R. G., & Gibson, R. J. (1998). Aggressive behavior in intellectually challenged patients with epilepsy treated with lamotrigine. *Epilepsia, 39,* 280–282.

Buchanan, N. (1995). The efficacy of lamotrigine on seizure control in 34 children, adolescents and young adults with intellectual and physical disability. *Seizure, 4,* 233–236.

Caplan, R., & Austin, J. K. (2000). Behavioral aspects of epilepsy in children with mental retardation. *Mental Retardation and Developmental Disabilities Research Reviews, 6,* 293–299.

Committee on Classification and Terminology (1981). Proposal for revised clinical and electroencephalographic classification of epileptic seizures. *Epilepsia, 22,* 489–501.

Committee on Classification and Terminology (1985). Proposal for classification of epilepsies and epileptic syndromes. *Epilepsia, 26,* 268–278.

Coppola, G., & Pascotto, A. (1997). Lamotrigine as add-on drug in children and adolescents with refractory epilepsy and mental delay: An open trial. *Brain and Development, 19,* 398–402.

Coulter, D. L. (1995). Carnitine deficiency in epilepsy: Risk factors and treatment. *Journal of Child Neurology, 10* (Suppl. 2), 2S32–2S39.

Coulter, D. L. (1997). Comprehensive management of epilepsy in persons with mental retardation. *Epilepsia, 38* (Suppl. 4), S24–S31.

Crawford, P., Brown, S., & Kerr, M. (2001). A randomized open-label study of gabapentin and lamotrigine in adults with learning disability and resistant epilepsy. *Seizure, 10,* 107–115.

Deb, S. (1997). Mental disorder in adults with mental retardation and epilepsy. *Comprehensive Psychiatry, 38,* 179–184.

Devinsky, O., & Westbrook, L. E. (Eds). (2002). *Epilepsy and developmental disabilities.* Boston: Butterworth-Heinemann.

Donat, J. F., & Wright, F. S. (1990). Episodic symptoms mistaken for seizures in the neurologically impaired child. *Neurology, 40,* 156–157.

Ettinger, A. B., Weisbrot, D. M., Saracco, J., Dhoon, A., Kanner, A., & Devinsky, O. (1998). Positive and negative psychotropic effects of lamotrigine in patients with epilepsy and mental retardation. *Epilepsia, 39,* 874–877.

Forsgren, L., Edvinsson, S. O., Nylstrom, L., & Blomquist, H. K. (1996). Influence of epilepsy on mortality in mental retardation: An epidemiologic study. *Epilepsia, 37,* 956–963.

French, J. A., Kanner, A. M., Bautista, J., Abou-Khalil, B., Browne, T., Harden, C. L., et al. (2004a). Efficacy and tolerability of the new antiepileptic drugs I: Treatment of new onset epilepsy. *Neurology, 62,* 1252–1260.

French, J. A., Kanner, A. M., Bautista, J., Abou-Khalil, B., Browne, T., Harden, C. L., et al. (2004b). Efficacy and tolerability of the new antiepileptic dugs II: Treatment of refractory epilepsy. *Neurology, 62,* 1261–1273.

Gaily, E., Granstrom, M. L., & Liukkonen, E. (1998). Oxcarbazepine in the treatment of epilepsy in children and adolescents with intellectual disability. *Journal of Intellectual Disability Research, 42* (Suppl. 1), 41–45.

Gibson, G. (2002). Efficacy of levetiracetam in developmentally disabled patients: A review of the literature and six case reports. *Epilepsy and Behavior, 3,* 280–284.

Gidal, B. E., Walker, J. K., Lott, R. S., Shaw, R., Speth, J., Marty, K. J., et al. (2000). Efficacy of lamotrigine in institutionalized, developmentally disabled patients with epilepsy: A retrospective evaluation. *Seizure, 9,* 131–136.

Harbord, M. G. (2000). Significant anticonvulsant side effects in children and adolescents. *Journal of Clinical Neuroscience, 7,* 213–216.

Hauser, W. A., & Hesdorffer, D. C. (1990). *Epilepsy: Frequency, causes, and consequences.* New York: Demos.

Holmes, G. L., McKeever, M., & Russman, B. S. (1983). Abnormal behavior or epilepsy? Use of long-term EEG and video monitoring with severely to profoundly mentally retarded patients with seizures. *American Journal of Mental Deficiency, 87,* 456–458.

Hosain, S. A., Green, N. S., Solomon, G., & Chutorian, A. (2003). Nitrazepam for the treatment of Lennox-Gastaut syndrome. *Pediatric Neurology, 28,* 16–19.

IASSID Working Group on Epilepsy (2001). Clinical guidelines for the management of epilepsy in adults with an intellectual disability. *Seizure, 10,* 401–409.

Iinuma, K., Minami, T., Cho, K., Kajii, N., & Tachi, N. (1998). Long-term effects of zonisamide in the treatment of epilepsy in children with intellectual disability. *Journal of Intellectual Disability Research, 42* (Suppl. 1), 68–73.

Ilvanainen, M. (1998). Phenytoin: Effective but insidious therapy for epilepsy in people with intellectual disability. *Journal of Intellectual Disability Research, 42* (Suppl. 1), 24–31.

Jancar, J. & Jancar, M. P. (1998). Age-related fractures in people with intellectual disability and epilepsy. *Journal of Intellectual Disability Research, 42,* 429–433.

Johnson, C. R., Lowengrub, J. A., & Lubetsky, M. J. (1995). Psychiatric and behavior disorders in children with mental retardation and seizure disorder. *Journal of Developmental and Physical Disabilities, 7,* 243–252.

Kalachnik, J. E., Hanzel, T. E., Harder, S. R., Bauernfeind, J. D., & Engstrom, E. A. (1995). Antiepileptic drug behavioral side effects in individuals with mental retardation and the use of behavioral measurement techniques. *Mental Retardation, 33,* 374–382.

Kurihara, M., Kumagai, K., Noda, Y., Watanabe, M., & Imai, M. (1998). Prognosis in severe motor and intellectual disabilities syndrome complicated by epilepsy. *Brain and Development, 20,* 519–523.

Lewis, J. N., Tonge, B. J., Mowat, D. R., Einfeld, S. L., Siddons, H. M., & Rees, V. W. (2000). Epilepsy and associated psychopathology in young people with intellectual disability. *Journal of Pediatrics and Child Health, 36,* 172–175.

Litzinger, M. J., Duvall, B., & Little, P. (1993). Movement of individuals with complex epilepsy from an institution into the community: Seizure control and functional outcomes. *American Journal on Mental Retardation, 98* (Suppl.), 52–57.

Matson, J. L., Bamburg, J. W., Mayville, E. A., & Khan, I. (1999). Seizure disorders in people with intellectual disability: An analysis of differences in social functioning, adaptive functioning, and maladaptive behaviours. *Journal of Intellectual Disability Research, 43,* 531–539.

McKee, J. R., & Bodfish, J. W. (2000). Sudden unexpected death in epilepsy in adults with mental retardation. *American Journal on Mental Retardation, 105,* 229–235.

McKee, J. R., Sunder, T. R., FineSmith, R., Vuong, A., Varner, J. A., Hammer, A. E., et al. (2003). Lamotrigine as adjunctive therapy in patients with refractory epilepsy and mental retardation. *Epilepsy and Behavior, 4,* 386–394.

Mikati, M. A., Choueri, R., Khurana, D. S., Riviello, J., Helmers, S, & Holmes, G. (1998). Gabapentin in the treatment of refractory partial epilepsy in children with intellectual disability. *Journal of Intellectual Disability Research, 42* (Suppl. 1), 57–62.

Neill, J. C., & Alvarez, N. (1986). Differential diagnosis of epileptic versus pseudoepileptic seizures in developmentally disabled persons. *Applied Research in Mental Retardation, 7,* 285–298.

Pary, R. (1993). Mental retardation, mental illness, and seizure diagnosis. *American Journal on Mental Retardation, 98* (Suppl.), 58–62.

Prasher, V. P. (1995). Epilepsy and associated effects on adaptive behaviour in adults with Down syndrome. *Seizure, 4,* 53–56.

Rutecki, P. A., & Gidal, B. E. (2002). Antiepileptic drug treatment in the developmentally disabled: Treatment considerations with the newer antiepileptic drugs. *Epilepsy and Behavior, 3,* S24–S31.

Sabaz, M., Cairns, D. R., Lawson, J. A., Bleasel, A. F., & Bye, A. M. E. (2001). The health-related quality of life of children with refractory epilepsy: A comparison of those with and without intellectual disability. *Epilepsia, 42,* 621–628.

Singh, B. K., & White-Scott, S. (2002). Role of topiramate in adults with intractable epilepsy, mental retardation, and developmental disabilities. *Seizure, 11,* 47–50.

Steffenburg, S., Gillberg, C., & Steffenburg, U. (1996). Psychiatric disorders in children and adolescents with mental retardation and active epilepsy. *Archives of Neurology, 53,* 904–912.

Ylinen, A. (1998). Antiepileptic efficacy of vigabatrin in people with severe epilepsy and intellectual disability. *Journal of Intellectual Disability Research, 42* (Suppl. 1), 46–49.

5

MENTAL HEALTH

Betsey A. Benson, PhD, FAAMR

The full range of mental illness is observed in persons with intellectual and developmental disability (I/DD). The co-occurrence of mental illness and I/DD has been referred to as "dual diagnosis." Many factors contribute to a vulnerability to mental health problems, including biological sources as well as prenatal and perinatal influences that may also cause I/DD. Psychosocial origins or precipitants of mental illness of persons with I/DD include short- and long-term stressors such as repeated failure experiences, an unstable environment with changing caretakers, abuse, and stigmatization (Deb, Matthews, Holt, & Bouras, 2001; Rush & Frances, 2000). The experience of stress, without the skills and social supports to cope with it, can trigger emotional problems that interfere with daily functioning.

WHAT IS THE PREVALENCE OF CO-OCCURRING MENTAL ILLNESS IN I/DD?

A considerable amount of research on the prevalence of dual diagnosis has been conducted around the globe. A prevalence range between 10% and 40% has been reported, with the wide range most likely due to the study methods (Borthwick-Duffy & Eyman, 1990; Day, 1985; Einfeld & Tonge, 1996; Jacobson, 1990; Koller, Richardson, Katz, & McLaren, 1983; Rutter, Tizard, Yule, Graham, & Whitmore, 1976). Investigations based on case files tend to obtain smaller prevalence rates than those that conduct clinical interviews. The gap between prevalence rates based on previously diagnosed disorders and those obtained from clinical interview has been attributed to a number of factors including unrecognized disorders, the lack of availability of mental health services, and diagnostic overshadowing. Diagnostic overshadowing refers to a phenomenon in which the symptoms of mental illness are ascribed to the individual's I/DD, thereby overlooking mental health needs. Prevalence studies also differ in the types of symptoms and problem behaviors that are studied. Investigations that include maladaptive behaviors, such as self-injurious behavior or aggression, in addition to diagnosed mental disorders, report higher rates. Finally, studies differ in the definition of I/DD that is used and whether other disabilities are included in the sample. For a more extensive discussion of these issues the reader is referred to Nezu, Nezu, and Gill-Weiss (1992).

WHAT ARE THE DIAGNOSTIC ISSUES?

It has been recognized that there are difficulties in applying existing psychiatric diagnostic classification systems to persons with I/DD. The individual interview is the cornerstone of psychiatric diagnosis. People who are unable to participate fully in the interview process, whether because of communication difficulties or cognitive limitations, present challenges to the diagnostician.

The use of informants can address some of the difficulty presented by a non-verbal patient. The quality of the informant report is critical. However, many psychiatric disorders are diagnosed based on the verbal report of symptoms by the individual. Informants may not have been able to observe the critical symptoms. In the case of major depression, for example, some of the symptoms include feelings of worthlessness or excessive guilt, inability to think or concentrate, and recurrent thoughts of death (American Psychiatric Association, 1994). An informant would have difficulty reporting these symptoms in the absence of an individual's self-report.

Some professionals have proposed that adaptations to the criteria for psychiatric diagnosis be permitted for persons with I/DD to take into account the limitations of verbal reports. For example, in the Diagnostic and Statistical Manual of Mental Disorders 4th ed. (DSM-IV) diagnosis of major depressive disorder, instead of five of nine symptoms being required to make a diagnosis, one of which must be depressed mood or loss of interest or pleasure in activities (American Psychiatric Association, 1994), the modification would allow three of nine to be sufficient for a diagnosis. It has also been suggested that some symptoms be permitted to serve as substitute criteria or behavioral indicators of depression for persons with I/DD (Clarke & Gomez, 1999), but others disagree with this approach (Tsiouris, Mann, Patti, & Sturmey, 2003).

In Great Britain, a consensus-based psychiatric diagnostic classification was developed for adults with I/DD called the Diagnostic Criteria for Psychiatric Disorders for Use with Adults with Learning Disabilities/Mental Retardation (DC-LD). The system is designed as a companion to the International Classification of Diseases, Tenth Revision (ICD-10) for adults with mild I/DD and as an alternative system for individuals who function in the moderate to profound range (Royal College of Psychiatrists, 2001). The DC-LD provides descriptive diagnostic criteria and is envisioned as a work in progress that will evolve as further information is obtained (Cooper, Melville, & Einfeld, 2003).

An expert panel comprised of members of the European Association for Mental Health in Mental Retardation (Deb et al., 2001) wrote *Practice Guidelines for the Assessment and Diagnosis of Mental Health Problems in Adults with I/DD*. The guidelines describe symptoms in some detail as they appear in adults with I/DD.

In the United States, the National Association for Dual Diagnosis (NADD) is working with the American Psychiatric Association to develop an alternative psychiatric diagnostic classification system for children and adults with I/DD. The NADD Web site will provide information on the progress of this collaboration: http://www.thenadd.org.

The challenges presented in the area of psychiatric diagnosis in persons with I/DD have motivated professionals to propose solutions. For an alternative diagnostic classification system to gain wide acceptance, it must demonstrate reliability and validity. Diagnostic issues are one obstacle to progress in the treatment of mental illness in persons with I/DD. Reliable and accurate psychiatric diagnosis is necessary to conduct assessment and treatment research and to advance the field to evidence-based clinical practice.

WHAT ARE THE ASSESSMENT ISSUES?

In many ways, the challenges in the area of assessment of persons with I/DD are similar to those in the area of psychiatric diagnosis. When selecting assessment instruments to be used the choices are: (1) use the assessment tools that were developed for the general population, (2) adapt tools for the general population for use with persons with I/DD, or (3) develop new tools designed specifically for persons with I/DD. For example, in the area of depression, the *Beck Depression Inventory* (Beck, Ward, Mendelson, Mock, & Erbaugh, 1961) is a widely used self-report instrument of the symptoms of depression for the general population. The scale consists of sentence stems that are completed by choosing one of four alternative statements. When administered to an adult with I/DD, the items are typically read to the individual. Because of the length of the items, it can be difficult for the listener to remember the four choices and to select the appropriate one. The *Children's Depression Inventory* (Kovacs, 1980/81) would be another choice. The individual needs to respond to only three options. Some of the questions are not age-appropriate for adults and require word substitutions, however. Alternatively, one could select the *Reynolds Depression Scale* (Reynolds & Baker, 1988) that was developed for persons with I/DD. The items are rated on a three-point response format according to how frequently the subject has the experience. Norms were obtained for persons with I/DD. Regardless of the instrument chosen, the demands on receptive and expressive language can present obstacles to accurate completion for many individuals.

WHAT IS THE STATE OF THE EVIDENCE IN MENTAL HEALTH?

Considering the difficulties in diagnosis and assessment of mental illness in persons with I/DD, it is not surprising that progress has been slow in the area of treatment. For many topics, case studies or case series are the only published works. In lieu of research evidence, professionals have collaborated to produce consensus documents that offer guidelines for practice based on current knowledge. Consensus guidelines can be useful to practitioners because although the published case studies and case series are valuable, it may be difficult to generalize from them to clinical practice. The combined experience of the experts is based on a larger number of individuals than a case report. On the other hand, expert consensus is subject to the biases of the experts and how representative and experienced they are. Expert opinion is described as "a bridge between research and clinical practice" (Rush & Frances, 2000). Expert consensus is likely to change in time in response to published research.

An international consensus conference on psychotropic medications in developmental disabilities at Ohio State University resulted in a volume edited by Reiss and Aman (1998). The book addressed the existing research and clinical experience with medications as well as the topics of epidemiology, diagnosis, consent, side effects, and drug interactions.

The American Academy of Child and Adolescent Psychiatry (1999) published practice parameters for the assessment and treatment of children, adolescents, and adults. The authors state that psychiatric diagnostic evaluation and treatment are in principle the same as for individuals without I/DD. Approaches are modified depending on the cognitive level and communications skills of the individual.

In May 2000, a special issue of the *American Journal on Mental Retardation* was published that presented expert consensus guidelines on the treatment of psychiatric and behavioral problems in mental retardation. Edited by John Rush and Allen Frances, the document surveyed two groups of experts on psychosocial interventions and on medication. Responses were obtained from 48 psychosocial experts and 45 medication experts. The respondents provided ratings on a scale from 1 to 9 of the appropriateness of various interventions. The results indicate which alternatives were treatments of choice (obtained the highest rating by at least half the experts), first line, second line, or third line based on the confidence interval of the ratings for each alternative.

The psychosocial experts rated applied behavior analysis, client and/or family education, and managed the environment as first-line treatments for most of the target symptoms that were included in the survey. Cognitive behavior therapy and classical behavioral therapy were first-line choices for the treatment of anxiety in clients with mild to moderate I/DD. The medication experts recommended medication as part of an initial treatment plan for psychotic, bipolar, and major depressive disorders and for some other symptoms in the absence of a clear psychiatric diagnosis, for example, suicidal ideation or behavior. The specific recommendations for medications were the same as those obtained in other surveys for treating individuals without I/DD. Thus, if diagnoses could be made with confidence, few differences would exist in medication selection in comparison to the general population.

Methods

A complete review of the state of the scientific evidence in mental health of persons with I/DD is beyond the scope of this chapter. Rather, two topics were selected as examples of the work that has been accomplished to date in the area of treatment. One topic represents psychosocial intervention and the other represents medication treatment. For each topic, an information specialist identified relevant research articles using the following databases: Medline, CINAHL, Sociofile, Health Star, PsychInfo, Pharmaceutical Abstracts, Web Science, Academic Search Premiere, Ingenta and GPO Access. The topics searched included mental retardation, developmental disabilities, and Down syndrome. In addition, recent review articles were consulted for references.

To address the question of the effectiveness of psychotherapy, only studies published since 1990 in which a control group was used were selected. The definition of psychotherapy written by Prout and Nowak-Drabik (2003) was used to frame this search: "planned direct face-to-face applications of psychological techniques . . . to modify feelings, values, attitudes, and behaviors" (p. 84). Interventions conducted by teachers or paraprofessionals were excluded.

For the second topic concerning medication treatment, the category atypical antipsychotics was chosen for examination because this classification of drugs is a consensus "first-line" treatment for psychotic disorders, self-injurious behavior, and aggression, according to the experts (Rush & Frances, 2000). The atypical antipsychotics are widely used because of reported advantages in comparison to the "typical" antipsychotic medications. There is said to be a more favorable side effect profile with these medications (Aman & Madrid, 1999). One specific drug, risperidone (Risperdal), was selected for inclusion here because of the level of activity that exists in research studies to date.

Results and Discussion

WHAT IS THE EVIDENCE FOR THE EFFECTIVENESS OF PSYCHOTHERAPY?

Three English language review articles were published in recent years that attempted to answer this question. Prout and Nowak-Drabik (2003) reviewed a 30-year period of psychotherapy research (1968–1998). A second review was authored by Beail (2003) and examined literature since 1996 that included psychodynamic and cognitive-behavioral psychotherapy. A third review, limited to anger control studies, was published by Whitaker (2001).

There were five psychotherapy studies of interventions that were based on a behavioral or cognitive-behavioral orientation. The target of treatment was social or interpersonal skills, including assertiveness, problem solving, dating skills, and anger control.

Table 5-1 contains a summary of the studies. The first two studies listed were conducted in the United States; the last three were completed in Great Britain. In most cases, a waiting-list control group was used with participants on the waiting list receiving the intervention after a delay period. In the case of the Taylor, Novaco, Gillmer, & Thorne (2002) and Rose, West, & Clifford (2000) studies, the comparison group received "routine care" during the waiting period. For the most part, the participants of the five studies were individuals functioning in the mild range of I/DD. The studies generally contained small sample sizes. The Rose et al. (2000) study was conducted over a period of 2 years to compile data on 44 subjects. The three anger

TABLE 5-1 *Psychotherapy: Summary of Studies*

STUDY	TREATMENT/CONTROL	PARTICIPANT	M/F	AGE (YRS)
Nezu et al., 1991	Assertiveness, Problem solving/ Wait list	Mild MR Various diagnoses	18/10	22–53
Valenti-Hein et al., 1994	Dating skills/Wait list	Moderate to borderline MR	13/12	18–50
Rose et al., 2000	Anger/Wait list with routine care	British Picture Vocabulary Scale score range 50–113	39/5	20–62
Taylor et al., 2002	Anger/Routine care	Inpatient, IQ range 55–80 Provocation Inventory < 55	20/0	18–60
Willner et al., 2002	Anger/Wait list	Community support, mean IQ 65	9/5	18–57

control treatment studies primarily worked with male participants. All of the studies were conducted with adults.

Table 5-2 presents some specifics about the design and interventions in the psychotherapy studies. In most cases, random assignment to the treatment and control conditions was used; the exception was the Rose et al. (2000) study. Four of the five studies provided a group therapy intervention. These interventions ranged in total duration from 10 to 32 hours. The one exception was the inpatient study by Taylor et al. (2002) in which 18 hours of individual therapy was provided. Two columns in Table 5-2 indicate the number of individuals in the treatment and control conditions. The first entry, by Nezu, Nezu, & Arean (1991), had two components

TABLE 5-2 *Psychotherapy: Research Methodology*

STUDY	DESIGN AND LEVEL OF EVIDENCE	DURATION	NO. OF TREATMENTS	NO. OF CONTROLS	FOLLOW-UP
Nezu et al., 1991	Random/control (I)	10, 1-hr group	9 Assert/Prob 9 Prob/Assert	10	3 mos
Valenti-Hein et al., 1994	Random/control (I)	12, 1.5-hr group	13	12	8 wks
Rose et al., 2000	Nonrandom/control (II-1)	16, 2-hr group	25	19	6, 12 mos
Taylor et al., 2002	Random/control (I)	18, 1-hr individual	9	10	1 mo.
Willner et al., 2002	Random/control (I)	9, 2-hr group	7	7	3 mos

TABLE 5-3 *Psychotherapy Outcomes*

STUDY	INDEX MEASURES	POST-TREATMENT COMPARISONS
Nezu et al., 1991	Brief Symptom Inventory, Subjective Units of Distress	T < C
	Problem Solving Test	PSA > PAS
	Role Play Test	T > C more assertive
	ABS-R Part II (caregiver)	T < C
Valenti-Hein et al., 1994	Role Play Test	T > C
	Stacking the Deck	T > C
	Social Avoidance and Distress	NS
	Waiting Room Observation (Dating Skills only)	Trend < interactions
Rose et al., 2000	Anger Inventory, Depression Scale	T < C
	Self-Concept	NS
Taylor et al., 2002	Provocation Inventory	T < C
	Ward Anger Scale (staff)	NS
Willner et al., 2002	Anger Inventory (self and other)	T < C
	Provocation Index (self and other)	T < C

C, Control; T, treatment.
NS, Not significant.

to the treatment that were offered in different orders: problem solving followed by assertiveness, or assertiveness followed by problem solving. In the last column, the length of the follow-up period is noted. Most of the studies obtained follow-up measures at 1–3 months, with the exception of Rose et al. (2000), in which measures were obtained at 6 and 12 months.

Table 5-3 summarizes the outcome measures used to compare the treatment and control conditions. A number of different types of measures were included. In addition to self-report, role play tests, observations, caregiver report, and clinician ratings were used. In the Nezu et al. study (1991), the self-report *Brief Symptom Index* and the *Subjective Units of Distress Scale* were completed as well as a test of problem solving. A caregiver completed Part II of the *Adaptive Behavior Scale* which is a section that focuses on problem behaviors. The expected differences were obtained; there were fewer symptoms and distress in the treatment group, as well as better role play performance and less caregiver report of problems. In this study, the group that received the problem solving intervention first did better on the problem solving test.

The Valenti-Hein, Yarnold, and Mueser (1994) study is noteworthy for including a behavioral observation component. Waiting room behavior was observed and interactions were coded. There was a trend for participants of the dating skills group to increase interactions.

The three interventions that focused on anger control found expected differences in the direction of fewer anger self-reports in the treatment conditions. Mixed results were obtained with staff ratings. In one study, improvement was significantly correlated with Verbal IQ (Willner, Jones, Tams, & Green, 2002).

In summary, there were few controlled trials of psychotherapy with persons with I/DD since 1990. The studies that were conducted can be characterized as group therapy with adults who function in the mild to moderate range of I/DD. Both inpatient and outpatient studies are represented. Outcome measures included self-report, but also behavioral enactment measures and staff or caregiver ratings. The follow-up period was generally short, on the order of weeks.

STRENGTH OF THE EVIDENCE—PSYCHOTHERAPY

The psychotherapy outcome effects tend to be significant, although modest. The studies may lack power to detect significant differences because of the small number of participants. Investigators used measures developed for the study or a combination of established measures and study-specific measures. The researchers could pay more attention to treatment fidelity issues—whether the interventions were delivered as described without variation. The psychotherapy treatments were not linked to a participant's psychiatric diagnosis. The focus of the interventions was not to treat a specific psychiatric disorder, but rather to improve interpersonal skills. Studies are needed on the treatment of specific diagnostic syndromes. The influence of cognitive functioning level on response to interventions should be examined to determine the boundaries of effective treatment.

WHAT IS THE EVIDENCE FOR THE EFFECTIVENESS OF PSYCHOTROPIC MEDICATIONS?

Psychotropic medication usage with persons with I/DD has generated much concern over the years. Studies indicate that a large percentage of individuals are prescribed psychotropic medication (e.g., Kiernan, Reeves, & Alborz, 1995). In addition to the widespread use of medications and the potential for overmedication, there is some debate about whether medications should be prescribed for treatment of a severe and persistent behavior, such as aggression, that is not linked to a specific psychiatric diagnosis (Santosh & Baird, 1999). In that case, medications are used symptomatically, which differs from the categorical diagnostic formulation currently in use. While the study of medications with persons with I/DD lags behind that of the general population, the published studies that are available tend to be open-label trials and case studies or case series designs.

Six studies were identified as randomized controlled trials (RCTs) of risperidone with persons with I/DD. The studies were conducted in Belgium, the Netherlands, Canada, and the United States. Table 5-4 provides a summary of the studies. The last study entry was authored by the Research Units on Pediatric Psychopharmacology (RUPP) Autism Network (2002). Two studies were conducted with inpatients, while the rest were outpatients. The investigations included participants from two diagnostic groups: those with conduct problems, including diagnoses of oppositional defiant disorder and disruptive behavior disorders, and participants with autism or pervasive developmental disorder plus severe behavior problems. Both of these diagnos-

TABLE 5-4 *Risperidone: Summary of Studies*

STUDY	TREATMENT/CONTROL	DIAGNOSIS	M/F	AGE (YRS)
McDougle et al., 1998	Risperidone/Placebo	Autism or Pervasive Dev Disorder	22/9	18–43
Buitelaar et al., 2001	Risperidone/Placebo	Conduct Disorder, ODD, ADHD	33/5	12–18
Van Bellinghen & de Troch, 2001	Risperidone/Placebo	Behavior Disturbance	5/8	6–14
Aman et al., 2002	Risperidone/Placebo	Conduct Disorder, ODD, Disruptive Disorder NOS	97/21	5–12
Research Unit on Pediatric Psychopharmacology (RUPP) Autism Network, 2002	Risperidone/Placebo	Autism plus Behavior Disturbance	82/19	5–17
Snyder et al., 2002	Risperidone/Placebo	Conduct Disorder, ODD, Disruptive Disorder NOS	83/27	5–12

tic groups include a greater number of males than females and the study participants reflected that distribution; more males than females were enrolled. Five of the six studies were conducted with children, ranging in age from 5 to 18 years.

All of the studies were double-blind randomized controlled trials (see Table 5-5). The three bottom entries were multisite studies which resulted in a larger number of participants in the treatment and placebo control conditions. The studies ranged in duration from 4 to 12 weeks, with 6 weeks being the most common.

TABLE 5-5 *Risperidone: Research Methodology*

STUDY	RESEARCH DESIGN AND LEVEL OF EVIDENCE	TREATMENT DURATION	NO. IN TREATMENT GROUP	NO. IN CONTROL GROUP
McDougle et al., 1998	Double-blind, Random (I)	12 wks	14	16
Buitelaar et al., 2001	Double-blind, Random (I)	6 wks	19	19
Van Bellinghen et al., 2001	Double-blind, Random (I)	4 wks	6	7
Aman et al., 2002	Multisite, Double-blind, Random (I)	6 wks	55	63
RUPP, 2002	Multisite, Double-blind, Random (I)	8 wks	49	52
Snyder et al., 2002	Multisite, Double-blind, Random (I)	6 wks	53	57

TABLE 5-6 *Risperidone: Outcomes*

STUDY	MEASURES	TREATMENT VS. CONTROL
McDougle et al., 1998	Clinical Global Impression Yale-Brown Obsessive Compulsive Scale SIB-Q Ritvo-Freeman Real-Life Rating Scale	57% vs. 0% Improved or Much Improved Decrease in repetitive behavior Decrease in total score Decrease in total and two subscales
Buitelaar et al., 2001	Clinical Global Impressions—Severity Aberrant Behavior Checklist—Teacher Overt Aggression Scale—M	T < C T < C total NS
Van Bellinghen et al., 2001	Clinical Global Impression Aberrant Behavior Checklist Personal Assessment Checklist	82% vs. 0% Improved or Much Improved Decrease in two subscales Two subscales improved
Aman et al., 2002	Clinical Global Impression Nisonger Child Behavior Rating Form Aberrant Behavior Checklist Behavior Problems Inventory	77% vs. 33% Improved All subscales improved Three subscales improved Aggression subscale improved
RUPP, 2002	Clinical Global Impression Aberrant Behavior Checklist	69% vs. 12% Improved or Much Improved Irritability subscale decrease
Snyder et al., 2002	Clinical Global Impression Nisonger Child Behavior Rating Form Aberrant Behavior Checklist Behavior Problems Inventory	77% vs. 25% Improved Conduct Scale 47% vs. 20% decrease All subscales improved Aggression subscale improved

C, Control; T, treatment

The study outcomes were tracked with multiple measures (see Table 5-6). For all, the *Clinical Global Impression-Improvement or Severity* rating was used. Several of the studies also used the *Aberrant Behavior Checklist* rating scale (Aman, Singh, Stewart, & Field, 1985). There are five subscales in this measure including hyperactivity, irritability, lethargy, stereotypy, and inappropriate speech. In some studies, the *Nisonger Child Behavior Rating Form* that contains a Conduct Problem subscale (Aman, Tassé, Rojahn, & Hammer, 1996) was used. The *Behavior Problems Inventory* is a rating scale that focuses on aggression and self-injurious behavior (Rojahn, Matson, Lott, Esbensen, & Smalls, 2001). The latter three measures were developed specifically for individuals with I/DD.

Table 5-6 summarizes the study outcomes. *Clinical Global Impression-Improvement* is often reported according to the percentage of participants who are rated "improved" or "much improved." Significant differences were obtained on this measure as well as several of the rating scales that were completed by an informant.

A high proportion of participants in both the treatment and placebo conditions reported some adverse effects (see Table 5-7). The reports indicated that most of these were transient and of mild intensity. One adverse effect that has prompted

TABLE 5-7 *Risperidone: Dosage and Adverse Effects*

STUDY	DOSAGE/DAY	% ADVERSE EFFECTS (TREATMENT VS. CONTROL), TYPE
McDougle et al., 1998	Mean, 2.9 mg	87% vs. 31%, agitation, weight gain, sedation
Buitelaar et al., 2001	Mean, 2.9 mg	89% vs. 58%, tired, headache, nausea
Van Bellinghen et al., 2001	Mean, 1.2 mg	67% vs. 29%, heart rate increase, sleepy
Aman et al., 2002	Mean, 1.16 mg	98% vs. 74%, headache, sleepy
RUPP, 2002	Mean, 1.8 mg	Significant difference for drowsy, fatigue, weight gain
Snyder et al., 2002	0.02– 0.06 mg/kg	87% vs. 74%, sleepy, appetite increase

further investigation is that of increased appetite and weight gain. The potential for hyperglycemia associated with treatment with the atypical antipsychotics is problematic and physicians have been alerted to the possibility.

STRENGTH OF THE EVIDENCE—RISPERIDONE

The strength of the evidence for the effectiveness of risperidone is substantial. Rapid and significant effects were reported consistently. Definite improvements were obtained in aggressive and disruptive behavior. The adverse effects in these relatively short-term studies are described as not significant. The issue of weight gain and possible hyperglycemia require further investigation. Although participants in some of the studies were diagnosed with autism or pervasive developmental disorder, the findings do not suggest that the drug is effective with core symptoms of autism, but rather has effects on disruptive behaviors.

Considerable progress has been made with regard to studying the safety and efficacy of risperidone. Less research progress has been made with respect to other classes of psychotropic medications, despite widespread use with persons with I/DD.

Summary and Directions of Future Research

Many of the issues presented in this chapter were identified at the 2001 National Institutes of Health workshop on emotional and behavioral health that immediately preceded the Surgeon General's conference on health and I/DD. At the conference, workgroups were organized on several topics including epidemiology, diagnosis and assessment, interventions research, ethical considerations, research design, and research training needs. Each group provided recommendations to advance research efforts. In the area of diagnosis, it was recommended that research be conducted to assess the validity and reliability of adaptations of standard diagnosis and assessment strategies and to develop direct observation instruments to identify overt characteristics of emotional disturbance. In the interventions area, it was suggested that efforts be made to assess genetic etiology effects on treatment outcomes, including neuroimaging studies. Researchers were encouraged to assess the effects of combining pharmacological treatment with behavioral interventions and other approaches. This is currently being done by the RUPP autism network. A summary of the conference report can be found at: *http://draft.ninds.nih.gov/news_and_events/Emotional_Behavioral_Health_2001.htm*

It will require many years of concerted effort to address the recommendations of the NIH workgroups. However, if the recommendations are carried out, significant progress will be made in mental health and I/DD. In addition to the efforts in the United States, work continues in other countries to improve the diagnosis, assessment, and treatment of mental illness in persons with I/DD. With committed professionals and dedicated resources, the necessary advancements can be achieved.

REFERENCES

Aman, M. G., de Smedt, G., Derivan, A., Lyons, B., Findling, R. L., & the Risperidone Disruptive Behavior Study Group. (2002). Double-blind, placebo-controlled study of risperidone for the treatment of disruptive behaviors in children with subaverage intelligence. *American Journal of Psychiatry, 159*, 1337–1346.

Aman, M. G., & Madrid, A. (1999). Atypical antipsychotics in persons with developmental disabilities. *Mental Retardation and Developmental Disabilities Research Reviews, 5*, 253–263.

Aman, M. G., Singh, N., Stewart, A. W., & Field, C. J. (1985). Psychometric characteristics of the Aberrant Behavior Checklist. *American Journal on Mental Deficiency, 89*, 492–502.

Aman, M. G., Tassé, M. J., Rojahn, J., & Hammer, D. (1996) The Nisonger CBRF: A child behavior rating form for children with developmental disabilities. *Research in Developmental Disabilities, 17*, 41–57.

American Academy of Child and Adolescent Psychiatry. (1999). Practice parameters for the assessment and treatment of children, adolescents, and adults with mental retardation and comorbid mental disorders. *Journal of the American Academy of Child and Adolescent Psychiatry, 38* (12 Suppl), 5S–31S.

American Psychiatric Association. (1994). *Diagnostic and statistical manual of mental disorders* (4th ed.). Washington, DC: Author.

Beail, N. (2003). What works for people with mental retardation? Critical commentary on cognitive-behavioral and psychodynamic psychotherapy research. *Mental Retardation, 41*, 468–472.

Beck, A. T., Ward, C. H., Mendelson, M., Mock, J., & Erbaugh, J. (1961). An inventory for measuring depression. *Archives of General Psychiatry, 4*, 561–571.

Borthwick-Duffy, S., & Eyman, R. K. (1990). Who are the dually diagnosed? *American Journal on Mental Retardation, 94*, 586–595.

Buitelaar, J. K., van der Gaag, R. J., Cohen-Kettenis, P., & Melman, C. T. M. (2001). A randomized controlled trial of risperidone in the treatment of aggression in hospitalized adolescents with subaverage cognitive abilities. *Journal of Clinical Psychiatry, 62*, 239–248.

Clarke, D. J., & Gomez, G. (1999). Utility of modified DCR-10 criteria in the diagnosis of depression associated with I/DD. *Journal of Intellectual Disability Research, 43*, 413–420.

Cooper, S., Melville, C. A., & Einfeld, S. L. (2003). Psychiatric diagnosis, intellectual disabilities, and Diagnostic Criteria for Psychiatric Disorders for Use with Adults with Learning Disabilities/Mental Retardation (DC-LD). *Journal of Intellectual Disability Research, 47*, 3–15.

Day, K. (1985). Psychiatric disorder in the middle-aged and elderly mentally handicapped. *British Journal of Psychiatry, 147*, 660–667.

Deb, S., Matthews, T., Holt, G., & Bouras, N. (Eds). (2001). *Practice guidelines for the assessment and diagnosis of mental health problems in adults with intellectual disability.* Brighton, Great Britain: Pavilion.

Einfeld, S. L., & Tonge, B. J. (1996). Population prevalence of psychopathology in children and adolescents with I/DD: II. Epidemiological findings. *Journal of Intellectual Disability Research, 40,* 99–109.

Jacobson, J. W. (1990). Do some mental disorders occur less frequently among persons with mental retardation? *American Journal on Mental Retardation, 94,* 596–602.

Kiernan, C., Reeves, D., & Alborz, A. (1995). The use of anti-psychotic drugs with adults with learning difficulties and challenging behaviour. *Journal of Intellectual Disability Research, 39,* 263–274.

Koller, H., Richardson, S. A., Katz, M., & McLaren, J. (1983). Behavior disturbance since childhood among a 5-year cohort of all mentally retarded young adults in a city. *American Journal of Mental Deficiency, 87,* 386–395.

Kovacs, M. (1980/81). Rating scales to assess depression in school-aged children. *Acta Paedopsychiatarica, 46,* 305–315.

McDougle, C. J., Holmes, J. P., Carlson, D. C., Pelton, G. H., Cohen, D. J., & Price, L. H. (1998). A double-blind, placebo-controlled study of risperidone in adults with autistic disorder and other pervasive developmental disorders. *Archives of General Psychiatry, 55,* 633–641.

National Institutes of Health. (2001). *Workshop on emotional and behavioral health in persons with mental retardation/developmental disabilities: Research challenges and opportunities.* Retrieved December 22, 2004, from *http://draft.ninds.nih.gov/news_and_events/Emotional_Behavioral_Health_2001.htm*

Nezu, C. M., Nezu, A. M., & Arean, P. (1991). Assertiveness and problem-solving training for mildly mentally retarded persons with dual diagnoses. *Research in Developmental Disabilities, 12,* 371–386.

Nezu, C. M., Nezu, A. M., & Gill-Weiss, M. J. (1992). *Psychopathology in persons with mental retardation: Clinical guidelines for assessment and treatment.* Champaign, IL: Research Press.

Prout, H. T., & Nowak-Drabik, K. M. (2003). Psychotherapy with persons who have mental retardation: An evaluation of effectiveness. *American Journal on Mental Retardation, 108,* 82–93.

Reiss, S., & Aman, M. G. (Eds). (1998). *Psychotropic medications and developmental disabilities: The international consensus handbook.* Columbus, OH: The Ohio State University.

Research Units on Pediatric Psychopharmacology Autism Network. (2002). Risperidone in children with autism and serious behavioral problems. *New England Journal of Medicine, 347*(5), 314–321.

Reynolds, W. M., & Baker, J. A. (1988). Assessment of depression in persons with mental retardation. *American Journal on Mental Retardation, 93,* 93–103.

Rojahn, J., Matson, J. L., Lott, D., Esbensen, A. J., & Smalls, Y. (2001). The Behavior Problems Inventory: An instrument for the assessment of self-injury, stereotyped behavior, and aggression/destruction in individuals with developmental disabilities. *Journal of Autism and Developmental Disorders, 31,* 577–588.

Rose, J., West, C., & Clifford, D. (2000). Group interventions for anger in people with intellectual disabilities. *Research in Developmental Disabilities, 21,* 171–181.

Royal College of Psychiatrists (2001). *The diagnostic criteria for psychiatric disorders for use with adults with learning disabilities/mental retardation.* Occasional Paper 48, London: Gaskell Press.

Rush, A. J., & Frances, A. (2000). Expert consensus guideline series: Treatment of psychiatric and behavioral problems in mental retardation. *American Journal on Mental Retardation, 105* (3), 159–226.

Rutter, M., Tizard, J., Yule, W., Graham, P., & Whitmore, K. (1976). Isle of Wight studies, 1964–1974. *Psychological Medicine, 6,* 313–332.

Santosh, P. J., & Baird, G. (1999). Psychopharmacotherapy in children and adults with intellectual disability. *Lancet, 354*, 231–240.

Snyder, R., Turgay, A., Aman, M., Binder, C., Fisman, S., Carroll, A., and the Risperidone Conduct Study Group. (2002). Effects of risperidone on conduct and disruptive behavior disorders in children with subaverage IQs. *Journal of the American Academy of Child and Adolescent Psychiatry, 41*, 1026–1036.

Taylor, J. L., Novaco, R. W., Gillmer, B., & Thorne, I. (2002). Cognitive-behavioural treatment of anger intensity among offenders with intellectual disabilities. *Journal of Applied Research in Intellectual Disabilities, 15*, 151–165.

Tsiouris, J. A., Mann, R., Patti, P. J., & Sturmey, P. (2003). Challenging behaviours should not be considered as depressive equivalents in individuals with intellectual disability. *Journal of Intellectual Disability Research, 47*, 12–21.

Valenti-Hein, D. C., Yarnold, P. R., & Mueser, J. T. (1994). Evaluation of the Dating Skills Program for improving heterosocial interactions in people with mental retardation. *Behavior Modification, 18*, 32–46.

Van Bellinghen, M., & de Troch, C. (2001). Risperidone in the treatment of behavioral disturbances in children and adolescents with borderline intellectual functioning: A double-blind, placebo-controlled pilot trial. *Journal of Child and Adolescent Psychopharmacology, 11*, 5–13.

Whitaker, S. (2001). Anger control for people with learning disabilities: A critical review. *Behavioural and Cognitive Psychotherapy, 29*, 277–293.

Willner, P., Jones, J., Tams, R., & Green, G. (2002). A randomized controlled trial of the efficacy of a cognitive-behavioural anger management group for clients with learning disabilities. *Journal of Applied Research in Intellectual Disabilities, 15*, 224–235.

6

PHYSICAL ACTIVITY AND FITNESS

James H. Rimmer, PhD, and S. Blythe Hiss, BS

The data supporting the health benefits of adequate amounts of daily physical activity leading to higher levels of fitness are now indisputable (Kesaniemi et al., 2001). Numerous studies have reported the benefits of increased physical activity and fitness in reducing both morbidity and mortality from all causes of disease (Blair, Cheng, & Holder, 2001; Wessel et al., 2004). Physical inactivity and poor physical fitness have been consistently associated with an increased risk of chronic diseases, including obesity, type 2 diabetes, and heart disease (U.S. Department of Health and Human Services, 1996).

Most individuals with intellectual and developmental disabilities (I/DD) have been reported to have below average levels of fitness (Fernhall & Pitetti, 2001; Pitteti & Campbell, 1991; Rimmer, Heller, Wang, & Valerio, 2004) and levels of daily physical activity that are similar to sedentary non-I/DD adults (Draheim, Williams, & McCubbin, 2002b; Frey, 2004; Temple, Anderson, & Walkley, 2000). Individuals with I/DD are potentially at greater risk for various types of diseases because of their generally sedentary lifestyle, low level of physical fitness, and overweight/obesity status (Rimmer et al., 2004; Traci, Geurts, & Seekins, 2001). Two of the most commonly reported secondary conditions among persons with I/DD are obesity and physical deconditioning. Rimmer and Liu (2001) examined a group of adults with Down syndrome (DS) and reported that more than 80% of the women were obese or overweight and more than 95% had very low levels of physical fitness. They noted that these secondary conditions likely increased the risk and/or severity of other secondary conditions (e.g., joint pain related to excess weight; fatigue; increased social isolation; type 2 diabetes; depression) and recommended that obesity, nutrition counseling, and physical fitness/physical activity be targeted in future health promotion research with this population (Rimmer & Liu, 2001).

It is important to begin to develop a systematic framework for identifying factors that are associated with poor health status among persons with I/DD. Reports from both the Special Olympics (Special Olympics, 2001) and Surgeon General (U.S. Public Health Service, 2002) emphasize the importance of addressing physical inactivity among persons with I/DD. Physical inactivity and low fitness have a dose-related, inverse relationship with poorer health status in the general population (Blair & Church, 2004), and there is a need to better understand how low fitness may affect the health of persons with I/DD.

Research Questions

The following research questions are addressed in this chapter:

1. What are the physical fitness and physical activity levels of adults with I/DD?

2. What are the physical fitness and physical activity levels of adults with I/DD compared to adults without I/DD?

3. What research has been performed on the physical fitness and physical activity levels of persons with I/DD?

4. What interventions have been shown to be effective?

5. Where are the gaps in the current knowledge and research?

Methods

We reviewed 67 studies that were related to physical activity/fitness and I/DD. An attempt was made to review every article that was published using the following search descriptors: *exercise, physical activity, fitness, mental retardation, developmental disabilities, intellectual disabilities,* and *Down syndrome.* The following databases were searched: Medline, PubMed, CINAHL, SocioFile, Health Star, PsychoInfo, Pharmaceutical Abstracts, Web Science, Academic Search Premiere, Ingenta, and GPO Access.

The pie chart illustrated in Figure 6-1 breaks out the studies we reviewed into descriptive and experimental research. The descriptive studies were then separated into two groups. The first group provides details of fitness levels by either population comparisons (i.e., comparing a population with I/DD to a population without I/DD or to general population data), program comparisons (i.e., comparing interventions such as walking with a pacer vs. walking without a pacer), or correlational research (i.e., examining a relationship between VO_2peak and leg strength). The second type of descriptive research examined the reliability and validity of specific

FIGURE 6-1 *Studies reviewed in physical activity and intellectual/developmental disability (67).*

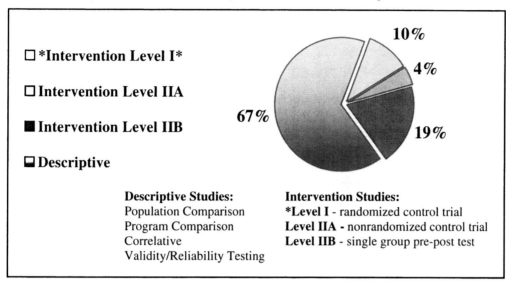

☐ *Intervention Level I*

☐ Intervention Level IIA

■ Intervention Level IIB

▣ Descriptive

10%

4%

67%

19%

Descriptive Studies:
Population Comparison
Program Comparison
Correlative
Validity/Reliability Testing

Intervention Studies:
*Level I - randomized control trial
Level IIA - nonrandomized control trial
Level IIB - single group pre-post test

fitness tests for populations with I/DD. A few of the descriptive studies also reported characteristics of a particular subgroup with I/DD. Experimental or training studies were categorized into three Intervention Levels: Level I—randomized control trial; Level IIA—nonrandomized control trial; and Level IIB—single-group pre–post test.

Studies were reviewed with the following criteria:

➤ Keyword—the fitness components that were targeted in the study were listed as keywords and included aerobic/cardiorespiratory, muscular strength/endurance, and flexibility.

➤ Sample—population details such as age, gender, and condition (i.e., DS, cerebral palsy) were included. The size of the total population, including controls, is listed under *N*. The tables then specify how many of each type of population was included. A typical example would be comparing the strength levels between 23 persons with I/DD to 25 persons without I/DD.

Age was classified into the following categories: Infant (0–2 years), Child (3–12 years), Adolescent (13–17 years), and Adult (18 and older). A "senior" category was not used because researchers did not record mean ages high enough to classify the entire sample as elderly.

The numbers of men and women within each study are also provided. As in the general population, men and women may have very different data depending on the fitness test or fitness component.

There were several studies comparing differences in fitness levels between individuals with DS to other subgroups with I/DD (Fernhall, Pitetti, Stubbs, & Stadler, 1996b; Stanish, 2004). Since DS presents a very unique perspective from the standpoint of health and fitness, we reported the number of individuals with DS within each study. Cerebral palsy (CP) was also mentioned in several studies and because of the variety of neurologic conditions associated with this condition, we also documented the number of persons with CP within each study population. Other information included:

> Testing Mode (intervention studies only)—the name of the fitness tests (i.e., modified Balke treadmill test, skinfolds)

> Intervention (intervention studies only)—mode of physical activity or exercise, including group aerobic classes, stationary bicycle, and so forth, as well as the frequency, intensity, duration, and length of time of the entire study

> Outcome Measures—measures obtained from the above-mentioned fitness tests, as well as other available information such as body mass index (BMI) or psychosocial outcomes (i.e., perceived barriers)

> Findings—significant findings, improvements, decreases, correlations, effect sizes (if given), percentages, and any other pertinent information (i.e., compliance or attendance rates)

NIH CRITERIA FOR EVALUATING RESEARCH STUDIES

We employed the National Institutes of Health, National Heart, Lung and Blood Institute (NHLBI) evidence-based categories for Research (Bouchard, 2001). Category A data includes a rich body of evidence from randomized controlled trials (RCTs), which involves a substantial number of studies and participants. Category B includes limited data from RCTs. This involves few RCTs, small sample sizes, and inconsistent results. Category C includes nonrandomized trials and observational studies. Studies are typically uncontrolled and/or cross-sectional or prospective observational. Category D is committee consensus, which usually occurs when there is no compelling scientific or clinical data. Recommendations are based on expert judgment of panel members.

Results

Tables 6-1 through 6-5 summarize the details and findings of the 67 reported studies. The discussion that follows focuses on levels of physical activity among persons with I/DD, how those levels may affect different aspects of physical fitness, and how research has attempted to improve fitness in persons with I/DD through various exercise interventions. Comparisons are made to the general population or to a population without I/DD.

DESCRIPTIVE STUDIES

Physical Fitness

Overall, data on persons with I/DD indicate lower VO_2peak (cardiorespiratory fitness) and strength levels, higher or similar levels of body weight or body fat, higher energy cost for performing various physical activities, a greater number of secondary conditions, similar levels of flexibility and blood lipids, and lower or equivalent levels of physical activity compared to the general population (population-based norms) or a comparative non-I/DD group (refer to Table 6-4). These comments are based on a review of 32 descriptive studies that contained various and sometimes conflicting findings, most likely because of sample selection, measurement error, and widely varying assessment tools or instruments used to collect baseline data. The samples in some studies were also extremely small. Six of the 32 studies had sample sizes (adults with I/DD) of fewer than or equal to 20 subjects. The smallest samples were from the intervention trials, in which 11 of the 23 studies had 12 or fewer subjects, and 5 of the studies had fewer than 6 subjects. A few studies reported that the fitness levels and/or levels of physical activity of persons with I/DD were similar to those of a sedentary group of persons without I/DD (Balic, Mateos, & Blasco, 2000; Faison-Hodge & Porretta, 2004; Frey, 2004). In other studies, although a specific group of sedentary non-I/DD persons was not tested, findings were similar to values of sedentary non-I/DD persons recorded from other studies.

Physical Activity

The data are somewhat inconsistent in reporting the actual amount of physical activity obtained by persons with I/DD. Stanish (2004) found that persons with I/DD (all DS) recorded significantly fewer steps per day than those without I/DD. Messent, Cooke, and Long (1998) administered an interview style survey to a group of 24 adults with mild to moderate ID and to their managers/caregivers and found that 93% recorded less than 3 days a week (20 min/day) of moderate physical activity (energy cost between 5 and 7.5 kcal/min) compared to 64% of the general population. Fujiura, Fitzsimons, Marks, and Chicoine (1997) reported that only 6% to 8% of 28 males with DS reported moderate to vigorous physical activity (MVPA). Of the 21 females, only 5.6% of 16- to 29-year-olds and none of the females 30–59 years of age engaged in MVPA.

Draheim, Williams, and McCubbin (2002a) found that fewer than 45% of a sample of 145 subjects with I/DD participated in the recommended amount of physical activity (according to the Centers for Disease Control and Prevention and American College of Sports Medicine's recommendation of MVPA, at least five or more times per week with MVPA being defined as activity greater than or equal to 3.5 metabolic equivalents [METs]; U.S. Department of Health and Human Services, 1996). In another study, Draheim et al. (2002b) found that among 150 adults with I/DD, only 1.3% of the males and 1.4% of the females reported regular vigorous activity, and no subjects older than 30 years of age reported any vigorous activity. About half the subjects (47% to 51%) reported little to no leisure time physical activity, while 13% reported no activity.

Frey (2004) was the first to use accelerometers to record intensity and duration of daily physical activity among adults with I/DD. She compared subjects' scores to a sedentary non-I/DD control group. She reported that there was no difference in physical activity patterns between adults with I/DD and a sedentary group of non-I/DD adults, but noted that neither group engaged in recommended levels of moderate to vigorous physical activity.

TABLE 6-1 Randomized Control Trials—Intervention Level I (7)

STUDY	KEY WORD	SAMPLE	TESTING MODE	INTERVENTION MODE	FREQUENCY	INTENSITY	DURATION	LENGTH	OUTCOME MEASURES	FINDINGS
Anchuthengil et al., 1992	Aerobic	$N=6$ Lag Ctrl = 3 Adult All male	Treadmill— Standard Balke	Treadmill	5×/wk	60–70% peak METs	10–30 min	12 wks	VO₂peak HR peak	Significant improvements: ► VO₂peak +38% ► HR peak +10%
Carmeli et al., 2002	Aerobic Strength Speed	$N=26$ Ctrl = 10 Adult 10 Men 16 Women All DS	Dynamometer "Get up and go" test	Treadmill Walking	3×/wk	0% grade Self-select speed	10–15 min up to 45 min	25 wks	Knee flexion Knee extension Walking duration Walking distance Walking speed	Significant increase: ► Strength ► Duration +150% ► Speed +86% ► Distance +180%
Heller et al., 2004	Psychosocial barriers	$N=53$ Ctrl = 21 Adult 24 Men 29 Women All DS	Scaled surveys and questionnaires	Aerobic + strength + health education	3×/wk	Not given	30–35 min aerobic + 15 min strength + 60 min education	12 wks	**Attitudes:** Barriers Outcome expectations Performance self-efficacy **Psychosocial:** Community integration Depression Life satisfaction	Significant differences: ► Barriers ► Outcome expectations ► Performance self-efficacy ► Life satisfaction
Millar et al., 1993	Aerobic	$N=14$ Ctrl = 4 Adolescent 11 Boys 3 Girls All DS	Treadmill— Modified Balke	Treadmill Walk/jog	3×/wk	65–75% HRmax	30 min	10 wks	VO₂max HRmax Workload Duration Weight	No significant improvements in metabolic measures; Significant increases: ► Duration ► % grade

Study	Domains	Sample	Mode	Assessment	Frequency	Intensity	Duration	Weeks	Measures	Results
Rimmer et al. 2004	Aerobic Strength Body Comp	$N = 52$ Ctrl = 22 Adult 23 Men 29 Women All DS	Step/bike/treadmill/elliptical + Weights (machine)	Ramped cycle 1 RM* Dynamometer Skinfold	3×/wk	50–70% VO$_2$peak + 70% 1 RM 10–20 reps/set; 1 set	30–35 min + 15–20 min	12 wks	VO$_2$peak HR peak Bench press Leg press Handgrip Workload Duration Weight BMI Skinfold	Significant improvements: ➤ VO$_2$peak +14% ➤ Duration +27% ➤ Max workload +27.1% ➤ Leg press +39% ➤ Bench press +43% ➤ Weight −1 kg avg
Rimmer & Kelly, 1991	Strength	$N = 24$ Ctrl = 12 Adult 11 Men 13 Women	Weights (machine)	1 RM	2×/wk	30% wks 1–3 60% wks 4–6 70% wks 7–9 8–10 reps/set 3 sets	60 min	9 wks	Leg extension; Leg curl; Pectoralis; Shoulder abduction; Pull-over; Bicep curl; Tricep extension	Significant group effect: ➤ $F = 3.23$; ➤ $df = 64, 29.56$, $p = .000$ Exercise group significantly higher: ➤ Shoulder abduction ➤ Pull-over ➤ Pectoralis deck ➤ Bicep curl ➤ Tricep extension
Varela et al., 2001	Aerobic Body Comp	$N = 16$ Ctrl = 8 Adult All men All DS	Rowing	Peak Treadmill Peak row Waist/forearm circumference	3×/wk	wks 1–4 55–60% VO$_2$peak; wks 5–16 70% VO$_2$ peak	15–25 min	16 wks	VO$_2$peak HR peak Weight Body fat % Workload Duration Distance	No significant changes in physiologic measures; Significant increases: ➤ Duration ➤ Distance ➤ Grade ➤ Resistance

*1 RM = One Repetition Maximum strength test (maximum amount of weight that can be lifted one time); DS, Down syndrome; HR, heart rate (measured in bpm = beats per minute); METs, metabolic equivalents

TABLE 6-2 *Nonrandomized Control Trials—Intervention Level IIA (3)*

STUDY	KEY WORD	SAMPLE	TESTING MODE	INTERVENTION MODE	FREQUENCY	INTENSITY	DURATION	LENGTH	OUTCOME MEASURES	FINDINGS
Cluphf et al., 2001	Aerobic	$N = 27$ Ctrl = 12 Intact groups Adult 15 Men 12 Women 7 DS	1-mile RFWT with partner	Aerobic dance	3×/wk	N/A	12–30 min (30 min by week 6)	12 wks	HR Walk time	RFWT times between groups: ▸ $F(4,100)$ 4.41, $p = .003$; ▸ $Eta^2 = .05$; ▸ Obtained power = .15 (statistically significant but not meaningful) Post-walk HR between groups: ▸ $F(4,100)$ 3.86, $p = .006$; ▸ $Eta^2 = .24$; ▸ Obtained power = .97 (statistically significant but not meaningful)
Halle et al., 1999	Aerobic	$N = 17$ Ctrl = 7 Adolescent 10 Boys 7 Girls DS, CP, Other	Submax Treadmill	Walk/jog (with non-ID)	3×/wk	70–85% THR zone	20 min	12–21 wks	HR	HR decreased with program; Significant changes in mean HR: ▸ Test 1–2 $t(5)$ = 2.74, $p = .04$; ▸ Test 2–3 $t(5)$ = 2.92, $p = .033$. Lower HR at same workload

Study	Focus	Sample	Measures	Type	Frequency	Intensity	Distance/Duration	Outcomes	Results
Silverthorn & Hornak, 1993	Aerobic Body Comp	N = 11 Ctrl = 5 Intact groups Adult 7 Men 4 Women All Prader-Willi	YMCA cycle ergometer Four-site Skinfolds	Group walking	2–4×/wk	20–23 min/km up to 13.5–16.5 min/km	2.4–4.8 km up to 10 km 6 mos	VO_2max RHR Workload Weight Muscle Girth	Significant improvements for experimental group: ▶ VO_2 +9.69 mL/kg/min ▶ RHR –5.33 bpm ▶ Max workload +145.83 watts ▶ Weight –5.2 kg ▶ Biceps skinfold –3.15 mm

CP, Cerebral palsy; DS, Down syndrome; HR, Heart rate (measured in bpm = beats per minute); ID, Intellectual disability; RFWT, Rockport Fitness Walking Test; RHR, resting heart rate (measured in bpm = beats per minute); THR, target heart rate (measured in bpm = beats per minute).

TABLE 6-3 *Single Group Pre–Post Test: Intervention Studies—Level IIB (13)*

| | | | | INTERVENTION | | | | | OUTCOME | |
STUDY	KEY WORD	SAMPLE	TESTING MODE	MODE	FREQUENCY	INTENSITY	DURATION	LENGTH	MEASURES	FINDINGS
Croce et al., 1994	Problem Solving	N = 16 Adolescent 10 Boys 6 Girls	Add/subtract equation; Canadian Step	None vs. walk/jog	1×	70% HR max (~55–60% VO$_2$ max)	20 or 30 min	1×	Time Accuracy	Time (not accuracy) to solve problems significantly better after 20 min of exercise, not 30 min
Deener & Horvat, 1995	Aerobic	N = 11 Adolescent 8 Boys 3 Girls	Timed Run/walk	Praise vs. praise + self-recording	3×/wk	Not controlled	8–15 min	6 wks	Distance	Both improved distance: ▶ $p < .05$ praise only ▶ $p < .01$ both Praise + self-recording = greater distance increase
Dyer, 1994	Aerobic	N = 10 Adolescent 4 Boys 6 Girls All DS	Step test 1 × RM	Walk/ jog/ bike, etc. Circuit weights	4×/wk	130–150 bpm 40% 1 RM	Cardio 22 min Strength 25 min	13 wks	RHR HRmax BP Workload	Significantly improved: ▶ RHR: 14.8% ▶ BP: 112/70 to 103/63 mm Hg ▶ HR: response to step test 7.7% Intervention withdrawn = decrease (but not all the way back to baseline)

Study	Focus	Sample	Method	Activity	Frequency	Intensity	Duration	Length	Measures	Results
Eberhard et al., 1997	Blood Lipids	$N = 11$ Adolescent 7 Boys 4 Girls All DS	Max cycle Chemical analysis	Walk/run games + Cycle	5×/wk 2×/wk	N/A 60% VO_2 max	60 min up to 60 min	12 wks	Plasma substrates Cate-cholamines Lipid metabolism SOD-1	➤ Low blood lactate at peak exercise ➤ Slow FFA mobilization ➤ Low HDL at rest ➤ High VLDL at rest ➤ Difference pre-/post- for SOD-1 ➤ *Adjust to normal lipid profiles with endurance exercise*
Horvat et al., 1993	Strength	$N = 6$ Adolescent 5 Boys 1 Girls	MMT (elbow + hip + knee) 1-min sit-ups	Circuit training	4×/wk	1 set/12 reps; up to 3 sets	40-min circuit	20 wks	No. of sit-ups Composite isometric strength	Group 1: ➤ 51% isometric increase ➤ 26% sit-up increase Group 2: ➤ 20% isometric increase ➤ 23% sit-up increase
Lancioni et al., 2000	Activity Levels Gait BMD Body Comp	$N = 2$ Adult All women Severe hearing, visual impairment		Independent indoor exercise; 2/3 travel 1/3 tasks	4×/day	N/A	30 min/session = 120 min/day	9 mos / 4.5 mos	% exercise Step width Rising assistance Weight Urinary Ca^{+2} BMD	Significant improvements: ➤ Independent exercise (12–94% and 19–88%) ➤ Step width (for 1 participant only); ➤ Assistance with rising; ➤ Urinary Ca^{+2} (42/49 to <10 mg/day) ➤ Weight decreased by 4 and 3 kg

(continued)

TABLE 6-3 *Continued*

STUDY	KEY WORD	SAMPLE	TESTING MODE	INTERVENTION					OUTCOME MEASURES	FINDINGS
				MODE	FREQUENCY	INTENSITY	DURATION	LENGTH		
Messent et al., 1998	Aerobic Body Comp	N = 24 Adults 14 Men 10 Women All LD	1-mile RFWT, BMI	Community-based	1×/wk	N/A	60 min	10 wks	VO$_2$max Body mass	Significantly improved: ▶ VO$_2$max: 6.1% Attendance > 85%
Owlia et al., 1995	Behavior	N = 5 Adolescent	Time-on-task Continuous cycling	None vs. audio vs. audio-visual reinforcers	10×	N/A	N/A	10×	On-task time	Audio and audio-visual significantly higher time-on-task than none No difference between
Peran et al., 1997	Aerobic Body Comp	N = 20 Adolescent 16 Boys 4 Girls	1000-m run 50-m run Vertical and long jump Ball throw Skinfolds	Athletics training (running, circuits, races)	2×/wk	N/A	90 min	1 yr	Weight % body fat Distance Time	Overall significant improvement for performance ($p<.001$): ▶ Times (1000 m) 13.33–8.35 min ▶ Mean improvement for 1000 m ~73%
Podgorski et al., 2004	Activity Levels Function	N = 12 Adults CP, ID	30-sec elbow flexion 30-sec chair rises ROM 3.1-m walk	Group aerobics + strength	4×/wk	N/A UB 1 set of 5 up to 2 sets of 10; LB 2 sets of 5	45 min total	12 wks	Timed elbow flexion Timed chair rises ROM Timed walk Weight	92% of participants improved in ≥ 1 functional skill (sustained > 1 yr) Attendance = 75%

Study	Outcome	Measures	Sample	Activity	Frequency	Intensity	Duration	Length	Variables	Results
Pommering et al., 1994	Aerobic Body Comp Flexibility	Max cycle Bioelectric impedance Sit and reach	N = 14 Adult 9 Men 5 Women	Alternate bike/row	4×/wk	85% THR	20–30 min	10 wks	VO₂max HR MaxO₂ pulse Time Flexibility Weight Body fat % Lean mass Body water%	80% still in P.A. sessions > 1 yr Mean weight change = +0.68 kg Significantly improved: ▸ VO_2: 12.8% ▸ $MaxO_2$ pulse: 2.1% ▸ Time: 17.9% ▸ Flexibility: 8.78 cm ▸ HR: 6.9–7.7% for 30–90 watts 1.29% at max watts Attendance = 91.3%
Stanish et al., 2001	Activity Levels	MVPA	N = 17 Adult 12 Men 5 Women	Aerobic Dance 1. Leader + video 2. Video only 3. Both 4. Video only	3×/wk	Not controlled	15–17 min	12 wks (2 wks of each)	Engagement in MVPA Attendance	Engagement in MVPA: ▸ Leader + video = 71%; ▸ Video only = 64%; ▸ Leader + video = 72%; ▸ Video only = 64%; Attendance: ▸ 9 attended avg 89% ▸ 8 others avg 75% Considering ease and cost of video only, 7% difference not meaningful

(continued)

99

TABLE 6-3 *Continued*

STUDY	KEY WORD	SAMPLE	TESTING MODE	INTERVENTION MODE	FREQUENCY	INTENSITY	DURATION	LENGTH	OUTCOME MEASURES	FINDINGS
Stopka et al., 1994	Strength	N = 12 Adult 11 Men 1 Woman DS, CP, Other	3 RM 50-yd dash 300-m run/ walk Sit and reach Sit-ups	Resistance + aerobics/ sports	2×/wk	1 set 10–15 reps	30 min + 15–20 min	23 wks	Chest press Leg extension Lat pulldown Chest press Sit-ups Sit and reach 50-yd dash 300-m run	Increased gains: ➤ Chest press ➤ Leg extension ➤ Lat pulldowns ➤ Sit-ups No increases in "untrained" activities; Mean attendance = 92.7%
Woodard et al., 1996	Postural control	N = 6 Adult	Two-legged stance (eyes open and closed)	Aerobic dance video	3×/wk	Moderate	45 min	8 wks	Sway ratios	Ratios significantly decreased for both eyes open and closed.

BMD, Bone mineral density; BMI, body mass index; BP, blood pressure (measured in mm Hg [millimeters of mercury]; 120/80 mm Hg for an adult is considered standard resting blood pressure); CP, cerebral palsy; DS, Down syndrome; FFA, free fatty acids; HDL, high-density lipoprotein ("good" form of cholesterol; measured in mg/dL – milligrams per deciliter of blood; maintaining > 40 mg/dL is optimal for HDL); HR, heart rate (measured in bpm = beats per minute); ID, intellectual disability; LB, lower body; LD, learning disability; MMT, manual muscle test; MVPA, moderate to vigorous physical activity; P.A., physical activity; RFWT, Rockport Fitness Walking Test; RHR, resting heart rate (measured in bpm = beats per minute); RM, repetition maximum (maximum amount of weight lifted in one repetition, or 3 repetitions for 3 RM); ROM, range of motion; *SOD-1*, gene allowing the making of an enzyme called superoxide dismutase, which removes superoxide radicals from body cells by converting them to a harmless form; THR, target heart rate (measured in bpm = beats per minute); UB, upper body; VLDL, very low density lipoprotein ("bad" form of cholesterol; measured in mg/dL [milligrams per deciliter of blood]).

Messent et al. (1998) described the types of activities performed by persons with I/DD and reported that 85% to 99.3% of all leisure activities were performed indoors. Draheim et al. (2002b) noted that the most popular forms of physical activity among adult with I/DD was walking and biking, and that these forms of physical activity probably served as a method of transportation since subjects were unable to drive. Frey (2004) reported that common leisure activities among individuals with I/DD included watching TV (estimated at 1–5 hr/day), shopping, eating out, visiting friends or family, and involvement in religious activities.

Persons with I/DD may encounter several more barriers to participation in physical activity compared to the general population. This is often related to their immediate support system. Heller, Hsieh, and Rimmer (2002) found that in a sample of 44 adults with DS, 41% did not participate in any type of structured exercise. Significant predictors of exercise participation were age, outcome expectations of the caregivers, and access barriers. Although access barriers (i.e., transportation and cost) were the most frequently cited barriers, attention must be given to developing effective age-adapted activities and programs as well as educating caregivers.

Messent, Cooke, and Long (1999) reported that the primary barriers to physical activity that were identified by caregivers were unclear policy guidelines about activities, financial constraints (personal, transportation, staffing), limited access to opportunities, and limited options for activities in the community.

Body Composition

Although a large percentage of participants with I/DD were considered overweight (BMI > 25 kg/m^2 according to the National Institutes of Health), in the 67 studies reviewed, percentages did not seem to differ markedly from national data sets of persons without I/DD (This is not a positive finding given that two-thirds of Americans are overweight.) However, there was a substantially higher frequency of obesity (BMI > 30 kg/m^2) among adults with I/DD. As shown in Figure 6-2, Yamaki (2005) reported comparative data from the National Health Interview Survey (NHIS) and concluded that the overall prevalence of obesity was significantly higher for adults with I/DD (34.6%) compared to adults without I/DD (20.58%). The incidence of obesity in adults with I/DD increased 15.17% from 1985 to 2000.

Yamaki (2005) also noted that the proportion of overweight individuals with I/DD (28.86%) was lower than in the general population (34.06%) and did not significantly increase between 1985 and 2000 (only a 1.54% increase). As shown in Figure 6-3, this lack of increase in overweight prevalence in adults with I/DD is in stark contrast to the significant increase in obesity and suggests that the level of weight gain has increased and that more individuals with I/DD qualify for the obese category instead of the overweight category.

There was only one study that examined the association between frequency of physical activity and body composition. Draheim et al. (2002a) reported that in subjects with I/DD who were more physically active, they were approximately one third less likely to have abdominal obesity.

Exercise interventions targeted at improving body composition in persons with I/DD have had minimal success on weight reduction (Messent et al., 1998; Peran,

TABLE 6-4 *Descriptive Studies (32)—Population Comparison, Program Comparison, Correlative*

STUDY	KEYWORDS	SAMPLE	MEASURES	FINDINGS
Balic et al., 2000	Aerobic Strength Body comp Power Special Olympics	$N = 20$ Adult 14 Men 6 Women All DS 13 S.O. Athletes vs. 7 sedentary non-S.O.	VO_2 peak—treadmill HR peak Test time Dynamometer (grip, low back, quadricep) Skinfold BMI Squat jump Counter movement jump	Significant differences between groups: ▸ VO_2 peak (34.3 vs. 27.4 mL/kg/min); "Highest VO_2 peak reported to date"; ▸ Lower back strength (72 vs. 41.3 kg); ▸ Strength index (sum of variables as a function of body weight) (3.5 vs. 2.6 kg) "Active group similar to non-ID sedentary persons of same age" Medium to large effect size for muscular strength and power and aerobic measures
Bergerson et al., 1996	Aerobic Strength Flexibility	$N = 22$ Child— "elementary" 11 ID vs. 11 non-ID	President's Challenge: ▸ 1-Mile run ▸ Sit-ups ▸ Sit and reach	Non-ID significantly higher in abdominal endurance
Braunschweig et al., 2004	Aerobic Body comp Lipid levels	$N = 48$ Adult 21 Men 27 Women DS vs. statistical non-ID data	BP BMI Waist circumference Total cholesterol LDL HDL Triglycerides Glucose	BMI = 33.5 kg/m² (men, 31.7; women, 36.8); Waist circumference = 102.4 cm vs. 102. 88 cm; BP = 106/68 mm Hg (vs. 130/85 mm Hg); Total cholesterol = 198 mg/dL (vs. <200); ▸ LDL = 126 mg/dL (vs. <130); ▸ HDL = 50 mg/dL (vs. >40 male or 50 female) Triglycerides = 109 mg/dL (vs. <150) Glucose = 89 mg/dL (vs. <110)

Author/Year	Domains	Measures	Sample	Results
				18.8% Overweight; 70.8% obese Within recommended ranges: ➤ LDL ➤ BP ➤ HDL ➤ Glucose ➤ Triglycerides
Castagno, 2001	Special Olympics Psychosocial	Self-Esteem Inventory Friendship Activity Basketball Skills	$N = 58$ Adolescent All male 24 ID vs. 34 non-ID	Both groups scored significantly higher on all tests after 8 wks of participation in S.O. program
Chaiwanichsiri et al., 2000	Aerobic Strength Body comp Flexibility	VO$_2$peak—treadmill HRmax Isometric leg strength Skinfold BMI Exercise time Sit and reach	$N = 42$ Adolescent 21 Boys 21 Girls 28 ID vs. 14 non-ID	ID had significantly higher level of obesity: ➤ Five girls had % body fat > 30. ➤ Eight girls with ID had a BMI > 27 kg/m^2 (vs. 1 non-ID). Mean VO$_2$peak for ID was 70% of non-ID. Poor: ➤ Leg strength = 40.1 vs. 109.4 kg ➤ Flexibility = −2.4 vs. 9.6 cm
Draheim et al., 2003	Aerobic Body comp Activity levels Blood lipids Special Olympics	RBP Weight BMI Total fat % Abdominal fat Fasting cholesterol Fasting insulin Activity levels S.O. participation	$N = 145$ Adult 73 Men 72 Women All ID 45 Active S.O. vs. 38 inactive non-S.O. vs. 62 active non-S.O.	Active S.O. < Inactive and active non-S.O.: ➤ DBP ➤ Insulin ➤ Fat % ➤ Triglycerides ➤ Abdominal fat Active S.O. < Active non-S.O.: ➤ Fat % Active non-S.O. < inactive non-S.O.: ➤ Triglycerides ➤ Insulin

(continued)

TABLE 6-4 *Continued*

STUDY	KEYWORDS	SAMPLE	MEASURES	FINDINGS
Draheim et al. (*continued*)				Active S.O.: ▶ MVPA = 7.2x/wk ▶ BMI = 28.0 kg/m² ▶ Fat % = 25.2% Active non-S.O.: ▶ MVPA = 6.8x/wk ▶ BMI = 30 kg/m² ▶ Fat % = 28.4% Inactive non-S.O.: ▶ MVPA = 0.4x/wk ▶ BMI = 32.5 kg/m² ▶ Fat % = 29.1 "BP similar to general population"
Draheim et al., 2002a	Body comp Blood lipids Activity Levels	*N* = 145 Adult 74 Men 71 Women ID (75 DS) vs. statistical non-ID data	BP Weight BMI Waist circumference Abdominal diameter Fasting insulin Activity survey Fat intake survey Fruit/vegetable survey	>40% had hyperinsulinemia. and low HDL 52% had abdominal obesity <37% ate recommended amounts of fruits/vegetables <45% reach recommended amount of P.A. More frequent P.A. or less dietary fat 1/3 as likely for hyperinsulinemia and abdominal obesity "Overweight" three to seven times as likely to have high triglycerides, hyperinsulinemia, hypertension

Study	Focus	Sample	Measures	Findings
Draheim et al., 2002b	Body comp Activity levels	$N = 150$ Adult 76 Men 74 Women ID (75 DS) vs. statistical non-ID data	Weight BMI LTPA	Physical activity: ▶ 1.3–1.4% reported regular vigorous activity ▶ 0% older than 30 yrs reported regular vigorous activity ▶ 47–51% reported little to no LTPA ▶ 13% reported none Mean BMI = 28 kg/m^2 males and 32.2 kg/m^2 in females Findings similar to general population
Dykens & Cohen, 1996	Special Olympics	$N = 137$ Adult 76 Men 61 Women All ID 104 S.O. vs. 33 non-S.O.	Questionnaires/tests Social competence Adaptive behavior Self-perception Intelligence Visual–motor skills Maladaptive behavior Resources Stress	IQ: ▶ Only significant predictor of adaptive behavior ▶ 24% of variance for adaptive behavior Length of time in S.O.: ▶ Most significant predictor of social competence S.O. Athletes: ▶ Higher social competence scores ▶ More positive self-perception
Faison-Hodge & Porretta, 2004	Activity levels	$N = 46$ Child 25 Boys 21 Girls 8 ID vs. 19 non-ID Low cardio vs. 19 non-ID high cardio	PE class vs. recess Observe Fitness Time MVPA Pacer Test	% MVPA: ▶ Between groups similar within settings ▶ Significantly different between settings (66% of recess vs. 24% of PE) Fitness levels of ID and non-ID with low cardio fitness similar in: ▶ % MVPA ▶ No. of PACER laps

(continued)

TABLE 6-4 *Continued*

STUDY	KEYWORDS	SAMPLE	MEASURES	FINDINGS
Fernhall & Pitetti, 2000	Aerobic Strength	$N = 26$ Adolescent 15 Boys 11 Girls All ID	VO_2peak—treadmill Isokinetic knee strength 600-yd run/walk 20-m shuttle run	Leg strength: ▶ Significantly related to both runs ▶ More significant contributor to 600-yd run/walk than to 20-m shuttle run
Fernhall et al., 2001	Aerobic	$N = 572$ Adult 276 ID (97 DS) vs. 296 non-ID	Treadmill Modified Bruce/individualized VO_2peak HRmax Prediction equations	Maximal responses significantly higher in non-ID ▶ MHR —ID 177 bpm vs. non-ID 185 bpm ▶ VO_2peak: —ID 33.8 vs. non-ID 35.6 mL/kg/min Adding DS significantly improved prediction Age poor predictor of MHR (though better in ID) Weight significant predictor in non-ID only
Fernhall et al., 1996a	Aerobic	$N = 111$ Adult 66 Men 45 Women 47 DS vs. 64 non-DS	VO_2peak—treadmill walk HR	Significantly higher in non-DS: ▶ VO_2peak; ▶ HR peak DS even lower VO_2peak levels IQ did not influence levels
Frey, 2004	Activity Levels Body comp	$N = 48$ Adult 11 Men 11 Women	7-day accelerometer Activity diary Weight BMI	ID and sedentary non-ID show similar P.A. patterns: ▶ Less active ▶ Less moderate to hard P.A. ▶ Fewer bouts of continuous MVPA

		22 ID (6 DS) vs. 17 sedentary non-ID vs. 9 active non-ID		BMI: ▶ ID = 34 kg/m² ▶ Sedentary non-ID = 28.6 kg/m² ▶ Active non-ID = 26.8 kg/m²
Frey et al., 1999	Aerobic Strength Body comp Flexibility	$N = 18$ Adult 14 Men 4 Women Trained runners 9 ID vs. 9 non-ID	VO₂peak—treadmill HR Knee extension/flexion Skinfold Sit and reach	No difference between groups on ▶ VO₂peak ▶ Flexibility ▶ % Fat Knee flexion/extension sign greater in non-ID
Fujiura et al., 1997	Body comp Health status Activity levels	$N = 49$ Adult 28 Men 21 Women DS vs. statistical non-ID data	BMI Weight Questionnaires	~1/3 exceeded BMI > 27 = "at risk" for obesity 100% of females ages 30–59 were "at risk" 44 reported > 1 secondary condition MVPA: ▶ Reported by only 6–8% of all males ▶ Females age 16–29 reported 5.6% ▶ Females age 30–59 reported 0% "Lifestyle" large predictor of BMI Covaried with BMI: ▶ Friendship; access to recreation; Social support

(continued)

TABLE 6-4 *Continued*

STUDY	KEYWORDS	SAMPLE	MEASURES	FINDINGS
Giordano et al., 2001	Aerobic	$N = 17$ Adolescent 8 Boys 9 Girls Williams syndrome vs. statistical non-ID data	HR BP Bruce treadmill test 24-hour ABPM	Compared to general population at same workload: ▶ Reduced total time of exercise ▶ Increased HR ▶ Increased max SBP Higher SBP during day and nighttime High risk for hypertension
Graham & Reid, 2000	Aerobic Strength Body comp Flexibility	$N = 32$ Adult 18 Men 14 Women 4 DS ID vs. statistical non-ID data	VO_2 predicted—step Grip strength Sit-ups Push-ups Weight Skinfold Sit and reach	Magnitude of change for ID over a 13-year span greater for males and females: ▶ BMI ▶ Fat % Magnitude of change for ID greater only for females: ▶ VO_2 ▶ Sit-ups
Heller et al., 2002	Activity levels Barriers	$N = 88$ Adult 26 Men 18 Women 44 DS vs. 44 non-ID	Exercise participation Demographics Secondary conditions Adaptive behaviors Perceived outcomes Exercise barriers	41% not currently participating in exercise Significant predictors for exercise participation: ▶ Age ▶ Outcome expectations of caregivers ▶ Access barriers (top two are transportation/cost)

Horvat & Franklin, 2001	Activity levels	$N = 23$ Child All ID	HR; Activity velocity Classroom vs. inclusive/noninclusive recess	Those in either recess scored higher in all measures No significant differences between inclusive and non-inclusive recess
Horvat et al., 1997	Strength	$N = 35$ Adult 9 DS vs. 13 ID non-DS vs. 13 non-ID	Isokinetic elbow flexion/extension Peak torque Mean power	Non-ID > ID (with and without DS) for peak torque and mean power (flexion and extension) No significant difference between groups in ratios
Iwaoka et al., 1998	Aerobic Body comp Blood lipids Energy cost Gait	$N = 46$ Adult All men 23 ID vs. 23 non-ID	VO_2max HR Submax bicycle Weight Skinfold BMI Circumference Energy cost (basal, lie, sit, stand, walk) Macronutrients	ID significantly lower: ➤ VO_2max ➤ Triacylglycerols ➤ Total cholesterol ➤ Albumin ID significantly higher: ➤ Waist to thigh ratio ➤ Stride frequency ➤ HR (for sitting, standing, walking only) Less economical metabolism = higher energy cost
Kunde & Rimmer, 2000	Aerobic	$N = 15$ Adult 8 Men 7 Women All ID	HR 1-mile RFWT with pacer vs. without	Significant difference in mean times: ➤ Walking with pacer faster by ~1 min ➤ Medium effect size = .53 with pacer = more likely to complete in fewer trials without pacer = 3 of 15 stopped completely

(*continued*)

TABLE 6-4 *Continued*

STUDY	KEY WORDS	SAMPLE	MEASURES	FINDINGS
Messent et al., 1998	Aerobic Body comp Activity level Barriers	$N = 24$ Adult 14 Men 10 Women ID vs. statistical non-ID data	VO_2 max BMI 1-mile RFWT Exercise barriers	VO_2 levels compared to general population: ➤ 20–28% lower for men ➤ 42% lower for women Overweight: ➤ 50% of men (57% of these obese) ➤ 70% of women (100% of these obese) Barriers: ➤ Transportation ➤ Staff ratios ➤ Cost ➤ Unclear policy guidelines 93% below 3 x 20 min MVPA/wk (64% general population) 22 below recommended minimum levels of P.A. 85.7–99.3% of all leisure activities were inside
Modell et al., 1997	Social integration	$N = 28$ Child All ID	Surveys —inclusive/ noninclusive recreation activities	Most children in segregated activities Those in socially integrated education in more inclusive recreational activities
Pitetti & Boneh, 1995	Aerobic Strength	$N = 37$ Adult 25 Men 12 Women All ID 13 DS	VO_2 peak treadmill Peak torque Mean power Isokinetic knee flexion/ extension Dynamometer Weight Skinfold	Significant positive relationship for VO_2 peak and leg strength ($r = .61$) Significance is mainly for DS ($r = .84$) Not significant VO_2 peak for females Leg strength may contribute to VO_2 peak for ID

Author/Year	Focus	Sample	Measures	Results
Pitetti et al., 2001	Aerobic Body comp	$N = 874$ Adolescent 458 Boys 416 Girls 268 ID vs. 606 non-ID	VO_2 predicted 20-m shuttle run Weight BMI	Non-ID in all age groups: ▸ Significantly more laps ▸ Significantly higher predicted VO_2peak Significant effect sizes (eta^2): ▸ Age = .879 ▸ BMI = .311 ▸ Weight = .462 ▸ Laps = .414 ▸ Predicted VO_2peak = .602 Females above cutoff for "overweight" BMI
Rimmer et al., 1994	Body comp Blood lipids Residential setting	$N = 329$ (+1786); Adult 186 Men (+896) 143 Women (+890) ID vs. non-ID (Framingham)	% Body fat Blood lipids Smoking	Cardiovascular risk similar to risk in non-ID Those in 16+ bed setting significantly below non-ID for: ▸ LDL ▸ Cholesterol ▸ Obesity Natural family significantly above non-ID in cholesterol
Shapiro, 2003	Special Olympics	$N = 147$ Adult 80 Men 67 Women All ID 30 DS	Sport motivation questionnaire Demographics	Reasons for participation = tasks and social integration No significant differences across age, sports, gender 91–94% of younger think winning is important Top 3 reasons for participation: ▸ Win medals ▸ Play with others on a team ▸ Exercise

(continued)

TABLE 6-4 *Continued*

STUDY	KEYWORDS	SAMPLE	MEASURES	FINDINGS
Stanish, 2004	Activity levels Pedometers	$N = 20$ Adult 8 Men 12 Women 9 DS vs. 11 non-DS	Step counts Distance Stride length Pedometers 400-m walk	No. of steps: ▶ All recorded more on weekdays ▶ 9 recorded > 10,000/day on weekdays ▶ Only 4 recorded > 1000 on weekend DS recorded significantly fewer steps than non-DS Pedometers highly consistent with steps (ICC > .05)
Temple et al., 2000	Activity levels	$N = 6$ Adult 3 Men 3 Women All ID	BMI Accelerometer Direct observation	ICC between observation and accelerometer = .83. Time spent on average: ▶ 10 hours/day lying ▶ 6 hours sitting ▶ 3 hours personal tasks ▶ 3 hours standing Other hours = light to moderate sport, leisure, work
Yun & Ulrich, 1997	Psychosocial	$N = 109$ Child 54 Boys 55 Girls All ID	Perceived vs. actual Physical competence (running, jumping, batting, skipping, etc.)	Significantly higher perceived competence in older boys Significant relationship between perceived/actual competence in older girls No gender differences in younger children

The symbol *r* is used to denote correlation quantifying degree of linear association between two variables. Value will range between −1 and +1. ABPM, Ambulatory blood pressure monitoring; BMI, body mass index (a measure of body composition equaling weight [kg] per meter of height squared – kg/m²); BP, blood pressure, forms include RBP (resting), DBP (diastolic), SBP (systolic), measured in mm Hg (millimeters of mercury) where SBP/DBP; 120/80 mm Hg for an adult is considered standard resting blood pressure; DS, Down syndrome; HDL, high-density lipoprotein ("good" form of cholesterol; measured in mg/dL – milligrams per deciliter of blood); HR, heart rate, includes RHR (resting), MHR (maximum), measured in bpm (beats per minute); ICC, interclass correlation coefficient; ID, intellectual disability; LDL, low-density lipoprotein ("bad" form of cholesterol; measured in mg/dL – milligrams per deciliter of blood); LTPA, leisure time physical activity; MVPA, moderate to vigorous (or strenuous) physical activity; P.A., physical activity; PACER, Progressive Aerobic Cardiovascular Endurance Run—a multistage fitness test adapted from the 20-m shuttle run test; RFWT, Rockport Fitness Walking Test; S.O., Special Olympics

112

TABLE 6-5 *Descriptive Studies—Test Validity and/or Reliability (11)**

STUDY	KEYWORD	SAMPLE	FITNESS TEST	FINDINGS
Draheim et al., 1999	Aerobic	$N = 23$ Adult 10 Men 13 Women All ID	1-mile RFWT (with pacers) vs. treadmill	Predicted and measured VO_2peak for prediction equations indicate general overestimation Times and HR did not significantly differ between ▶ 1 pacer: 1 walker; and ▶ 1 pacer: 5 walkers.
Fernhall et al., 2000	Aerobic	$N = 17$ Adolescent 9 Boys 8 Girls All ID (6 DS)	20-m shuttle run vs. Treadmill max	Regression analysis: ▶ 20-m shuttle run valid indicator of VO_2peak ▶ Prediction accuracy lower in non-ID. Relationship between measured/predicted VO_2peak: ▶ $r = .86$ ▶ SEE = 6.2. (no significant difference)
Fernhall et al., 1996b	Aerobic	$N = 23$ Adolescent 13 Boys 10 Girls All ID (8 DS)	½ mile run/walk	½- Mile run/walk reliable, but questionable validity Test-retest correlation: ▶ VO_2max $r = .90$ ▶ MaxHR $r = .81$ ▶ Run/walk $r = .96$ Correlation between VO_2max and run/walk: $r = -.60$
Fernhall et al., 1998	Aerobic	$N = 34$ Adolescent 22 Boys 12 Girls All ID (8 DS)	20-m shuttle run 600-yd walk/run Modified 16-m shuttle run vs. treadmill	VO_2peak significantly related to all field tests All field tests valid and reliable for aerobic capacity Significant predictors of VO_2peak: ▶ Field test performance ▶ BMI ▶ Gender (not age or weight)

(continued)

113

TABLE 6-5 *Continued*

STUDY	KEYWORD	SAMPLE	FITNESS TEST	FINDINGS
Kittredge et al., 1994	Aerobic	$N = 25$ Adult 12 Men 13 Women All ID	1-mile RFWT Prediction Equations	Significant correlation between measured and predicted VO_2peak Significant differences: 28% (absolute) and 36% (relative) of measured values fell into predicted values (over-estimated VO_2peak)
MacDonncha et al., 1999	Aerobic Strength Flexibility Body comp	$N = 85$ Adolescent All boys 63 ID vs. 22 non-ID	20-m shuttle run (Eurofit): ▶ Long jump ▶ Height ▶ Weight ▶ Sit-ups ▶ Sit and reach ▶ Handgrip ▶ Skinfolds ▶ Number laps	ICC: % Error for all items: ▶ ID = .94–.99; ▶ ID = 0.5–47.5%; ▶ Non-ID = .85–.99 ▶ Non-ID = 0.4–32.2% Reliable but large error for sit and reach and shuttle run ID scored lower on: ▶ Long jump ▶ Sit-ups ▶ Sit and reach ▶ Handgrip ▶ 20 m shuttle run ▶ Number of laps
Montgomery et al., 1992	Aerobic	$N = 28$ Adult 18 ID vs. 10 non-ID	Treadmill max Shuttle run max Cycle submax Submax step	All 4 modes similar in VO_2max values (ICC = .90–.97) Step and shuttle correlate significantly with treadmill Submax step recommended over: ▶ Max shuttle ▶ Submax cycle
Pitetti et al., 1997	Aerobic	$N = 24$ Adolescent 13 Boys 11 Girls All ID (8 DS)	Submax step test	Measured VO_2peak significantly different from estimated values Correlation between HR and VO_2peak significant, not valid Step test is feasible, but not valid for VO_2peak

114

Study	Type	Sample	Test	Findings
Pitetti et al., 2000	Aerobic	$N = 46$ Adolescent 24 Boys 22 Women 23 ID (2 DS) vs. 23 non-ID	Treadmill max	No difference between ID and non-ID in reliability and accuracy for peak performance treadmill test Test-retest reliability: ➤ ID $r = .85-.99$ ➤ Non-ID $r = .55-.99$
Rintala et al., 1997	Aerobic	$N = 19$ Adult All men All ID	1-mile RFWT vs. Treadmill max	Significant + correlation between measured and predicted VO_2peak on both 1-mile walks ($r = 0.91$ and 0.93) Underestimated actual cardio levels in 74–79% of all subjects Only 58% of measured VO_2peak within predicted range Test not statistically valid
Teo-Koh & McCubbin, 1999	Aerobic	$N = 40$ Adolescent All boys All ID	1-mile walk test vs. Treadmill max	High test-retest reliability: ➤ Times $r = .97$ ➤ Relative VO_2peak $r = .90$ 1-mile walk is reliable field test for sample

*Studies that reported descriptive characteristics of the I/DD population are also listed in findings.

The symbol r is typically used to denote a correlation quantifying the degree of linear association between two variables. It will have a value ranging between -1 and $+1$. BMI, Body mass index (a measure of body composition equaling weight [kg] per meter of height squared [kg/m²]); DS, Down syndrome; HR, heart rate; includes RHR (resting), MHR (maximum, measured in bpm [beats per minute]); ICC, interclass correlation coefficient; ID, intellectual disability; RFWT, Rockport Fitness Walking Test; SEE, standard error of the estimate

FIGURE 6-2 *Proportion of obese adults (BMI ≥ 30) by the presence of intellectual disability (ID), US, 1985–2000 (Yamaki, in press)*

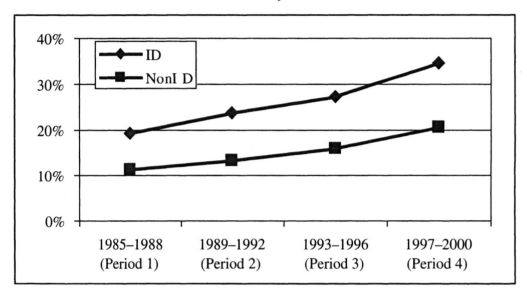

DATA: 1985–2000 NATIONAL HEALTH INTERVIEW SURVEY

FIGURE 6-3 *Proportion of overweight adults (BMI = 25–30) with intellectual disability (ID), United States, 1985–2000 (Yamaki, 2005)*

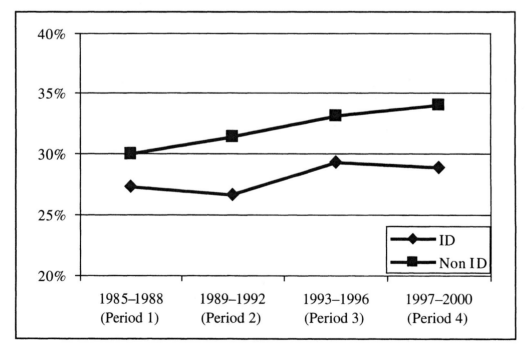

Gil, Ruiz, & Fernandez-Pastor, 1997; Podgorski, Kessler, Cacia, Peterson, & Henderson, 2004; Pommering et al., 1994; Varela, Sardinha, & Pitetti, 2001). However, the investigators had targeted increases in physical activity or improvements in cardiorespiratory fitness and/or strength rather than weight reduction.

Three studies did report slight decreases in body weight (Lancioni, Gigante, O'Reilly, Oliva, & Montironi, 2000; Rimmer et al., 2004; Silverthorn & Hornak, 1993), but one of these studies had only two subjects (Lancioni et al., 2000). Varela, Sardinha, and Pitetti (2001) conducted a 16-week study using a rowing exercise and did not report any significant changes in percent body fat. In a study involving a 12-week training program for 12 adults with I/DD, researchers reported that 4 participants lost weight and 7 gained weight. The mean change in weight for all participants after the intervention was a gain of 0.68 kg (Podgorski et al., 2004).

Training Studies

Of the 67 studies reviewed, only 7 were Level I studies (randomized controlled trials). Of these 7, sample sizes ranged from 6 to 53 with a mean of 27. VO_2peak, the gold standard for aerobic capacity or cardiorespiratory fitness, was measured in 4 of the 7 studies (Anchuthengil, Nielsen, Schulenburg, Hurst, & Davis, 1992; Millar, Fernhall, & Burkett, 1993; Rimmer et al., 2004; Varela et al., 2001). Two of these training studies found significant improvements post-intervention of 38% and 14%, respectively (Anchuthengil et al., 1992; Rimmer et al., 2004). The other two studies (Millar et al., 1993; Varela et al., 2001) did not find increases in VO_2peak but reported significant increases in other aerobic measures such as exercise duration, workload, and/or distance.

The two studies that found an increase in VO_2peak after training used the following interventions:

MODALITY	FREQUENCY	STUDY LENGTH	INTENSITY	DURATION
Treadmill walking	5×/wk	12 wks.	60–70% peak MET level	10–30 min

MODALITY	FREQUENCY	STUDY LENGTH	INTENSITY	DURATION
Step/bike/TM/ elliptical (+ weights)	3×/wk	12 wks.	50–70% VO_2peak	30–35 min

The two studies that did not find increases in VO_2peak used the following interventions:

Treadmill walk/jog	3×/wk	10 wks	65–75% HRmax	30 min
Rowing	3×/wk	16 wks	55–70% VO_2peak	15–25 min

It is difficult to contrast the findings from these studies since subject selection, age, number of males/females, training volume, modality, and level of supervision differed between studies.

Muscular strength was shown to increase in three of the four training studies. Rimmer et al. (2004) reported a 39% and 43% increase, respectively, in the lower (leg press) and upper body (bench press) after a 12-week aerobic plus machine-based weight training program. Rimmer and Kelly (1991) reported significantly higher strength scores for the intervention group compared to the control group on five different strength machines using following a 9-week program using only resistance training. Carmeli, Kessel, Coleman, and Ayalon (2002) reported a significant increase in knee flexion and extension after a 25-week treadmill walking program, which did not incorporate any specific resistance training component.

Three nonrandomized controlled studies were reported in the literature (Cluphf, O'Connor, & Vanin, 2001; Halle, Gabler-Halle, & Chung, 1999; Silverthorn & Hornak, 1993), with sample sizes of 11, 17, and 27. The reason for nonrandomization was that the groups were intact by either residence or participation in another program, which made testing and intervention more conducive if applied to whole groups in their particular setting. All three training studies found positive gains in targeted aerobic measures, which included a measure of cardiorespiratory fitness, heart rate, and/or workload. One study also found decreases in body weight and biceps skinfold in a group of individuals with Prader-Willi syndrome after a 6-month intervention involving group walking (Silverthorn & Hornak, 1993). Body composition was not measured in the other two studies.

Thirteen single-group pre–post training studies were identified. Sample sizes ranged from 2 to 24 subjects. Only two studies measured VO_2. Both studies reported significant improvements in VO_2max (6.1% and 12.8%, respectively) after 10 weeks of training (Messent et al., 1998; Pommering et al., 1994). One study involved a community-based exercise program (Messent et al., 1998), while the other study used an alternate biking/rowing program (Pommering et al., 1994). The other two studies (Dyer, 1994; Peran et al., 1997) reported significant improvements in heart rate, blood pressure, walk distance, and exercise time after a training program that involved some combination of walking/jogging/biking in addition to circuit weight training and sports training.

Discussion

All three levels of intervention studies showed some type of improvement in aerobic fitness and/or strength. However, given the wide variety of interventions that have shown some type of benefit, more research is needed to identify specific doses of exercise that have the greatest effect in persons with I/DD. Since most of this evidence is from small, nonrandomized studies involving a specific cohort (i.e., Down syndrome, Prader-Willi syndrome), more research is needed from larger RCTs to identify key factors that increase health and function. As a composite, these studies had several limitations:

➤ Most of the interventions used very small sample sizes;

➤ 5/7 RCTs involved subjects with DS only;

➤ Interventions were 12 weeks or less with minimal to no long-term follow up;

➤ Randomization was lacking;

➤ Several studies combined disabilities (i.e., DS and non-DS, CP and mental retardation [MR]), limiting generalizability;

➤ Lack of self-monitoring protocols that encouraged individuals with I/DD to self-initiate and maintain their own exercise regimen.

These comments are by no means a criticism of the extant body of research. As with any research agenda, studies must build on a foundation of previous work. When there are few studies available on a particular topic, researchers can address various areas with little risk of redundancy. However, as the field matures and begins to identify key research questions involving individuals with I/DD, future research must build from these studies and focus on stronger experimental research designs that have a clear purpose, hypotheses based on previous work, randomized studies with control or comparison groups, accurate assessment tools, appropriate sampling procedures, clearly defined endpoints, and enough power to detect statistical significance.

The impact of physical activity and physical fitness among children, adults, and seniors with I/DD is an important area of research. Overweight/obesity, poor nutrition, and low physical fitness are major health concerns in this population. These secondary conditions have a substantial negative impact on quality of life and must be targeted in future intervention research. While more and more Americans are becoming increasingly aware of the need to participate in regular physical activity, it is clear that physical activity and physical fitness must also be a primary health-promoting factor among people with I/DD.

Obesity is a major concern among adults with I/DD. It would be interesting to know if this higher incidence is associated with lower levels of physical activity. While approximately one third of Americans are obese, close to one half of individuals with mental retardation are classified as obese. Environmental factors could play a major role in the development of obesity in individuals with I/DD.

The overall low level of fitness among persons with I/DD raises serious concerns. Not only are these individuals at risk medically, but there is also concern about their level of social integration being negatively affected by their poor physical fitness (Rimmer, Braddock, & Fujiura, 1993). Integrating individuals with I/DD who are obese into the community is made more difficult given prevailing negative attitudes in this society concerning obese individuals.

Research Recommendations

Given the growing importance in improving the health and quality of life of people with I/DD (Special Olympics, 2001; U.S. Public Health Service, 2002), there is a need to address key research questions related to physical activity and fitness among persons with I/DD. We must begin to develop a systematic plan for closing gaps in the literature. Physical activity can have enormous health benefits for individuals with I/DD, but the evidence remains limited regarding what types of programs and activities are most effective and sustainable in this population.

There is a profound need for more RCTs and prospective observational studies that will provide a stronger level of evidence. Participation in regular physical activity could be an important behavior for maintaining functional independence, work productivity, and quality of life among individuals with I/DD across the lifespan, but without strong evidence, this treatment strategy will have limited utility among practitioners and health care professionals. As noted in this chapter, the majority of studies that have been conducted in this area have been descriptive in nature. Substantially less experimental/intervention work has been completed and no large-scale longitudinal or epidemiological research has been initiated regarding the effects of various doses of physical activity on health and function.

There are four primary gaps in the current knowledge on I/DD and physical activity/fitness related to dose–response. First, the ability to draw conclusions about the relationship between physical activity/physical fitness and cardiovascular risk reduction and improvements in functional status in persons with I/DD is limited by the lack of prospective randomized exercise studies. Second, it is unclear if gains in cardiorespiratory fitness will translate into improvements in functional status (i.e., performing daily tasks at a lower energy cost). Third, the understanding of how to increase exercise adherence among persons with I/DD so that the program is sustainable beyond the intervention component must be examined. Short-term gains are clearly much easier to achieve than longer, sustainable outcomes. Fourth, the balance between benefits and risks of aerobic exercise in persons with I/DD is not well understood, and this lack of information limits its utility in enhancing health. Research addressing these four critical areas will significantly advance the use of exercise and physical activity as an integral component of health promotion among persons with I/DD, and has the potential to improve functional status and quality of life in this population.

RESEARCH AREAS

1. There is a need for large cohort prospective observational studies to examine the effects of various levels of physical activity on health outcomes among persons with I/DD. While observational studies are typically not considered as scientifically rigorous as RCTs, there is merit in identifying a large cohort of persons with I/DD and tracking their physical activity patterns over time. This would allow investigators to better understand issues related to the most common types of physical activities chosen, barriers that may prevent ongoing and sustainable participation, and most important, the potential to order the dose of physical activity and associate it with improvements in specific health outcomes.

2. There is an absence of longitudinal research on the physical activity behavior of persons with I/DD. The majority of studies are less than 12 weeks in duration and there is a lack of information on sustainability of these programs after the study is completed. Likewise, it is not clear if training studies can be continued independent of the structured research setting, and if individuals with I/DD can sustain the program on their own initiative. Because of the nature of living arrangements for persons with I/DD (i.e., group homes, large congregate facilities,

living with an older family member, supported living), it would be interesting to know if different settings result in greater or lesser participation in physical activity. Similarly, it is important to know what impact physical activity has on modifying the complications/secondary conditions associated with subgroups of individual with I/DD such as Prader-Willi syndrome or DS.

One way to address this question is to recruit a large cohort of individuals with I/DD and subcategorize individuals with I/DD by age, health, etiology, and participation level. Special Olympics International has access to a large group of participants with I/DD and this might be a good starting point for ordering the various participation levels (i.e., some individuals participate in an occasional Special Olympics event while other individuals train and participate on a more regular basis) and associating these levels of participation with various health measures (i.e., body weight, fitness, cardiovascular risk factors).

3. There is a need to follow individuals longitudinally to identify what health issues may result from a sedentary lifestyle. Since the nature of federal funding is to provide support for only 3–5 years, sponsored research must support the concept of renewable grant applications that will allow a greater length of monitoring in order to better understand the effects of aging in adults with I/DD and to examine what conditions (i.e., health complications) might occur across the lifespan. A particularly interesting question relates to what happens to the health and physical activity behavior of individuals with I/DD when they move to various settings such as group homes, large residential facilities, or small apartments where there is a greater or lesser level of independence.

4. More work needs to be done on the contextual factors (person–environment) that affect participation in physical activity (Heller, Hsieh, & Rimmer, 2004). Given the rapidly developing focus in research, public policy, and practice concerning the role of the environment in determining participation in physical activity, there is a need to increase the accessibility of fitness and recreation facilities and programs for people with I/DD. Numerous barriers have been identified in various cohort groups regarding the lack of physical activity in daily behavior. There is substantially less work involving persons with I/DD. In one of the few studies that examined barriers to participation in physical activity among persons with I/DD, Heller et al. (2004) reported a reduction in the number of barriers to physical activity after a 12-week health education intervention. It would be interesting to know what barriers would recur after the training period and what methods can be used to overcome them. Identifying ways to maintain physical activity after a study or training program has ended should be a high research priority.

5. To our knowledge, there are no studies that have trained adults with I/DD to self-initiate their own physical activity regimen. In this era of empowerment and self-determination, it is critical for researchers to identify strategies for teaching individuals with I/DD to be team leaders, trainers, and coaches, and to take some responsibility for assisting roommates or housemates in increasing their physical activity behavior. With the use of technology, there may be several innovative ways

that would allow adults with I/DD to capture their daily physical activity levels and to assist others who reside or work in the same setting to increase their own physical activity. One strategy for starting this effort may be to work with organizations such as People First, which is involved in getting adults with I/DD more involved in making their own choices and living a more independent lifestyle.

6. Physical activity can be beneficial for reducing cardiovascular disease, obesity, low bone mineral density, some forms of depression, and many other conditions. Clearly defined endpoints must be established based on the specific needs of individuals with I/DD. Research must target individuals with specific secondary conditions rather than using intact groups (i.e., group home, sheltered workshop) in which all the participants, including those individuals who do not have a certain condition (i.e., obese), receive the intervention. In some instances an individual who is underweight and at risk for osteoporosis may need more resistance exercise to increase muscle mass and bone mineral density. In other cases, reduction in social isolation may be the primary endpoint and may require more group activity sessions to enhance socialization rather than an individualized program. This may require a more complex study design but will likely achieve greater effects since measurable gains in high-risk groups will not be "washed out" by subjects who do not need the specific intervention.

7. There is a need to use more accurate assessment tools for monitoring physical activity levels in individuals with I/DD. New and emerging technologies such as wireless networks using PDAs and cell phones, geographical information system (GIS) and global positioning system (GPS), accelerometers and pedometers, would be helpful in obtaining accurate data on the physical activity patterns of persons with I/DD. These technologies, however, must be easy enough to use by individuals with I/DD and/or their caregivers. Simple picture cues for identifying certain physical activities and selecting different time intervals would be helpful for recording various "doses" of physical activity which could then be assessed in terms of health improvements and risk reduction.

8. It is important to begin to target "at-risk" subgroups of individuals with ID who have low levels of physical activity. Not every individual with I/DD is unhealthy and inactive. Greater resources must be directed at those with the most extreme sedentary behaviors. With good assessment tools, we should be able to define "extreme" sedentary behaviors more accurately and develop simple, targeted interventions for certain subgroups with the greatest need. Clearly, increasing physical activity among those with the lowest level of physical activity can achieve the greatest overall health benefits.

9. A key issue today in many research interventions is sampling. Often, individuals who could benefit the most from a physical activity intervention are less likely to volunteer for these types of studies. For example, in a recent physical activity intervention, researchers targeted a day habilitation program that consisted of 47 workers. Out of these 47 individuals, only 15 (32%) were eligible for the study. The reasons that the other 68% of the program attendees were not eligible

included 12 workers (25.5%) who were uncooperative; 12 others were denied consent (25.5%); four individuals had poor physical health (8.5%); and four workers (8.5%) were excluded for other reasons (Podgorski et al., 2004). It is plausible that individuals with the most need for physical activity are those who typically do not join studies or drop out. There is an enormous need to identify strategies for recruiting participants with I/DD who are typically not volunteering for research studies because of their low interest level, behavior, difficulty obtaining consent, lack of awareness of the importance of physical activity, or apathy toward participating in research. Amazingly, most of our knowledge on physical activity and I/DD has occurred with a small cohort of volunteers. How representative this group is to the general population of individuals with I/DD is unclear. Successful behavioral strategies for increasing participation among those with the greatest need is crucial to ensuring that future research is targeted to these high-risk subgroups.

Conclusion

This is a promising time for researchers to learn more about how physical activity and physical fitness can affect the health and quality of life of individuals with I/DD. There are significant health disparities observed among persons with I/DD and physical activity research must be supported to address these critical gaps.

The lack of evidence-based data on quantifying the dose–response effects of physical activity in relationship to various health outcomes such as reduced body weight, greater work productivity, and lower cardiovascular risk limit its utility by health practitioners. For guidelines/recommendations to be established for this diverse population who reside in multiple settings with various levels of support, evidenced-based data and "best practice" programs must be the highest priority so that practitioners and health care providers can develop similar programs in their communities. This will require more RCTs and prospective observational studies that evaluate the effects of multiple levels of intervention and controlling for impairments/etiologies and levels of physical activity/fitness. The ultimate goal for having solid evidence-based data documenting the benefits of physical activity among persons with I/DD is to encourage health maintenance organizations (HMOs), Medicaid, and other insurers to provide subsidized memberships to health clubs and fitness facilities along with accessible transportation so that individuals with I/DD can actively engage in this important health enhancing behavior without restriction.

ACKNOWLEDGMENTS

This work was supported, in part, by the Centers for Disease Control and Prevention, National Center on Birth Defects and Developmental Disabilities, Division of Human Development and Disability, Grant no. R04CCR514155, and the National Institute on Disability and Rehabilitation Research, RRTC on Aging with Developmental Disabilities, Grant no. H133B980046.

REFERENCES

Anchuthengil, J. D., Nielsen, D. H., Schulenburg, J., Hurst, R., & Davis, M. J. (1992). Effects of an individualized treadmill exercise training program on cardiovascular fitness of adults with mental retardation. *The Journal of Orthopaedic and Sports Physical Therapy, 16,* 220–228.

Balic, M. G., Mateos, E. C., & Blasco, C. G. (2000). Physical fitness levels of physically active and sedentary adults with Down syndrome. *Adapted Physical Activity Quarterly, 17,* 310–321.

Bergerson, M. J., Folsom-Meek, S. L., & Kalakian, L. (1996). Health-related physical fitness of children with mental retardation and children without disabilities: A comparative study. *Research Quarterly for Exercise and Sport, 67,* A-115–116.

Blair, S. N., Cheng, Y., & Holder, J. S. (2001). Is physical activity or physical fitness more important in defining health benefits? *Medicine and Science in Sports and Exercise, 33*(6 Suppl), S379–S399, discussion S419–S420.

Blair, S. N., & Church, T. S. (2004). The fitness, obesity and health equation. Is physical activity the common denominator? *Journal of the American Medical Association, 292,* 1232–1234.

Bouchard, C. (2001). Physical activity and health: Introduction to the dose-response symposium. *Medicine and Science in Sports and Exercise, 33*(6 Suppl), S347–S350.

Braunschweig, C. L., Gomez, S., Sheehan, P., Tomey, K. M., Rimmer, J. H., & Heller, T. (2004). Nutritional status and risk factors for chronic disease in urban-dwelling adults with Down syndrome. *American Journal on Mental Retardation, 109,* 186–193.

Carmeli, E., Kessel, S., Coleman, R., & Ayalon, M. (2002). Effects of a treadmill walking program on muscle strength and balance in elderly people with Down syndrome. *Journal of Gerontology, 57A,* M106–M110.

Castagno, K. S. (2001). Special Olympics Unified Sports: Changes in male athletes during a basketball season. *Adapted Physical Activity Quarterly, 18,* 193–206.

Chaiwanichsiri, D., Sanguanrungsirikul, S., & Suwannakul, W. (2000). Poor physical fitness of adolescents with mental retardation at Rajanukul School, Bangkok. *Journal of the Medical Association of Thailand, 83,* 1387–1392.

Cluphf, D., O'Connor, J., & Vanin, S. (2001). Effects of aerobic dance on the cardiovascular endurance of adults with intellectual disabilities. *Adapted Physical Activity Quarterly, 18,* 60–71.

Croce, R., Horvat, M., & Roswal, G. (1994). A preliminary investigation into the effects of exercise duration and fitness level on problem solving ability in individuals with mild mental retardation. *Clinical Kinesiology, 48,* 48–54.

Deener, T. M., & Horvat, M. (1995). Effects of social reinforcement and self-recording on exercise duration in middle school students with moderate mental retardation. *Clinical Kinesiology, Spring,* 28–33.

Draheim, C. C., Laurie, N. E., McCubbin, J. A., & Perkins, J. L. (1999). Validity of a modified aerobic fitness test for adults with mental retardation. *Medicine and Science in Sports and Exercise, 31,* 1849–1854.

Draheim, C. C., Williams, D. P., & McCubbin, J. A. (2002a). Physical activity, dietary intake, and the insulin resistance syndrome in nondiabetic adults with mental retardation. *American Journal of Mental Retardation, 107,* 361–375.

Draheim, C. C., Williams, D. P., & McCubbin, J. A. (2002b). Prevalence of physical inactivity and recommended physical activity in community-based adults with mental retardation. *Mental Retardation, 40,* 436–444.

Draheim, C. C., Williams, D. P., & McCubbin, J. A. (2003). Cardiovascular disease risk factor differences between Special Olympians and non-Special Olympians. *Adapted Physical Activity Quarterly, 20,* 118–133.

Dyer, S. M. (1994). Physiological effects of a 13-week physical fitness program on Down syndrome subjects. *Pediatric Exercise Science, 6,* 88–100.

Dykens, E. M., & Cohen, D. J. (1996). Effects of Special Olympics International on social competence in persons with mental retardation. *Journal of the American Academy of Child and Adolescent Psychiatry, 35,* 223–229.

Eberhard, Y., Eterradossi, J., & Debu, B. (1997). Biological changes induced by physical activity in individuals with Down syndrome. *Adapted Physical Activity Quarterly, 14,* 166–175.

Faison-Hodge, J., & Porretta, D. L. (2004). Physical activity of students with mental retardation and students without disabilities. *Adapted Physical Activity Quarterly, 21,* 139–152.

Fernhall, B., McCubbin, J. A., Pitetti, K. H., Rintala, P., Rimmer, J. H., Millar, A. L., et al. (2001). Prediction of maximal heart rate in individuals with mental retardation. *Medicine and Science in Sports and Exercise, 33,* 1655–1660.

Fernhall, B., Millar, A. L., Pitetti, K. H., Hensen, T., & Vukovich, M. D. (2000). Cross validation of the 20-m shuttle run test for children and adolescents with mental retardation. *Adapted Physical Activity Quarterly, 17,* 402–412.

Fernhall, B., & Pitetti, K. H. (2000). Leg strength is related to endurance run performance in children and adolescents with mental retardation. *Pediatric Exercise Science, 12,* 324–333.

Fernhall, B., & Pitetti, K. H. (2001). Limitations to physical work capacity in individuals with mental retardation. *Clinical Exercise Physiology, 3,* 176–185.

Fernhall, B., Pitetti, K. H., Rimmer, J. H., McCubbin, J. A., Rintala, P., Millar, A. L., et al. (1996a). Cardiorespiratory capacity of individuals with mental retardation including Down syndrome. *Medicine and Science in Sports and Exercise, 28,* 366–371.

Fernhall, B., Pitetti, K., Stubbs, N., & Stadler, L. (1996b). Validity and reliability of the 1/2-mile run-walk as an indicator of aerobic fitness in children with mental retardation. *Pediatric Exercise Science, 8,* 130–142.

Fernhall, B., Pitetti, K. H., Vukovich, M. D., Stubbs, N., Hensen, T., Winnick, J. P., et al. (1998). Validation of cardiovascular fitness field tests in children with mental retardation. *American Journal of Mental Retardation, 102,* 602–612.

Frey, G. C. (2004). Comparison of physical activity levels between adults with and without mental retardation. *Journal of Physical Activity and Health, 1,* 235–245.

Frey, G. C., McCubbin, J. A., Hannigan-Downs, S., Kasser, S. L., & Skaggs, S. O. (1999). Physical fitness of trained runners with and without mild mental retardation. *Adapted Physical Activity Quarterly, 16,* 126–137.

Fujiura, G. T., Fitzsimons, N., Marks, B., & Chicoine, B. (1997). Predictors of BMI among adults with Down syndrome: The social context of health promotion. *Research in Developmental Disabilities, 18,* 261–274.

Giordano, U., Turchetta, A., Giannotti, A., Digilio, M. C., Virgilii, F., & Calzolari, A. (2001). Exercise testing and 24-hour ambulatory blood pressure monitoring in children with Williams syndrome. *Pediatric Cardiology, 22,* 509–511.

Graham, A., & Reid, G. (2000). Physical fitness of adults with an intellectual disability: A 13-year follow-up study. *Research Quarterly for Exercise and Sport, 71,* 152–161.

Halle, J. W., Gabler-Halle, D., & Chung, Y. B. (1999). Effects of a peer-mediated aerobic conditioning program on fitness levels of youth with mental retardation: Two systematic replications. *Mental Retardation, 37,* 435–448.

Heller, T., Hsieh, K., & Rimmer, J. (2002). Barriers and supports for exercise participation among adults with Down syndrome. *Journal of Gerontological Social Work, 38,* 161–179.

Heller, T., Hsieh, K., & Rimmer, J. H. (2004). Attitudinal and psychological outcomes of a fitness and health education program on adults with Down syndrome. *American Journal on Mental Retardation, 109,* 175–185.

Horvat, M., Croce, R., & McGhee, T. (1993). Effects of a circuit training program on individuals with mental retardation. *Clinical Kinesiology, Fall,* 71–77.

Horvat, M., & Franklin, C. (2001). The effects of the environment on physical activity patterns of children with mental retardation. *Research Quarterly for Exercise and Sport, 72,* 189–195.

Horvat, M., Pitetti, K. H., & Croce, R. (1997). Isokinetic torque, average power, and flexion/extension ratios in nondisabled adults and adults with mental retardation. *Journal of Orthopaedic and Sports Physical Therapy, 25,* 395–399.

Iwaoka, H., Yokoyama, T., Masayasu, S., Fuchi, T., Nakayama, T., & Tanaka, H. (1998). Characteristics of energy metabolism in males with mental retardation. *Journal of Nutritional Science and Vitaminology, 44,* 151–164.

Kesaniemi, Y. K., Danforth, E. J., Jensen, M. D., Kopelman, P. G., Lefebvre, P., & Reeder, B. A. (2001). Dose-response issues concerning physical activity and health: An evidence-based symposium. *Medicine and Science in Sports and Exercise, 33*(6 Suppl), S351–S358.

Kittredge, J. M., Rimmer, J. H., & Looney, M. A. (1994). Validation of the Rockport Fitness Walking Test for adults with mental retardation. *Medicine and Science in Sports and Exercise, 26,* 95–102.

Kunde, K., & Rimmer, J. H. (2000). Effects of pacing vs. nonpacing on a one-mile walk test in adults with mental retardation. *Adapted Physical Activity Quarterly, 17,* 413–420.

Lancioni, G. E., Gigante, A., O'Reilly, M. F., Oliva, D., & Montironi, L. (2000). Indoor travel and simple tasks as physical exercise for people with profound multiple disabilities. *Perceptual and Motor Skills, 91,* 211–216.

MacDonncha, C., Watson, A. W. S., McSweeney, T., & O'Donovan, D. J. (1999). Reliability of Eurofit physical fitness items for adolescent males with and without mental retardation. *Adapted Physical Activity Quarterly, 16,* 86–95.

Messent, P. R., Cooke, C. B., & Long, J. (1998). Physical activity, exercise and health of adults with mild and moderate learning disabilities. *British Journal of Learning Disabilities, 26,* 17–22.

Messent, P. R., Cooke, C. B., & Long, J. (1999). Primary and secondary barriers to physically active healthy lifestyles for adults with learning disabilities. *Disability and Rehabilitation, 21,* 409–419.

Millar, A. L., Fernhall, B., & Burkett, L. N. (1993). Effects of aerobic training in adolescents with Down syndrome. *Medicine and Science in Sports and Exercise, 25,* 270–274.

Modell, S. J., Rider, R. A., & Menchetti, B. M. (1997). An exploration of the influence of educational placement on the community recreation and leisure patterns of children with developmental disabilities. *Perceptual and Motor Skills, 85,* 695–704.

Montgomery, D. L., Reid, G., & Koziris, L. P. (1992). Reliability and validity of three fitness tests for adults with mental handicaps. *Canadian Journal of Sports Science, 17,* 309–315.

Owlia, G., French, R., Ben-Ezra, V., & Silliman, L. M. (1995). Influence of reinforcers on the time-on-task performance of adolescents who are profoundly mentally retarded. *Adapted Physical Activity Quarterly, 12,* 275–288.

Peran, S., Gil, J. L., Ruiz, F., & Fernandez-Pastor, V. (1997). Development of physical response after athletics training in adolescents with Down syndrome. *Scandinavian Journal of Medicine and Sports Science, 7,* 283–288.

Pitetti, K. H., & Boneh, S. (1995). Cardiovascular fitness as related to leg strength in adults with mental retardation. *Medicine and Science in Sports and Exercise, 27,* 423–428.

Pitetti, K. H., & Campbell, K. D. (1991). Mentally retarded individuals—a population at risk? *Medicine and Science in Sports and Exercise, 23,* 586–593.

Pitetti, K. H., Fernhall, B., Stubbs, N., & Stadler, L. V. (1997). A step test for evaluating the aerobic fitness of children and adolescents with mental retardation. *Pediatric Exercise Science, 9,* 127–135.

Pitetti, K. H., Millar, A. L., & Fernhall, B. (2000). Reliability of a peak performance treadmill test for children and adolescents with and without mental retardation. *Adapted Physical Activity Quarterly, 17,* 322–332.

Pitetti, K. H., Yarmer, D. A., & Fernhall, B. (2001). Cardiovascular fitness and body composition of youth with and without mental retardation. *Adapted Physical Activity Quarterly, 18,* 127–141.

Podgorski, C. A., Kessler, K., Cacia, B., Peterson, D. R., & Henderson, C. M. (2004). Physical activity intervention for older adults with intellectual disability: Report on a pilot project. *Mental Retardation, 42,* 272–283.

Pommering, T. L., Brose, J. A., Randolph, E., Murray, T. F., Purdy, R. W., Cadamagnani, P. E., et al. (1994). Effects of an aerobic exercise program on community-based adults with mental retardation. *Mental Retardation, 32,* 218–226.

Rimmer, J. H., Braddock, D., & Fujiura, G. (1993). Prevalence of obesity in adults with mental retardation: Implications for health promotion and disease prevention. *Mental Retardation, 31,* 105–110.

Rimmer, J. H., Braddock, D., & Fujiura, G. T. (1994). Cardiovascular risk factor levels in adults with mental retardation. *American Journal on Mental Retardation, 98,* 510–518.

Rimmer, J. H., Heller, T., Wang, E., & Valerio, I. (2004). Improvements in physical fitness in adults with Down syndrome. *American Journal on Mental Retardation, 109,* 165–174.

Rimmer, J. H., & Kelly, L. E. (1991). Effects of a resistance training program on adults with mental retardation. *Adapted Physical Activity Quarterly, 8,* 146–153.

Rimmer, J. H., & Liu, Y. (2001). *Center on Health Promotion Research for Persons with Disabilities: Final report.* Chicago: University of Illinois at Chicago.

Rintala, P., McCubbin, J. A., Downs, S. B., & Fox, S. D. (1997). Cross validation of the 1-mile walking test for men with mental retardation. *Medicine and Science in Sports and Exercise, 29,* 133–137.

Shapiro, D. R. (2003). Participation motives of Special Olympics athletes. *Adapted Physical Activity Quarterly, 20,* 150–165.

Silverthorn, K. H., & Hornak, J. E. (1993). Beneficial effects of exercise on aerobic capacity and body composition in adults with Prader-Willi syndrome. *American Journal on Mental Retardation, 97,* 654–658.

Special Olympics. (2001). *Hearing before a subcommittee of the Committee on Appropriations, United States Senate One Hundred Seventh Congress.* Washington, DC: U.S. Government Printing Office.

Stanish, H. I. (2004). Accuracy of pedometers and walking activity in adults with mental retardation. *Adapted Physical Activity Quarterly, 21,* 167–179.

Stanish, H., McCubbin, J. A., Draheim, C. C., & van der Mars, H. (2001). Participation of adults with mental retardation in a video- and leader-directed aerobic dance program. *Adapted Physical Activity Quarterly, 18,* 142–155.

Stopka, C., Limper, L., Siders, R., Graves, J., Goodman, A., & Silverstone, E. (1994). Effects of a supervised resistance training program on adolescents and young adults with mental retardation. *Journal of Strength and Conditioning Research, 8,* 184–187.

Temple, V. A., Anderson, C., & Walkley, J. W. (2000). Physical activity levels of individuals living in a group home. *Journal of Intellectual & Developmental Disabilities, 25,* 327–341.

Teo-Koh, S. M., & McCubbin, J. A. (1999). Relationship between peak VO2 and 1-mile walk test performance of adolescent males with mental retardation. *Pediatric Exercise Science, 11,* 144–157.

Traci, M. A., Geurts, S., & Seekins, T. (2001). *The health status of adult Montanans in supported and semi-independent living arrangements.* Final report.

U.S. Department of Health and Human Services. (1996). *Physical Activity and Health: A Report of the Surgeon General.* Atlanta: Centers for Disease Control and Prevention.

U.S. Public Health Service. (2002). *Closing the gap: A national blueprint for improving the health of individuals with mental retardation. Report of the Surgeon General's conference on health disparities and mental retardation.* Rockville, MD: Author.

Varela, A. M., Sardinha, L. B., & Pitetti, K. H. (2001). Effects of an aerobic rowing training regimen in young adults with Down syndrome. *American Journal on Mental Retardation, 106,* 135–144.

Wessel, T. R., Arant, C. B., Olson, M. B., Johnson, B. D., Reis, S. E., Sharaf, B. L., et al. (2004). Relationship of physical fitness vs body mass index with coronary artery disease and cardiovascular events in women. *Journal of the American Medical Association, 292,* 1179–1187.

Woodard, R., Lewis, C., Koceja, D. M., & Surburg, P. R. (1996). The effects of an aerobic dance program on the postural control of adults with mental retardation. *Research Quarterly for Exercise and Sport, March Supplement,* A124–A125.

Yamaki, K. (2005). Body weight status among adults with intellectual disability in the community. *Mental Retardation, 43*(1), 1–10.

Yun, J., & Ulrich, D. A. (1997). Perceived and actual physical competence in children with mild mental retardation. *Adapted Physical Activity Quarterly, 14,* 285-297.

7

ACCESS TO HEALTH CARE

Sheryl A. Larson, PhD, FAAMR, Lynda Anderson, MPH, MA, and Robert Doljanac, PhD

Between 1967 and 2003, the number of people with intellectual and developmental disabilities (I/DD) living in publicly operated institutional settings declined from 194,650 to 43,289 (Prouty, Smith, & Lakin, 2004). Similarly, between 1982 and 2003 the number of people with I/DD living in nursing homes declined from 40,538 to 35,005. Meanwhile, the number of people with I/DD receiving residential supports in community settings increased from 63,703 in 1982 to 325,611 in 2003 (Prouty et al., 2004). In addition, an estimated 3.9 million individuals with I/DD (including an estimated 938,000 whose reported health status was fair or poor) lived in their own homes or with family members in 1995 (Larson, Lakin, Anderson, & Kwak, 2001). The change in focus from institutional to community supports, coupled with an increasing lifespan for people with I/DD (e.g., Patja, 2001) and increased supports for families (particularly the provision of a free and appropriate public education for all children with I/DD), has had a dramatic impact on where people with I/DD live and where they receive medical and dental care. In the last quarter of the 20th century, medical and dental services for people with I/DD were often provided on institutional campuses, or in the pediatric units of hospitals and medical practices. Between 1960 and 2003, however, the number of large state institutions declined from 357 to 186, and by 2002, only 25% of public residential facilities offered medical or nursing treatment to people not residing in the facility, while 39% offered dental services to nonresidents (Larson, Coucouvanis, &

Prouty, 2003). Today, the vast majority of children and adults with I/DD live, go to school, work, play, and receive medical and dental services in community settings.

These changes have not come without challenges. The literature is replete with stories about the poor health care received by people with I/DD, ranging from how some health care providers appear ignorant about disability to accounts of dentists who refuse patients with Medicaid, effectively denying access to dental care for people with I/DD. A 2002 report from the U.S. Surgeon General noted that the health care system "has not been updated to reflect the progress of people with intellectual disabilities" (U.S. Public Health Service, 2002, p. xi). The report further states that the nation's health care system is "fragmented" and "primary and specialty sources of care are often poorly distributed, inadequate in number, and ill-equipped" to respond to the needs of people with I/DD (U.S. Public Health Service, 2002, p. 12). Other studies report that few doctors are trained to understand the needs of people with I/DD (Beange, 1996).

People with I/DD face attitudinal, communication, architectural, and physical barriers to accessing health care (Kaye, 2001). In this chapter, we summarize research examining access to preventive care, medical or dental care, and insurance. We also summarize research on satisfaction with health care, quality of care, consequences of inadequate access to care, and unmet health care needs. In addition we summarize research findings detailing the types of barriers people with I/DD face in accessing appropriate medical and dental care. The information is organized by whether the study focused on medical care or dental care, by whether the individual or a personal representative was queried, whether the study involved screenings or document reviews, or whether medical or dental providers were queried. Finally, the barriers to health care access and consequences of barriers identified are clustered and summarized.

Methods

DEFINING ACCESS TO HEALTH CARE AND BARRIERS

Andersen's Behavioral Model of Access to Care describes both external and internal factors related to the ability of people to access the care they need (Horwitz, Kerker, Owens, & Zigler, 2000). External factors are those related to continuity of care, coordination of the health care delivery system, and how the health care system is structured. Internal factors include predisposing factors in the individual (e.g., level of comfort with medical providers), enabling resources (e.g., health insurance), and the extent to which an individual recognizes his or her need for care. Barriers to health care can be external, such as people lacking insurance and therefore being unable to afford health care, or internal, such as a person with an I/DD not knowing symptoms of a particular illness and thus not recognizing the need for medical care.

Yeatts, Crow, and Folts (1992) propose a model for access to health care in which people must have (1) knowledge of services and procedures; (2) access to services through transportation and availability and affordability of health care services; and (3) the intent to use the services, meaning the services are "attractive" because they are culturally appropriate and user-friendly. Attitudes toward service use, such as belief in its relative beneficence, are also related to an individual's intent to use health care. A person with I/DD might face barriers to care under this model through not understanding what a particular procedure is for (e.g., mammograms), lack of transportation to and from a clinic (particularly if the person lives independently in the community), or finding a health care system that is not attractive to him or her because medical providers either do not understand the individual's needs or do not have adequate time to explain medical terminology and treatment plans to him or her.

Even in most European countries, despite the existence of universal health care coverage and provision, the health service system does not always deliver adequate health or dental care to individuals with I/DD (Meijer, Carpenter, & Scholt, 2004). A group of European researchers recently developed a "manifesto" on health care for people with I/DD. This manifesto included five standards or recommendations that would increase both access to and quality of health care for people with I/DD: (1) optimal availability and accessibility are ensured; (2) health professionals are competent in I/DD and in the specific health problems related to I/DD; (3) specialists in I/DD are available for consultation and referral for general practitioners; (4) health care for people with I/DD is multidisciplinary to reflect the myriad needs often present in this population; and (5) health care is proactive, meaning that people with I/DD are offered the same level of health care screenings and preventive medicine as the general population. The manifesto specifically includes measuring access and outcomes; understanding factors associated with access barriers; preventing undiagnosed health conditions through screening; and improving client satisfaction, quality of health care, and access to preventive care as important factors related to increasing the availability and accessibility of health care for people with I/DD (Meijer et al., 2004).

Access to health care might most simply be defined as "the actual use of personal health services and everything that facilitates or impedes the use of health services" (Andersen, Rice, & Kominski, in Ulrich, Blewett, & Carrizales, 1999). This is the definition of access used for selecting articles for this chapter.

RESEARCH QUESTIONS

The following research questions are addressed in this chapter:

1. What factors are associated with community-dwelling people with I/DD accessing preventive care, medical and dental care, and insurance?

2. To what extent are community-dwelling people with I/DD satisfied with their health care?

3. How do people with I/DD and people who support them rate the quality of health care?

4. What are the consequences of inadequate access to health care?

5. What are the key unmet medical and dental needs of people with I/DD?

6. What barriers do people with I/DD experience in accessing medical and dental care?

DATA COLLECTION STRATEGIES

Several strategies were used to gather studies for this literature review. As in the other chapters in this volume, this chapter used the services of a research librarian who reviewed results of online searches conducted for the project at the following Web sites: Medline, CINAHL, SocioFile, Health Star, PsychInfo, Pharmaceutical Abstracts, Web Science, Academic Search Premiere, Ingenta, and GPO Access. In addition, articles were identified for inclusion by using the ancestry approach (reviewed reference lists of relevant articles), reviewing in-house research (National Health Inventory Survey-Disabilities [d-D] studies, deinstitutionalization studies, evaluation studies), searching relevant Web sites (Administration on Developmental Disabilities [ADD], American Association on Mental Retardation [AAMR], Down Syndrome Society, The Arc, Centers for Disease Control and Prevention, National Organization on Disability, Kaiser Family Foundation, Human Services Research Institute [HSRI], Mathematica, National Center for the Dissemination of Disability Research) for recent papers on access to health care, and accessing papers identified in an earlier literature review that made requests to all state developmental disabilities planning councils, University Centers of Excellence in Developmental Disabilities, and state directors of mental retardation/developmental disabilities programs (Hayden & Kim, 2002).

INCLUSION/EXCLUSION CRITERIA

Articles were included if they were published in 1990 or later; if they clearly focused on populations with I/DD (as opposed to general Medicaid populations); if they included people with I/DD; and if they involved data collection and analysis. Study participants included people with I/DD, caregivers, and/or health care providers. Some articles discussed factors associated with differences in access to health care (e.g., deinstitutionalization studies). Articles defining the meaning of access to health care for people with I/DD were used to set the context. Studies of disease prevalence, models of care, health care financing, health status, health care utilization (other than preventive care), and psychotropic medication use were excluded.

Several studies were conducted by international researchers, primarily in the United Kingdom. Despite the differences in health care systems, many of the barriers were identified across health care systems and cultures and are, therefore, instructive to medical educators, practitioners, and policy makers in the United States and were included in this review.

Results

The studies were initially separated by whether they focused on medical (including mental health) care or dental care. Some studies are presented in multiple tables or in tables more than once depending on the kinds of information presented. For example, some studies were surveys of both individuals and providers; others used both surveys and health screenings. Tables 7-1 and 7-2 show country and year published, population studied, sample size, age of interest, and any interventions given for medical care and dental care, respectively. Studies that included both medical and dental care outcomes are included in both tables. Articles were further organized by the following categories: studies of individuals, studies using screenings and record reviews, and studies of health care providers.

STUDY CHARACTERISTICS

Medical Care Study Characteristics

Table 7-1 summarizes the characteristics of 35 studies of individuals with disabilities or the people who supported them, 7 studies using screenings or record reviews, and 10 studies of health care providers all focusing on medical care and access. Fourteen of the 52 studies focusing on medical care included children. Thirty-five of the studies were conducted in the United States, 10 in the United Kingdom, and the remainder in Australia, New Zealand, or Canada. All but four of the medical studies explicitly included people with I/DD as the focus of study. Three of the other studies focused on children with special health care needs, and one focused on people with disabilities more generally. In four studies, people with I/DD were included, although other types of disabilities were also represented. Across the studies on Table 7-1, the sample size ranged from 47 to 202,560, with 16 studies including more than 1000 people. Some of the larger studies included both people with I/DD and people with other disabilities or sometimes people with no disabilities. Among the screening and record review studies, sample sizes ranged from 63 to 589. Among the studies of health care providers, the sample sizes ranged from 19 to 536. Six of the studies focused on outcomes of deinstitutionalization, six provided clinical exams or screenings, and one used a chart review and interviews to assess medical care needs.

Dental Care Study Characteristics

Table 7-2 summarizes four studies of individuals, four studies using screenings or record reviews, and two studies of health care providers focusing on dental care and access. Six studies were conducted in the United States, two in the United Kingdom, one in Singapore, and one in France. Most of the studies of dental care focused on both children and adults. Two studies included only adults. All of the dental care studies focused specifically on people with I/DD. Sample sizes for the dental care studies ranged from 60 to 12,539. Four of the dental care studies assessed dental care needs using a clinical oral examination.

STRENGTH OF EVIDENCE

Forty of the 64 studies included Level of Evidence II information. Most Level of Evidence II studies were either surveys of people with I/DD and/or their family members and caregivers or they were surveys of health care providers. One study using medical evaluation was classified as Level of Evidence III. Nine additional studies that included direct exams, screenings, or evaluations of study participants were classified as Level of Evidence IV. Fifteen studies of individuals or health care

TABLE 7-1 *Access to Medical Care: Summary of Country, Subject Information, and Interventions*

AUTHORS	COUNTRY	POPULATION STUDIED	NUMBER OF SUBJECTS	AGE OF SUBJECTS, YRS	LEVEL OF EVIDENCE	DIMENSION OF DISABILITY	INTERVENTION
Studies of Individuals							
Anderson et al., 2003	USA	General population, people with disabilities	202,650; ID, 3,076	All	II	Disability/participation	NA
Bradley et al., 2000	USA	People with ID	600 individuals with ID, 600 family members	19–86	II	Disability/participation	NA
Broughton & Thomson, 2000	UK caregivers	Women with ID, caregivers	52 women with ID, 35 caregivers	20–64	IV	Disability/participation	NA
Brown & Bretting, 1998	USA	Adults with ID discharged from state institutions	Year 1, 32 families; Year 2, 36 families; Year 3, 42 families; Year 4, 43 families (70 unique respondents)	25–57	IV	Disability/participation	Deinstitutionalization (pre–post)
Brown & Bretting, 1999	USA	Adults with ID discharged from state institutions	Baseline (in institution) 60, Time 1, 90; Time 2, 96; Time 3, 93; Time 4, 84; Time 5, 36	All ages	II	Disability/participation	Deinstitutionalization (pre–post)
Conroy, 1995	USA	People with ID	382	All ages	IV	Disability/participation	Deinstitutionalization (pre–post)
Conroy, 1996	USA	People with ID	455 movers, 395 stayers	All ages	II	Disability/participation	Deinstitutionalization (experimental contrast group)
Conroy et al., 1991	USA	Adults with ID	101 family members	22–93	II	Disability/participation	Deinstitutionalization
Conroy et al., 1995	USA	People with ID	745 community-dwelling individuals, 255 institution-dwelling individuals	All ages	II	Disability/participation	Deinstitutionalization (experimental contrast group)
Conroy et al., 1998	USA	People with ID	1073 community-dwelling individuals	All ages	II	Disability/participation	Deinstitutionalization (experimental contrast group)

Reference	Country	Population	Sample	Age		Topic	
Davies & Duff, 2001	UK	Women with ID	58	Women older than age 50	II	Disability/participation	NA
Edgerton et al., 1994	USA	Older adults with mild ID	17 adults living alone, 30 adults living with family members or in residential facilities	Mean age 65	IV	Disability/participation	NA
Fortune, 1996	USA	People with ID	6332	All ages	II	Disability/participation	NA
Hanson et al., 2003	USA	People with disabilities	2481	18–64	II	Disability/participation	NA
Hanson et al., 2003	USA	Adults with disabilities (19% had ID)	1505	18–64	II	Disability/participation	NA
Hewitt et al., 2000	USA	People with ID	372 adults with ID, 184 residential providers, 82 vocational providers, 183 families, 486 case managers, 288 direct support staff, 21 county HCBS Waiver coordinators	All ages	II	Disability/participation	NA
Iacono & Davis, 2003	Australia	Adults with DD	328 adults, 295 surveys completed by a support person, 11 interviews, 119 had recent hospital experiences	Adults	II	Disability/participation	NA
Jaskulski et al., 1990	USA	People with ID	13,075	All ages	II	Disability/participation	NA
Kaye, 2001	USA	Working age adults with disabilities	NS	18–64	II	Disability/participation	NA
Kennedy & Erb, 2002	USA	Adults with disabilities (including ID)	25,805	Adults	II	Disability/participation	NA
Kim & Cooker, 2001	USA	Adults with DD	People with DD weighted $N = 534$; people without DD weighted $N = 5127$;	Adults	II	Disability/participation	NA

(continued)

TABLE 7-1 *Continued*

AUTHORS	COUNTRY	POPULATION STUDIED	NUMBER OF SUBJECTS	AGE OF SUBJECTS, YRS	LEVEL OF EVIDENCE	DIMENSION OF DISABILITY	INTERVENTION
Kopac et al., 1998	USA	Women with DD, service providers	127 women with DD; 155 provider agency responses	18–80	II	Disability/participation	NA
Krauss et al., 2003	USA	Families of children with SHCN	2220	18 and younger	II	Disability/participation	NA
Larson et al., 2001	USA	National household population including people with ID/DD	202,560	All ages	II	Disability/participation	NA
Larson et al., 2003	USA	Adults with ID and other disabilities	9950	Adults	II	Disability/participation	NA
Lee et al., 1993	USA	Children with special needs	182	0–21	IV	Pathophysiology	NA
National Association of State Directors of Developmental Disabilities Services, 2003	USA	People with ID	7732	18–103	II	Disability/participation	NA
Neri et al., 2001	USA	Adults with cerebral palsy, MS, or SCI	477	18–64	II	Disability/participation	NA
Newachek et al., 2000	USA	Children with special health care needs	57,553	Children younger than 18	II	Disability/participation	NA

136

Reference	Country	Sample	N	Age	Level	Framework	Notes
National Organization on Disability, 2000	USA	Adults with disabilities	997 adults with disabilities, 953 adults without disabilities	Adults	II	Disability/participation	NA
Noll & Deschenes-Desmond, 1993	USA	People with ID in licensed community settings	274 people with ID	Not specified	II	Disability/participation	NA
Perry et al., 2003	USA	Adults with disabilities	98	18–64	IV	Disability/participation	NA
Reichard & Turnbull, 2004	USA	Family members Case managers	335, 38	Children and adults	IV	Disability/participation	NA
Roy et al., 1997	Australia	Adults with ID	127	19–89	IV	Impairment	NA
Thomas & Payne, 1998	USA	Adults receiving home health services	2013	All ages	II	Disability/participation	NA
Screenings and Record Reviews							
Beange et al., 1995	Australia	Adults with ID	202	20–50	III	Impairment	Medical evaluation
Kerr et al., 2003	UK	People with ID, 23 related conditions	589	Adults	IV	Impairment	Health, Vision and Hearing Checks, "plain English" reports for caregivers
Lewis et al., 2002	USA	People with ID	353	Adults	IV	Impairment/societal limitations	Physical and Dental exams; health and mental health histories
Martin et al., 1997	UK	People with ID	132 people with ID examined, 52 people with ID interviewed, 170 unpaid caregivers surveyed	Adults	IV	Disability/participation	Adults with ID were given physical and mental health check by local GPs; if risks were found, appropriate interventions given

(continued)

TABLE 7-1 *Continued*

AUTHORS	COUNTRY	POPULATION STUDIED	NUMBER OF SUBJECTS	AGE OF SUBJECTS, YRS	LEVEL OF EVIDENCE	DIMENSION OF DISABILITY	INTERVENTION
McCulloch et al., 1996	UK	Adults with ID	63	20–85	IV	Pathophysiology	Vision screening and chart review
Paxton & Taylor, 1998	UK	Adults with DD	71	Adults	IV	Pathophysiology	Chart review and interview
Studies of Health Care Providers							
Cook & Lennox, 2000	UK	GP registrars	157	Adults	II	Disability/participation	NA
Dovey & Webb, 2000	New Zealand	General practitioners	137	All ages	IV	Disability/participation	NA
Hewitt et al., 2000	USA	Direct support professionals	288	All ages	II	Disability/participation	NA
Lennox & Chaplin, 1995	Australia	Psychiatrists and trainee psychiatrists	116	Adults	II	Disability/participation	NA
Lennox et al., 1997	Australia	General practitioners	526	Adults	II	Disability/participation	NA
Muir & Ogden, 2001	UK	Registrars and trainers	19	Adults	IV	Disability/participation	NA
Noll & Deschenes-Desmond, 1993	USA	Physicians and dentists	102	Not specified	II	Disability/participation	NA
Powrie, 2003	UK	Nurses	107	Adults	II	Disability/participation	NA
Reichard & Turnbull, 2004	USA	Physicians	40	Children and adults	II	Disability/participation	NA

Sparks & Temple, 2000	Canada	Providers of elder services	44	Adults	II	Disability/participation	NA
Stein, 2000	UK	General practitioners	64	Not specified	IV	Disability/participation	NA
Thornton, 1996	UK	Health care providers	20	Adults	IV	Disability/participation	NA
Tyler et al., 1999	USA	Family practice residency program directors	274	Adults	IV	Disability/participation	NA
Walsh et al., 2000	USA	Registered nurses	538	Not specified	IV	Disability/participation	NA

HCBS, home and community based; MS, multiple sclerosis; SCI, spinal cord injury; SHCN, special health care needs

TABLE 7-2 *Access to Dental Care: Summary of Country, Subject Information, and Interventions*

AUTHORS	COUNTRY	POPULATION STUDIED	NUMBER OF SUBJECTS	AGE OF SUBJECTS, YRS	LEVEL OF EVIDENCE	DIMENSION OF DISABILITY	INTERVENTION
Studies of Individuals							
Allison et al., 2000	France	Children with DS	204	Children	II, IV	Disability/participation	NA
Hewitt et al., 2000	USA	People with ID	372 adults with ID, 183 families, 486 case managers, 288 direct support staff	All ages	II	Disability/participation	NA
Reichard et al., 2001	USA	People with ID	335 parents, 40 case managers, 70 DDS for surveys: 3 DDS, 9–15 family members, 9–15 case managers for surveys	All ages	II	Disability/participation	NA
Schultz et al., 2001	USA	Children with DD	12,539	2–17	II	Disability/participation	NA
Screenings and Record Reviews							
Cumella et al., 2000	UK	Adults with ID	60 for interview, 50 for oral exam	Adults	IV	Pathophysiology	Oral examination
Feldman et al., 1997	USA	People with ID at national Special Olympics competition	713	Not stated	IV	Pathophysiology	Oral examination
Vignehsa et al., 1991	Singapore	Children with disabilities	322	6–18	IV	Pathophysiology	Oral examination
White et al., 1998	USA	People with ID at regional Special Olympics competition	385	9–49	IV	Pathophysiology	Oral examination
Studies of Health Care Providers							
Ferguson et al., 1991	USA	Dentists	139	All ages	IV	Disability/participation	NA
Russell & Kinirons, 1993	UK	Dentists	60	Adults	II	Disability/participation	NA

providers that used focus groups or methods that did not use random samples of study subjects were also classified as Level of Evidence IV.

DIMENSIONS OF DISABLEMENT

Most studies reviewed focused on the inability of people with I/DD to access the health care system. These studies were classified as meeting the disability/participation dimension of disablement as the principal barrier to health care and was related to the health care system's inability to structure itself to fully meet the needs of this group of health care consumers. Studies of vision and dental health were primarily related to pathophysiology and identifying undiagnosed or untreated health conditions or diseases. The remainder of the studies fell into the impairment category in which records or in-person health assessment screened for and identified particular diagnoses to understand the level of monitoring and follow-up people received for these conditions.

ACCESS TO MEDICAL CARE

Tables 7-3 and 7-4 summarize studies of individuals with I/DD and/or their caregivers regarding access to medical or dental care. The tables include information on research design, measures used in the study, and findings for medical care and dental care, respectively. The studies are grouped by the type of findings reported.

Fifteen medical care studies reported on access to preventive care, 9 reported on access to other types of medical care, 6 reported on access to health care insurance, 8 reported satisfaction with access to medical care, 15 reported on the quality of health care, 15 reported on unmet health needs, and 16 reported on barriers to accessing health care for people with I/DD. The studies used a variety of research designs (most commonly surveys, longitudinal studies, reviews of registries, reviews of medical charts, and physical examinations or screenings). Some of the studies used convenience samples of various sizes while others used more sophisticated methods such as multistage random household samples designed to accurately represent the population of interest.

ACCESS TO PREVENTIVE CARE

The first set of studies reported information about access to preventive care. Studies in group homes and other licensed facilities reported high rates of people with I/DD having had physical exams in the last year. People in community residential settings were also more likely to have had preventive care such as TB tests, flu vaccinations, and Ob/GYN exams than those living with family members (e.g., Hewitt, Larson, & Lakin, 2000; Lewis, Lewis, Leake, King, & Lindemann, 2002). Many of the studies reported that women with I/DD had had Pap smears or OB/GYN exams less often than people in the general population. People with I/DD living with families were least likely to have had such exams. Similarly men living on their own or with family members rarely had prostate exams (e.g., Edgerton, Gaston, Kelly, & Ward, 1994; Hanson, Newman, & Voris, 2003). One clinical study and one study that examined health

TABLE 7-3 Access to Medical Care: Summary of Evidence and Research Design

AUTHORS	RESEARCH DESIGN	DATA SOURCE	MEASURES USED	RESULTS
Preventive Care				
Bradley et al., 2000	Survey	Individual	Core indicators survey	94% of adults with ID/DD had a physical exam in the last year. 63% of women had an OB/GYN exam during the last year. Overall one fifth of women had never had an OB/GYN exam; one third of women living with parents or relatives had never had an OB/GYN exam.
Broughton & Thomson, 2000	Registry	Individual	Survey	40% of the women with disabilities interviewed had a Pap smear test, far below the national UK average of 85%.
Davies & Duff, 2001	Survey	Individual	NA	30% of the women had never been referred for mammography, although for the 30 individuals who had been referred 90% completed the screening. 21% did not know what mammography was. 66% of the women did not do monthly breast exams and 64% reported that their physician had not done a breast exam.
Edgerton et al., 1994	Intensive longitudinal participant-observation ethnographic research	Individual	Interview and direct observation of health care	Among independent living participants only 3 of 17 received care from the same physician or clinic more than two or three times. Few received thorough physical exams. Only a few of the women had ever had Pap smears. Only one man had had a prostate exam in recent years.
Hanson et al., 2003	Survey (National Household—random digit dialing)	Individual	Telephone survey	44% of women had had a mammogram, and 34% of men had had a prostate exam during the past year.
Hewitt et al., 2000	Survey and interview	Individual	Consumer interview	98% of people living in corporate foster care settings had a physical exam in the last year compared with 84% of individuals living in a family home, foster home, or their own home. Adults who were older were more likely to have had a physical exam while people in the large urban counties were less likely to have had an exam. Overall, 74% of adult women had received an OB/GYN exam in the past year while 7% had never had one. Older women with less severe mental retardation living in corporate foster care settings were more likely to have had an OB/GYN exam than those with more severe MR; those living in family, foster, or own home, and younger women. 18% of women living with family members, with a foster family or in a home of their own had never had an OB/GYN exam.

Kaye, 2001	Survey	Individual	NHIS 1998	Among women with severe mobility impairments who had seen a doctor in the last 2 yrs, 51% had a mammogram compared with 78% of women with no mobility impairments. Similarly, 65% reported they had a Pap smear, compared to 86% of women with no mobility limitations.
Kopac et al., 1998	Survey	Individual		Nurses and caregivers provide the majority of gynecological care giving and advice. Only one half of provider agencies provided health education to women, with only one fourth saying it was accessible to ALL women. Most agencies did not provide STD screening or counseling.
Larson et al., 2003	Survey	Individual	NHIS—Phase 2 Follow back 1994,1995	Among adults with ID/DD, 24.3% had had a flu shot in the last 12 months, 14.3% had had a pneumonia vaccination ever, and 64.9% had had a tetanus shot in the past 10 yrs. None of these items differed significantly from adults with no functional limitations once age, gender, overall health status, race, and economic status were taken into account.
Lee et al., 1993	Random sample of client charts	Screen or record	Standardized protocol to assess clinical and dietary information to assess nutrition risk	Children identified at nutritional risk were frequently not referred for appropriate services. Monitoring of nutritional risk was lacking for many children with special needs. 127 charts had insufficient information to determine nutritional risk. 25% lacked height/weight information. 84% lacked biochemical data. 44% lacked feeding information. Only 33% of charts had adequate information to identify nutritional risk. General nutrition guidance was provided by nurses (50%), occupational therapists (5%), dieticians (27%), and other providers (18%).
Lewis et al., 2002	Case series	Screen or record	Health markers—obesity, blood laboratory tests, urinalysis, chart reviews	People on their own or with family were more likely to be obese. People living in community care facilities were more likely to have TB tests and flu vaccines. Only one third of women had a Pap smear in the previous 3 yrs. Fewer than one third of women did breast exams and only 23% of women older than 40 had a mammogram. About one fourth of people living with family or friends did not have a personal health care provider.
McCulloch et al., 1996	Pilot Study/convenience sample	Screen or record	Visual acuity tests, ocular health exams	Only 2 had received an eye exam in previous 2 yrs and only 7 in the previous 5 yrs. None of the people with severe/profound ID had records of any eye exams.

(continued)

143

TABLE 7-3 *Continued*

AUTHORS	RESEARCH DESIGN	DATA SOURCE	MEASURES USED	RESULTS
National Association of State Directors of Developmental Disabilities Services, 2000	Survey	Individual	National core indicators survey	52% of women had an OB/GYN exam in the previous year, 8% had never had one. 86% had a physical exam in the past year.
National Association of State Directors of Developmental Disabilities Services, 2003	Survey	Individual	National core indicators survey	52% of women had an OB/GYN exam in the previous year, 7% had never had one.
Paxton & Taylor, 1998	Registry, chart review and Interview/ health assessment	Screen or Record	Health assessments—three categories, no abnormality detected, "known" problem, "new" problem	Twenty had their eyes checked in the last 2 yrs while 51 had never had eyes checked (including 24 who were reported to be unlikely to tolerate an exam due to challenging behavior). Of 71 screened, 10 had had their hearing assessed; none of the others had a hearing test since finishing school. Thirty-nine had wax in one or both ears requiring treatment. The screening identified two individuals with high blood pressure. Of the 71 studied, 23 had completed a full course of tetanus immunization. Six had had a partial course of immunization; the others did not have medical records showing their immunization status available. Four women were within the age range for which mammography is recommended; one had had a mammogram. Seven people were underweight including some who were severely underweight who had not been weighed for several months. At least one unmet health need was identified in all people screened.
Medical Care				
Brown & Bretting, 1998	Longitudinal survey	Individual	Family survey	Proportion saying access to medical services is somewhat better or better in the community increased from 35% in Year 1 to 48% in Year 4 (14% reported worse or somewhat worse in Year 4). Proportion saying that by Year 4 access to special therapies was better or somewhat better, 44%; no change, 24%; worse or somewhat worse, 22%.

Conroy, 1996	Longitudinal study	Individual	Personal life quality protocol	Movers reported it was significantly more difficult to get medical care than stayers (4.0 vs. 4.9' 5 is very easy). Overall quality of health care for stayers and leavers (4.4 and 4.5) was not statistically different.
Conroy, et al., 1998	Longitudinal study	Individual	Personal life quality protocol	There were no significant differences between setting types for percent who said health care is very easy to get (30% for supported living, 26% for others). Differences in how easy it is to find medical care were not significant (4.0 for ICF-MR, 3.5 for HCBS Waiver settings).
Edgerton, et al., 1994	Intensive longitudinal participant-observation ethnographic research	Individual	Interview and direct observation of health care	Seventeen individuals living independently had great difficulty locating appropriate care.
Hanson et al., 2003	Survey (National Household—random digit dialing)	Individual	Telephone survey	25% of working age adults with disabilities reporting having trouble finding a doctor who understands their disability and 15% did not have a regular doctor.
Hanson et al., 2003	Survey	Individual		25% reported difficulty finding a doctor who understands their disability.
Hewitt et al, 2000	Survey and interview	Individual	Individual case manager survey, general case manager survey	Case manager reports: 8% of case managers reported some or much difficulty finding health and physician services for a specific sampled individual with ID; 4% reported difficulty obtaining nursing or home health aide services. There was no difference between ICF-MR and HCBS Waiver funding in access to health care services.
Krauss et al., 2003	Telephone survey	Individual	Access to specialty medical care, child characteristics, family characteristics, health care coverage	More than 30% of children with autism and more than 20% of children with MR and other conditions had problems accessing specialty care.
Reichard & Turnbull, 2004	Surveys and focus groups	Individual	Family survey, case manager survey	Most reported that there were enough physicians to serve people with DD in the area (74% of parents, 72% of case managers). Most families did not have trouble locating a physician.

(*continued*)

145

TABLE 7-3 *Continued*

AUTHORS	RESEARCH DESIGN	DATA SOURCE	MEASURES USED	RESULTS
Insurance Coverage				
Anderson et al., 2003	Survey	Individual	National Health Interview Survey	10% of people with ID or DD had no health insurance compared with 9% of people with disabilities other than ID or DD and 14% of people with no disabilities. People with ID, DD, or both and people with functional limitations but not ID/DD were less likely than people with no functional limitations to be enrolled in an HMO-based health care program and much more likely to be in a public insurance program.
Hanson et al., 2003	Survey (National Household—Random digit dialing)	Individual	Telephone survey	5% of working age adults with disabilities were uninsured, 33% had private insurance; 59% had Medicare and/or Medicaid. 17% reported the doctor would not accept their health insurance. Serious problems were reported in paying for the following services needed in the previous 12 months: prescription drugs (32%), dental care (29%), equipment (21%), mental health care (17%), and home care (16%).
Kaye, 2001	Survey	Individual	National Health Interview Survey— Disability Supplement	17% of working age adults with disabilities lack any type of health insurance. 55% of working age adults with disabilities had private insurance vs. 73% of working age adults without disabilities. Among working age adults with disabilities, 13% who had a private individual insurance plan, 11% of those with no insurance, 4% of those with public insurance, and 3.5% of those with private group plans were turned down for insurance or had coverage restricted during the prior 2 yrs. Although 70% of nondisabled working age adults have employment-based group health insurance, only 31% of adults with disabilities have coverage in their own names and 19% get coverage through a family member.
Larson et al., 2001	NHIS-D	Individual	National Health Interview Survey	People with intellectual or developmental disabilities were significantly more likely to be on Medicaid than people in the general U.S. population (52.2% vs. 9.8%)
National Organization on Disability, 2002	Telephone survey	Individual	2000 NOD/Harris Survey of Americans with Disabilities	People with and without disabilities are equally likely to have health insurance of some kind (90% vs. 89%, respectively). People with disabilities are four times more likely to have special needs that are not covered by their health insurance (28% vs. 7%).

146

Newachek et al., 2000	NHIS-D	Individual	National Health Interview Survey	Uninsured children and children with public insurance were more likely to be without a usual source of care than privately insured children.
Noll & Deschenes-Desmond, 1993	Random sample of residents of licensed facilities	Individual	Client survey (individuals, family members)	All individuals in licensed community settings had some type of medical insurance.
Satisfaction				
Anderson et al., 2003	Survey	Individual	NHIS 1994, 1995 Adult—Phase 2	Level of satisfaction with primary health care for adults with I/DD and adults with other significant functional limitations were not statistically different once age, gender, economic status, race, health status, and health coverage were considered. The percentage of adults with I/DD who said their primary health care services were excellent (as opposed to good, fair, or poor) was 48% for respect and privacy, 46% for the doctor's interest in the person and his or condition, 43% for thoroughness of the exam, 41% for availability of transportation to the clinic, 40% for availability of the physician in an emergency, 35% for ability to get answers to medical questions over the phone, 29% for time waiting for an appointment, and 26% for time waiting to see doctor.
Fortune, 1996	Longitudinal study using administrative data set	Individual	Inventory for client and agency planning; family survey	Among 97 families whose children were receiving waiver-funded services, 81% were satisfied with skilled nursing services and 87.5% were satisfied with specialized medical equipment.
Jaskulski et al., 1990	Survey	Individual	National consumer survey	22% of people surveyed were dissatisfied with payment for or provision of medical equipment or supplies. 20% of those with private health insurance were dissatisfied with it compared to 13% who were dissatisfied with Medicaid.
Martin et al., 1997	Participants identified through registries; Given health check; Randomly selected group surveyed; unpaid caregivers surveyed	Individual	Body mass index, physical activity measures, GP consultation protocol, Psychiatric Assessment Scale for Adults with a Developmental Disability (PAS-ADD)	In general, people with ID and their caregivers were satisfied with care given, but had concerns about rudeness, inaccessibility, and lack of information/knowledge of GP. Caregivers also reported that GPs didn't know about other services and didn't provide enough information about medications.

(continued)

TABLE 7-3 *Continued*

AUTHORS	RESEARCH DESIGN	DATA SOURCE	MEASURES USED	RESULTS
National Organization on Disability, 2000	Telephone survey	Individual	2000 NOD/Harris Survey of Americans with Disabilities	People with disabilities are more likely than people without disabilities to be somewhat or very dissatisfied with their health care (26% vs. 16%).
Neri et al., 2001	Survey	Individual	Survey	Among adults with CP, MS, and SCI, 50% in fee for service plans and 37% in managed care plans were extremely satisfied with their primary care doctor.
Reichard & Turnbull, 2004	Surveys and focus groups	Individual	Family survey, case manager survey	19% of those who required communication facilitators were not satisfied. 20% of families were dissatisfied with physician's communication directly with family members.
Changes Associated with Deinstitutionalization				
Brown & Bretting, 1998	Longitudinal survey	Individual	Family survey	Overall health: 49% somewhat better or better vs. 20% somewhat worse or worse in Year 4. Quality of medical services: 60% somewhat better or better vs. 17% worse or somewhat worse.
Brown & Bretting, 1999	Longitudinal study	Individual	Interview/observation	Between Time 4 and Time 5 (both community observations) the rating for staff being knowledgeable about health care needs declined significantly. The proportion of individuals in community settings scored as excellent in providing information to encourage personal well-being (exercise, diet) was significantly higher than in the institution. More than 70% of community residents reported that their doctor always listened to them. More than 70% reported that their doctor always helped them with what is wrong. There were no significant differences between institution- and community-dwelling individuals. The percentage of individuals reporting that their doctor always spends enough time with them increased from 67% in the first year after deinstitutionalization to 74% in the fourth year. The difference was not statistically significant.
Conroy, 1995	Longitudinal study	Individual	Interview	The proportion of individuals reporting occasional or frequent problems in recent medical services was 5.8% in 1995 after deinstitutionalization, which is significantly higher than the percentage in 1990.

148

Citation	Study type	Level	Method	Findings
Conroy, 1996	Longitudinal study	Individual	Personal life quality protocol	Overall quality of health care for stayers and leavers (4.4 and 4.5) was not statistically different. The general health of movers was significantly better than for stayers.
Conroy, et al., 1991	Longitudinal survey	Individual	Family survey	Family satisfaction with the quality of medical care their family member received increased significantly between the time the family member first moved to community to an assessment 4 yrs later.
Conroy et al., 1998	Longitudinal study	Individual	Personal life quality protocol	Community-dwelling individuals reported significant improvements in the quality of health care in the previous year (from 3.9 to 4.2 on a five-point scale). There were no significant differences between setting types for percentage who said health care is excellent (36% for ICF-MR vs. 48% for HCBS Waiver Settings).
Conroy et al., 1995	Longitudinal study	Individual	Survey	The proportion of individuals who could identify their primary care physician was 99% for those in the institution compared with 94% for those in the community. Both community and institution dwelling individuals reported that their physician's knowledge of DD, sensitivity, and taking enough time was good.
Quality of Care				
Hewitt et al., 2000	Survey and interview	Individual	Individual case manager survey, general case manager survey	Case manager reports: Overall quality of health care services were rated 3.06 on a four-point scale. Overall the quality of health care and physicians were rated excellent by 26% of case managers and good by 62% of case managers. Individuals with relatively more medical support needs were reported to have received higher quality medical services.
Iacono & Davis, 2003	Survey	Individual	Survey questions: needs and access to special utensils, communicating with hospital staff, dependence on support person, leaving hospital. Interviews asked about hospital experience.	Most people with ID (79) wanted a support person with them when they were in the hospital. Having a support person available was a significant predictor for getting some needs met (enough to drink and moving from the bed). Support people reported that they thought their presence necessary because hospital staff members were too busy and not experienced with ID.

(continued)

149

TABLE 7-3 *Continued*

AUTHORS	RESEARCH DESIGN	DATA SOURCE	MEASURES USED	RESULTS
Kaye, 2001	Survey	Individual	National Health Interview Survey— Disability Supplement	The percentage of working age adults with disabilities rating the quality of health care as excellent was 54% for those with private coverage, 49% for Medicare only, 40% for Medicaid only, 43% for those who are uninsured.
Lee et al., 1993	Random sample of client charts	Screen or record	Standardized protocol to assess clinical and dietary info to assess nutrition risk	One hundred and twenty-seven charts for children with special needs had insufficient information to determine nutritional risk. 25% lacked height/weight information; 84% lacked biochemical data; 44% lacked feeding information; only 33% of charts had adequate information to identify nutritional risk.
Noll & Deschenes-Desmond, 1993	Random sample of residents of licensed facilities	Individual	Client information (individuals, family members)	Individuals rated physician and dental services higher when provided in an office than in a clinic (physician services: 4.36 vs. 3.88 for clinic; dental 4.2 vs. 5.1 for clinic).
Paxton & Taylor, 1998	Registry, chart review and interview/health assessment	Screen or record	Health assessments— three categories, no abnormality detected, "known" problem, "new" problem	There were patterns of lack of medical follow-up for a variety of diseases—cardiovascular, cancer. Twenty-one people had mental health needs but only 12 had psychiatric assessment; 35 had challenging behavior, but 29 had never had a specialist contact; 34 had epilepsy treated by anticonvulsants but only 13 had had blood anticonvulsant levels checked in the previous year and there was no evidence that any were monitored with regard to education, advice, regular review, seizure patterns, etc.
Perry et al., 2003	Focus groups (12 total)	Individual	Focus group	Many participants had difficulty forming a close relationship with their primary care providers and specialists. Those who use mental health services are frustrated by a lack of time with their providers, and are concerned that their treatment plans place too much emphasis on medication.
Reichard & Turnbull, 2004	Surveys and focus groups	Individual	Family survey, case manager survey	The percentage who said various medical services were good (rather than neutral or poor) were: how well consumers' needs are met (case manager, 51.3%; family, 65%); physical/structural accessibility of the office (case managers, 81%; family, 80%), distance to the office (case managers, 62%; families, 70%), ease in accessing transportation to care (case managers, 46%; families, 54%), ease in making appointments (case managers, 54%; families, 68%). 40% of case managers reported that physicians

Unmet Health Needs

				communicate poorly or very poorly with individuals with ID, 45% said physicians were poor at allowing extra time for communication barriers, 36% reported physicians were poor at making accommodations for communication when necessary, and 22% said emergency care was poor. 17% of families and 41% of case managers said physicians had poor or very poor knowledge of people with ID. Almost all said physicians were effective in handling ordinary health maintenance, meeting extraordinary health challenges, and in making necessary but special accommodations. 26% of families said physicians did not allow extra time to compensate for communication barriers.
Anderson et al., 2003	Survey	Individual	National Health Interview Survey	People with ID but not DD were more likely to report unmet health care needs (4.6%) than people with no functional limitations (2.2%) once demographic variables (age, gender, economic status, race, overall health status, and type of health care) were taken into consideration. People with ID and DD were more likely than others to report unmet mental health care needs (2.1%) than people with no functional limitations (0.4%) once demographic variables were controlled. People with DD but not ID were more likely to report unmet needs in all areas (health (6.7% vs. 2.2%), dental (12.9% vs. 7.0%), mental health (3.4% vs. 0.4%), and prescription medication (5.2% vs. 1.8%) than the people with no functional limitations once demographic variables were controlled.
Beange et al., 1995	Medical exam of randomly selected adults (stratified sample) comparison results from studies of general population	Screen or record	Physical exam, routine blood tests (full blood count, biochemical screen, thyroid function test, hepatitis B profile), chromosome analysis and other special tests if clinically indicated	A total of 1103 health impairments were identified in the 202 individuals. Of those, 42% had not been diagnosed previously, 51% were not adequately managed, and 26% required specialist care. 69% of individuals with hypertension had not previously been diagnosed. Adverse drug effects were present in 11% of the sample; 50% of drug levels tested were in the nontherapeutic range. In 15.5% of the sample, symptoms and signs such as abdominal pain, headache, and localized swelling had not been investigated or treated. The sample had a mean of 5.4 health impairments per person but 65% of the subjects reported no symptoms and 24% of caregivers said there were no problems.

151

(continued)

TABLE 7-3 *Continued*

AUTHORS	RESEARCH DESIGN	DATA SOURCE	MEASURES USED	RESULTS
Edgerton et al., 1994	Intensive longitudinal participant-observation ethnographic research	Individual	Interview and direct observation of health care	Of the 17 independently living adults studied longitudinally, one woman who had been under the care of a physician for 10 yrs had never had a Pap smear and developed cancer of the uterus. Another woman developed breast cancer while under regular medical care that did not include mammograms.
Hanson et al., 2003	Survey (National Household—random digit dialing)	Individual	Telephone survey	Results of cost barriers: 46% went without needed equipment (e.g., eye glasses), 37% postponed care due to cost, 36% skipped doses, split pills, or did not fill a prescription due to cost, 36% spent less on basic needs (food, heat) to pay for health care. These were significantly more common for those who were uninsured and for those on Medicare as opposed to private insurance or Medicaid.
Jaskulski et al., 1990	Survey	Individual	National consumer survey	18% reported needing health insurance but not having it, 18% reported needing dental care but not getting it.
Kaye, 2001	Survey	Individual	National Health Interview Survey—Disability Supplement	Overall, 12% of working age adults with disabilities had unmet mental health care needs (27% of those who were uninsured and 8% of those with insurance). Working age adults with disabilities were more likely to have unmet health care needs than working age adults without disabilities regardless of insurance type: of uninsured adults, 48% of adults with disabilities had unmet needs vs. 20% of adults without disabilities; of those on public insurance, 20% had unmet needs vs. 6%; of those on private insurance, 15% had unmet needs vs. 5%.
Kennedy & Erb, 2002	Survey	Individual	NHIS Disability Follow back 1994,1995	4.4% of adults with prescriptions failed to take them as prescribed due to cost. 8.7% failed to take them as prescribed for other reasons (forgot, side effects, perceived lack of need, cannot get medication from drug store).
Kerr et al., 2003	Case record review	Screen or record	Audiometric tests Barry McCormick Speech discrimination test, tympanometer, Cardiff cards for visual acuity, a variety of optometric tools	Overlooked vision, hearing loss and other health conditions discovered. Unmet nutritional needs discovered. Access should include specialist services since so many conditions were overlooked. No subjects had a recent neurologic assessment despite a third having epilepsy. Other unmet needs included untreated cataracts (28%), needed eyeglasses (21%), and needed hearing aids (14%).

152

Author	Method	Unit	Instrument	Findings
Kim & Cooker, 2001	Survey	Individual	NHIS questions related to access to MH care	8% of people with DD reported unmet needs compared to 6% of general population. There were no differences in types of mental health providers accessed.
Larson et al., 2003	Survey	Individual	NHIS—Phase 2 Follow back 1994, 1995	6.2% of adults with ID/DD were waiting for mental health services compared with 2.9% of adults with functional limitations other than ID/DD. This difference was statistically significant once age, gender, overall health status, race, and economic status were taken into account.
Lee et al., 1993	Random sample of client charts	Screen or record	Standardized information protocol to assess clinical and dietary info to assess nutrition risk	Children identified at nutritional risk were frequently not referred for appropriate services.
National Organization on Disability, 2000	Telephone survey	Individual	2000 NOD/Harris Survey of Americans with Disabilities	People with disabilities are three times more likely than people without disabilities to have not received needed care on at least one occasion in the last year (19% vs. 6%). People with disabilities are more likely than people without disabilities to postpone or put off seeking needed health care because they could not afford it (28% vs. 12%).
Newachek et al., 2000	NHIS-D	Individual		8.1% of uninsured children or children with public insurance reported unmet dental needs, 4.1% reported unmet eyeglass and prescription needs, 3.2% reported unmet medical needs, and 1.2% unmet mental health needs.
Roy et al., 1997	Registry	Screen or record	PAS-ADD	33% were identified as having some possible psychiatric disorder but nearly half of those screened as having some psychiatric disorder had no contact with any related specialist service.
Thomas & Payne, 1998	Survey	Individual	Home health patient classification system —ratings by nurses	Of 2013 individuals receiving home health care services, 14.6% had an unmet need for home health aide services; 9.4% for mental health services; 7.3% for nutrition, dietary, or meals on wheels services; 3% for occupational therapy; 5.3% for physical therapy; and 1.9% for speech therapy. Overall, almost one half of those visited had one or more unmet needs.
Health Care Barriers				
Bradley et al., 2000	Survey	Individual	Core indicators survey	Individuals living independently, in community residences, or in nursing homes were more likely than those living with family members to have had a recent physical.

153

(continued)

TABLE 7-3 *Continued*

AUTHORS	RESEARCH DESIGN	DATA SOURCE	MEASURES USED	RESULTS
Edgerton et al., 1994	Intensive longitudinal participant-observation ethnographic research	Individual	Interview and direct observation of health care	Seventeen individuals living independently had little understanding of the relationships among smoking, exercise, diet, and health. Few had more than the most rudimentary understanding of health matters in general. All 17 had difficulty determining when they need health care, communicating their needs to care providers, and understanding how to cooperate with treatment plans. Most were not sufficiently literate to follow written instructions and few could remember doctor's instructions well enough to carry them out. Access to medical coverage was also hampered by the difficulty of completing the paperwork.
Fortune, 1996	Longitudinal study using administrative data set	Individual	Inventory for client and agency planning; family survey	In 1996, 18% of individuals with ID/DD reported that health problems were a barrier to participating in social activities compared to 15% in 1988.
Hanson et al., 2003	Survey (National Household—Random digit dialing)	Individual	Telephone survey	Serious problems were reported in paying for the following services needed in the previous 12 months: prescription drugs (32%), dental care (29%), equipment (21%), mental health care (17%), and home care (16%). These were significantly more common for those who were uninsured and for those on Medicare as opposed to private insurance or Medicaid.
Jaskulski et al., 1990	Survey	Individual	National consumer survey	Barriers reported included: lack of health care in rural areas or variations across regions, lack of various types of health care including maternal and child health, early periodic screening, diagnostic and treatment, dental care and prescriptions, lack of access to prevention of disability and other preventive health measures, low reimbursement rates and red tape for Medicaid, lack of health insurance, lack of transportation, eligibility barriers to Medicaid and other public health financing programs, eligibility barriers for private insurance, high premiums for insurance for people with disabilities, above average costs for health care, limitations in the scope of coverage, institutional bias in health care financing, lack of knowledge of DD among health care providers, unmet needs for people with dual diagnosis, lack of data on health care.

Kaye, 2001	Survey	Individual	National Health Interview Survey—Disability Supplement	More than 77% of working age adults with disabilities who have no insurance reported they cannot afford the premiums.
Kopac et al., 1998	Survey	Individual		Barriers include financial—lack of insurance or health care providers that don't take Medicaid, Medicare. Other barriers included family perceptions of sexual health needs of women with DD. 11% of agencies reported women were uncooperative during exams. Finding a physician willing to treat this population (excluding financial reasons) was also mentioned as a barrier.
Krauss et al., 2003	Telephone survey	Individual	Access to specialty medical care, child characteristics, family characteristics, health care coverage	The most common insurance barrier to specialist care was getting referrals. The most common barrier to provider access was problems finding skilled and experienced practitioners. 25% of children with autism had problems getting referrals and finding skilled and experienced specialists. Parents of children with autism were three times as likely to report difficulties with care coordination. Odds of experiencing a health care problem increased when "parents were in fair or poor health, had multiple children with special health care needs, for children with unstable health, children with autism and for children without secondary health care coverage."
Lee et al., 1993	Survey	Individual	NHIS—1988 Child Health Supplement	Children with special health care needs reported to have a regular provider were more likely to have seen a doctor and taken prescribed medicines. Children without health care coverage were the least likely to have seen a doctor or taken prescribed medicine. Other factors that were related to not accessing care included poverty level, minority status, and children living with their mother or with someone other than their parents.
Martin et al., 1997	Participants identified through registries. Given health check. Randomly selected group surveyed. Unpaid caregivers surveyed.	Screen or record	Body mass index, physical activity measures, GP consultation protocol, PAS-ADD	GPs with relatively high patient loads of people with ID believed that these patients were more time consuming and they didn't have the time to do health checks (which take about 30 minutes).

(continued)

TABLE 7-3 *Continued*

AUTHORS	RESEARCH DESIGN	DATA SOURCE	MEASURES USED	RESULTS
Newachek et al., 2000	NHIS-D	Individual		5.6% of uninsured children and children with public insurance reported delays in getting care because of costs. Another 1.4% reported not receiving care because of costs, with uninsured children five times more likely to report this as a problem.
Noll & Deschenes-Desmond, 1993	Random sample of residents of licensed facilities	Individual	Client survey (individuals, family members)	Important or very important challenges included previous experience and training for medical provider, 60%; administrative issues such as DNR policies, 58%; getting reimbursement from medical insurers, 53% clients; patient needs (e.g., special scheduling, extra treatment time, extra support), 53%; support staff issues (familiarity with person and needs, follow-up), 48%; medical information (e.g., individual able to provide information, current health information available), 45%; transportation causing missed appointments, 40%.
Perry et al., 2003	Focus groups (12 total)	Individual	Focus group	Specific problems included provider turnover, provider lack of knowledge about the patient's disability, and difficulty finding a provider who would accept their coverage. Participants identified many problems with durable medical equipment coverage and feel they must fight for every piece of equipment they need or else pay large sums of their own money for it.
Reichard & Turnbull, 2004	Surveys and focus groups	Individual	Family survey, case manager survey	Case managers report struggles to find physicians who would serve new patients with Medicaid funding. Some families struggled to find a physician who would serve new patients with Medicaid funding. Transportation was especially difficult for individuals who lived with elderly parents, those who did not like to ride in a car, and those who lived alone in places with poor public transportation. Physical access barriers included the door at the entrance of the building, rooms too small to accommodate wheelchairs, lack of convenient parking, and examination tables too high for people in wheelchairs.

156

Roy et al. 1997	Registry	Screen or record	PAS-ADD	Referrals were made for 42 people screened as having some psychiatric disorder but no contact with any related specialist service but none followed through because they reported it was an inappropriate referral, caregivers were unprepared, or there were delays in the referral being made.
Thomas & Payne, 1998	Survey	Individual	Home health patient classification system —ratings by nurses	Individuals under 20 yrs old were significantly more likely to have an unmet need. Among 2013 individuals receiving home health care services, factors associated with increased unmet needs included: being on Medicaid and receiving maternal/child health services, having an acute condition, being visited for an admission visit, and belonging to an HMO.

ICF; intermediate care facility; HCBS, home and community based services; MR, mental retardation

TABLE 7-4 Access to Dental Care Summary of Evidence and Research Design

AUTHORS	RESEARCH DESIGN	DATA SOURCE	MEASURES USED	RESULTS
Preventive Care				
Bradley et al., 2000	Survey	Individuals	Core indicators survey	74% of adults had had a dental exam in the previous 6 months. Individuals living in community residences or specialized facilities were the most likely to have had a recent dental visit.
Conroy, et al. 1998	Longitudinal study	Individuals	Personal life quality protocol	Individuals in supported living settings averaged two dental visits per year; other movers averaged 1 visit per year (this is not a significant difference because the sample sizes were very different for the two groups). There were no differences for ICF/MR residents compared with HCBS Waiver recipients in the number of dentist visits.
Conroy et al., 1995	Longitudinal study	Individuals	Survey	Institution residents saw the dentist an average of 3.7 times per year compared to 2.1 times per year for community dwelling residents.
Cumella et al., 2000	Registry	Screen or record	Oral exams surveys	Identification of dental problems tended to be based on presence of pain and unattractive teeth. Incidence of caries and gingivitis was higher than in general population.
Feldman et al., 1997	Convenience sample	Screen or record	Oral exam	5% of the participants reported difficulties seeking dental care. 70% had been to the DDS in the previous year. High levels of gingivitis and low levels of sealants suggested preventive care should be improved. 13% of subjects needed urgent dental care and 30% hadn't seen the DDS in over a year.
Hanson et al., 2003	Survey (National Household—random digit dialing)	Individual	Telephone survey	41% of working age adults with disabilities had had a dental exam in the past year.
Hewitt et al., 2000	Survey and interview	Individuals	Consumer interview	Overall, 89% of adults had been to the dentist within the previous 6 mo.
Hewitt et al., 2000	Survey and Interview	Individuals	Individual case manager survey, general case manager survey	11.5% of case managers reported that they had some or much difficulty finding dental services for a specific sampled person with ID (more than for any of the other 14 services).
National Association of State Directors of Developmental Disabilities Services, 2000	Survey	Individuals	National core indicators survey	45% had not had a dental exam in the previous 6 mo.

National Association of State Directors of Developmental Disabilities Services, 2003	Survey	Individuals	National core indicators survey	31% had not had a dental exam in the previous 6 mo.
Paxton & Taylor, 1998	Registry, chart review, and interview/health assessment	Screen or record	Health assessments—three categories, no abnormality detected, "known" problem, "new" problem	Only 1 of 71 individuals with I/DD had not had a dental check within the past 6 mo.
Access to Dentist				
Allison et al., 2000	Cross-sectional survey of a convenience sample	Individuals	Oral assessment—Down syndrome Questionnaire	Parents of children with DS reported that it was twice as often more difficult to find dental care than medical care for their children without DS.
Cumella et al., 2000	Registry	Screen or record	Oral exams surveys	A few caregivers (four) reported that it was difficult to access a DDS.
Hewitt et al., 2000	Survey and interview	Individuals	Individual case manager survey, general case manager survey	Dental services were more difficult to find than case management, day training and habilitation, health care, supported employment, recreation activities, and facility-based residential and in-home residential services. 11.5% of case managers reported that they had some or much difficulty finding dental services for a specific sampled person with ID (more than for any of the other 14 services).
Schultz et al., 2001	NHIS survey	Individuals	1997 NHIS questions related to dental care	About half of children with DD do not have regular access to dental health care. Children with DD more likely to have seen or have consulted a DDS in last 6 mo (80% vs. 71%). 3% of children with DD and 51% of children without had seen or talked to DDS in last 6 mo. 11% had never had contact with a DDS (DD children vs. 15% for children without DD) compared with fewer than .5% who had never seen a physician.
Quality of Care				
Conroy et al., 1998	Longitudinal study	Individuals	Personal life quality protocol	Community-dwelling individuals reported significant improvements in the quality of dental care in the previous year (from 3.9 to 4.2 on a five-point scale).

(continued)

159

TABLE 7-4 *Continued*

AUTHORS	RESEARCH DESIGN	DATA SOURCE	MEASURES USED	RESULTS
Hewitt et al., 2000	Survey and interview	Individuals	Individual case manager survey, general case manager survey	Overall quality of dental care services was rated 2.86 on a four-point scale (between fair and good). 21% of case managers reported that dental care services received by the designated individual were excellent, 63% said good, 14% said adequate, and 2% said poor. Quality of dental care did not vary by age, level of mental retardation, level of challenging behavior, or region of the state.
Reichard et al., 2001	Survey, focus groups	Individuals	Survey, focus groups	Case managers reported that DDS did not communicate directly with people with ID (29%) nor did they allow adequate time for communication (34%). 26% of case managers reported that DDS did not use accommodations such as American Sign Language (ASL) interpreters. 17% of families thought that DDS's communication was poor or very poor. 46% of case managers and 24% of families thought that DDS were not adequately trained to work with people with ID. 34% of case managers reported that dealing with the extraordinary needs of people with ID (e.g., sedation) was poor or very poor.
Unmet Needs				
Feldman et al., 1997	Convenience sample	Screen or record	Oral exam	13% of subjects needed urgent dental care and 30% hadn't seen the DDS in over a year.
White et al., 1998	Convenience sample	Screen or record	Oral health screening	12% of children (9–20) and 7% of adults (20–49) had urgent dental treatment needs. (Twenty-year-olds were included in both groups for analysis.)
Barriers to Dental Care				
Cumella et al., 2000	Registry	Screen or record	Oral exams Surveys	People with ID tended not to go to DDS because of experiences with pain or because of fear. Caregivers were untrained in oral health care.
Hewitt et al., 2000	Survey and interview	Individuals	Consumer interview	People with less severe MR and less challenging behavior were more likely to have seen the dentist. The likelihood also varied by type of setting and region of the state.

Study	Method	Unit	Measure	Findings
Hewitt et al., 2000	Survey and interview	Individuals	Individual case manager survey, general case manager survey	Case manager assessments of the quality of dental care were lower for people living with a family member (rather than in a small group home), lower for people who used a wheelchair, higher for people who were white, and higher for people who needed on-call medical services. Case managers in smaller urban communities reported more difficulty finding dental services than those in large urban communities and those in rural communities.
Perry et al., 2003	Focus groups (12 total)	Individual	Focus group	Parents reported difficulty finding a provider who would accept their coverage. Most report their dental coverage is inadequate. Those with dental benefits claim only minimal services are covered. Several participants have found it challenging to find a dentist who accepts Medicaid payment.
Reichard et al., 2001	Survey, focus groups	Individuals	Survey, focus groups	93% of case managers reported funding as the largest barrier to dental care. Both families and case managers report that availability of DDS is a concern in both urban and rural areas. Availability both in terms of numbers of providers as well as the ease in making appointments with providers were concerns for both case managers and families. 33% of DDS reported barriers to care for people with I/DD that included remuneration from Medicaid, their own lack of knowledge and training, patient resistance to treatment, and structural barriers (e.g., small exam rooms). A small number reported difficulties maintaining insurance and hospital privileges that allowed them to do the extraordinary care for people with ID as a barrier.
Schultz et al., 2001	NHIS survey	Individuals	1997 NHIS questions related to dental care	22% of children with Down syndrome and 10% with MR and autism had not received DDS services because of cost considerations. Children with DD in poorest families twice as likely to not have received DDS care. Lack of access to DDS services for children with DD worsens as the socioeconomic of the family decreases. Children with DD are less likely to have received dental care at all income levels except upper middle class. Children with DD more likely to have seen or have consulted a DDS in the last 6 mo than children without DD (80% vs. 71%).
Vignehsa et al., 1991	Representative sample	Screen or record	Oral health screening	Overall, children with disabilities were found to have poorer dental health status than children without disabilities. Children with intellectual disabilities and multiple disabilities had more dental health problems than other disability groups.

care records revealed most adults with I/DD had not had routine vision or hearing screenings as adults (McCulloch, Sludden, McKeown, & Kerr, 1996; Paxton & Taylor, 1998). One study corroborated the survey research findings that people with I/DD had not received recommended preventive screenings such as blood pressure checks, immunizations, or mammograms. One study reported that children with I/DD who were at nutritional risk were not referred for needed services (Lee, Freeman, Cialone, & Lichtenwalter, 1993).

ACCESS TO MEDICAL CARE

The second set of studies examined access to ongoing medical care. These studies reported that a substantial minority (typically between 20% and 30%) of adults with I/DD had difficulty finding a doctor who understood their conditions and had difficulties accessing specialists. One study reported that people moving from institutions reported no change or improved access to medical services over time (Brown & Bretting, 1998). Another study reported that people in institutions were more likely to say it is very easy to get medical care than people who had moved to community settings (Conroy, 1996). Studies that compared Intermediate Care Facility-Mental Retardation (ICF-MR) and Home and Community-Based Waiver settings found no significant differences in access to health care (Conroy, Seiders, & Yuskauskas, 1998; Hewitt et al., 2000). Whereas 70% of parents with children with I/DD reported there were enough physicians to serve people with I/DD (Reichard & Turnbull, 2004), studies of people with I/DD living independently reported they had substantial difficulty locating appropriate care (e.g., Edgerton et al., 1994).

ACCESS TO INSURANCE

The third set of studies examined access to health care insurance. Most studies reported similar rates of access to health care insurance for people with and without I/DD. The key differences were that people with I/DD were much more likely to receive publicly funded health care through programs such as Medicaid and much less likely to receive private health care such as through Health Maintenance Organizations (Anderson, Larson, Lakin, & Kwak, 2003; Kaye, 2001; Larson et al., 2001; National Organization on Disability, 2000). But whether a person had insurance was only part of the story. These studies also reported that even those who had insurance had serious difficulties in paying for various types of medical services using their insurance (e.g., Hanson et al., 2003). Others reported that uninsured children and children with public insurance were more likely to have special needs not covered by their health insurance (National Organization on Disability, 2000).

SATISFACTION WITH HEALTH CARE

The fourth set of studies reported on satisfaction with the quality of health care. Most of those studies reported satisfaction levels of between 70% and 85%. One study reported that people with I/DD were more likely than people without I/DD to be dissatisfied with their health care. Despite overall satisfaction with health care, people with I/DD were more likely to be dissatisfied with their care than were people without I/DD (National Organization on Disability, 2000). Specific areas of dissatisfaction included physician communication, knowledge of general practitioners (GPs), inaccessibility, and rudeness (e.g., Martin, Roy, & Wells, 1997).

In a national study, level of satisfaction with primary health care for adults with I/DD and adults with other significant functional limitations were not statistically different once age, gender, economic status, race, health status, and health coverage were considered. The percentage of adults with I/DD who said their primary health care services were excellent (as opposed to good, fair, or poor) was 48% for respect and privacy, 46% for the doctor's interest in the person and their condition, 43% for thoroughness of the exam, 41% for availability of transportation to the clinic, 40% for availability of the physician in an emergency, 35% for ability to get answers to medical questions over the phone, 29% for time waiting for an appointment, and 26% for time waiting to see doctor (Anderson, Larson, Lakin, & Kwak, 2003).

CHANGES ASSOCIATED WITH DEINSTITUTIONALIZATION

Studies of deinstitutionalization address some of the systemic challenges of accessing adequate health care as people have moved from institutions to the community. Some studies of people with I/DD and/or their families and caregivers reported that on leaving institutions to live in the community, in general, it was more difficult to obtain health care and fewer were able to identify a primary care physician (Conroy, 1995; Conroy, Seiders, Jones, & Thomas, 1995). Conversely, others reported that community care was easy to get, that medical care was better in the community, and their access to specialty care was better or no worse than in the institution and that their general health had improved (Brown & Bretting, 1999; Conroy, 1996; Conroy, Seiders, & Yuskauskas, 1998). These findings were particularly true the longer individuals had lived in the community. Family members and caregivers of people with I/DD moving from institutions to the community reported increased levels of satisfaction with care (Conroy, Lemanowicz, Feinstein, & Bernotsky, 1991). People living in the community, people moving from institutions, as well as those remaining in institutions also reported that their health care providers' level of knowledge was good, that the length of time health care providers spent with them was adequate, and they had good knowledge of I/DD (Anderson et al., 2003; Brown & Bretting, 1998; Conroy, Seiders, Jones, & Thomas, 1995; Fortune, 1996; Hewitt et al., 2000; Neri, Beatty, & Dhont, 2001).

QUALITY OF HEALTH CARE

Studies on the quality of health care reported several different types of findings. The two studies that examined charts or did clinical assessments reported several findings suggesting that the quality of health care needed improvement. Specifically, a review of 137 charts for children with special needs lacked biochemical data (84%), feeding information (44%), and height and weight data (25%) (Lee et al., 1993). A study using clinical exams reported a pattern of lack of medical follow-up for a variety of diseases (Paxton & Taylor, 1998). In another study, 12% of case managers reported that the overall quality of health care services for specific individuals was fair or poor (Hewitt, Larson, & Lakin, 2000). In a study of families and case managers, most reported that physicians were effective in handling ordinary health maintenance, meeting extraordinary health challenges, making necessary but special accommodations, and having offices that were accessible and in close proximity (Reichard & Turnbull, 2004). A substantial minority of case managers, however, reported that physicians communicated poorly or very poorly with individuals with I/DD (40%), were poor at making accommodations for communication when necessary (41%), and were poor at providing emergency care (22%). Similarly, 26% of families reported that physicians did not allow extra time to compensate for communication barriers.

Factors Associated with Quality of Health Care

Among studies that identified factors associated with poorer or better quality of health care, some reported no differences based on type of I/DD (Anderson et al., 2003) or type of residence (institution vs. community residential settings) (Conroy, 1996). Other studies did find differences. For example, studies by Brown and Bretting (1998, 1999) reported that overall health and quality of medical services improved over time but that knowledge of caregivers regarding health care needs declined. Another study found that working age adults with I/DD on Medicaid only (40%) or who were uninsured (43%) were less likely to rate the quality of health care as excellent than those with private coverage (54%) or Medicare only (49%) (Kaye, 2001). A study of residents of licensed facilities reported that the quality of health care was higher for care provided in medical offices than when provided in clinic settings (Noll & Deschenes-Desmond, 1993).

UNMET HEALTH NEEDS

Fifteen of the medical care studies reported unmet health needs of people with I/DD. Studies reported lack of preventive care for women such as Pap smears and mammograms, the lack of preventive care for men such as prostate exams, and the general lack of preventive care for people with I/DD such as immunizations and health screenings (Broughton & Thomson, 2000; Davies & Duff, 2001; Edgerton, Gaston, Kelly, & Ward, 1994; Hanson, Neuman, & Voris, 2003; Hewitt, Larson, & Lakin, 2000; Kopac, Fritz, & Holt, 1998; Larson, Lakin, & Huang, 2003; Lewis et al., 2002; National Association of State Directors of Developmental Disabilities Services [NASDDS] and Human Resources Research Institute, 2000; Paxton & Taylor, 1998). Unmet nutritional needs, mental health care needs, adaptive and assistive equipment, prescription drug needs, and needed eyeglasses and vision care were also reported (Anderson et al., 2003; Cumella, Ransford, Lyons, & Burnham, 2000; Feldman et al., 1997; Jaskulski, Metzler, & Zierman, 1990; Kaye, 2001; Kennedy & Erb, 2002; Kerr et al., 2003; Krauss, Gulley, Sciegaj, & Wells, 2003; Lee, Freeman, Cialone, & Lichtenwalter, 1993; McCulloch, Sludden, McKeown, & Kerr, 1996; Newacheck, McManus, Fox, Hung, & Halfon, 2000; Paxton & Taylor, 1998; Roy, Martin, & Wells, 1997; Thomas & Payne, 1998; Vignehsa, Soh, Lo, & Chellappah, 1991; White, Beltran, Malvitz, & Perlman, 1998).

Several studies reported higher rates of unmet needs for individuals with I/DD than for the general population (Anderson et al., 2003; Kaye, 2001; Kim & Cooker, 2001; National Organization on Disability, 2000) or individuals with other types of disabilities (Larson et al., 2003). One qualitative study found that participants with I/DD living independently had not received cancer screenings despite having had regular medical visits (Edgerton et al., 1994).

Studies in the United Kingdom and Australia in which the researchers examined people with I/DD frequently found undiagnosed/untreated conditions such as cataracts, mental health disorders, seizure disorders, vision and hearing loss, diseases of the teeth and gums, and numerous other diseases (Cumella et al., 2000; Feldman et al., 1997; Kerr et al., 2003; McCulloch et al., 1996; Paxton & Taylor, 1998; Roy et al., 1997). One Australian study reported 1103 health impairments in 202 people including 42% that had not been previously diagnosed and 51% that were not adequately managed (Beange, McElduff, & Baker, 1995). Only one U.S. clinical study on preventive care focused on obesity, vaccinations, and OB/GYN (Lewis et al., 2002).

HEALTH CARE BARRIERS

Study participants identified several types of health care barriers including individual barriers, systemic barriers, and financial barriers. People with I/DD or their caregivers often reported challenges finding health care providers willing to take patients with I/DD or accessing the health care system (Allan, 1997; Allison, Hennequin, & Faulks, 2000; Cumella, Ransford, Lyons, & Burnham, 2000; Feldman et al., 1997; White, Beltran, Malvitz, & Perlman, 1998). In one study, family members reported that the lack of knowledge on the part of the health care provider regarding other services and medications was a problem. Participants in another study reported that once a need was identified, accessing care was not a problem (Paxton & Taylor, 1998). The main concern was unidentified needs.

Individual Barriers

Barriers to appropriate health care on the individual level included fear of specific procedures (i.e., pelvic exams and Pap smears) (Broughton & Thomson, 2000; Kopac et al., 1998) and general fear of seeing a provider for care (Lennox, Diggens, & Ugoni, 1997). Communication was also a problem for individuals who were unable to provide health histories, understand medical terms, and had difficulties following the directions of the health care providers (Lennox et al., 1997; Martin et al., 1997; Muir & Ogden, 2001; Paxton & Taylor, 1998; Roy et al., 1997). People with I/DD often demonstrated a lack of knowledge about basic health and prevention activities (such as the association between diet or smoking and health), which in turn limited their ability to seek appropriate health care (Edgerton et al., 1994). One study reported that family perceptions of sexual health needs were a barrier to some getting needed health care (Kopac et al., 1998). Certain demographic characteristics were associated with lack of access to care, including minority status and children living only with their mother or with someone other than a parent.

Systemic Barriers

Systemic barriers to health care for people with I/DD included difficulties accessing specialty care or getting needed referrals. Finding health care providers who were experienced and skilled in meeting their particular health care needs was also a barrier (Noll & Deschenes-Desmond, 1993). Lack of coordination of care, continuity of care, and consistency of care were all reported as concerns for people with I/DD. Systemic health care barriers also included barriers that prevented people with I/DD from accessing health care regardless of the presence or lack of other types of barriers (e.g., financial, willing provider, individual recognition of need for care). These barriers included lack of transportation or inconvenient parking, physical access barriers such as treatment rooms that were too small, examination tables that were too high, and/or inaccessible offices and clinics (Anderson et al., 2003; Noll & Deschenes-Desmond, 1993). Other systemic barriers included support staff issues (turnover for caregivers, familiarity with the person, follow up or lack thereof), lack of care in rural areas and waiting lists to see health care providers (Jaskulski et al., 1990; Noll & Deschenes-Desmond, 1993; Perry, Dulio, & Hanson, 2003; Reichard & Turnbull, 2004).

Financial Barriers

Financial barriers were also cited as reasons individuals did not access needed health care. Individuals with I/DD cited costs as a factor in delaying or not accessing care (Hanson et al., 2003; National Organization on Disability, 2000; Newacheck et al., 2000). In addition, type of insurance (public vs. private) and lack of insurance were factors in unmet health care needs in the United States (Hanson, Neuman, Dutwin, & Kasper, 2003; Hanson et al., 2003; Kaye, 2001; Krauss et al., 2003; Newachek et al., 2000; Perry et al., 2003). People with I/DD report that obtaining health insurance can be difficult because the cost of premiums is too high or because of preexisting condition exclusions (Jaskulski et al., 1990; Kaye, 2001).

ACCESS TO DENTAL CARE

Ten articles discussed preventive care for people with I/DD, one reported on access to general dental care, three discussed quality of care, four covered unmet needs, and six reported on barriers to dental care (see Table 7-4).

Access to Preventive Dental Care

The proportion of individuals with I/DD reported to have seen a dentist in the most recent 6 months ranged from 55% to 99% across the studies. One study reported that 70% of people with I/DD who were directly screened had seen a dentist in the prior year (Feldman et al., 1997). That study reported high levels of gingivitis and low levels of sealants, suggesting that preventive care should be improved. A study of people with all types of disabilities found that 41% of working age individuals with disabilities had a dental exam in the previous year (Hanson et al., 2003).

Access to Dentists

Four studies examined access to dentists. Two of those studies were of children. One study found that parents had more difficulty finding dentists for children with Down syndrome than for their children without I/DD (Allison et al., 2000). The other study reported that half of children with I/DD do not have regular access to dental services, with 3% of children with I/DD reporting they had seen a dentist in the past 6 months compared with 51% of children without I/DD (Schultz, Shenkin, & Horowitz, 2001). Case managers reported that dental services were more difficult to find than many other types of services for community-dwelling individuals with I/DD (Hewitt et al., 2000).

QUALITY OF DENTAL CARE

Overall, 21% of case managers rated dental care for individuals with I/DD receiving services funded by the Medicaid Home and Community Based Waiver Program as excellent; 63% reported it was good (Hewitt et al., 2000). Surveys and focus groups with case managers and families revealed that the quality of dental care for persons with I/DD was reduced because of poor communication and limited skills of dentists in working with people with I/DD (Reichard, Turnbull, & Turnbull, 2001). In a longitudinal study, community-dwelling individuals with I/DD reported the quality of dental care improved over time (Conroy et al., 1998).

UNMET DENTAL CARE NEEDS

Two studies that did clinical dental exams found several unmet dental needs. One reported that 13% of those examined had urgent needs for dental care (Feldman et al., 1997). The other reported that 12% of children and 7% of adults had urgent dental treatment needs (White et al., 1998).

BARRIERS TO DENTAL CARE

Studies of dental care reported that key barriers or factors associated with poorer dental care included having disabilities, having more severe disabilities, having more challenging behavior, living with family members, wheelchair use, and a non-European or American background. Lack of insurance coverage for dental care and lack of funding for dental services were reported to be major barriers. Individual barriers such as fear or pain were mentioned as problems in two studies (Cumella et al., 2000; Reichard, Turnbull, & Turnbull, 2001). As with barriers to medical care, dentists reported structural barriers (e.g., small exam rooms).

STUDIES OF HEALTH AND DENTAL CARE PROVIDERS

Table 7-5 summarizes studies of providers of health and dental care providers. This table includes information on research design, measures used in the study, and

TABLE 7-5 *Studies of Health Care Providers: Summary of Evidence and Research Design*

AUTHORS	RESEARCH DESIGN	MEASURES USED	RESULTS
Cook & Lennox, 2000	Survey	GP survey	70% of community nurses did not know if there were unmet health care needs for patients with DD. Nurses reported that caring for patients with DD was challenging because of communication problems, particularly with history-taking. 90% found it harder to provide care to people with ID. Communication difficulties with patients as well as with other health care providers made it difficult. 94% believed further education would improve health care. 44% reported that continuity of care is a problem and establishing doctor–patient relationships was difficult. About half reported remuneration was inadequate for level of care required and 85% reported that communication with other professionals was a problem.
Dovey & Webb, 2000	Survey	Survey	42% agreed (rather than remained neutral or disagreed) that including patients with an ID makes more demands on a GPs time than the average patient.
Ferguson et al., 1991	Survey	Survey	Of those who provided dental care to people with ID, 91% said training through the dental care for the developmentally disabled program helped a great deal or somewhat compared with 61% of dentists who had gone through the program who were not providing dental care for people with ID.
Hewitt et al., 2000	Survey and interview	Direct support professional survey	7.3% of DSPs reported not being proficient in medication administration, 7.8% were not proficient in CPR, 6.9% were not proficient in first aid, 6.9% were not proficient in health issues, and 21% were not proficient in identifying when a person needed medical supports.
Lennox & Chaplin, 1995	Survey	NA	93% reported difficulties working with community caregivers, leading most (81%) to agree that antipsychotics were prescribed for this reason and 75% to agree that antipsychotics were overused to control aggressive behavior. Most felt inadequately trained to work with people with ID and the people with ID receive relatively poor standards of care. Nearly a third of psychiatrists and trainees would not want to provide services to people with ID. Most report that the current system is inadequate to meet the needs of people with dual diagnoses and that better care would be given with an emphasis on specialization for psychiatric care for people with ID.

Citation			
Lennox et al. 1997	Survey	NA	Main barriers to care include communication–both understanding and obtaining information, poor patient comprehension, lack of compliance, lack of knowledge related to conditions common in ID, and lack of time. Insufficient funding, poor care coordination, poor continuity of care, patient fear, and lack of cooperation for exams were also mentioned. Solutions included better training and education, increased consultation times, and more involvement of family and caregivers in consultation. Better documentation at residential facilities was needed.
Muir & Ogden, 2001	Purposeful sample interviews, critical incident technique	NA	Factors related to helping or hindering care included patient characteristics (appearance, caregivers, speech or mental impairments, etc.), aspects of the doctor (level of knowledge, time pressure, perception of role, perception of patient, emotional reactions), and historical context (prior experiences of doctor and patient and caregiver). Better training is needed for doctors to further understand disability and to increase ability to communicate with people with ID and their caregivers.
Noll & Deschenes-Desmond, 1993	Random sample of physicians and dentists serving DMR clients	Practitioner survey	Reported the percentage who said each item was an important or very important challenge to community medical or dental services. For reimbursement, 58% said the issue was important; administrative issues such as DNR policies, 60%; transportation causing missed appointments, 40%; patient needs (e.g., special scheduling, extra treatment time, extra support), 36%; medical information (e.g., individual able to provide information, current health information available), 59%; support staff issues (familiarity with person and needs, follow-up), 55%; previous experience and training for medical provider, 30%. Top barriers rated by physicians: reimbursement (especially inadequate reimbursement rates), administrative issues (paperwork and documentation), and support staff issues (lack of familiarity with the person). 49% of physicians reported they needed future education in issues of mental retardation (e.g., on psychiatric and behavioral interventions, end of life issues, types and availability of ancillary services.
Powrie, 2003	Survey	Survey of nurses	Nurses want better training about disabilities. Nurses want more effective communication and cooperation between caregivers and medical personnel, which would improve health care for people with ID. Places to provide care should be extended since so many people living at home/with families are isolated. Difficulties providing health promotion because of time constraints/level of disability.

(continued)

TABLE 7-5 *Continued*

AUTHORS	RESEARCH DESIGN	MEASURES USED	RESULTS
Reichard & Turnbull, 2004	Survey	Survey	Physicians reported that treatment barriers included lack of training on ID (37%), lack of exposure to people with ID (32%), and Medicaid reimbursement policies (63%). 13% reported being generally uncomfortable working with people with ID. 17% believed there were not enough primary care physicians to meet the needs of people with ID. Barriers identified in focus groups included insufficient time, and insufficient follow-up through community coordinators. Physicians with limited training or experience in developmental medicine reported not being proactive soon enough to get interventions started when indicated. Those physicians also did not refer parents appropriately and may have not understood important needed services. Physicians reported there were too few developmental specialists. Waiting lists to see the physician, poor reimbursement, and funding for families for preventive care were also noted as barriers.
Reichard et al., 2001	Survey, focus groups	Survey	33% of DDS reported barriers to care for people with ID that included remuneration from Medicaid, their own lack of knowledge and training, patient resistance to treatment, and structural barriers (e.g., small exam rooms). A small number reported difficulties maintaining insurance and hospital privileges that allowed them to do the extraordinary care for people with ID as a barrier. 14% of DDS reported feeling uneasy providing care to people with ID.
Russell & Kinirons, 1993	Health board/registry for DDS	Survey	DDS reported their lack of experience and knowledge as the largest barriers to providing care. DDS perceived greater difficulty treating ID or medically compromised individuals than individuals with other disabilities.
Sparks et al., 2000	Survey		Better training is needed for aging caregivers, geriatric and DD service agencies, and the medical system about needs of aging and people with DD. Although respondents expressed concern about medical needs, they are very similar to the general aging population.
Stein, 2000	Survey	Mail survey	Fewer than half of the respondents reported screening for hypothyroidism in persons with Down syndrome. The GPs were asked if they would be prepared to offer annual assessments to people with ID on their list. 7% said they already do so, 27% that they are prepared to do so in the future, 12% that they would not but another member of the practice would, and 44% that they would not be willing to offer annual assessments, nor would any members of the practice team. 54% said they would offer a woman ages 20–64 a Pap smear if she had not had one in the

		past, 4% were unsure, and 42% said depending on the circumstances (sexual activity).
		The percentage who strongly agreed or partly agreed with the following statements were: people with ID consult the clinic more often than the general population, 44.7%; people with ID request more home visits than the general population, 46.8%; people with ID request more inappropriate home visits than the general population, 36.2%; special knowledge and skills are required to meet the needs of people with ID, 18.8%; and GPs do not see enough people with ID to justify going to a training course, 52.1%; all aspects of care for people with ID should be met by professionals working with learning disability services, 29.7%; GPs should meet the primary health care needs of people with ID as part of general medical services, 61.7%.
Thornton, 1996	Focus groups	NA — Health care providers identified shortfalls in time, remuneration, and expertise as significant problems in providing health care to people with ID. Concerns about the effects of large numbers of people with ID on the rest of the practice were expressed owing to increased need for services/care of people with ID.
Tyler et al., 1999	Population survey	Survey — 60% of the programs indicated that their residents are specifically instructed about health care issues related to adults with ID. Directors of residency programs whose trainees cared for adults with mental retardation in their own residency-based clinics and hospital in-patient services were more likely to view education about this population as valuable.
Walsh et al., 2000	Stratified random sample mail survey	Mail survey — Among nurses who encountered people with ID, 27% were very comfortable, 56% were somewhat comfortable, 14% were not too comfortable, and 1% were not at all comfortable in dealing with people with ID. Among the nurses, 10% received a great deal of education in developmental disabilities, while 59% received little or no preemployment training in supporting individuals with ID. Nurses reported having had the following experiences in their pre-service education: visited inclusive or community programs for people with ID, 49%; completed a rotation in a general health care setting that served people with ID, 39%; completed a rotation in a specialty health care setting treating people with ID, 36%; visited the home of a person with a disability, 17%; attended meetings or conferences of disability organizations, 17%; worked with a mentor with special training or experience in ID,13%. Fewer than 5% reported receiving continuing education unit (CEU) or in-service training since licensure, while between 6% and 29% had participated in DD specific learning as part of their orientation in their current job setting (most commonly self-study materials on DD).

171

findings. The findings describe barriers to health and dental care for people with I/DD from the provider point of view.

Barriers to Providing Medical or Dental Care

Providers reported a number of barriers to providing care to people with I/DD. Communication was a significant barrier. Health care providers reported two main areas in which communication proved especially challenging with this population. The first was the inability of the health care provider to communicate with people with I/DD (Cook & Lennox, 2000; Lennox et al., 1997; Muir & Ogden, 2001). This barrier is not a surprise considering the finding from the National Health Interview Survey on Disability that 38.3% of people with I/DD have substantial functional limitations in language or communication (Larson et al., 2001). Communication was also reported to be troublesome between providers and other professionals, including community care givers (paid staff or family members) (Cook & Lennox, 2000; Paxton & Taylor, 1998; Perry et al., 2003; Powrie, 2003). Health care providers believed that this not only made it more difficult for them to provide appropriate care, but that it also hindered the continuity of care for people with I/DD.

A second barrier identified by providers was lack of knowledge and training on their part. Many providers did not believe that they had the expertise to provide adequate care and were therefore uncomfortable doing so (Lennox & Chaplin, 1995). In one study of psychiatrists, nearly a third reported that they would not provide mental health services to people with I/DD because of lack of training and knowledge or general discomfort working with the population (Lennox & Chaplin, 1995). One survey of dentists had similar findings in that dentists did not believe that they had adequate knowledge and expertise to treat people with I/DD and therefore perceived greater difficulties in treating these patients (Russell & Kinirons, 1993). A minority of direct support professionals also reported a lack of proficiency in caring for specific medical needs. For example, 21% reported they were not proficient in identifying when a person needed medical supports (Hewitt et al., 2000).

Health care providers also identified a variety of other barriers. Providers reported that it often took longer per appointment for individuals with I/DD and therefore they were unable to provide adequate care because of time constraints (Lennox et al., 1997; Martin et al., 1997; Thornton, 1996). Health care providers, regardless of the country in which they practiced, reported that remuneration for people with I/DD was not adequate for the needs and length of time needed to accommodate people with I/DD at their appointments (Cook & Lennox, 2000; Hanson, Neuman, Dutwin, & Kasper, 2003; Lennox, Diggens, & Ugoni, 1997; Martin, Roy, & Wells, 1997; Thornton, 1996). Other barriers reported included transportation for individuals, administrative paperwork and documentation barriers, and skill deficits for community care givers leading to overuse of antipsychotic medication.

Needed Changes

Providers suggested several solutions to the barriers presented to people with I/DD when accessing health care.

TRAINING Providers and recipients of health care and their caregivers believed that medical care providers needed better training to be more knowledgeable about I/DD, to be able to work with people with I/DD, and to be more aware of services available to people with I/DD. Many providers thought that specialists in providing health care to people with I/DD would reduce some of the unmet health care needs.

IMPROVED COMMUNICATION Providers of medical care thought that improving communication systems and continuity of care would reduce barriers to accessing health care. This was particularly true in the area of obtaining health histories. Health care providers in countries in which registries are common believed that registries of people with I/DD that included pertinent medical information would decrease unmet health care needs. Another area in which improved communication is critical is from the community caregivers.

FINANCIAL Providers all believed that increased reimbursement for people with I/DD would decrease unmet health care needs. Much of this related to the amount of time a provider must spend with a person with I/DD, making them more expensive as a patient, as well as the needs for extra visits and support during those visits (e.g., the presence of a person to support the individual during the exam). Access to adequate health insurance proved to be an important barrier in the United States. Underinsured and uninsured people with disabilities all reported higher levels of unmet health care needs.

BARRIERS TO HEALTH CARE ACROSS STUDY TYPES AND RESPONDENTS

Table 7-6 summarizes the barriers to adequate health and dental care from all of the studies reviewed. Those barriers include demographic characteristics, communication and comprehension challenges, support staff and other care provider issues, knowledge and attitude barriers for health care providers, communication barriers, lack of time to meet the needs of patients with I/DD, difficulties accessing specialty care, lack of stability and consistency in care provision, financial barriers, and insurance barriers. Insurance barriers included lack of insurance, insufficient insurance coverage, physicians who would not accept Medicare, Medicaid or another type of insurance plan, and being turned down for insurance coverage or having insurance coverage restricted. Other types of barriers included transportation, physical accessibility, lack of care providers, waiting lists, and lack of information about health care.

CONSEQUENCES OF BARRIERS TO HEALTH CARE

The final table summarizes the many consequences or negative outcomes associated with problems in accessing health or dental care. Like Table 7-6, Table 7-7 pulls information from three of the earlier tables. People who did not have adequate access to medical or dental health care did not receive preventive care and screenings. The results included higher rates of obesity, unmanaged instances of underweight, and cancers that were not detected early. Individuals studied reported unmet needs in the areas of medical care, mental health, dental health, prescription medication, and

TABLE 7-6 *Barriers to Health Care for People with Disabilities*

Demographic Characteristics
Minority status was associated with not accessing care, as was children living with only their mother or
    with someone other than their parents.

Communication and Comprehension Challenges
Fear of specific procedures
Communication—ability to read/follow directions
Communication—ability to understand medical terminology
Speech impairments
Ability to give health histories, availability of current health information
Compliance with prescribed therapies or treatments
Difficulty understanding health issues
Difficulties recognizing need for medical care

Support Staff and Other Care Provider Issues
Family perceptions of sexual health needs of women with DD
DSPs reported not being proficient in medication administration, CPR, first aid, health issues, and in
    identifying when a person needed medical supports
Support staff issues: familiarity with person and needs, follow-up
Support staff lack of knowledge about health care needs
Psychiatrists and trainees reported difficulties working with community caregivers regarding
    psychotropic medications
Lack of training for caregivers to monitor health conditions and report needs to health providers

Knowledge and Attitude Barriers
Lack of knowledge and training about disabilities
Families and case managers said physicians had a poor or very poor knowledge of people with ID
GPs were asked if they would be prepared to offer annual assessment to people with ID on their list;
    7% said they already do so, 27% that they are prepared to do so in the future, 12% that they would not
    but another member of the practice would, and 44% that they would not be willing to offer annual
    assessment, nor would any members of the practice team
Physicians reported that lack of training on ID was a barrier
Physicians reported that lack of exposure to people with ID was a barrier
Not offering routine preventive screenings
Inadequate training on people with disabilities for health care providers
Emotional reactions, perception of the patient
Among nurses who encountered people with ID, 27% were very comfortable, 56% were somewhat
    comfortable, 14% were not too comfortable, and 1% were not at all comfortable in dealing with people
    with ID
Physicians reluctant or unwilling to treat people with ID/DD
Physicians did not know about other services and did not provide enough information about
    medications
General discomfort serving the population
Only 25% of physicians believed that the regular assessment of hearing and vision for people with DD is
    the responsibility of the GP
Case managers and families said that DDS were ineffective in dealing with extraordinary needs such as
    sedation, were not flexible in making unexpected accommodations, and had poor knowledge about
    people with ID

TABLE 7-6 *Continued*

Communication Barriers
Difficulties communicating with individuals with disabilities
Physicians often did not allow extra time to compensate for communication difficulties
Physicians were often poor at making accommodations for communication when necessary
Most nurses reported that communication with other professionals was a problem
Most community residents said their doctor always listened to them
Poor communication with/from caregivers
Physicians were rude, inaccessible, and lacked the needed information

Lack of Time to Meet Needs of Patients with ID
Special scheduling needs, extra treatment time, or extra support needs
Hospital staff were too busy and not experienced with people with ID
Most said the doctor always spends enough time with the person
Inadequate time with physician
Administrative barriers such as DNR policies

Difficulty Accessing Specialty Care
Difficulty finding skilled and experienced doctors
Difficulties with care coordination
One third of children with autism had difficulty accessing specialty care; one fifth of children with MR
Difficulty getting referrals
Mental health professionals place too much emphasis on medications

Stability and Consistency of Care
Turnover
99% of individuals in institutions could identify their primary care physician vs. 94% of individuals in
    community settings
Nearly half of nurses reported that a lack of continuity of care made establishing doctor–patient
    relationships difficult

Financial Barriers
Poverty level was associated with lack of access to care
Insufficient remuneration for providers
A majority of physicians reported that Medicaid reimbursement policies were a barrier
Costs of care for individuals
Difficulty finding dentists and prescription drugs because of cost
Above average costs for people with disabilities
Most case managers said funding was the biggest barrier to dental care

Insurance Barriers
Lack of insurance:
10% of people with ID/DD had no health insurance compared with 9% of people with disabilities other
    than IDD and 14% of people without disabilities
Children without health care coverage were the least likely to have seen a doctor or taken prescribed
    medication
17% of working age adults with disabilities lack health insurance
Eligibility barriers for Medicaid, other public insurance, and private insurance
High premiums for insurance for people with disabilities

(*continued*)

TABLE 7-6 *Continued*

Insufficient insurance coverage:
77% with no insurance reported they cannot afford the premiums
People with disabilities are four times more likely to have special needs not covered by insurance
   (28% vs. 7%)
Dental coverage is not comprehensive enough
Inadequate coverage for durable medical equipment

Physicians would not accept Medicare or Medicaid or other insurance plan:
Physicians would not accept new patients with Medicare or Medicaid
Red tape and low reimbursement rates for Medicaid
Administrative issues (paperwork and documentation)
Institutional bias in health care financing
37% of DDS reported that Medicaid offered insufficient remuneration

Turned down for insurance or had coverage restricted in last 2 yrs:
13% with private individual insurance
11% with no insurance
4% with public insurance
3.5% with private group plan

Other
Transportation causing missed appointments
Transportation was especially difficult for individuals who lived with elderly parents, those who did not
   like to ride in a car, and those who lived in places that lacked public transportation
Physical access barriers
Entrance doors not accessible
Exam rooms too small to accommodate wheelchairs
Lack of convenient parking
Examination tables too high for people using wheelchairs
Lack of health care in rural areas
Lack of access to preventive care
Lack of data on health care
Waiting lists to get in to see the doctor

equipment. Consequences of these unmet needs included poor health, poor dental health, going without needed medications, and doing without basic equipment such as eyeglasses. Finally, because of poor medical or dental care or lack of thorough screenings, several studies identified previously undiagnosed or untreated dental, mental health, or health conditions of varying levels of severity (ranging from lack of nutritional services to use of nontherapeutic dosages of medications, untreated cataracts, and untreated hearing loss).

Directions for Future Research and Practice

The studies reviewed here identify several key concerns for adequate access to health care for people with I/DD. While financial barriers and health care payment systems

TABLE 7-7 *Consequences of Barriers to Health Care*

Lack of Preventive Care and Screenings
- ➤ Cancer of the uterus, breast cancer
- ➤ People living on their own or with family members were more likely to be obese.

Unmet Medical Needs
- ➤ 37% postponed care because of cost.
- ➤ 5.6% delayed getting care because of cost.
- ➤ 4.6% with I/DD reported unmet health care needs vs. 2.2% for people with no disabilities.
- ➤ 1.4% did not get needed care because of cost.
- ➤ 19% of people with disabilities vs. 6% with no disabilities did not get needed care at least once last year.
- ➤ 3.2% had unmet medical needs.
- ➤ 48% of working age adults with disabilities had unmet needs vs. 20% for other adults.
- ➤ More than one half of people receiving home health care services had one or more unmet needs.
- ➤ People 20 years of age and younger were more likely to have unmet needs than older people receiving home health care.
- ➤ People with disabilities were more likely to postpone seeking needed care because of cost (28% vs. 12%).
- ➤ Physicians reported that they were not proactive enough in referring families to get interventions when indicated.

Unmet Mental Health Needs
- ➤ 1.2% had unmet mental health needs.
- ➤ 2.1% with I/DD had unmet mental health needs vs. 0.4% of people with no disabilities.
- ➤ 12% of working age adults had unmet mental health needs (27% of those without insurance; 7% with insurance).
- ➤ 8% of people with DD reported unmet mental health needs vs. 6% of the general population.
- ➤ 6.2% of adults with I/DD were waiting for mental health services vs. 2.9% of adults with no disabilities.

Unmet Dental Health Needs
- ➤ People with DD but not ID were more likely to have unmet dental needs (12% vs. 7% for people without disabilities).
- ➤ 18% needed dental care but did not receive it.
- ➤ 8.1% had unmet dental needs.
- ➤ 11.5% of case managers reported they had some or much difficulty finding dental services for a person with ID.
- ➤ 13% of subjects needed urgent dental care and 30% had not seen the DDS in more than a year.
- ➤ Overall, children with disabilities were found to have poorer dental health status than children without disabilities. Children with intellectual disabilities and multiple disabilities had more dental health problems than other disability groups.
- ➤ Identification of dental problems tended to be based on presence of pain and unattractive teeth. Incidence of caries and gingivitis was higher than in general population.

Unmet Prescription Medication Needs
- ➤ 36% skipped doses, split pills or did not fill a prescription.
- ➤ 36% spent less on basic needs for shelter and food to pay for prescriptions.
- ➤ 4.4% of adults with prescriptions failed to take them as prescribed because of cost.
- ➤ 8.7% of adults with prescriptions failed to take them because they forgot, side effects, perceived lack of need, or difficulty obtaining the medication.

(*continued*)

TABLE 7-7 *Continued*

Unmet Equipment Needs
➤ 4.1% had unmet needs for eye glasses or medications.
➤ 46% went without needed equipment (e.g., eyeglasses).
➤ 37% of those examined needed new eyeglasses; 14% needed further treatment.

Undiagnosed/Untreated Dental, Mental Health, and Health Conditions
➤ Children at risk nutritionally were not referred for appropriate services; nutrition risks were not monitored.
➤ Lack of follow-up for a variety of diseases—cardiovascular, cancer, testicular cancer
➤ A total of 1103 health impairments were identified in the 202 individuals. Of those, 42% had not previously been diagnosed, 51% were not adequately managed, and 26% required specialist care. 69% of individuals with hypertension had not been previously diagnosed. Adverse drug effects were present in 11% of the sample; 50% of drug levels tested were in the nontherapeutic range. In 15.5% of the sample, symptoms and signs such as abdominal pain, headache, and localized swelling had not been investigated or treated. The sample had a mean of 5.4 health impairments per person but 65% of the subjects reported no symptoms and 24% of caregivers said there were no problems.
➤ (1) Overlooked vision, hearing loss, and other health conditions discovered. (2) Unmet nutritional needs discovered. (3) Better caregiver training needed. (4) Access should include specialist services since so many conditions were overlooked. No subjects had a recent neurologic assessment despite a third having epilepsy. (5) Other unmet needs included untreated cataracts (28%), needed eyeglasses (21%), and needed hearing aids (14%).
➤ 12% of children (9–20) and 7% of adults (20–49) had urgent dental treatment needs.

Conclusions
➤ While people with I/DD were at least as likely as the general population to have health insurance, and while those receiving residential supports received routine physical exams (and immunizations), access to preventive cancer screenings for adults with I/DD lagged behind that for the general population.
➤ Type of setting matters. People living on their own or with family members were less likely to get routine physical and dental care than those in community, residential, or institutional settings.
➤ For dental care especially, type and severity of disability mattered (mobility limitation, challenging behavior, severe intellectual disability).
➤ The clinical studies made it clear that just visiting the doctor is not enough. Even those who went to the doctor had basic undiagnosed conditions and needs.
➤ Estimates of unmet needs varied widely depending on the group studied, the type of study (survey, longitudinal study, clinical exam), and the location (USA, Australia/New Zealand, Asia, UK, Canada).

are often blamed for the lack of access to health care for people with I/DD (especially for providers), the most frequently identified barriers related to attitudes and knowledge on the part of health care providers, caregivers, and people with I/DD. There are some specific things the health care system could do to improve access to people with I/DD that address the Surgeon General's concerns (see U.S. Public Health Service, 2002) as well as concerns of those both receiving and providing health care.

PRACTICE

Deinstitutionalization has caused a change in how people with I/DD receive health care, exacerbating systemic barriers and increasing systemic challenges to meeting health care needs of people with I/DD. Prior to deinstitutionalization, care was provided to the residents of state hospitals by on-site staff of these facilities. Community health care providers saw relatively few people with I/DD and they were relatively dispersed. As institutions have closed, the community health care system has had to provide care for a population with which it was relatively inexperienced and unprepared to serve.

Future efforts to address access to health care for people with I/DD should focus on three educational opportunities. The first is to teach health care literacy and advocacy to people with I/DD. People with I/DD should have at least basic information and understanding about the health care system, health care procedures, and identifying when they are in need of care. For example, Davies and Duff (2001) found women who had participated in mammography did not know why they were having the procedure. Beyond basic information, self-advocacy skills in relation to health care access should be taught so that people with I/DD can both understand their rights as consumers of health care and can assert those rights—that is, expecting health care information and explanation of medical orders in a format that is understandable.

The second educational opportunity is to provide this same type of instruction to caregivers. Since many people with I/DD depend on caregivers to be intermediaries with the health care system, caregivers must also be able to understand the health care system and health care procedures and have advocacy skills to ensure that the people for whom they are caring receive access to the appropriate medical care.

The third opportunity is for better training for health care providers about the needs of people with I/DD, both in terms of specific health care needs that may arise from the condition(s) as well as the accommodation needs people with I/DD have to adequately access the health care system. These range from improved communication practices to using alternative or augmentative communication formats to ensure people understand the health care directives given them.

Financial structures of the health care system undoubtedly play a role in the ability of people with I/DD to receive health care. Providers with remuneration insufficient to cover the basic costs of providing care are going to be less likely to provide that care and are certainly going to be less likely to provide the additional time it may take for a person with I/DD to communicate their health concerns and to fully understand any information and orders from the health care providers. Beange (1996) suggests that for people with I/DD to have access to health care they need interpreters and advocates, and more time and resources. One option might be the development of a "health care advocate," who would be able to bill for services at a rate lower than medical providers, and who would be charged with ensuring that people with I/DD (and other populations with access to health care challenges) fully understand diagnoses, procedures, and orders. It is possible that such a person would, in the end, save money for the health care system by increasing compliance which may in turn decrease further health problems.

RESEARCH

A better understanding of the barriers to health care access from the perspective of people with I/DD and their families is needed. Much of the current research describes the barriers from the providers' point of view. It may be that consumers of health care have a different view. More applied research is also needed. Education programs and alternative information delivery methods need to be put into practice and measured for their effectiveness in order to find the tools that are cost-effective and efficacious. Among the many studies reviewed for this chapter, relatively few were clinical studies of controlled samples. Most of those that were available had been conducted in Europe. Few of the studies examine health care needs in the context of other factors such as age, gender, ethnicity, and health status.

In addition to these specific types of research, federal and state health monitoring programs and surveys should increase their capability to identify and describe the health care needs of persons with I/DD. The National Health Inventory Survey-Disabilities (NHIS-D) provided a unique opportunity to look at these needs. Unfortunately it is now more than 10 years old and there are no plans to repeat it. To monitor the health status of community-dwelling children and adults with I/DD, a more proactive approach is needed.

Conclusions

The studies reviewed for this chapter reported a variety of gaps between what individuals with I/DD living in community settings needed and what they were able to get in terms of health and dental care. Among the challenges identified were a lack of preventive care and screenings (cancer, obesity for some groups of individuals with I/DD), unmet medical needs (reported as between 3.2% and more than 50% of participants across various studies), unmet mental health needs (1.2% to 27%), unmet dental health needs (8.1% to 18%), unmet prescription medication needs (4.4% to 36%), unmet equipment needs (4.1% to 46%), and undiagnosed/untreated dental, mental health, and health conditions.

The United States has been very successful in the past four decades in deinstitutionalizing its residential support system for persons with I/DD. However, the studies reviewed here clearly show that the system for providing community-based medical care has lagged behind in several areas. Full implementation of the New Freedom Initiative and the Olmstead decision, which focus on providing community supports for people with I/DD rather than nursing home or institutional services, will require continued changes and improvements in how medical and dental services are offered for people with I/DD. It is time to deinstitutionalize medical and dental care for persons with I/DD.

REFERENCES

Allan, E. (1997). A health clinic for people with learning disabilities. *Nursing Standard, 11*(30), 34–37.

Allison, J., Hennequin, M., & Faulks, D. (2000). Dental care access among individuals with Down syndrome in France. *Special Care in Dentistry, 20*(1), 28–34.

Anderson, L. L., Larson, S. A., Lakin, K. C., & Kwak, N. (2003). Health insurance coverage and health care experiences of persons with disabilities in the NHIS-D. *DD Data Brief, 5* (1). Minneapolis: University of Minnesota, Research and Training Center on Community Living.

Andersen, R., Rice, T., & Kominski, G. (1996). *Changing the US health care system: Key issues in health services, policy and management.* San Francisco: Jossey-Bass.

Beange, H. (1996). Caring for a vulnerable population: Who will take responsibility for those getting a raw deal for the health care system? *Medical Journal of Australia, 164,* 159–160.

Beange, H., McElduff, A., & Baker, W. (1995). Medical disorders of adults with mental retardation: A population study. *American Journal on Mental Retardation, 99,* 595–604.

Bradley, V. J., Taub, S., Chawla, D., Freedman, R., Chassier, D., & Little, F. (2000). *Evaluation of services and supports to people with mental retardation and their families in Massachusetts.* Boston: Human Services Research Institute.

Broughton, S., & Thomson, K. (2000). Women with learning disabilities: Risk behaviors and experiences of the cervical smear test. *Journal of Advanced Nursing, 32,* 905–912.

Brown, J. R., & Bretting, J. G. (1998). *The Jackson family survey: Final report on four years of research.* Albuquerque, NM: State of New Mexico Developmental Disabilities Planning Council.

Brown, J. R., & Bretting, J. G. (1999). *The Jackson longitudinal study: Findings of five years of research.* Albuquerque, NM: State of New Mexico Developmental Disabilities Planning Council.

Conroy, J. W. (1995). The people who moved from Hissom Memorial Center to community: Are they better off? *The Hissom outcomes study: A report on six years of movement into supported living, 1.* Ardmore, PA: Center for Outcome Analysis.

Conroy, J. W. (1996). *Qualities of life among Coffelt class members who moved from developmental centers to community homes, 1993–1995.* Ardmore, PA: Center for Outcome Analysis.

Conroy, J. W., Lemanowicz, J. A., Feinstein, C. S., & Bernotsky, J. M. (1991). 1990 result of the CARC v. Thorne longitudinal study. *Connecticut Applied Research Project, 10.* Narberth, PA: Conroy & Feinstein Associates.

Conroy, J. W., Seiders, J. X., Jones, J. C., & Thomas, D. (1995). *Longitudinal assessment of consumer satisfaction with health care services during deinstitutionalization of people with developmental disabilities.* Report No. 2. New York: Columbus Medical Services.

Conroy, J. W., Seiders, J. X., & Yuskauskas, A. (1998). *Patterns of community placement IV: The fourth annual report on the outcomes of implementing the Coffelt settlement agreement.* Bryn Mawr, PA: Center for Outcome Analysis.

Cook, A., & Lennox, N. (2000). General practice registrars' care of people with intellectual disabilities. *Journal of Intellectual and Developmental Disability, 25*(1), 69–77.

Cumella, S., Ransford, N., Lyons, J., & Burnham, H. (2000). Needs for oral care among people with intellectual disability not in contact with community dental services. *Journal of Intellectual Disability Research, 44*(1), 45–52.

Davies, N., & Duff, M. (2001). Breast cancer screening for older women with intellectual disability living in community group homes. *Journal of Intellectual Disability Research, 45,* 253–257.

Dovey, S., & Webb, O. (2000). General practitioners' perception of their role in care for people with intellectual disability. *Journal of Intellectual Disability Research, 44,* 553–561.

Edgerton, R. B., Gaston, M. A., Kelly, H., & Ward, T. W. (1994). Health care for aging people with mental retardation. *Mental Retardation, 32,* 146–159.

Feldman, C., Ginger, M., Sanders, M., Saporito, R., Zohn, K., & Perlman, S. (1997). Special Olympics, special smiles: Assessing the feasibility of epidemiological data collection. *Journal of the American Dental Association, 128,* 1687–1696.

Ferguson, F., Berentsen, B., & Richardson, P. (1991). Dentists' willingness to provide care for patients with developmental disabilities. *Special Care in Dentistry, 11,* 234–237.

Fortune, J. (1996). *State of Wyoming quality enhancements for community services for persons with developmental disabilities and mental retardation.* Cheyenne, WY: Division of Developmental Disabilities, State of Wyoming.

Hanson, K. W., Neuman, P., Dutwin, D., & Kasper, J. D. (2003). Uncovering the health challenges facing people with disabilities: The role of health insurance. *Health Affairs Web Exclusive, W3,*

552–565. Retrieved December 8, 2004 from http://content.healthaffairs.org/cgi/reprint/hlthaff.w3.552v1.pdf

Hanson, K., Neuman, T., & Voris, M. (2003). *Understanding the health care needs and experiences of people with disabilities: Findings from a 2003 survey.* Menlo Park, CA: The Henry J. Kaiser Family Foundation.

Hayden, M. F., & Kim, S. H. (2002). Health status, health care utilization patterns and health care outcomes of persons with intellectual disabilities: A review of the literature. *Policy Research Brief, 13 (1).* Minneapolis: University of Minnesota, Research and Training Center on Community Living.

Hewitt, A., Larson, S. A., & Lakin, K. C. (2000). *An independent evaluation of the quality of services and system performance of Minnesota's Medicaid home and community based services for persons with mental retardation and related conditions.* Minneapolis: University of Minnesota, Research and Training Center on Community Living.

Horwitz, S., Kerker, B., Owens, P., & Zigler, E. (2000). *The health status and needs of individuals with mental retardation.* New Haven, CT: Departments of Epidemiology and Public Health and Psychology, Yale University School of Medicine.

Iacono, T., & Davis, R. (2003). The experiences of people with developmental disability in emergency departments and hospital wards. *Research in Developmental Disabilities, 24,* 247–264.

Jaskulski, T., Metzler, C., & Zierman, S. A. (1990). *The 1990 reports forging a new era.* Washington, DC: National Association of Developmental Disabilities Councils.

Kaye, H. S. (2001). *Disability watch: The status of people with disabilities in the United States* (Vol. 2). Oakland, CA: Disability Rights Advocates.

Kennedy, J., & Erb, C. (2002). Prescription noncompliance due to cost among adults with disabilities in the United States. *American Journal of Public Health, 92,* 1120–1124.

Kerr, A., McCulloch, D., Oliver, K., McLean, B., Coleman, E., Law, T., et al. (2003). Medical needs of people with intellectual disability required regular reassessment, and the provision of client- and carer-held reports. *Journal of Intellectual Disability Research, 47,* 134–145.

Kim, S., & Cooker, P. (2001). Accessibility and appropriateness of community-based mental health services to persons with developmental disabilities. *Mental Health Aspects of Developmental Disabilities, 4,* 108–118.

Kopac, C., Fritz, J., & Holt, R. (1998). Gynecologic and reproductive services for women with developmental disabilities. *Clinical Excellence for Nurse Practitioners, 2*(2), 88–95.

Krauss, M., Gulley, S., Sciegaj, M., & Wells, N. (2003). Access to specialty medical care for children with mental retardation, autism, and other special health care needs. *Mental Retardation, 41,* 329–339.

Larson, S. A., Coucouvanis, K., & Prouty, R. W. (2003). Staffing patterns, characteristics, and outcomes in large state residential facilities in 2002. In R. W. Prouty, G. Smith, & K. C. Lakin (Eds). *Residential services for persons with developmental disabilities: Status and trends through 2002.* Minneapolis: University of Minnesota, Research and Training Center on Community Living, Institute on Community Integration.

Larson, S. A., Lakin, K. C., Anderson, L., & Kwak, N. (2001). Characteristics of and service use by persons with MR/DD living in their own homes or with family members: NHIS-D analysis. *MR/DD Data Brief, 3* (1). Minneapolis: University of Minnesota, Research and Training Center on Community Living.

Larson, S. A., Lakin, K. C., & Huang, J. (2003). Service use by and needs of adults with functional limitations or ID/DD in the NHIS-D: Difference by age, gender, and disability. *MR/DD Data Brief, 5 (2).* Minneapolis: University of Minnesota, Research and Training Center on Community Living.

Lee, M., Freeman, R., Cialone, J., & Lichtenwalter, L. (1993). Nutrition care for children with special health needs: A chart review. *Public Health Nursing, 10,* 177–182.

Lennox, N., & Chaplin, R. (1995). The psychiatric care of people with intellectual disabilities: The perceptions of trainee psychiatrists and psychiatric medical officers. *Australian and New Zealand Journal of Psychiatry, 29,* 632–637.

Lennox, N., Diggens, J., & Ugoni, A. (1997). The general practice care of people with intellectual disability: Barriers and solutions. *Journal of Intellectual Disability Research, 41,* 380–390.

Lewis, M., Lewis, C., Leake, B., King, B., & Lindemann, R. (2002). The quality of health care for adults with developmental disabilities. *Public Health Reports, 117,* 174–184.

Martin, D., Roy, A., & Wells, M. (1997). Health gain through health checks: Improving access to primary health care for people with intellectual disability. *Journal of Intellectual Disability Research, 41,* 401–408.

McCulloch, D., Sludden, P., McKeown, K., & Kerr, A. (1996). Vision care requirements among intellectually disabled adults: A residence-based pilot study. *Journal of Intellectual Disability Resources, 40,* 140–150.

Meijer, M. M., Carpenter, S., & Scholte, F. A. (2004). European manifesto on basic standards of health care for people with intellectual disabilities. *Journal of Policy and Practice in Intellectual Disabilities, 1*(1), 10–15.

Muir, E., & Ogden, J. (2001). Consultation involving people with congenital disabilities: Factors that help or hinder giving care. *Family Practice, 18,* 419–424.

National Association of State Directors of Developmental Disabilities Services & Human Services Research Institute. (2000). *Consumer survey: Summary report 2000.* Alexandria, VA: Author.

National Association of State Directors of Developmental Disabilities Services. (2003). *Consumer outcomes: Phase IV final report, fiscal year 2001–2002 data.* Alexandria, VA: Author.

National Organization on Disability. (2000). *NOD/Harris survey of Americans with disabilities.* (*www.nod.org*).

National Organization on Disability. (2002). *Executive Summary: 2000 N.O.D./Harris survey of Americans with disabilities. (www.nod.org*).

Neri, M., Beatty, P., & Dhont, K. (2001). Individuals with disabilities are less likely to have the primary care doctor of their choice—especially in managed care. *Health and Disability Brief.* Washington, DC: National Rehabilitation Hospital Center for Health and Disability Research. (*www.nrhchdr.org*).

Newacheck, P., McManus, M., Fox, H., Hung, Y., & Halfon, N. (2000). Access to health care for children with special health care needs. *Pediatric, 105,* 760–766.

Noll, P., & Deschenes-Desmond, D. (1993). *DMR community medical survey report.* Hartford, CT: State of Connecticut, Department of Mental Retardation.

Patja, K. (2001). *Life expectancy and mortality in intellectual disability* (Academic Dissertation). Finnish Association on Mental Retardation Research Publications 81/2001. Helsinki, Finland: Kehitysvammaliitto ry.

Paxton, D., & Taylor, S. (1998). Access to primary health care for adults with a learning disability. *Health Bulletin, 56,* 686–693.

Perry, M., Dulio, A., & Hanson, K. (2003). *The role of health coverage for people with disabilities: Findings from 12 focus groups with people with disabilities.* Menlo Park, CA: Henry J. Kaiser Family Foundation.

Powrie, E. (2003). Primary health care provision for adults with a learning disability. *Journal of Advanced Nursing 42,* 413–423.

Prouty, R. W., Smith, G., & Lakin, K. C. (Eds.) (2004), *Residential services for persons with developmental disabilities: Status and trends through 2003.* Minneapolis: University of Minnesota, Research and Training Center on Community Living, Institute on Community Integration.

Reichard, A., & Turnbull, H. R. III (2004). Perspectives of physicians, families, and case managers concerning access to health care by individuals with developmental disabilities. *Mental Retardation, 42,* 181–194.

Reichard, A., Turnbull, H. R., & Turnbull, A. P. (2001). Dentist, family, and case manager perspectives on dental care for individuals with developmental disabilities in Kansas. *Mental Retardation, 39,* 268–285.

Roy, A., Martin, D., & Wells, M. (1997). Health gain through screening—mental health: Developing primary health care services for people with intellectual disability. *Journal of Intellectual and Developmental Disability, 22,* 227–239.

Russell, G., & Kinirons, M. (1993). The attitudes and experience of community dental officers in Northern Ireland in treating disabled people. *Community Dental Health, 10,* 327–333.

Schultz, S., Shenkin, J., & Horowitz, A. (2001). Parental perceptions of unmet dental need and cost barriers to care for developmentally disabled children. *Pediatric Dentistry, 20,* 321–325.

Sparks, B., Temple, V., Springer, M., & Stoddart, K. (2000). Service provision to older adults with developmental disabilities: A survey of service providers. *Canadian Journal on Aging, 19,* 210–222.

Stein, K. (2000). Caring for people with learning disability: A survey of general practitioners' attitudes in Southampton and Southwest Hampshire. *British Journal of Learning Disabilities, 28,* 9–15.

Thomas, C., & Payne, S. (1998). Home alone: Unmet need for formal support services among home health clients. *Home Health Care Services Quarterly, 17*(2), 1–20.

Thornton, C. (1996). A focus group inquiry into the perceptions of primary health care teams and the provision of health care for adults with learning disability living in the community. *Journal of Advanced Nursing, 23,* 1168–1176.

Tyler, C. V., Jr., Snyder, C. W., & Zyzanski, S. J. (1999). Caring for adults with mental retardation: Survey of family practice residency program directors. *Mental Retardation, 37,* 347–352.

Ulrich, E. M., Blewett, L. A., & Carrizales, P. J. (1999). *Public health and health care access: Minnesota's Latino community.* Minneapolis: School of Public Health, University of Minnesota.

U.S. Public Health Service. (2002). *Closing the gap: A national blueprint for improving the health of individuals with mental retardation. Report of the Surgeon General's conference on health disparities and mental retardation.* Washington, DC: Author.

Vignehsa, H., Soh, G., Lo, G., & Chellappah, N. (1991). Dental health of disabled children in Singapore. *Australian Dental Journal, 36,* 151–156.

Walsh, K., Hammerman, S., Josephson, F., & Krupka, P. (2000). Caring for people with developmental disabilities: Survey of nurses about their education and experience. *Mental Retardation, 38*(1), 33–41.

White, J., Beltran, E., Malvitz, D., & Perlman, S. (1998). Oral health status for special athletes in the San Francisco Bay area. *Canadian Dental Association Journal, 26,* 347–353.

Yeatts, D. E., Crow, T., MA, & Folts, E. (1992). Service use among low-income minority elderly: Strategies for overcoming barriers. *The Gerontological Society of America, 32*(1), 24–32.

8

WOMEN'S HEALTH

Sheryl White-Scott, MD, FACP, FAAMR

There has been increased visibility in the area of women's health over the last few years. Many hospitals have established comprehensive women's health centers to provide primary medical services, obstetrics/gynecology, and subspecialty services specifically for women. Women with intellectual and developmental disabilities (I/DD) often remain invisible in the health care system, even those areas geared for women, and are even less likely to have their needs addressed. Guidelines and protocols developed for screening do not address the special needs of women with I/DD. Research, which drives clinical practice, usually does not include individuals with I/DD. This may occur because difficulties with identification, tracking, and consent which presents challenges to researchers. Thus, the development of clinical guidelines that are based on scientific research evidence specific to women with I/DD is essential to provide quality care to all women.

Background

DEFINITIONS

The population of women with I/DD varies depending on the definition and geographic location of the studies. A major challenge in reviewing the literature is defining the population in order to make comparisons between studies. The definitions identified for the purpose of this review are the American Association on Mental Retardation definition of *mental retardation* (Luckasson et al., 2002) and the federal definition of *developmental disabilities* from the Developmental Disabilities Act of 2000.

The United Kingdom/Great Britain defines individuals with I/DD as those with a *learning disability* as opposed to mental retardation or other related terms. Studies reviewed from this area were evaluated for the level of impairment of participants and location because of the difference in definitions. Learning disability is defined as ". . . the presence of developmental disability originating early in life, resulting in significant intellectual impairment, the presence of learning disabilities, and delayed and/or impaired development of living and/or social skills' (Lifespan Health Care NHS Trust, 1998, p. 2).

WOMEN'S HEALTH/REPRODUCTIVE HEALTH

Individuals with I/DD face many barriers in obtaining adequate health care. *Healthy People 2010* (U.S. Department of Health and Human Services [DHHS], 2000) looked at the health status of people with I/DD and addressed the barriers that undermine their health, well being, and participation in life activities: (1) lack of information about services, (2) shortage of appropriately educated health providers, (3) transportation and access problems, (4) lack of or limitations of health insurance coverage, (5) cultural and language barriers, (6) limited patient education materials, and (7) lack of health care standards/guidelines.

These barriers impact on the access to health care and delivery of healthcare for adults with I/DD. Women with disabilities, and in particular women with I/DD, have many challenges in obtaining health care.

BARRIERS TO GYNECOLOGIC CARE

Welner (1999) identified several of the barriers that prevent women with I/DD from receiving adequate screening and preventive care:

➤ Lack of accessible equipment (e.g., hydraulic tables)

➤ Lack of understanding by health care providers about I/DD

➤ Lack of assistance during health care visits

➤ Bias of health care providers that all health problems are due to I/DD

➤ Failure of health providers to address general, sexual, or reproductive health because of focus on I/DD

➤ Belief on part of women that many health problems are inevitable

➤ Failure to be proactive and advocate for their own health and health care

Additional barriers to care include the level of retardation, difficulty with patient understanding and cooperation, and orthopedic abnormalities (e.g., scoliosis and contractures) that may contribute to technical difficulties. Lack of a medical history will limit ability to assess risk factors for cervical cancer including multiple sex partners, sex at an early age, human immunodeficiency virus (HIV), smoking, and alcohol abuse. These behaviors are less likely in more severely impaired individuals, but are complicated by the incidence of sexual abuse, noted to be as high as 35% to 60% in this population. Sexual abuse appears to be more common in women with mild cognitive impairments, but additional screening is required to confirm this assumption (see Chapter 9). Difficulty with informed consent and inadequate training of professionals in the clinical care of women with I/DD are also barriers. Time for adequate explanation and questions, and tools to assist with anxiety for women with I/DD are potential solutions to these challenges.

Clinical management and interventions are based on evidence from research trials. Many of the barriers that make obtaining health care difficult can also prevent involvement in research trials. This review of the current literature reflects a limited pool of studies that specifically address the needs of women with I/DD.

Methods

HOW THE LITERATURE SEARCH WAS CONDUCTED

The initial search was completed by an information specialist hired to identify all relevant research articles for this topic from any available source. The following databases were searched: Medline, CINAHL, SocioFile, Health Star, PsychInfo, Pharmaceutical Abstracts, Web Science, Academic Search Premiere, Ingenta, and GPO Access. The following search terms were used besides the topic: *mental retardation, developmental disabilities,* and *Down syndrome*. Additional searches were completed using the term *learning disabilities* to identify related articles in the United Kingdom and *physical disabilities* to identify related articles on women's health.

INCLUSION/EXCLUSION CRITERIA

The focus of this review was to identify studies involving individuals with I/DD. This included individuals identified with mental retardation, learning disabilities (from the UK), and developmental disabilities. The ages of the subjects included adolescents and adults. The time range for articles was initially set for the past five years and then expanded to the last 10 years owing to the limited data. Studies that were limited only to individuals with physical disabilities were reviewed for common issues, additional resources, and references but not included in the detailed review.

RESEARCH QUESTIONS

The articles retrieved were categorized into four areas: (1) cervical cancer, (2) contraception and gynecologic issues, (3) HIV/AIDS, and (4) sexuality. The research questions per category were as follows:

1. Cervical cancer

   ➤ What are the rates of screening and incidence of cervical cancer in women with I/DD?

   ➤ How good is our ability to perform pelvic examinations in woman with I/DD?

   ➤ What is the quality of our cervical cytology tests?

   ➤ What is the incidence of abnormal smears in this population?

   ➤ At what age can cervical cancer screening be eliminated?

2. Contraception and gynecologic issues

   ➤ Are fertility rates the same in women with I/DD as those without I/DD?

   ➤ What is the prevalence of contraceptive use in women with I/DD?

   ➤ What is the frequency and efficacy of different methods of contraception in women with I/DD?

   ➤ What are the most effective management strategies for menstrual and contraceptive issues in women with I/DD?

   ➤ Can specific education programs increase the use of birth control when clinically indicated for women with I/DD?

   ➤ Are medical contraindications for birth control the same in women with I/DD?

3. HIV/AIDS

   ➤ What is the risk of HIV/AIDS in individuals with I/DD?

   ➤ Are the risk factors for HIV in the general population the same or different for individuals with I/DD?

   ➤ What is the incidence and prevalence of HIV in individuals with I/DD?

   ➤ Are HIV prevention programs effective for adults with I/DD?

   ➤ Are treatment protocols for HIV/AIDS accessible and effective for adults with I/DD?

4. Sexuality

   ➤ What is the level of knowledge of adults with I/DD about reproductive health?

   ➤ How does this compare to individuals without disabilities?

   ➤ What methods are effective to teach individuals with I/DD about sexuality and reproductive health?

   ➤ What are effective ways to educate family members and caregivers about issues of reproductive health?

Results and Discussion

CERVICAL CANCER

The recommendations for cervical cancer screening vary among leading organizations. The United States Preventive Services Task Force (USPSTF) and the American Academy of Family Practitioners (AAFP) recommend Pap tests at least every three years for all women who have ever had sexual intercourse and who have a cervix. USPSTF recommends discontinuing regular Pap testing after age 65 in women who have had consistently normal results on previous tests. American College of Obstetricians and Gynecologists (ACOG) recommends annual screening with a Pap test and pelvic examination in all women who are or who have been sexually active, or who are 18 years of age or older. The frequency of Pap tests may be decreased at the discretion of the physician after two or three consecutive normal tests (American Academy of Family Practitioners, 2004; American College of Obstetricians and Gynecologists, 1997; U.S. Preventive Health Services Task Force, 1996).

Screening guidelines should be individualized for each patient. In general practice, a dialogue occurs between practitioner and patient to identify the best screening intervention. Women with developmental disabilities often do not have this opportunity and practitioners are limited by a lack of evidence to guide practice.

The evaluation of risks and benefits along with the support of evidence should drive best practice.

The risk of cervical cancer is related to multiple factors including sexual activity, number of partners, smoking, and diet. Women with I/DD who are not sexually active should have a low risk of cervical cancer. The barriers presented above indicate a few of the difficulties in obtaining adequate gynecologic exams; the quality of the cervical sampling and interventions requires additional testing. Guidelines to determine risk factors, screening, and time frames require additional research. This is evidenced by the few studies available (Broughton & Thomson, 2000; Jaffe, Timell, Eisenberg, & Chambers, 2002; Quint & Elkins, 1997; Stein & Allen, 1999) (see Tables 8-1 and 8-2).

The levels of evidence for the four studies reviewed were limited to levels IV and V (see Table 8-3). The research designs were limited mainly to retrospective chart reviews and there was limited comparison data to the general population. Additional

TABLE 8-1 *Sample and Setting for Studies of Cervical Cancer in Women with I/DD*

STUDY	LOCATION	SAMPLE	TOTAL N	AGES, YRS	SETTING
Broughton & Thomson, 2000	England	Women with LD and caregivers	52 with LD 34 caregivers	20–64	Majority in group home, remainder with family
Jaffe et al., 2002	New York	Women with ID (mild to profound)	162	28–92	ICF-MR
Quint & Elkins, 1997	Michigan	Women with MR (mild to severe)	574	7–88	Not reported*
Stein & Allen, 1999	England	Women with LD	389	18–94	Not reported**

*Specific living situation not reported. Population drawn from community-based clinic to address reproductive health issues of women with mental retardation (MR), ICF, Intermediate Care Facility
**Population drawn from all residents with learning difficulties in one English Health District

TABLE 8-2 *Outcomes of Cervical Cancer Studies*

STUDY	MEASURE USED	RESULTS	CLINICAL IMPORTANCE	SIGNIFICANT STATISTICS
Broughton & Thomson, 2000	Semistructured questionnaire, Interview		Interventions for clinicians to increase screening	
Jaffe et al., 2002		310 satisfactory smears 40% had endocervical cells 3 abnormal smears (0.97%) 1 with dysplasia (0.32%)	Low incidence of cervical dysplasia similar to other studies Rates of cervical cancer in women with I/DD vary according to factors including level of I/DD and sexual activity Possibility of HPV screening for cervical cancer	
Quint & Elkins, 1997	Standardized form	706 smears with 243 (34%) with endothelial cells done without sedation 124 smears with 40 (32%) with endothelial cells done with sedation 254 standard—164 standard 93 (58%) with endothelial cells —93 cotton swab 17(18%) with endothelial cells 2 abnormal smears (0.3%) both with HPV	Blind cotton swab technique is suboptimal Incidence of abnormal Pap tests 2.8/1000 vs. 8–137 in general population. Frequency of cervical screening needs to be individualized	Effect of sedation not statistically significant Difference between techniques significant $p = .001$
Stein & Allen, 1999		49 (13%) of 389 eligible women were screened vs. 88% screened in general population 2 (4%) had inadequate smears	Lowers screening for women with LD Needs clarification to assist with screening	No significant difference in age of screened vs. not screened

190

TABLE 8-3 *Research Design and Levels of Evidence for the Studies Concerning Cervical Cancer*

STUDY	RESEARCH DESIGN	LEVEL OF EVIDENCE	DURATION OF TREATMENT
Broughton & Thomson, 2000	Qualitative	V	1997–1999
Jaffe et al., 2002	Retrospective chart review	V	April 1996–March 2001
Quint & Elkins, 1997	Retrospective chart review	V	Nov. 1985–Oct. 1992
Stein & Allen, 1999	Retrospective chart review	V	

research is needed to answer the research questions proposed for cervical cancer and women with I/DD.

Women with I/DD require screening and preventive care like any other women in the community. Current guidelines for screening apply until evidence supports alternate levels of intervention. The lack of data to support guidelines at this time is apparent in this limited review of current data. The research questions for this section are representative of standard practice for women without I/DD. For example, are three negative smears with low risk for human papillomavirus (HPV) or cervical cancer sufficient to change the interval for screening? Level of sexual activity for women with I/DD is an important factor in determining the screening for cervical cancer. Taking into consideration the possibility of sexual abuse for any woman, regardless of level of intellectual disability, impacts greatly on screening. The ability to comprehend and participate in screening also needs to be taken into consideration when implementing guidelines. Training and sensitivity is thought to improve the yield of screening but studies are needed to support this hypothesis. Guidelines for practitioners to adequately screen for cervical cancer can be developed. Additional information is required to support interventions and frequency of screening.

CONTRACEPTION AND GYNECOLOGIC ISSUES

Women with I/DD have the same contraception and gynecologic needs as other women. Little research has been done to evaluate sexuality and fertility in women with I/DD. The expression of sexuality may vary depending on level of disability. Behaviors may be labeled as disorders without accurate diagnosis and interventions. Fertility would be assumed to be similar to women without I/DD. Genetic syndromes, hormonal dysfunction, and medications may impact fertility. Many research questions can be studied to begin to identify gaps in clinical knowledge, effective interventions, and ongoing management.

The evidence that exists in the current literature is limited and can be used to stimulate discussion about the research studies that need to be designed (see Tables 8-4 and 8-5). The variability of access to health care for people with I/DD is a major

TABLE 8-4 *Sample and Setting in Studies of Gynecologic and Contraceptive Practices in Women with I/DD*

STUDY	LOCATION	INTERVENTION	CONTROL	SAMPLE	TOTAL N	AGES, YRS	SETTING
Grover, 2002	Australia			Women with significant I/DD and mod/high support needs	107	6–34	Not reported*
Huovinen, 1993	Finland			Women with MR	510 (255 cases, 255 controls)	22–46	
McDermott et al., 1994	South Carolina, USA	Home visits, Instruction at day program, group instruction and accompany to doctor	Women on waiting list with no intervention	Women with MR (IQ, 70, deficits in two or more adaptive skills areas and onset prior to 18 yrs of age)	99 (47 cases, 52 controls)	—**	Medicaid-funded family planning program
Servais et al., 2002	Brussels and Belgium			Women with I/DD Using DSM-IV IQ criteria	397	18–46	Government-funded facilities
Shearer et al., 2002	USA			Women bearing a child before 18th birthday (early) / Women with second birth before 20th birthday (late)	***Early —2089 (706 cases, 1383 controls) / Repeat (336 cases, 379 controls)	14–22	
Smith & Polloway, 1993	Virginia, USA			Women and men with MR discharged from institution	212	14–39	Institution

* Patients required referral to specialist at gynecologic clinic at local hospital or private office
** Mean age reported as 32 yrs
***Data from the National Longitudinal Survey of Youth from 1982 to 1990. Cognitive ability from the Armed Services Vocational Aptitude Battery Test, composite score based on 4 of 10 subsets from test, then used percentile rankings.

TABLE 8-5 *Research Design, Levels of Evidence, and Outcomes of Studies of Gynecologic and Contraceptive Practices*

STUDY	RESEARCH DESIGN	LEVEL OF EVIDENCE	TREATMENT DURATION	TREATMENT GROUP N	CONTROL GROUP N	RESULTS	CLINICAL IMPORTANCE
Grover, 2002	Case series	IV				2/107 required surgical intervention after medical attempts	Management of gynecologic issues for mod/severe women with ID primarily medical; similar to general population
							Information and resources helpful for education of patients and caregivers
Huovinen, 1993	Case control study	III				Therapeutic amenorrhea more often the reason for consultation for cases	Therapeutic amenorrhea common previously, now safer with Depo-provera and has been reduced with guidelines and practice changes.
						Smoking less common, fewer pregnancies, deliveries, and abortions	
						Extremely small hymenal ring (82.4% vs. 18%) for cases	
						Lower incidence of genital infection, tumor, and neoplasm ($p < .001$)	
McDermott et al., 1994	Case control study	III	1 yr	47	52	Upward trend in birth control use in the treatment group from baseline to year (permanent birth control use from 42.5% to 68%)	Change in birth control use occurred with intense intervention; long-term impact and effectiveness of interventions need to be tracked.
						Compared to a national sample, 8% used no birth control compared to 32% in baseline of this study	Rates of birth control use, pregnancy and births would determine effectiveness of interventions in future

(continued)

TABLE 8-5 *Continued*

STUDY	RESEARCH DESIGN	LEVEL OF EVIDENCE	TREATMENT DURATION	TREATMENT GROUP *N*	CONTROL GROUP *N*	RESULTS	CLINICAL IMPORTANCE
Servais et al., 2002	Population-based study	IV				Women with ID less often under contraception (60% vs. 68%), method is less often oral contraceptives (OC) (18.5% vs. 46%) More often sterilization (22.2% vs. 7%) or depomedroxyprojesterone acetate (DMPA) (17.6% vs. < 2%)	Results stratified by level of MR and by type of facility. Implications for birth control usage depending on severity of MR and facility policy regarding sexual activity. Medical indications should be used in choice of birth control.
Shearer et al., 2002	Case control study	III				Early childbearings had significantly lower cognitive scores (22th percentile) compared to controls (37th percentile) Repeat early cases even lower with 70% in two lowest quartiles vs. only 7% of mothers in highest quartile Lower cognitive ability linked to earlier initiation of sex, fewer years of school and higher level of poverty.	Implication of low cognition, related to less exposure to sex education or less likely to remember or effectively use information Health education programs need to be designed for teens with low cognition, could help decrease sexual abuse, and decrease pregnancy and births. Poverty linked to low cognition and limited resources Limited capacity to comprehend implications of sexual behavior, fend off unwanted sex and increased risk of STD

194

Smith & Polloway, 1993	Retrospective chart review	V	Women (125/925—13.51% were more likely to be sterilized than men (87/1262— 6.89%)	Involuntary sterilization no longer continues, with changes in laws and practices that now govern clinicians and protect rights of individuals with MR
			Sterilizations more common in the 1940s—1960s (68 in 1950 vs. 5 in 1970s)	
			Majority done between 15 and 24 yrs (146—69%)	
			Higher level of MR more likely to be sterilized than lower level including 13 without MR	
			Majority placed in community settings, sterilization unlikely to have been a positive feature in less restrictive settings	

barrier to assessing contraceptive use and ongoing medical services. The past practices of sterilization and therapeutic abortion noted in Smith and Polloway (1993) give a historical perspective but are no longer, morally or ethically, the standard of care. The method of counseling, contraception, and interventions for women with disabilities varies from country to country. The studies from Grover (2002), Huovinen (1993), and Servais et al. (2002) provide interesting information about practices in different countries. There is such a small amount of literature that any data are helpful; however, the timing of the studies and differences in clinical practice and health care delivery make it difficult to directly apply this information to clinical guidelines in the United States. Interventions to inform women with cognitive disabilities about sexuality, healthy sex practices, contraception, and pregnancy require education programs designed for this population. McDermott, Kelly, and Spearman (1994) and Shearer et al. (2002) show that there is a need for this information and suggest that interventions can be measured to assess positive outcomes.

The levels of evidence to support contraceptive management in women with I/DD are limited to levels III, IV, and V in the five studies reviewed (see Table 8-5). There are limited sample sizes with a lack of control groups and difficulty applying these findings to clinical practice. There are helpful descriptions of segments of the population with I/DD. Studies need to be designed with the assistance of women with I/DD to evaluate contraceptive practices and fertility issues.

HIV/AIDS

HIV/AIDS remains a worldwide epidemic and continues to be a major public health issue. Individuals with I/DD are not recognized in epidemiologic studies, educational interventions, and clinical treatment trials. This is in part due to the fact that I/DD is not a medical diagnosis and consensus on definitions of I/DD remains problematic. The need to know accurate data on incidence is essential. This is especially true now that there are interventions that can improve the quality of life for individuals living with HIV/AIDS.

These four studies provide a representation of the limited literature available on adults with I/DD with HIV/AIDS (see Tables 8-6 and 8-7). Kastner, Hickman, and Bellehumer (1989) reported on two case studies. Brown and Jemmott (2002) and Cambridge (1998) provide insight into the service system and individual needs around HIV/AIDS. Walkup, Sambamoorthi, and Crystal (1999) attempt to identify characteristics about individuals with mental retardation and HIV/AIDS from a statewide perspective. But there are major limitations with the data, such as use of administrative datafiles for data collection, concern regarding the credibility of diagnostic information in claims files, questions about the verification of the clinical diagnosis, and lack of statistical testing because of small cell size. Therefore, only descriptive comparisons were done. This is an ongoing theme for many studies involving adults with I/DD. The levels of evidence for these four studies are level V. This limits the use of this information to develop guidelines for HIV/AIDS for people with I/DD. These studies give an overview of the issues, but additional research is needed to develop guidelines and evaluate efficacy.

TABLE 8-6 *Sample and Settings for Studies Concerning Screening, Incidence, and Prevention of HIV in Adults with I/DD*

STUDY	LOCATION	POPULATION	TOTAL N	AGES	SETTING
Brown & Jemmott, 2002	Philadelphia, PA, USA	Adults with DD Service providers	7 Adults with I/DD 9 Providers	Adult	
Cambridge, 1998	UK, USA	Adults with LD		Adults	
Kastner et al., 1989	USA	Adults with HIV and MR	2	Adult	Group home
Walkup et al., 1999	New Jersey, USA	Adults with HIV and MR	119	Adult	

HIV/AIDS will continue to be a major clinical issue for the United States and throughout the world for decades to come. Major advancements have been made in treatment but not a cure or a vaccine. This leaves prevention as a major focus for efforts to limit the spread of HIV. Adults with I/DD are living their lives in the community and this includes having sex. Women with I/DD in the mild range are at increased risk for sexual abuse and are vulnerable to sexually transmitted disease (STD), including HIV (see Chapter 9). The lack of information about the rates of HIV, efficacy of treatment regimens, and educational interventions leaves the population vulnerable. HIV intervention strategies need to be developed based on current scientific research literature, with an emphasis on prevention, implementation, and evaluation. Such studies need to be completed to bridge this major gap in knowledge.

SEXUALITY

As noted previously, sexuality and individuals with I/DD are often ignored. The feelings of women with I/DD with regard to their own sexuality and level of sexual knowledge is important when developing guidelines for women's health. Letting women with I/DD speak about their own needs and wants is the first step in establishing a working relationship between patients and practitioners.

The area of sexuality and reproductive health, similar to the other areas of women's health and I/DD, remains limited with regard to the scientific research literature. The evidence from available studies is mixed. McCabe (1999) presents an interesting comparison between adults with cognitive disabilities, adults with physical disabilities, and adults in the general population. This type of study identifies possible comparison groups and a basis for further research to identify the needs of individuals with I/DD around sexuality. Dotson, Stinson, and Christian's (2003) study, based on direct interviews, provides to a small sample of women an opportunity

TABLE 8-7 *Research Design, Level of Evidence, and Outcomes of HIV/AIDS Studies*

STUDY	RESEARCH DESIGN	LEVEL OF EVIDENCE	MEASURE USED	CLINICAL IMPORTANCE	SIGNIFICANT STATISTICS
Brown & Jemmott, 2002	Qualitative descriptive study	V		Identification of risk factors for HIV/AIDS HIV prevention strategies	
Cambridge, 1998	Descriptive study	V		Awareness and sexuality of adults with I/DD Homosexuality has not been recognized or accepted in I/DD Education and intervention for HIV is necessary along with system change to recognize the rights of adults with I/DD	
Kastner et al., 1989	Case reports	V		Education about HIV for persons with MR Need to assess efficacy of educational training HIV testing presents challenges that need to be addressed Agencies that serve adults with MR need policies to address issues and concerns.	
Walkup et al., 1999	Descriptive study	V	Only descriptive comparisons	Major limitations with data People with mild MR, more common in HIV sample in this study Higher proportion of blacks than whites in HIV group Females higher than males in HIV group in contrast to the reverse in MR in general Coordination of medical treatment for this group required	No statistical tests owing to small cell size

198

TABLE 8-8 *Sample and Setting for Studies on Awareness and Knowledge of Sexuality in Persons with I/DD*

STUDY	LOCATION	SAMPLE	TOTAL *N*	AGES	SETTING
Cheng & Udry, 2003	USA	High school students grouped by IQ, 55–111	18,924	*	School-based
Dotson et al., 2003	California, USA	Women with I/DD	8	32–40 yrs	Not reported**
McCabe, 1999	USA	Adults with I/DD Adults with physical disabilities Adults from general population	220	Mean age: 27.62 (I/DD) 28.65 (physical disability) 30.10 (general population)	Living independently in the community

*7th–12th graders in school-based national cohort
** All participants received supported living, supported employment, or behavior management day services from a human service agency

to discuss their individual feelings and needs. This can help shape the future research agenda. Cheng and Udry (2003) illustrate how a large nationwide sample can identify issues and needs to shape the future (see Table 8-8 and 8-9).

The levels of evidence for these studies range from II to V. There is a variation in the design and the populations that make it difficult to do a direct comparison. It is clear that there is a need for additional education around sexuality that is developed for and by individuals with I/DD. Additional scientific studies can produce the scientific evidence needed to design effective sexual education programs.

Sexual knowledge is learned through many resources. Adolescents often obtain information from peers, with parents and school also providing information. These formative years are often a time for sexual exploration. For adults, additional information about sex is obtained through various sources. Both adolescents and adults with I/DD are often at a disadvantage in many ways, especially learning about their own sexuality. Educational programs in school settings should be adapted to the learning needs of individuals across the spectrum of cognitive levels. Evaluation of the effectiveness of these programs would be an important component. Adults with I/DD, especially women, require opportunities to express concerns, fears, and needs around sexuality.

Summary and Directions for Future Research and Practice

It is clear from this literature review that there are major gaps in the area of reproductive health for women with I/DD. The focus here was on women; however, it is also clear that there is limited information available about men with I/DD as well. This review of the scientific research literature on women's health illustrates many of

TABLE 8-9 *Research Design, Level of Evidence, and Outcomes on Studies on Awareness and Knowledge of Sexuality*

STUDY	RESEARCH DESIGN	LEVEL OF EVIDENCE	MEASURE USED	RESULTS	CLINICAL IMPORTANCE
Cheng & Udry, 2003	Survey	II		Lower % of teenagers with MR reported learning about AIDS and pregnancy in school than teens of average IQ	Lack of sex education, education needed at home and in school
				Parents of teenagers with MR think of themselves as less knowledgable talking about sex and birth control	Negative attitudes toward sex education for adolescents with MR has impact on information shared and lack of information or misinformation common
				Higher % of parents with teenagers with MR have not discussed premarital sex and implication	Sexual activity still occurs in teenagers with MR and lack of knowledge may lead to STDs, unwanted pregnancy, and sexual abuse.
				Lower % teenagers with MR have had sexual intercourse (24% vs. 37% of boys) and (8% vs. 38% of girls)	
Dotson et al., 2003	Chart review and interviews	V	Direct interviews	3/8 had been to gynecologic screening in last year, 4/8 many years ago; 1/8 had never been	Lack of gynecologic screening
				5/8 sexually active	Difficulty with understanding medical terms and professionals

200

| McCabe, 1999 | Case control study | III | Sexual knowl-edge, experiece, and needs scale for people with intellectual disability (SexKEN-I/DD), SexKEN-PD (physical disability), SexKEN-GP (general population) | Analyses were conducted from knowledge, experience, feelings, and needs for each subscale

Significant differences were noted on almost all subsets between I/DD, physical disability, and general population

Sexual experiences noted more experience for general population than for people with physical disability than for I/DD | People with I/DD had lower level of knowledge than people with physical disability and in turn lower than that of the general population

Still require effort to improve sexual knowledge base of people with disabilities

People with disabilities get their information from other sources rather than parents, friends, and others of general population

Information needs to be provided by reliable sources and more discussion of sexuality for people with disabilities

Evaluation of sex education classes necessary

People with disabilities have sexual needs that are not being met for many reasons, including lack of knowledge and opportunity |

201

the difficulties with current research. These difficulties include small sample sizes, variable use of instruments, lack of statistical significance, and a lack of control groups. This provides limited scientific evidence on which to base guidelines and recommendations for clinical practice.

There are several areas of additional interest that need to be evaluated:

➤ Breast cancer

➤ Osteoporosis

➤ Menopause

➤ Testicular and prostate cancer

➤ Sexually transmitted diseases

➤ Sexual abuse

➤ Fertility

Additional research questions should be identified from researchers, clinicians, adults with I/DD, and their family members to define a research agenda. Research design and specific populations should be identified to help evaluate outcomes and use this in information. Priorities should be set to address needs, develop guidelines, and improve clinical practice.

REFERENCES

American Academy of Family Practice. (2004). *Summary of policy recommendations for periodic health Examinations.* Retrieved January 6, 2005, from: *http://www.aafp.org/exam.xml.*

American College of Obstetricians and Gynecologists. (1997). *Routine cancer screening.* ACOG Opinion, No. 185. Washington, DC: Author

Broughton, S., & Thomson, K. (2000). Women with learning disabilities: Risk behaviors and experiences of the cervical smear test. *Journal of Advanced Nursing, 32,* 905–912.

Brown, E., & Jemmott, L. (2002). HIV prevention among people with developmental disabilities. *Journal of Psychosocial Nursing, 40,* 15–21.

Cambridge, P. (1998). Challenges for safer sex education and HIV prevention in services for people with intellectual disabilities in Britain. *Health Promotion International, 13,* 67–74.

Cheng, M., & Udry, J. (2003). How much do mentally disabled adolescents know about sex and birth control? *Adolescent & Family Health, 3*(1), 28–38.

Developmental Disabilities Assistance and Bill of Rights Act Amendments of 2000. (2000). P. L. No. 106-402, 114 Stat. 1677.

Dotson, L., Stinson, J., & Christian, L. (2003). "People tell me I can't have sex": Women with disabilities share their personal perspectives on health care, sexuality and reproductive rights. *Women and Therapy, 26,* 195–209.

Grover, S. (2002). Menstrual and contraceptive management in women with an intellectual disability. *Medical Journal of Australia, 176,* 108–110.

Hartman, K., Hall, S., Nanda, K., Boggess, J., & Zolnoun, D. (2002) *Screening for cervical cancer.* Systematic Evidence Review. No. 25. (Prepared by the Research Triangle Institute—University of North Carolina Evidence-based Practice Center under contract No. 290-97-0011). Rockville, MD: Agency for Healthcare Research and Quality. Retrieved January 6, 2005, from *http://www.ahrq.gov/clinic/serfiles.htm*

Huovinen, K. (1993). Gynecological problems of mentally retarded women. *Acta Obstetrica Gynecologica Scandnavia, 72,* 475–480.

Jaffe, J., Timell, A., Eisenberg, M., & Chambers, J. (2002). Low prevalence of abnormal cervical cytology in an institutionalized population with intellectual disability. *Journal of Intellectual Disability Research, 46,* 569–574.

Kastner, T., Hickman, M., & Bellehumer, D. (1989). The provision of services to persons with mental retardation and subsequent infection with human immunodeficiency virus. *American Journal of Public Health, 79,* 491–494.

Lifespan Health Care NHS Trust. (1998). *Specialist health care services for adults with learning disabilities: Community teams for adults with learning disabilities.* Cambridgeshire, England: Author.

Luckasson, R., Borthwick-Duffy, S., Buntinx, W. H. E., Coulter, D. L., Craig, E. M., Reeve, A., et al. (2002). *Mental retardation: Definition, classification and systems of support* (10th ed). Washington, DC: American Association on Mental Retardation.

McCabe, M. (1999). Sexual knowledge, experience, and feelings among people with disability. *Sexuality and Disability, 17,* 157–170.

McDermott, S., Kelly, M., & Spearman, J. (1994). Evaluation of a family planning program for individuals with mental retardation. *Sexuality and Disability, 12,* 307–314.

Quint, E., & Elkins, T. (1997). Cervical cytology in women with mental retardation. *Obstetrics and Gynecology, 89,* 123–126.

Servais, L., Jacques, D., Leach, R., Conod, L., Hoyois, P., Dan, B., et al. (2002). Contraception of women with intellectual disability: Prevalence and determinants. *Journal of Intellectual Disability, 46,* 108–119.

Shearer, D., Mulvihill, B., Klerman, L., Wallender, J., Hovinga, M., & Redden, D. (2002). Association of early childbearing and low cognitive ability. *Perspectives on Sexual and Reproductive Health, 34,* 236–243.

Smith, J., & Polloway, E. (1993). Institutionalization, involuntary sterilization, and mental retardation: Profiles from the history of the practice. *Mental Retardation, 31,* 208–214.

Stein, K., & Allen, N. (1999). Cross sectional survey of cervical cancer screening in women with learning disability. *British Medical Journal, 318,* 641.

U.S. Department of Health and Human Services. (2000). *Healthy people 2010: Disability and secondary conditions, Chapter 6.* Washington, DC: Author.

U.S. Preventive Health Services Task Force. (1996). *Guide to clinical preventive services* (2nd ed). Baltimore: Williams & Wilkins.

Walkup, J., Sambamoorthi, U., & Crystal, S. (1999). Characteristics of persons with mental retardation and HIV/AIDS infection in a statewide Medicaid population. *American Journal on Mental Retardation, 104,* 356–363.

Welner, S. (1999). *A provider's guide for the care of women with physical disabilities and chronic medical conditions.* Wilmington, NC: North Carolina Office on Disability and Health.

9

VIOLENCE

Richard Sobsey, PhD

For many years, researchers and clinicians noted a strong association between disability and violence. Children and adults with disabilities in general and intellectual and developmental disabilities (I/DD) in particular have been shown to have an increased lifetime incidence of victimization. Recent studies confirm the existence of this relationship, but they provide little guidance about the reason for this association. Researchers and clinicians have often assumed the association results from increased risk among individuals with preexisting developmental disabilities. However, it is important to recognize that three kinds of causal pathways might explain this association.

First, it is possible that violence is a major cause of disability. While violence is clearly known to result in injuries that can produce long-term or permanent disabilities, current estimates attribute fewer than 1% of I/DD to violence (e.g., Centers for Disease Control and Prevention, 1996), far less than would be required to play any significant part in the strong relationship between the two. Several recent lines of research, however, suggest the possibility that violence is an unacknowledged causal factor in many more cases. These raise the possibility that violence could be a major, but well concealed, etiologic factor.

Second, it is possible that common factors increase the risk for both disability and violence and thereby increase the probability of an association between the two. Factors such as maternal substance abuse are known to increase the risk for both violence and for disability. Other global factors such as poverty or general family dysfunction may also contribute to risk for both disability and family violence.

Finally, existing disabilities may directly or indirectly increase risk for violence. Direct effects may include impairments that limit an individual's ability to avoid, escape from, or resist victimization. Indirect effects may result from social responses to disability. For example, children with disabilities often live in foster families, group homes, or institutions, where rates of victimization appear to be increased (Sobsey, 1994).

The first part of this chapter is a systematic review of research linking violence, particularly child maltreatment, to I/DD. The second part of this chapter reviews research suggesting that violence might contribute to many more cases of I/DD than currently acknowledged through a variety of mechanisms that are not well understood. The role of other mutual causal factors that increase risk for both violence and disability and the role of I/DD in contributing to risk and vulnerability are not addressed in this chapter, but have received considerable attention elsewhere (e.g., Petersilia, 2001; Sobsey, 2002).

Methods and Research Questions

In preparing this chapter, I conducted a series of searches of electronic databases in addition to consulting previous reviews to answer three questions. First, is I/DD associated with high rates of victimization by violence? Second, is violence a significant cause of I/DD? Third, might other factors increase risk for both disability and violence? Primary databases that were searched included Medline, Child Welfare and Adoption, and Web of Science. Medline searches used both an Endnote interface to search on free-text phrases and an Ovid interface to allow advanced Boolean-logic searches of key words. Studies were categorized using the 1998 criteria established by the Centre for Evidence-Based Medicine (2004), based on earlier work by the Canadian Task Force on Periodic Health Examination (1979).

Results and Discussion

ASSOCIATING VIOLENCE WITH DISABILITIES

Child Abuse and I/DD

DISABILITIES AMONG MALTREATED CHILDREN Caffey's (1946) work in radiology, reporting that many children seen for head injuries had large numbers of healed fractures, was an important first step in our modern recognition of a massive child abuse problem. It was not until the 1960s, however, when the battered child syndrome was widely publicized (Kempe, Silverman, Steele, Droegemueller, & Silver, 1962) that major clinical and research efforts accelerated rapidly. Within a few years, researchers began noting the strong association between child abuse and I/DD. Classic studies of child abuse and disability identified samples of abused children and determined the percentage of children within these samples who previously were diagnosed or who exhibited symptoms of various disabilities. Table 9-1 summarizes selected examples of these studies. This table and those that follow in this chapter list studies in chronological order.

TABLE 9-1 *Selected Studies of Abused Children with I/DD*

STUDY	STUDY TYPE AND LEVEL OF EVIDENCE	PARTICIPANTS	MEASURES	RELEVANT FINDINGS
Elmer & Gregg, 1967	Level IV Case series	USA: follow-up of 50 physically abused children	Examination and record review	50% were diagnosed as mentally retarded.
Birrell & Birrell, 1968	Level IV Case series	Australia: 42 abused children younger than 3 yo	Record review	25% had congenital disabilities, 24% experienced developmental delay as a result of abuse.
Johnson & Morse, 1968	Level IV Case series	USA: review of 101 cases of child abuse	Unclear	70% had a physical disability or mental retardation.
Gil, 1970	Level IV Survey	USA: 12,610 abused children ages 0.5–15 yrs	Survey	22% had mental retardation or physical disability.
Morse et al., 1970	Level IV Case series	USA: 25 abused children	Family perceptions of children	71% were considered to have behavior problems or mental retardation.
Martin et al., 1974	Level IV Case series	USA: 37 abused children without known head trauma	Psychological testing	43% showed neurologic dysfunction.
Sangrund et al., 1974	Level IIIb Controlled case series	60 abused, 30 neglected, 30 nonabused children	Psychological testing	25% of abused, 20% of neglected, and 3% of controls had mental retardation.
Davies, 1979	Level IIIb Case series with controls	USA: 22 incest survivors + control group of other hospital admissions	Electroencephalograms and seizure histories	77% had abnormal EEG readings and 27% had overt seizures. These rates were 3 to 4 times those in a control group of other hospital admissions.
Green et al., 1981	Level IIIb Controlled case series, blind examinations	60 physically abused, 30 neglected, 30 nonabused children	Neurologic examinations	50% of abused , 37% of neglected, and 14% of control children had moderate to severe neurologic dysfunction.

Note: Prior to 1977, the −1 standard deviation definition of mental retardation increased the expected rate to about 16%.

Among early examples, Elmer and Gregg (1967) reported that 50% of the physically abused children whom they followed had been diagnosed with mental retardation, and Johnson and Morse (1968) reported that 70% of the abused children in their sample had an identified mental or physical disability. Only Gil's (1970) study, however, had a large sample size, and none of these studies sampled randomly from a clearly defined population. Only a few of the studies used internal control groups, making comparisons of findings to the general population difficult. Green, Voeller, Gaines, and Kubie (1981) used some of the most sophisticated control procedures with neurologic examinations conducted by examiners who did not know whether they were examining abused children or members of the control group.

In spite of methodologic limitations, the consistency and strength of association reported by these studies provide a strong indicator that some relationship existed. The nature of this association remained unclear. A few studies attempted to determine if disability preexisted or resulted from abuse. For example, Birrell and Birrell (1968) concluded that about half of the children in their study had disabilities that predated abuse and the other half had disabilities that resulted from maltreatment. Martin, Beezley, Conway, and Kempe (1974) selected maltreated children who had no known history of head injury to attempt to control for the effects of traumatic brain injury, yet they found that 43% of children they studied showed significant neurologic dysfunction. While this and other similar attempts were commendable, they could not adequately address the complexities of determining which came first, whether other intervening variables may have increased risk for both abuse and disability, or how spiraling interactions might lead to increasing abuse and disability with each contributing to the other.

Most of these studies had small samples and none had an internal control group for comparison. While almost all pointed to more children with disabilities than might be expected among samples of abused children, the specific percentages reported varied drastically from study to study. In 1970, Gil published information on a large sample of abused children, reporting that 22% had a mental or physical disability.

The finding of considerable neurologic dysfunction among children with no known head injuries (Martin et al., 1974) was somewhat puzzling at the time, but even more puzzling was Davies' (1979) study of incest survivors. Although seizures had been frequently reported among incest survivors, they were generally assumed to be psychogenic (without electroencephalographic [EEG] evidence) rather than neurogenic (with electroencephalographic evidence). Davies' study set out to document this, but rather than finding non-epileptic EEGs among incest survivors who exhibited seizures, he found clear evidence of seizure-related EEG activity in 77%. More surprisingly, he found similar atypical EEG patterns in 27% of incest survivors who showed no overt signs of seizures. In the absence of any evidence of head injury or known mechanism for incest to affect EEG patterns, Davies concluded that these differences in brain activity must have preexisted and somehow increased vulnerability to incest. Davies' finding, however, foreshadowed contemporary theories and studies addressed later in this chapter linking extreme levels of emotional stress in abused children with damage to the developing central nervous system.

MALTREATMENT AMONG CHILDREN WITH DISABILITIES A second approach to studying the association between child maltreatment and I/DD was used in another series of studies, summarized in Table 9-2. These studies began with samples of children known to have childhood I/DD, and attempted to determine the rate of child maltreatment among these samples. They generally found high rates of maltreatment among children with I/DD. This series of studies provided similar evidence of an association between maltreatment and I/DD.

Buchanan and Oliver's (1977) study, for example, found that 22% of 140 children younger than 16 years of age who had been diagnosed with mental retardation had a known history of physical abuse. They estimated that between 3% and 11% (half of the abused children) had I/DD caused by abuse. Frisch and Rhoads (1982) reviewed the records of 430 children who had been identified as having special needs in school and found a rate of known child maltreatment 3.5 times as high as that found in the general population, a finding that comes very close to the best current estimates. Like the first set of studies, these studies generally used small and nonrandom samples. In one notable exception, Andre (1985) used a stratified random sample of children receiving social services and found that 23% of children with disabilities and 16% of children without disabilities had a history of maltreatment. While the difference was statistically significant, it was modest. Sampling from a social services population rather than the general population would be likely to reduce the extent of the difference.

Balogh et al. (2001) provide an example of a recent study following this general method. It was not intended as an incidence study, and the very high rates of sexual victimization reported are partly attributable to the sampling of a clinical population. Nevertheless, it has been included here for two reasons. First, it provides evidence that victimization of individuals with I/DD is not unique to young children and extends well into late adolescence. Second, it suggests that gender distributions among abused children with I/DD may be very different from those expected in the general population. Sobsey, Randall, and Parrila (1997) found similar gender distribution differences between abused children with and without I/DD. They found particularly that boys with I/DD experienced particularly high rates of physical abuse, and although boys were a minority of sexual abuse victims, they comprised a larger minority than expected from their proportion among sexual abuse victims in the general population.

A second series of studies indicating high rates of child maltreatment among children with disabilities provides additional evidence of an association between child abuse and disability. However, this group of studies also shares many of the same methodologic limitations; in addition, the degree of association varies greatly, and some studies failed to demonstrate any significant association. Benedict, White, Wulff, and Hall (1990), for example, found only 10.6% of the 500 children with multiple disabilities whom they studied had a history of abuse, a percentage not clearly above the rate in the general population. In contrast, Ammerman, Hersen, Van Hasselt, Lubetsky, and Sieck (1994) reported strong evidence of abuse in 61% of their sample of children and adolescents with multiple disabilities.

LARGE-SCALE STUDIES Three large-scale studies (summarized in Table 9-3) have been undertaken to clarify the relationship between childhood disability and child

TABLE 9-2 *Selected Studies of Maltreatment Among Children with I/DD*

STUDY	STUDY TYPE AND LEVEL OF EVIDENCE	PARTICIPANTS	MEASURES	RELEVANT FINDINGS
Buchanan & Oliver, 1977	Level IV Case series	UK: 140 children with mental retardation younger than 16 yo	Record review	22% had a history of physical abuse. Between 3% and 11% had disabilities that resulted from abuse.
Frisch & Rhoads, 1982	Level IV Case series	USA: 430 children referred for learning problems in Hawaii	Record review	The rate of referrals for child abuse was 3.5 times the rate in the general population.
Diamond & Jaudes, 1983	Level IV Case series	86 children with cerebral palsy	Record review	19% had a history of maltreatment.
Andre, 1985	Level IIb Stratified random sample of children receiving social services	USA: 609 children with disabilities, 614 without	Correlation with Social Services records	23% of children with disabilities were abused, 16% of children without disabilities were abused.
Ammerman et al., 1989	Level IV Case series	USA: 150 children with dual diagnoses	Record review	19% had definite history of maltreatment, another 9% were rated as probable abuse, and another 11% were rated as possibly abused.
Benedict et al., 1990	Level IV Case series	USA: 500 children with multiple disabilities	Record review	10.6% had known histories of abuse.
Ammerman et al., 1994	Level IV Case series	USA: 138 adolescents with dual diagnoses including developmental disability	Child and parent interview	61% had experienced some form of abuse by a caregiver.
Balogh et al., 2001	Level IV Case series	UK: 43 in-patients with intellectual disabilities	History, examination, interview	86% (17/23 males and 20/20 females) had experienced sexual abuse or sexual assault.

TABLE 9-3 *Large-Scale Studies on the Association of Child Maltreatment and I/DD*

STUDY	STUDY TYPE AND LEVEL OF EVIDENCE	PARTICIPANTS	MEASURES	RELEVANT FINDINGS	COMMENTS
Crosse, et al., 1993	Level Ib Prospective cohort study Compared to data from external Department of Education study of school-aged children.	1834 abused children ages 0–17 from a nationally representative sample of U.S. child abuse reporting districts	Caseworkers' identification of childhood disabilities	Children with disabilities were 1.7 times as likely to experience abuse. Children with mental retardation had no increased risk. While this was a prospective cohort study of maltreated children, the inappropriate control data used lowers the value of its Ib rating for comparison purposes.	While this study had good internal validity, the comparison of abused children (ages 0–17) to a school-aged (ages 6–17) sample is inappropriate.
Sullivan & Knutson, 1997, 2000	Level IIb Cohort study (Information summarized here comes from two reports of the same study.)	40,211 school-aged children in Omaha	Child abuse registry, police, and foster care review records of child maltreatment crossed with school records indicating absence or presence of special needs	Children with identified disabilities were 3.4 times as likely to have a known history of maltreatment. 31% of all special needs students had a history of maltreatment. Children with intellectual disabilities are 3.7 times as likely to be neglected, 3.8 times as likely to be physically abused, 3.8 times as likely to be emotionally abused, and 4.0 times as likely to be sexually abused compared to children without disabilities.	Excellent internal validity. Generalization outside of Omaha is unclear. Generalization to preschool children (before age of compulsory education) is questionable.
Trocmé et al., 2001	Level Ib Stratified cluster sample of Canadian child abuse reports Not valid for comparison to non-maltreated children	7672 cases of suspected maltreatment from a nationally representative sample of Canadian child abuse reports	Child functioning checklist completed by caseworkers	8% of abused children had developmental delays. 4% had physical/developmental disabilities, 2% had substance abuse-related birth defects, and 4% had other health conditions.	Excellent internal validity but does not provide basis for comparison of these figures to figures from external studies.

211

maltreatment. Crosse, Kaye, and Ratnofsky (1993) investigation, also commonly referred to as the Westat study, was undertaken to provide a definitive answer to questions about the association between child maltreatment and childhood disability. Like the first group of studies discussed, it started with a sample of maltreated children and attempted to determine the frequency of various disabilities among these children. Careful attention to demographics ensured that the sample was representative of abused and neglected children from the whole of the United States. Caseworkers used a formal protocol to determine if children belonged in various disability categories. The study included a number of measures important to ensure good internal validity and probably represents very accurate estimates of the prevalence of various disabilities among maltreated children. Unfortunately, the study also provides a powerful example of the threat to external validity posed by the use of an external and nonequivalent control group. The prevalence of various disabilities among the maltreated children in this sample was compared to national prevalence estimates provided by the United States Department of Education (1991). This resulted in two major problems.

First, the ages of the children in the two samples were radically different. The abused children ranged in age from birth to 17 and approximately 40% of the children were younger than 6 years old. The U.S. Department of Education (1991) data included only children 6–17 years of age. Comparing the two assumes that mental retardation, learning disabilities, and other categories used by the Department of Education are diagnosed in preschool children from the moment of birth at roughly the same rate found among school children. Ironically, the Department of Education data used as the source for the control statistics used in this study clearly indicate that even after school entry at age 6, mental retardation is still identified at a rate only about half of the rate identified by age 11, when the prevalence rate levels off. Epidemiologic studies of mental retardation and other I/DD (e.g., Larson et al., 2001) provide much more appropriate prevalence comparison figures for preschool children, suggesting rates about half those used for school-aged children. Without controlling for age, meaningful comparison of the two samples is impossible. This is aptly illustrated by the study's spurious finding that learning disabilities occur more than twice as frequently among nonabused children as among abused children. While the study reported a nonsignificant difference in mental retardation between abused and non-abused children, simply controlling for age would increase the difference to a level of statistical significance.

Second, the Crosse et al. (1993) study used categories of disability that did not exist in the U.S. Department of Education data. These extra categories included language delay, motor delay, failure to thrive, human immunodeficiency virus (HIV) positive status, and drug or alcohol toxicity at birth. Since only the primary diagnostic category was used for analysis, children in these categories were excluded from the mental retardation category although many of them would be placed in this category in the Department of Education sample.

Kendall-Tackett (2002) points out other difficulties with results of this study, such as the issue that using only child welfare data undersamples abuse in foster care and institutional environments and is likely to underestimate maltreatment of children with disabilities because a larger percentage of them live in these environments.

These problems compound the major concerns of failure to control for age or to use equivalent categories.

The Crosse et al. (1993) study concluded that the prevalence of disability was 1.7 times higher among maltreated children than in the general population, but the rate of mental retardation among maltreated children (13.3/1000) was not significantly higher than in the general population (11.4/1000). Our own attempts to control for age and compensate for the differences in categories using the original data set from this study (Sobsey & Mansell, 1997), however, suggest that the relative prevalence of mental retardation was probably three to four times higher among abused children than would be expected. Adjustments based on controls for age differences can be made reasonably using this dataset; however, adjustments for differences in categories and definitions are much more subjective and imprecise, so no definitive estimate of relative risk can be gleaned from this data. The failure of this study to produce useful information on relative risk points out three important considerations for future studies. First, epidemiologic studies should be based on a general population in which children with and without disabilities and with and without abuse histories have equal chances of being sampled. Second, consistent categories and criteria of disabilities must be applied to all children in the sample. The use of comparisons with statistics from other studies must be limited, carried out only with great caution, and, if done at all, subjected to minimal standards of age controls and common categories and definitional criteria.

Sullivan and Knutson's (1997, 2000)[1] study addressed many of these problems. While it is not without its own limitations, it unquestionably provides the soundest approach to determining relative risk. It is a true epidemiologic study combining some elements of a cohort study and some elements of a cross-sectional study. These researchers started with a cohort of 40,211 children enrolled in Omaha schools. School records were checked against child welfare, foster care review, and police records for a history of maltreatment. The schools' identification of children with various categories of special needs was used to determine whether children had disabilities and, if so, which category of disability. Among children without identified disabilities, 9% had a history of maltreatment. Among children with identified disabilities, 31% had a history of maltreatment. The relative risk for children with disabilities was 3.44 times the risk of children without disabilities. The highest relative risk (6.3 times the rate among children without disabilities) was for children with behavior disorders. Children diagnosed with mental retardation were 3.7 times as likely to be neglected, 3.8 times as likely to be physically abused, 3.8 times as likely to be emotionally abused, and four times as likely to be sexually abused. Overall, they were 3.3 times as likely to experience at least one form of maltreatment as children without disabilities. This combined relative risk is lower than the relative risk for any of the individual categories because children with mental retardation were also somewhat more likely to experience multiple forms of abuse.

---

[1]The original and more comprehensive grant report for this study was published in 1997, and the more readily available but shorter journal article was published in 2000. They are jointly referenced in this chapter because not all information is included in both versions.

Three limitations need consideration in interpreting these results: (1) subject mortality, (2) generalization across settings, and (3) generalization across ages. The ideal epidemiologic cohort study is prospective because the potential loss of participants might be differentially related to one of the variables examined. In this case, for example, fatal child abuse is not well addressed because children who died as a result of maltreatment would no longer be in school. Similarly, if abused children were more likely to drop out of school or be sent outside the school system, they would no longer be included in school records. Disability status could affect inclusion or exclusion in the cohort. While this is a real limitation, its effect is likely to be small. De Haan's (1997) study provides some indication of the possible effects of fatal child maltreatment. De Haan reported that about 4.5% of the confirmed maltreatment cases he studied involved fatalities. He also reported, however, that in "40 of the 42 fatal cases, the victim had a documented physical or mental condition" (p. 96). This suggests that the effect of fatal child abuse determined from the sample would probably be small, but would be more likely to lead to an underestimate than overestimate of relative risk for children with disabilities.

While this cohort included virtually the whole population of Omaha school children, generalizing results beyond Omaha is somewhat risky. The question of generalization across settings would be best answered by systematic replications of the study in other settings. There are several pieces of evidence, however, that encourage generalization. First, the results of the study are generally consistent with the findings of the studies summarized in Tables 9-1 and 9-2, which suggest some significant degree of association. Second, while the conclusion regarding intellectual disabilities appears to differ from the Crosse et al. (1993) study, it is quite similar to the revised interpretation of that data with age controls (Sobsey & Mansell, 1997). In addition, the Crosse et al. (1993) study, which used a nationally representative sample, did not identify large geographic differences, suggesting that generalization across the United States may be less problematic than might otherwise be assumed. Finally, the most methodologically similar study, Frisch and Rhoads (1982), of children referred for learning problems in school produced remarkably consistent results. Children with identified learning problems in Hawaii in 1982 were estimated to have a relative risk for maltreatment of 3.5 times and children in Omaha in 2000 were estimated to have a relative risk for maltreatment of 3.44 times.

The final limitation regarding generalization across ages raises the most serious issue. Because this study involved all children in Omaha schools, it included some very young children, but inclusion of children younger than 6 years of age in the school system is far from universal and, more problematically, may be related to the presence of disability or to other risk factors. Because preschoolers were a small part of the total sample, this is unlikely to have had a large effect on the general findings, but the generalization of these findings to preschool children must be done with extreme caution unless and until subsequent studies support it. While these limitations require consideration, the Sullivan and Knutson (1997, 2000) study clearly appears to be the soundest methodologically, and it is generally viewed as the best (e.g., Kendall-Tackett, 2002).

The Canadian Incidence Study (Trocmé et al., 2001) provides a final large-scale study with useful data for examining the association between I/DD and child maltreatment. In this study, disabilities are only one of many variables considered and appear under the general topic of child functioning characteristics. Like the Crosse et al. (1993) study, there is no internal control group and the categories do not easily equate to those used in other studies. At least four categories probably include at least some children who would fit classic definitions of developmental disabilities: (1) 8% of abused children were identified as having a "developmental delay," (2) 4% of abused children were identified as having a "physical/developmental disability," (3) 2% of abused children were identified as having a "substance abuse-related birth defect," and (4) 4% of abused children were identified as having an "other health condition." Although the categories and definitions, along with the lack of non-abused controls make any precise estimate of relative risk impossible from this data, the overall finding that 26% of abused children were identified as having at least one "physical, emotional, or cognitive health issue" is remarkably consistent with Sullivan and Knutson finding that 22% of the abused children had identified special needs.

In her review, Kendall-Tackett (2002) includes one other large-scale study (Embry, 2001). While the Embry study is not included here because it is primarily a study of deaf adults' histories of abuse as children, its findings also support the association between abuse and disability.

Violence Against Adults with I/DD

There is very little formal research addressing the relative risk of violence for adults with I/DD. There have been a few reports of the percentages of various convenience samples experiencing a particular form of violence, most frequently sexual assault. In many cases, statistics commonly used come from unpublished reports or conference presentations, which are difficult to assess for methodologic soundness. Such evidence should not be dismissed, but well-controlled studies are badly needed. Two commonly quoted studies are those of Hard (1986) and Cowardin (1987).

Hard (1986) reviewed the records of 95 adults between 17 and 48 years old who had I/DD and attended the same work program. In addition, she interviewed about two thirds of these individuals using a structured survey. She determined that 86% of the women and 32% of the men had a history of having been sexually abused or sexually assaulted.

Cowardin's (1987) report used archival data from the Seattle Rape Relief Crisis Centre and compared it to general incidence figures from the state of California, concluding that individuals with I/DD reported sexual abuse at a rate four times the rate of the general population. Comparing data from one treatment center, particularly one with a program dedicated to serving people with I/DD, to general incidence data from another state raises some obvious concerns with interpretation of this finding.

While both of these studies (Cowardin, 1987; Hard, 1986) have obvious limitations, they are fairly consistent with each other and reasonably consistent with what is known from child abuse research. Since we know that the rate of victimization of children with I/DD is approximately three to four times the rate of victimization of other children, and there is no evidence that this relative risk is diminishing as children approach adulthood, similar findings among adults are hardly surprising.

Another kind of extrapolation also lends support. Research using samples of individuals with other disabilities also suggests high rates of abuse among adults. For example, a study of adults with severe mental illness reported rates of sexual assault well over 20 times the national incidence. It indicated that 20.3% of women and 7.6% of men had been sexually assaulted within the last year (Goodman et al., 2001). However, extrapolating from adolescence to adulthood or from other disabilities to I/DD is risky and more research is required to provide clearer evidence.

McCarthy and Thompson (1997) provide a step toward a more structured and controlled study, but their sample of 65 women and 120 men with I/DD referred for sex education also introduces unpredictable bias into the sample. Their finding that 61% of the women and 25% of the men had been sexually abused or assaulted, however, is generally consistent with the other studies.

Other studies of abuse of adults explore patterns of abuse but do not directly address incidence (e.g., Brown, 1992; Furey, 1994; Marchetti, & McCartney, 1990; Sobsey & Doe, 1991; Turk & Brown, 1992). These studies, however, suggest that demographics and characteristics of victimization of people with disabilities are substantially different than those observed in other populations, making comparisons across populations difficult. For example, these studies suggest that group homes and other congregate living arrangements may have distinct risk factors, yet these settings are generally systematically excluded from generic surveys of criminal victimization.

Probably the most useful study of violence against adults is Wilson and Brewer's (1992) Australian study of 174 adults with I/DD from three sheltered workshops. They administered an adapted form of the Australian national crime victimization survey and compared the results with those from the national survey. They concluded that the relative risk across all categories of violent crime was 4.7 times the risk in the general population. People with I/DD were 2.8 times as likely to be assaulted, 10.7 times as likely to be sexually assaulted (only women were included in this calculation), and 12.8 times as likely to be robbed with threat of personal harm.

These results appear to contrast sharply with findings from the U.S. National Crime Victimization Survey as analyzed by McCleary and Weibe and reported by Petersilia (2001). They compared the results for Americans reporting by proxy because of incapacitation to the results for other Americans. While the relative risk for sexual assault was almost doubled (1.95 times) for the proxy group, their relative risks for assault (0.14 times) and robbery (0.21 times) were much lower than in the general population. These results are not really surprising, however, considering victimization characteristics apparent from the pattern studies. These suggest that people with mild I/DD may be victimized by casual acquaintances or strangers, while people with more severe I/DD are abused primarily by caregivers in home settings and other people with I/DD in congregate settings. People in congregate settings are not included in this study. People with mild I/DD do not need proxies to take the survey for them. Thus, the proxies who respond for them may in some cases be unaware of the individual's victimization and in other cases actually be the perpetrators. We should be no more surprised at this finding than we would be to find that a survey of husbands found a relatively low incidence of male violence toward women.

Conclusions on Violence and I/DD

There is now more than adequate evidence to conclude that children with I/DD are more likely to have experienced maltreatment than children without I/DD. The exact difference in lifetime incidence is unclear, but Sullivan and Knutson's (1997, 2000) estimate of 3.3 times appears to be a good estimate. In fact, the exact ratio is very dependent on the categories and criteria included. Measures that include milder forms of abuse and longer time periods for incidence tend to lower the ratio, while restriction to shorter time periods and more severe forms of abuse tend to raise the ratio because of ceiling effects. For example, some retrospective studies of sexual abuse of children cover ages from birth to 18 and any sexually inappropriate acts or suggestions. These tend to result in base rates in the general population of 50% or more. Since it is impossible to have more than 100% of a sample report a history of maltreatment, it is impossible to have a rate of more than two times a 50% base rate.

The great weight of available evidence suggests that the association between violence and I/DD continues into adulthood and throughout the lifespan. There is even some reason to suspect that the association between I/DD and violence is even stronger for adults than for children, but the evidence of this association in the adult population is much weaker than the available evidence for children.

Furthermore, there is little evidence to clarify the nature of the correlation between violence and I/DD. While terms such as "relative risk" seem to imply that having an I/DD somehow increases risk for violence, the same association might occur if large numbers of I/DD were the result of violence. In addition, there could be other factors that contribute to the risk for both I/DD and violence. A family history of alcohol or other substance abuse is a good example. This has been shown to increase the risk both for I/DD and for family violence (Sobsey, 1994). In fact, each of these three pathways (violence to disability, disability to violence, third factor to disability and violence) appears to contribute some cases to the correlation, but whether any one of the three contributes a large or small percentage of cases remains unclear. The remainder of this chapter addresses one of these three pathways. While violence has generally been considered only a minor cause of I/DD, there is no reason to suspect that it may play a larger role.

VIOLENCE AS A CAUSE OF I/DD

Generally accepted current professional opinion recognizes violence as a causal factor in only about 1% of cases of I/DD. For example, in a study of 3- to 10-year-old children with I/DD in Atlanta, researchers reported that only 4.8% of the children with mental retardation and/or cerebral palsy had any postnatal etiologic factor, and only 0.9% of children with I/DD had "child battering" as an etiologic factor (Centers for Disease Control and Prevention, 1996). Specifically, child battering was identified as a causal factor in 1.7% of cases of cerebral palsy and in 0.6% of cases of mental retardation.

If we assumed a similar rate among the Omaha children, the effect would be negligible in explaining the strong association between mental retardation and abuse reported by Sullivan and Knutson (1997, 2000). Dividing the total number of children with mental retardation in their sample into the expected numbers of maltreated and non-maltreated children based on the overall rate of maltreatment and adjusting the numbers to reflect the 0.6% who might have I/DD caused by violence would add less than one child to the number of abused children with mental retardation. Yet, the actual data indicate more than 170 abused children with mental retardation.

The simplest way to reconcile the two findings is to assume that violence rarely causes mental retardation or other I/DD and to assume that violence-induced I/DD are virtually irrelevant to the strong association between the maltreatment and I/DD. To account for any significant part of this large discrepancy, at least one of the following would have to be true: (1) traumatic brain injury caused by violence is vastly underdiagnosed as a causal factor in mental retardation and other I/DD or (2) violence acts through some mechanism, other than traumatic brain injury, to become a causal factor in mental retardation and I/DD.

Violence-Induced I/DD

In fact, there is considerable evidence to suggest that violence causes more disability through traumatic brain injury than has been recognized and that mechanisms other than postnatal battering injuries may contribute to the phenomenon. First, several of the studies already discussed present attempts to estimate the number of disabilities caused by maltreatment or violence. All of them suggest a much stronger role for violence as a cause of disability. Birrell and Birrell (1968), for example, estimated about half of the abused children with disabilities that they studied had disabilities resulting from violence, and Buchanan and Oliver (1977) estimated that at least one-seventh and very possibly as much as one-half of the abused children with disabilities whom they studied had disabilities that resulted from violence. Eppler and Brown (1977) found that child abuse and neglect were likely causes or causal factors in 65 (14.9%) of a series of 436 cases of mental retardation they saw. Hansen's (1980) review drew on available data and concluded that child abuse was probably both a significant "cause and effect" (p. 549) of mental retardation.

More recently, Crosse et al. (1993) also addressed maltreatment as a cause of disability, and, while dependence on the caseworkers' judgment is a limitation, the external validity issues that compromised the estimation of relative risk do not affect this aspect of the study. They reported that 601 (32.8%) of the 1834 maltreated children in their sample had injuries resulting from maltreatment and, of those, 36.6% had disabilities that were judged to definitely or probably have resulted from the abuse. This represented 12% of the total sample, and since 16.4% of the children in the total sample were identified as having a disability, it represented most (73%) of the children with disabilities in the sample.

All of these studies have methodologic limitations, primarily related to their dependence on making clinical judgments about the causes of children's disabilities. Most of these studies were designed primarily to test other hypotheses and added a component related to violence-induced developmental disabilities without the same careful consideration of methodology that were applied to primary variables in the same study. But before dismissing their results, it is important to consider the vast clinical implications that would follow from them, if they are right. Returning to the Sullivan and Knutson (1997, 2000) data, one can model the possible results if half of maltreated children had disabilities resulting from violence. Since about 31% of all children with mental retardation in Omaha schools had a history of maltreatment, if half had violence-induced I/DD, violence would be a causal factor in more than 15% of all mental retardation. It would be one of the largest and quite probably the single largest etiologic factor. While it is clearly premature to conclude that this is the case on the basis of available evidence, there is far too much currently available scientific support from different lines of research to ignore this possibility.

INFLICTED TRAUMATIC BRAIN INJURY Table 9-4 summarizes selected studies on outcomes of inflicted traumatic brain injury in children. These articles are fairly typical of a larger body of research. Collectively, these researchers suggest that inflicted traumatic brain injury is a fairly common occurrence and that the outcomes for inflicted traumatic brain injury are much more serious and much more likely to produce long-term disability than accidental traumatic brain injury. Maltreatment is clearly the most frequent cause of serious head injury in young children (e.g., Billmire & Myers, 1985) and continues to be a significant cause of serious head injury in older children. Based on the incidence suggested by Keenan et al. (2003), and the likelihood of these injuries producing I/DD summarized in Table 9-4, there does appear to be some discrepancy with the Atlanta study. Even assuming that the incidence of violence-inflicted injuries continued to decrease after the age of 2 years, these figures are consistent with the notion that several percent of all cases of mental retardation result from inflicted head injury, but this still falls far short of the percentage required for this pathway to account for any larger portion of the association between maltreatment and disability, such as the 15% of cases speculated above.

For this to be the case, many intentionally inflicted head injuries that cause I/DD would have to go undiagnosed or many disabilities resulting from intentionally inflicted head injuries would have to be unrecognized. In fact there is some evidence for both of these theories. Rubin, Christian, Bilaniuk, Zazyczny, and Durbin (2003) studied a group of 51 children known to have been abused but who had no clinical history or overt symptoms of head injury. With the aid of computed tomography (CT) scans and magnetic resonance imaging (MRI), they found that 37% had occult head injuries. Specific injuries were skull fractures (74%) and intracranial damage (53%). This suggests that among maltreated children, there may be large numbers of unidentified brain injuries, and these injuries could substantially increase the number of disabilities resulting from violence.

Until recently, most of the studies of neurologic and developmental outcomes of brain injury for infants and young children have been based in whole or in part on outcome at the time of release from the hospital or short-term follow-up. If the child's neurologic assessment was normal at the time of release from the hospital or short-term follow-up, the child was deemed to have recovered and no further follow-up was considered to be necessary. This practice led to an unfortunate underestimate of the morbidity associated with inflicted brain injury. Bonnier, Nassogne, and Evrard (1995) followed 13 cases of shaken-infant syndrome for an average of

TABLE 9-4 *Selected Studies of Pediatric Head Injury*

STUDY	STUDY TYPE AND LEVEL OF EVIDENCE	PARTICIPANTS	MEASURES	RELEVANT FINDINGS
Billmire & Myers, 1985	Level IV Case series	USA: children under age 1 admitted to hospital for head injury in 2-yr period	CT scans and medical records	64% of all head injuries and 95% of serious traumatic brain injuries were intentionally inflicted.
Ewing-Cobbs & Barnes, 2002	Level Ib Prospective case series—some of the evaluation done by blind examiners	40 children, 1 mo–6 yrs, admitted to Texas hospital with TBI (20 inflicted and 20 non-inflicted)	Physical exam, CT or MRI, case records	Inflicted injury group was significantly younger. 80% of inflicted TBI children sustained moderate to severe disability. 45% of non-inflicted TBI children sustained moderate to severe disability. 45% of inflicted TBI children and 5% of the non-inflicted TBI children tested as mentally retarded. Average post-inflicted TBI IQ was 78 (88 for non-inflicted group).
Perez-Arjona et al., 2002	Level IIIa Systematic review of (mostly) U.S. case series studies. Some studies included in review were weak.	Varied by study	Glasgow outcome scores Various measures of neurologic function and intellectual disability	20% of children with intentionally inflected head injuries incurred no disability, 65% developed moderate disabilities, and 15% developed severe disabilities. 45% of children with intentional head injuries developed mental retardation but only 9% of children with accidental head injuries developed mental retardation.
Hanks et al., 2003	Level Ib Prospective case series	1229 Americans who survived traumatic brain injury	Review of medical records and interviews	26% of TBI was intentional. Those who sustained intentional injuries required more care and had more disability.

Study	Design	Sample	Method	Findings
				Those with intentional injuries were more likely to have multiple TBI history, to be poor, or to be minority group members
Keenan et al., 2003	Level Ib Two-year prospective case series	All North Carolina children under age 2 who died from traumatic brain injury (TBI) or who were admitted to hospital with TBI	Review of records	53% of serious TBI was intentional. 17.0 children per 100,000 experience serious brain injury as a result of battery before age 2. Fatality rate was 22.5%.
Libby et al., 2003	Level IV Case series	1097 children < 3 yo admitted to Colorado hospitals with head trauma	Review of records	25.8% were known to be intentional. 15% of intentional injuries were rated at lowest severity level compared to 67% of accidental injuries. 20% of intentional injuries were rated at highest severity level compared to 5% of accidental injuries.

7 years. They described a typical pattern in which brain growth slowed significantly beginning 4 months after the injury; lesions in the long pathways of the central nervous system appeared after 6 months to a year; and behavioral, developmental, and neuropsychological signs developed 3–6 years after the injury. After long-term follow-up, 12 of the 13 children (92%) showed significant neurologic problems. While this and other long-term follow-up studies have generally been small in scale, the finding that problems emerge long after acute care ends have been consistent. Lo, McPhillips, Minns, and Gibson (2003), for example, found acquired microcephaly in 94% and clear cerebral atrophy in 50% of children on follow-up examination at approximately 1 year after acute inflicted brain injury. The development of microcephaly after acute trauma in infants and young children has been repeatedly documented in case studies since the 1970s (e.g., Oliver, 1975).

These and other recent studies of longer-term follow-up of maltreated children suggest that we may have substantially underestimated the effects of child maltreatment in producing I/DD. While most of the studies are relatively small-scale case series studies, they provide consistent and fairly convincing evidence when considered collectively because of the uniformly large effects. While the studies are consistent in suggesting that child maltreatment is having a substantial effect, the limitations of nonrandom sampling and variation in outcome measures and effect sizes, however, make it difficult to create meaningful estimates of overall population effects on child development, beyond concluding that the effect is probably quite large.

The logic that suggests that the strong association between child maltreatment and violence is related to the damaging effects of brain trauma on children, however, must consider another important aspect of the epidemiologic studies. The studies showing that long-term outcomes of violence-induced brain injuries are typically severe provide a convenient explanation for the association between physical abuse and violence, but a poor explanation of the strong association between sexual abuse or emotional abuse and violence. As previously discussed, the Sullivan and Knutson (1997, 2000) study indicated that children with mental retardation are 3.8 times as likely to be physically abused as children without I/DD, but they are also 3.8 times as likely to be emotionally abused, and 4 times as likely to be sexually abused. If head injuries from shaking and impact were major factors in producing this association, we would expect the association for physical abuse to be much stronger than the others. In fact, it is precisely the lack of this difference that led previous investigators away from concluding that maltreatment caused neurological and developmental harm. For example, when Davies (1979) found that incest survivors without known head injury had atypical brain wave patterns and no known mechanism was available to explain them, he assumed that those patterns could not be the result of maltreatment. More recent research, however, has pointed toward causal mechanisms that do not require gross or apparent physical injury.

POSTTRAUMATIC STRESS–INDUCED I/DD Research on child maltreatment, stress, and development of the central nervous system suggests another important mechanism. Although Davies' (1979) findings of central nervous system atypicalities in incest survivors were difficult to explain in the 1970s, early evidence began to emerge within a short period of time that provided a possible explanation. Miller, Kaplan, and Grumbach (1980) reported high levels of cortisol and suppression of the pituitary gland in maltreated children. Other researchers found that the extreme stress experienced by adult torture victims produced such high levels of cortisol that their brains actually shrank. Posttraumatic stress, constructed primarily as a psychological phenomenon in 1980, gradually began to be understood as a physiologic reality (Perry, 1994; Yehuda, 1998). In the last two decades of the 20th century, well over 100 studies have followed that have begun to map the pathway between child maltreatment and effects on child development. Collectively, these studies have been remarkably consistent in demonstrating that very high levels of stress experienced by maltreated children produce physiological, electrochemical, and anatomical changes in their developing brains, even when no direct physical injury occurs. These changes have substantial effects on learning and behavior. Researchers have not reached a clear consensus on the precise nature and extent of these changes, but a review by Teicher et al. (2003) provides an excellent summary of consistent findings. They describe the substantial and often long-enduring physiological, electrochemical, and structural changes in the developing central nervous system resulting from the extreme stress of maltreatment, including reduction in the corpus callosum, reduction in development of the left neocortex, reduced volume of the hippocampus, and reduced volume of the amygdala. These are accompanied by increased irritability of the limbic system and reduced electrical activity of the cerebellar vermis and manifest themselves in problems with learning, behavior, and affect. Nevertheless, the authors point out that the effects are variable and the reasons for this variability is not well understood.

Glaser (2000) suggested that the presence of a secure attachment might play an important role in mitigating the harm done by the stress response. However, the hyperstressed child may also have difficulty in forming attachments. Much more remains to be learned about factors that may moderate or influence the stress–maltreatment phenomena. While the central nervous system effects described seem to have a large potential for producing mental retardation and other developmental disabilities, and many authors have speculated on cognitive deficits (e.g., Bugental, Martorell, & Barraza, 2003), there is a surprising lack of research directly addressing these effects. Most researchers have concentrated on behavioral and affective outcomes.

These stress effects do not require direct injury to the brain. In fact, there has been some evidence that the effect can be significant even when the primary target of the violence is someone else. Koenen, Moffitt, Caspi, Taylor, and Purcell (2003) studied 1116 pairs of twins and measured IQ for exposure to domestic violence. They concluded that 4% of variability in IQ was attributable to exposure to domestic violence. This meant that children exposed to high levels of domestic violence lost 8 IQ points, about half of one standard deviation. Since the children were not the direct victims of the violence, the researchers assumed that the emotional effects caused the differences.

While much more work is needed to assess the cognitive impact of stress resulting from exposure to violence, another clue about the possible magnitude of the effect can be found in the Sullivan and Knutson (1997, 2000) study. They found that abused children without disabilities scored about one standard deviation lower than their peers on verbal and nonverbal achievements tests. This may have been larger than the half-standard deviation effect in the twin study because of less stringent controls or because the children experienced the violence directly. However, this magnitude of effect between one-half and one standard deviation might be large enough to make child maltreatment a major contributor to I/DD, yet small enough to escape major attention. Based on current estimates there are well over 1,000,000 children newly subjected to maltreatment each year, and assuming a normal distribution, about 136,000 of them would be expected to have cognitive abilities in a "borderline" range between 1 and 2 standard deviations below average. A loss of another half standard deviation would add another 50,000–60,000 cases of mental retardation each year, making violence a major contributor. For now, any such analysis remains highly speculative, but there is more than enough evidence to justify research to test this theory.

It should be pointed out that this suppression of cognitive potential due to extreme stress probably operates throughout the distribution of intelligence. There is no reason to believe that the loss is any greater for the child whose intelligence is in the borderline or mild cognitive deficit range than for the average or high performing child; the only difference is that the child in the borderline range is more likely to be judged as having a disability because of this loss. Because this appears to produce a shift in the normal distribution, it would be expected to add the most cases to the mild range of I/DD. While the gross injuries described above resulting from inflicted traumatic brain injury appear to produce fewer I/DD, those produced are much more likely to be added to the severe I/DD. Taken together, they might be expected to have a bimodal effect.

Already available research on posttraumatic stress–induced I/DD requires a major paradigm shift to expand our thinking because it suggests that violence could be a potent cause of I/DD, even when there is no gross physical injury and even when the child is not the primary target of the violence. However, another line of research may require an even greater shift in our thinking. It provides evidence that violence is a substantial prenatal as well as postnatal etiologic factor.

PRENATAL VIOLENCE-INDUCED I/DD Research on the outcomes for babies born to mothers subjected to violence during their pregnancy suggests another pathway connecting violence with disability. It has long been observed that babies born to mothers who were maltreated during their pregnancy had more than their share of difficulties. While this general observation has been well demonstrated, isolating the effects of violence from a wide variety of potentially confounding variables (e.g., socioeconomic status, quality of prenatal care, maternal nutritional status, maternal substance abuse) has been difficult and requires caution in interpreting these results.

Table 9-5 lists selected studies related to violence against women in pregnancy and relevant birth outcomes. While this general area of research has a large number of studies, the findings have been complex and lack uniformity. In general, the following conclusions have been supported. First, a large number of women experience some form of violence during pregnancy. The prevalence rates reported in these studies, however, vary from about 5.6% to about 20%. These differences appear to result in part from the populations sampled, but more substantially from differences in definitions of violence (e.g., some studies include only battery; others include threat of physical harm), the time frame (e.g., some studies survey the women only on the first prenatal care visit), and the screening method (e.g., detailed screening instrument vs. single question). In addition, there are some confounding variables that have been difficult to control. Mothers who are abused during pregnancy are also more likely to smoke, drink, and have other substance abuse problems, and are less likely to receive early prenatal care and proper nutrition during pregnancy (e.g., McFarlane, Parker, & Soeken, 1996). Some have argued that these other factors result, at least in part, from the abuse, and so they should be seen as pathways by which violence affects pregnancy rather than as confounders (Murphy, Schei, Myhr, & Du Mont, 2001). Even after controlling for these factors, however, there is clear evidence that abuse during pregnancy results in low birthweight (Murphy, Schei, Myhr, & Du Mont, 2001), and fairly consistent evidence that it increases preterm births (e.g., Fernandez & Krueger, 1999). In addition, there is some evidence that abuse during pregnancy leads to increases in other negative outcomes such as fetal distress and detachment of the placenta (Rachana, Suraiya, Hisham, Abdulaziz, & Hai, 2002). Unfortunately, while all of these outcome measures might be expected to increase I/DD among the offspring, none of these studies directly measures subsequent child development. Since low-birthweight and preterm status are not perfect predictors of I/DD and the likelihood of either depends on the underlying cause, it is difficult to predict the extent to which spousal abuse during pregnancy contributes to I/DD, but the high prevalence of violence during pregnancy leaves open the possibility that this may be a significant contributor.

In addition to the less common gross injury to the fetus as a result of violence during pregnancy, two major and closely related mechanisms appear to have the potential for causing I/DD. First, the high levels of maternal stress result in elevated maternal cortisol, which directly results in reduced umbilical blood flow (Teixeira, Fisk, & Glover, 1999), particularly during periods of reduced oxygenation when the placental blood supply normally increases (Jellyman, Gardner, Fowden, & Giussani, 2004). Second, although the placenta acts to partially protect the fetus from elevated maternal cortisol, high levels of maternal cortisol do cross the placenta into the fetus, where they can be expected to affect the developing nervous system adversely (e.g., Sun, Yang, & Challis, 1998), much as they do in traumatized children. In a sense, these children may be born with posttraumatic stress disorder. In addition, the high levels of cortisol increase blood pressure in the fetus and may increase the risk of stroke before, during, or after birth.

Animal model experiments suggest that the effects cortisol produced by severe or prolonged maternal trauma may be quite large. One study followed the offspring of rhesus monkey mothers that had been given large does of dexamethasone (i.e., cortisol equivalent) during the third trimester of pregnancy (Uno et al., 1994). Monkeys born to these mothers were compared to those born to mothers given a placebo. At 9 months of age the monkeys born to treated mothers had elevated cortisol levels and were hypersensitive to stress. These monkeys developed atypical brain anatomy with "irreversible deficiency in hippocampal neurons" (p. 336). At the age of 20 months the hippocampus in these animals averaged 30% smaller than in

TABLE 9-5 *Selected Studies of Spousal Violence During Pregnancy*

STUDY	STUDY TYPE AND LEVEL OF EVIDENCE	PARTICIPANTS	MEASURES	RELEVANT FINDINGS
Uno et al., 1994	Animal model	8 rhesus monkey mother and offspring pairs	Cortisol levels in offspring MRIs and other measures of brain development	Cortisol levels of offspring of mothers with high cortisol levels were elevated, endocrine stress responses of these primates were extreme, hippocampal volumes in offspring of treated mothers were 305 smaller than in controls at age 20 months.
McFarlane et al., 1996	Prospective cohort study	1203 pregnant women	Screened for abuse repeatedly during pregnancy Health history and birth outcomes	16% of women experienced abuse during pregnancy (60% of these described recurrent violence during pregnancy). Abused women were twice as likely to begin prenatal care in the third trimester. Abused women were more likely to have low-birthweight infants (mean birthweight was reduced by 133 g). Reduced birthweight was present for abused women in White, African-American, and Hispanic groups of abused women, but the largest effect was in the White group. More severe abuse was followed by a larger reduction in birthweight.
Fernandez & Krueger, 1999	Prospective case series	489 low-income, predominately white women, screened to eliminate substance abuse	Self-report of domestic violence history Gestational age at birth, birthweight	20% reported domestic violence. Among those experiencing domestic violence, 22% had preterm deliveries and 16% had low-birthweight infants. Among those without domestic violence, 9% had preterm deliveries and 6% had low-birthweight infants.

226

Study	Study type	Sample	Measures	Findings
Grimstad et al., 1999	Case control study	83 women who delivered low-birthweight (< 2500 g) infants and 92 women who delivered other infants	History of physical abuse History of smoking and alcohol use during pregnancy	Women who were abused were much more likely to smoke during pregnancy and more likely to drink during pregnancy. Alcohol and tobacco use during pregnancy were associated with low birthweight. Abuse history was not significantly associated after control for tobacco and alcohol use.
Teixeira et al., 1999	Prospective case series	100 pregnant women	Spielberger stress questionnaire, uterine artery flow	Mothers with high levels of anxiety had decreased uterine blood flow. Trait anxiety had lesser effect compared to state anxiety. Mean increase in resistance to blood flow was 24%.
Murphy et al., 2001	Meta-analysis of case-control and cohort studies	14 high-quality studies (sample sizes 178–1897) were selected for inclusion from an initial pool of 537 articles.	Rates of abuse during pregnancy Pregnancy outcomes	Prevalence of abuse during pregnancy ranged from 5.6% to 16.6%. After regression to control for other factors, abuse during pregnancy is associated with lowered birthweights (adjusted odds ratio 1:4).
Jellyman et al., 2004	Animal model	23 ewes	Umbilical conductance and fetal blood pressure with and without dexamethasone (cortisol equivalent)	Maternal dexamethasone interfered with normal blood flow in the placenta and prevented normal increase in blood flow in response to hypoxia.
Neggers et al., 2004	Level Ib Prospective cohort study	3149 low-income, low-risk, predominately African-American pregnant women older than 14 yrs of age	Abuse assessment screen Gestational age at birth, birthweight	5.9% women reported. Abuse during pregnancy was associated significantly with low birthweight (adjusted odds ratio 1:8) and preterm birth (adjusted odds ratio 1:6)

controls. The essential role of the hippocampus in memory and learning suggests the likelihood that this process could contribute substantially to I/DD.

Taken together, the evidence of these studies suggests that prenatal violence-induced I/DD may be an important link between violence and I/DD. If confirmed, it could be conceptualized as having two major components. The first has been described as fetal disruption sequence (e.g., Gabis, Gelman-Kohan, & Mogilner, 1997). It appears to be relatively rare and likely to produce severe I/DD. It occurs when a mother experiences gross trauma during pregnancy, resulting in a period of severe fetal hypoxia as a result of maternal shock and other associated changes in the fetal environment. While these episodes often result in miscarriage, when the fetus survives, microcephaly and I/DD are typical outcomes. The second postnatal component would be prenatal traumatic stress–induced I/DD. It may prove to be much more common but to typically have subtler effects.

The state of the available evidence on prenatal violence-induced I/DD is more than adequate to place a high priority on further and more detailed study. However, there are many gaps in the currently available research to make it possible to draw firm conclusions regarding whether prenatal violence contributes substantially as a causal factor. Until more information becomes available, implications for prevention and clinical practice remain unclear.

Summary

Current research indicates that there is a strong association between I/DD and exposure to maltreatment, but no clear causal pathway has been demonstrated to account for the major portion of the association. Although researchers have generally assumed that I/DD typically preexists and increases vulnerability to the maltreatment, a significant component of this association may result from violence acting as a causal factor in I/DD. Current estimates of the role of violence in causing I/DD, however, suggests violence is an etiologic factor in fewer than 1% of cases, far less than would be required to make a significant contribution to the strong association between I/DD and violence. Three areas of research now suggest that violence may be making a much larger contribution to the etiology of I/DD than previously estimated.

First, research on outcomes of children sustaining head injury as a result of maltreatment suggests that a significant delay in appearance of neurologic disabilities of several months to several years led to an overly optimistic estimation of recovery from these injuries. This has probably led to an underestimation of the role of child maltreatment in producing severe I/DD due to brain injury.

Second, research on physiologic responses to the extreme stress of maltreatment has demonstrated that physiologic responses to violence, including emotional violence and in some cases witnessing violence, can produce enduring biochemical, electrochemical, and anatomical changes in the developing central nervous system. Although these effects are subtler than the gross brain injuries associated with head injury, they are enduring and affect a much larger group of children. These are more likely to contribute to large numbers of milder I/DD.

Finally, there is a large body of research on extreme stress and spousal abuse during pregnancy suggesting that these phenomena have significant negative effects on pregnancy outcomes. This research suggests that extremely high levels of stress associated with violence during pregnancy significantly increase the number of infants at risk for I/DD and are likely to add many more cases, most in the mild range of I/DD. The actual number of these at-risk infants who develop I/DD, however, remains unknown.

While these three mechanisms by which violence can produce I/DD are conceptually distinct from each other, it is likely that they overlap and compound each other in a variety of ways as they affect the actual development of children. For example, the child who experiences gross brain injury as a result of shaking or striking is not immune to the emotional–endocrine stress responses associated with maltreatment, and the child who is exposed to high levels of cortisol may have anatomical and physiological effects that increase vulnerability to future physical trauma and reduce resilience to gross brain injury.

Taken together, these three mechanisms could account for many more cases of I/DD than are currently attributed to violence. While it is premature and speculative to estimate a percentage of cases attributable to violence, the contribution of violence could easily prove to be as great as or greater than that of genetic causes or alcohol-related birth defects, based on current evidence. Nevertheless, while current evidence is adequate to allow for that possibility, it falls far short of providing any conclusive proof. Research is urgently needed in many areas to fill in the current gaps in research. There are too many areas in need of study to list here, but the following examples would help to clarify the current picture.

First, carefully conductive prospective studies of child cohorts analyzed by age would help to identify the early indicators of abuse and of disability and might help clarify whether maltreatment preceded or followed the emergence of disability. A study similar to that of the Sullivan and Knutson (1997, 2000) study, but with repeated data collection over 6 years at annual or biannual intervals, would be ideal.

Second, studies of maternal abuse of mothers during pregnancy need to follow low-birthweight and normal birthweight infants of abused and non-abused mothers over time to determine if I/DD emerges in these at-risk infants. This would clarify whether the risk factors actually produce disability in babies born to maltreated mothers.

Finally, long-term studies of abuse rates in children whose I/DD can be clearly diagnosed and results from a nonviolence-related cause (e.g., Down syndrome) would help determine the association between violence and I/DD filtering out the effects of violence as an etiologic factor. Comparing current incidence of victimization among these individuals with the incidence among those for whom violence may have been a contributing factor might help separate the cases attributable to one pathway or the other.

The potential implications of violence-induced I/DD for prevention programs and clinical practice are vast. With the exception of "don't-shake-the-baby" campaigns, violence prevention has received very little attention as a means of preventing I/DD. Even using current estimates of etiology with no revision, child battering is a causal factor in more than four times as many cases of mental retardation in young children than motor vehicle accidents and in more than seven times the number of cases as encephalitis (Centers for Disease Control and Prevention, 1996), yet much more attention is given to those causes. Confirmation of some or all of violence-induced I/DD mechanisms discussed in this chapter could easily multiply those ratios by a factor of 10 or 20. Perhaps then society would be willing to include violence prevention among its approaches to preventing I/DD.

The overall finding that about one third of children with mental retardation have a confirmed history of maltreatment and that most of the abuse occurs within families (e.g., Sullivan & Knutson, 1997, 2000) is a sobering finding whether maltreatment causes, follows, or merely coincides with I/DD. We must be cautious not to indict all families and recognize that healthy families still represent the best living alternative for children with I/DD. We must also recognize that some families, specifically but not exclusively some families of children with I/DD, require support to remain healthy families. Nevertheless, we must also recognize that there is also a group of children with I/DD living within families that do harm to them. Just as it does injustice to well-functioning families and families with the potential to be healthy families to blame them for the abuse problem among children with I/DD, it is an injustice to ignore the harm done to large numbers of children with I/DD by their families. Children with I/DD need the same protection as all other children.

Current child-welfare efforts are only beginning to recognize that about one quarter of maltreated children have diagnosed disabilities (e.g., 22.5% in Sullivan & Knutson, 1997, 2000). Most child-welfare systems, however, are poorly equipped to address the needs of children with I/DD. Support programs for families of children with I/DD need to be seamlessly integrated with child welfare programs so that children who have needs for both can receive a blended program suited to their needs, rather than being assigned one or receiving uncoordinated services from both that create inefficiencies and often work against each other.

The next decade may be critical in filling the gaps in evidence and determining the actual contribution of violence to I/DD. Nevertheless, unless and until a great deal of additional study provides evidence, this proposition can be considered only a strong possibility.

REFERENCES

Ammerman, R. T., Hersen, M., Van Hasselt, V. B., Lubetsky, M. J., & Sieck, W. R. (1994). Maltreatment in psychiatrically hospitalized children and adolescents with developmental disabilities—Prevalence and correlates. *Journal of the American Academy of Child and Adolescent Psychiatry, 33,* 567–576.

Ammerman, R. T., Van Hasselt, V. B., Hersen, M., McGonigle, J. J., & Lubetsky, M. J. (1989). Abuse and neglect in psychiatrically hospitalized multihandicapped children. *Child Abuse & Neglect, 13,* 335–343.

Andre, C. E. (1985). Child maltreatment and handicapped children: An examination of family characteristics and service provision. *Dissertation Abstracts International, 46(3),* 792A.

Balogh, R., Bretherton, K., Whibley, S., Berney, T., Graham, S., Richold, P., et al. (2001). Sexual abuse in children and adolescents with intellectual disability. *Journal of Intellectual Disability Research, 45*(Pt 3), 194–201.

Benedict, M., White, R. B., Wulff, L. M., & Hall, B. J. (1990). Reported maltreatment in children with multiple disabilities. *Child Abuse & Neglect, 14,* 207–217.

Billmire, M. E., & Myers, P. A. (1985). Serious head injury in infants: Accident or abuse? *Pediatrics, 75,* 340–342.

Birrell, R., & Birrell, J. (1968). The maltreatment syndrome in children: A hospital survey. *Medical Journal of Australia, 2,* 1023–1029.

Bonnier, C., Nassogne, M. C., & Evrard, P. (1995). Outcome and prognosis of whiplash shaken infant syndrome: Late consequences after a symptom-free interval. *Developmental Medicine and Child Neurology, 37,* 943–956.

Brown, H. (1992). Abuse of adults with learning difficulties. *Mental Handicap Bulletin, 86*(4), 18–19.

Buchanan, A., & Oliver, J. E. (1977). Abuse and neglect as a cause of mental retardation: A study of 140 children admitted to subnormality hospitals in Wiltshire. *British Journal of Psychiatry, 131,* 458–467.

Bugental, D. B., Martorell, G. A., & Barraza, V. (2003). The hormonal costs of subtle forms of infant maltreatment. *Hormones and Behavior, 43*(1), 237–244.

Caffey, J. (1946). Multiple fractures in long bones of infants suffering from chronic subdural hematomas. *American Journal of Roentgenology, 56,* 163–168.

Canadian Task Force on Periodic Health Examination. (1979). The periodic health examination. *Canadian Medical Association Journal, 121,* 1193–1254.

Centers for Disease Control and Prevention. (1996). Postnatal causes of developmental disabilities in children aged 3–10 years—Atlanta, Georgia, 1991. *MMWR Weekly, 46,* pp. 130–134.

Centre for Evidence-Based Medicine. (2004). Levels of evidence and grades of recommendation. Retrieved April 28, 2004 from http://www.cebm.net/levels_of_evidence.asp

Cowardin, N. W. (1987). *Preventing sexual exploitation of adolescents with exceptional needs.* (Report). Seattle: Seattle Rape Relief Crisis Centre.

Crosse, S. B., Kaye, E., & Ratnofsky, A. C. (1993). *A report on the maltreatment of children with disabilities* (Contract No.: 105-89-1630). Washington, DC: National Center on Child Abuse and Neglect.

Davies, R. K. (1979). Incest and vulnerable children. *Science News, 116,* 244–245.

de Haan, B. (1997). Critical and fatal child maltreatment in Oregon: Escalating violence or distinct behavior? *Dissertation Abstracts International, 58,* 3307.

Diamond, L. J., & Jaudes, P. K. (1983). Child abuse in a cerebral-palsied population. *Developmental Medicine and Child Neurology, 25,* 169–174.

Elmer, E., & Gregg, G. S. (1967). Developmental characteristics of abused children. *Pediatrics, 40*(4, Pt I), 596–602.

Embry, R. A. (2001, July). Examination of risk factors for maltreatment of deaf children: Findings from a National Survey. Paper presented at the 7th International Family Violence Research Conference, Portsmouth, NH.

Eppler, M., & Brown, G. (1977). Child abuse and neglect: Preventable causes of mental retardation. *Child Abuse & Neglect, 1*(2–4), 309–313.

Ewing-Cobbs, L., & Barnes, M. (2002). Linguistic outcomes following traumatic brain injury in children. *Seminars in Pediatric Neurology, 9,* 209–217.

Fernandez, F. M., & Krueger, P. M. (1999). Domestic violence: Effect on pregnancy outcome. *Journal of the American Osteopathic Association, 99,* 254–256.

Frisch, L. E., & Rhoads, F. A. (1982). Child abuse and neglect in children referred for learning evaluation. *Journal of Learning Disability, 15,* 538–541.

Furey, E. M. (1994). Sexual abuse of adults with mental retardation: Who and where. *Mental Retardation, 32,* 173–180.

Gabis, L., Gelman-Kohan, Z., & Mogilner, M. (1997). Microcephaly due to fetal brain disruption sequence. *Journal of Perinatal Medicine, 25,* 213–215.

Gil, E. (1970). *Violence against children: Physical child abuse.* Cambridge, MA: Harvard University Press.

Glaser, D. (2000). Child abuse and neglect and the brain—a review. *Journal of Child Psychology and Psychiatry, 41*(1), 97–116.

Goodman, L. A., Salyers, M. P., Mueser, K. T., Rosenberg, S. D., Swartz, M., Essock, S. M., et al. (2001). Recent victimization in women and men with severe mental illness: Prevalence and correlates. *Journal of Traumatic Stress, 14,* 615–632.

Green, A. H., Voeller, K., Gaines, R., & Kubie, J. (1981). Neurological impairment in maltreated children. *Child Abuse & Neglect, 5,* 129–134.

Grimstad, H., Schei, B., Backe, B., & Jacobsen, G. (1999). Anxiety, physical abuse, and low birth weight. *Scandinavian Journal of Public Health, 27,* 296–300.

Hanks, R. A., Wood, D. L., Millis, S., Harrison-Felix, C., Pierce, C. A., Rosenthal, M., et al. (2003). Violent traumatic brain injury: Occurrence, patient characteristics, and risk factors from the Traumatic Brain Injury Model Systems project. *Archives of Physical Medicine and Rehabilitation, 84,* 249–254.

Hansen, C. (1980). Child abuse: A cause and effect of mental retardation. In M. K. McCormack (Ed.), *Prevention of mental retardation and other developmental disabilities* (pp. 549–568). New York: Dekker.

Hard, S. (1986, Oct.). Sexual abuse of the developmentally disabled: A case study. Paper presented at the National Conference of Executives of Associations for Retarded Citizens, Omaha, NE.

Jellyman, J. K., Gardner, D. S., Fowden, A. L., & Giussani, D. A. (2004). Effects of dexamethasone on the uterine and umbilical vascular beds during basal and hypoxemic conditions in sheep. *American Journal of Obstetrics and Gynecology, 190,* 825–835.

Johnson, B., & Morse, H. (1968). Injured children and their parents. *Children, 15,* 147–152.

Keenan, H. T., Runyan, D. K., Marshall, S. W., Nocera, M. A., Merten, D. F., & Sinal, S. H. (2003). A population-based study of inflicted traumatic brain injury in young children. *Journal of the American Medical Association, 290,* 621–626.

Kempe, C. H., Silverman, F. N., Steele, B. F., Droegemueller, W., & Silver, H. K. (1962). The battered child syndrome. *Journal of the American Medical Association, 181,* 17–24.

Kendall-Tackett, K. (2002). Abuse and neglect of children with disabilities. *Rehabilitation Psychology News, 29,* 12–13.

Koenen, K. C., Moffitt, T. E., Caspi, A., Taylor, A., & Purcell, S. (2003). Domestic violence is associated with environmental suppression of IQ in young children. *Developmental Psychopathology, 15,* 297–311.

Larson, S. A., Lakin, K. C., Anderson, L., Kwak, N., Lee, J. H., & Anderson, D. (2001). Prevalence of mental retardation and developmental disabilities: Estimates from the 1994/1995 National Health Interview Survey Disability Supplements. *American Journal of Mental Retardation, 106,* 231–252.

Libby, A. M., Sills, M. R., Thurston, N. K., & Orton, H. D. (2003). Costs of childhood physical abuse: Comparing inflicted and unintentional traumatic brain injuries. *Pediatrics, 112*(1, Pt 1), 58–65.

Lo, T. Y., McPhillips, M., Minns, R. A., & Gibson, R. J. (2003). Cerebral atrophy following shaken impact syndrome and other non-accidental head injury (NAHI). *Pediatric Rehabilitation, 6*(1), 47–55.

Marchetti, A. G., & McCartney, J. R. (1990). Abuse of persons with mental retardation: Characteristics of the abused, the abusers, and the informers. *Mental Retardation, 28,* 367–371.

Martin, H. P., Beezley, P., Conway, E. F., & Kempe, C. H. (1974). The development of abused children. Part 2. Physical, neurologic, and intellectual outcome. *Advances in Pediatrics, 21,* 44–73.

McCarthy, M., & Thompson, D. (1997). A prevalence study of sexual abuse of adults with intellectual disabilities referred for sex education. *Journal of Applied Research in Intellectual Disabilities, 10,* 105–124.

McFarlane, J., Parker, B., & Soeken, K. (1996). Abuse during pregnancy: Associations with maternal health and infant birth weight. *Nursing Research, 45*(1), 37–42.

Miller, W. L., Kaplan, S. L., & Grumbach, M. M. (1980). Child abuse as a cause of post-traumatic hypopituitarism. *New England Journal of Medicine, 302,* 724–728.

Morse, C. W., Sahler, O. Z., & Friedman, S. B. (1970). A three-year follow-up study of abused and neglected children. *American Journal of Diseases of Children, 120,* 439–446.

Murphy, C. C., Schei, B., Myhr, T. L., & Du Mont, J. (2001). Abuse: A risk factor for low birth weight? A systematic review and meta-analysis. *Canadian Medical Association Journal, 164,* 1567–1572.

Neggers, Y., Goldenberg, R., Cliver, S., & Hauth, J. (2004). Effects of domestic violence on preterm birth and low birth weight. *Acta Obstetrica et Gynecologica Scandinavica, 83,* 455–460.

Oliver, J. E. (1975). Microcephaly following baby battering and shaking. *British Medical Journal, 2*(5965), 262–264.

Perez-Arjona, E., Dujovny, M., Vinas, F., Park, H. K., Lizarraga, S., Park, T., et al. (2002). CNS child abuse: Epidemiology and prevention. *Neurological Research, 24*(1), 29–40.

Perry, B. D. (1994). Neurobiological sequelae of childhood trauma: Post traumatic stress disorders in children. In M. Murburg (Ed.), *Emerging concepts: Catecholamine function in post traumatic stress disorder* (pp. 253–276). Washington, DC: American Psychiatric Press.

Petersilia, J. (2001). Crime victims with developmental disabilities—A review essay. *Criminal Justice and Behavior, 28,* 655–694.

Rachana, C., Suraiya, K., Hisham, A. S., Abdulaziz, A. M., & Hai, A. (2002). Prevalence and complications of physical violence during pregnancy. *European Journal of Obstetrics, Gynecology, and Reproductive Biology, 103*(1), 26–29.

Rubin, D. M., Christian, C. W., Bilaniuk, L. T., Zazyczny, K. A., & Durbin, D. R. (2003). Occult head injury in high-risk abused children. *Pediatrics, 111*(6 Pt 1), 1382–1386.

Sangrun, A., Gaines, R. W., & Green, A. H. (1974). Child abuse and mental retardation: A problem of cause and effect. *American Journal of Mental Deficiency, 19,* 327–330.

Sobsey, D. (1994) *Violence and abuse in the lives of people with disabilities: The end of silent acceptance?* Baltimore: Paul H. Brookes.

Sobsey, D. (2002). Exceptionality, education, & maltreatment. *Exceptionality, 10*(1), 29–46.

Sobsey, D., & Doe, T. (1991). Patterns of sexual abuse and assault. *Journal of Sexuality and Disability, 9,* 243–259.

Sobsey, D., & Mansell, S. (1997, May). Patterns of abuse of children with developmental disabilities. Paper presented at the 121st annual meeting of the American Association on Mental Retardation, New York.

Sobsey, D., Randall, W., & Parrila, R. K. (1997). Gender differences in abused children with and without disabilities. *Child Abuse & Neglect, 21,* 707–720.

Sullivan, P. M., & Knutson, J. F. (1997). Maltreatment and disabilities: A school-based epidemiological study. Report of Grant 90-CA-1562-01. Washington, DC: National Center on Child Abuse and Neglect.

Sullivan, P. M., & Knutson, J. F. (2000). Maltreatment and disabilities: A population-based epidemiological study. *Child Abuse & Neglect, 24,* 1257–1273.

Sun, K., Yang, K., & Challis, J. R. (1998). Glucocorticoid actions and metabolism in pregnancy: Implications for placental function and fetal cardiovascular activity. *Placenta, 19*(5–6), 353–360.

Teicher, M. H., Andersen, S. L., Polcari, A., Anderson, C. M., Navalta, C. P., & Kim, D. M. (2003). The neurobiological consequences of early stress and childhood maltreatment. *Neuroscience and Biobehavioral Reviews, 27*(1–2), 33–44.

Teixeira, J. M., Fisk, N. M., & Glover, V. (1999). Association between maternal anxiety in pregnancy and increased uterine artery resistance index: cohort based study. *British Medical Journal, 318*(7177), 153–157.

Trocmé, N., MacLurin, B., Fallon, B., Daciuk, J., Billingsley, D., Tourigny, M., et al. (2001). *Canadian incidence study of reported child abuse and neglect: Final report.* Ottawa: Minister of Public Works and Government Services, Canada.

Turk, V., & Brown, H. (1992). Sexual abuse and adults with learning disabilities: Preliminary communication of survey results. *Mental Handicap, 20*(June), 56–58.

Uno, H., Eisele, S., Sakai, A., Shelton, S., Baker, E., DeJesus, O., & Holden, J. (1994). Neurotoxicity of glucocorticoids in the primate brain. *Hormones & Behavior, 28,* 336–348.

U.S. Department of Education. (1991). *Thirteenth annual report to Congress on the implementation of the Individuals with Disabilities Education Act.* Washington, DC: Author.

Wilson, C., & Brewer, N. (1992). The incidence of criminal victimisation of individuals with an intellectual disability. *Australian Psychologist, 27*(2), 114–117.

Yehuda, R. (1998). Psychoneuroendocrinology of posttraumatic stress disorder. *Psychiatric Clinics of North America, 21,* 359–379.

10

CASE MANAGEMENT, CARE COORDINATION, AND MANAGED CARE

Ruth Northway, PhD, MSc, RNLD, ENB 805, Cert Ed(FE)

A ppropriate access to care, quality of, and costs of health care for persons with intellectual and developmental disabilities (I/DD) can be examined by the success or lack of success of case management, care coordination, and managed care systems in the United States and internationally. As discussed in this chapter, a small amount of research has been done to test the efficacy of these systems.

Case management has been defined as: "a delivery system that focuses on outcomes by providing coordination of health care services and resources to meet the needs of a person with developmental disabilities and/or mental retardation by decreasing fragmentation, enhancing the person's quality of life, and containing costs. Case management also involves the provision of information to family members and to agencies regarding the person across settings and time" (Nehring et al., 1998, p. 13). Case management is thus concerned with outcomes related to enhanced quality of life and cost containment. The provision of information and a coordinated approach are also viewed as keys to successful case management. Each of these factors should be taken into account when reviewing the scientific evidence.

Care coordination has been defined as "coordinating or providing linkage among the various services required to meet individual needs" (Kastner, Walsh, &

| 235 |

Criscione, 1997a, p. 363). It may form part of a formal process of case management or the planning and delivery of other systems of care.

Managed care also emerged as a relevant concept in the literature search for this chapter and hence is included. It has been defined as "a series of interrelated financial and health decisions, linkages or agreements between health insurers, consumers, service providers and individual states, designed to decrease payer costs by rationing access to, and use of, services" (Goel & Keefe, 2003, p. 77).

As with case management, cost containment is a key emphasis within managed care. However, unlike in case management, there is no overt emphasis on enhancing quality of life. Indeed there is explicit reference to rationing of service provision that has the potential to negatively impact a person's quality of life.

Within the United Kingdom, the term *care management* is used in preference to case management to reflect the view that it is the care, rather than the person (or "case"), that is being managed (Department of Health Social Services Inspectorate, 1991). In the UK literature, therefore, "care management" should be taken as meaning the same as *case management*.

Methods

The literature search for this chapter took place in two stages. In the first stage, an information specialist undertook a search using the following parameters: (1) databases (Medline, CINAHL, Sociofile. Health Star, PsychInfo, Pharmaceutical Abstracts, Web Science, Academic Search Premiere, Ingenta, and GPO Access); and (2) search terms (*mental retardation, developmental disabilities,* and *Down syndrome + case management/care coordination*). Other terms such as *cerebral palsy* were used where appropriate. This resulted in the identification of 23 papers.

In the second stage, the author undertook a further search of the literature using the following parameters: (1) databases (CINAHL, Medline, Embase, ASSIA); and (2) search terms (*mental retardation, developmental disability(ies), learning disability(ies), intellectual disability(ies), mental handicap + care management/care coordination/managed care*). Additional search terms were included here to access wider international literature. Managed care was also included since it was apparent from the first stage search that this was a closely related issue. After duplicate references from the first stage were excluded, a further 49 references were identified that warranted examination.

INCLUSION/EXCLUSION CRITERIA

To be included in the review, studies had to be: (1) published since 1992, (2) written in English, (3) focused on people with I/DD and/or their families/caregivers, and (4) focused on the process or outcomes of case management/care coordination/managed care. Studies were excluded if they: (1) focused generally on the organization of services rather than specifically on case management/care coordination/managed care or (2) focused on an aspect of case management/care coordination/managed care not directly related to the promotion of health or the utilization of health care services. Thirty-two papers meeting the inclusion criteria were identified (13 from Stage 1, 19 from Stage 2). One further paper was identified from scanning the reference list of a paper already included. The identification of 19 papers in Stage 2 indicates the importance of using a wide range of search terms in order to access the international literature.

REVIEW QUESTIONS

The 33 papers meeting the inclusion criteria were reviewed and the following research questions were identified:

1. What effect does care coordination have on the use of health care facilities by people with I/DD?

2. What contribution does case management make to the care of people with I/DD who also have mental illness?

3. What contribution can case management make to the health and well-being of people with I/DD and their families/care-givers?

4. Can effective and acceptable case management systems be developed?

5. What impact does managed care have on the health and well-being of people with I/DD?

Results and Discussion

Studies were reviewed in relation to each of these questions. Key information is set out in the tables below and a commentary is provided in relation to each question highlighting key points and drawing conclusions. The studies are set out in chronological sequence so that the reader can assess the research over time.

1. What effect does care coordination have on the use of health care facilities by people with I/DD?

The seven papers in this section (see Table 10-1) all originate from the United States, with five papers authored by researchers working on one program of research during the 1990s at the Center for Human Development at the Morristown Memorial Hospital (Criscione, Kastner, Walsh, & Nathanson, 1993; Criscione, Kastner, O'Brien, & Nathanson, 1994; Criscione, Walsh, & Kastner, 1995; Kastner & Walsh, 1999; Walsh, Kastner, & Criscione, 1997). While it is positive to see a program of research focusing on this area over a sustained period of time, it is disappointing to note that similar studies do not appear to have been undertaken elsewhere. This may limit the extent to which the findings can be generalized to other areas and highlights the need for replication. Jackson, Finkler, and Robinson (1995) also note limitations in respect to their research design, which means that caution should be applied when considering the implications of the findings.

Despite these limitations, some conclusions can be drawn from these papers:

➤ The provision of health care coordination appears to have a positive impact in relation to admissions to the hospital, length of hospital stay, and hospital costs.

TABLE 10-1 *Studies Addressing the Relationship of Care Coordination to the Use of*

STUDY INFORMATION	RESEARCH DESIGN	LEVEL OF EVIDENCE	POPULATION STUDIED	TOTAL NUMBER OF SUBJECTS	AGES OF SUBJECTS	INTERVENTION
Criscione et al., 1993 (USA)	Retrospective analysis of case data (records of hospitalizations)	Level III Group research	People with intellectual disabilities	86	1–75 yrs	Health care coordination through Developmental Disabilities Center ($N = 36$)
Criscione et al., 1994 (USA)	Review of range of studies undertaken by research team	Level V— Nonempirical (although does report upon empirical studies)	People with intellectual disabilities	NA	NA	Health care coordination
Jackson et al., 1995 (USA)	Evaluation of a system of care coordination; Data gathered via staff completion of an activity log	Level IV Group research	Children with developmental disabilities and chronic illnesses	31	Birth– 27 mos at point of entry to the service	Service coordination across settings
Criscione et al., 1995	Retrospective analysis of case data (records of hospitalizations)	Level III Group research	People with developmental disabilities	370	Birth to 55+	Health care coordination through Developmental Disabilities Center ($N = 102$)

GROUP INTERVENTION	CONTROL OUTCOMES OF INTEREST	RESULTS	CLINICAL IMPORTANCE
Usual care (*N* = 50)	1. Hospital/ practice variables 2. Cost variables 3. Readmission rates	Patients receiving care coordination had shorter hospital stays, fewer admissions, and were less severely ill upon admission. Costs of care coordination were partially offset by reductions in in-patient utilization.	This study suggests that care coordination may have both clinical and financial benefits.
NA	1. Financial implication 2. Clinical outcomes 3. In-patient and out-patient utilization rates 4. Social service utilization rates	Retrospective analysis of case data reveals that care coordination leads to improvement in client health, reduced hospital stays, readmissions, and costs. Nurse practitioners as both primary care providers and care coordinators are most cost-efficient.	This review suggests that nurse practitioners acting as case coordinators can have a positive impact on both health status of clients and on usage of hospital facilities.
NA	Time costs in relation to: 1. Service coordination activities 2. Diagnosis 3. Family variables 4. Age of child	The most time-consuming service coordination activities involved providing family support and exchanging information. Costs varied according to the age of the child and his or her diagnosis. The time and costs incurred were almost double for those families with multiple problems.	Limitations include sample size and the exclusion of administrative and overhead costs from the analysis. However, the study does illustrate that it is possible to analyze service coordination functions and costs.
Usual care (*N* = 268)	1. Length of hospital stay 2. Hospital charges 3. Case mix adjusted variables	The intervention group had shorter lengths of stay and lower hospital charges especially when charges were adjusted for case mix.	This study suggests that the lack of well-managed and coordinated services can lead to increased hospitalizations. It also suggests that community based services can be provided in a cost-effective and efficient manner. However, it stresses that while this study has indicated that care coordination can lead to more efficient use of health care services, future research needs to focus upon the quality of health outcomes achieved and consumer satisfaction. Methodologically it suggests that 'outliers' or 'influential cases' may need to be excluded from analyses of data if findings are not to be skewed by such unusual cases.

(*continued*)

TABLE 10-1 *Continued*

STUDY INFORMATION	RESEARCH DESIGN	LEVEL OF EVIDENCE	POPULATION STUDIED	TOTAL NUMBER OF SUBJECTS	AGES OF SUBJECTS	INTERVENTION
Walsh et al., 1997 (USA)	Interrogation and analysis of datasets (one statewide and one coordinated care maintained by one hospital) —longitudinal analysis	Level IV— group research	People with developmental disabilities	22,986 admissions	Birth to death	Health care coordination (*N* = 692)
Anon., 1997 USA	Report of program of work at Morristown (see studies above)	Level V Nonempirical	People with developmental disabilities	NA	NA	Focuses on the program of work under-taken in relation to health care coordination
Kastner & Walsh, 1999 (USA)	Commentary on research paper	Level V Nonempirical	Children with special health care needs	NA	NA	Targeted case management

NA, Not applicable.

➤ In the studies at the Morristown Memorial Hospital, health care coordination was usually undertaken by nurse practitioners. Criscione and colleagues (1994) conclude that nurse practitioners working in this capacity can have a positive impact on both the health of clients and on hospital usage.

➤ The outcomes measured in these studies relate primarily to service usage rather than to impact on health of people with I/DD and consumer satisfaction. These are thus identified as areas for future research (Criscione et al., 1995).

➤ Some methodological challenges exist when undertaking research in this area, most notably the need to consider the impact of unusual cases or outliers on the overall results and the consequent advisability of including them in the analysis.

GROUP INTERVENTION	CONTROL OUTCOMES OF INTEREST	RESULTS	CLINICAL IMPORTANCE
Usual care (N = 22,294)	1. Admissions 2. Hospital days 3. Length of stay 4. Costs of care	Over the study period (1983–1991) an increase in hospital admissions and hospital days were found for people with developmental disabilities and their hospital charges rose by almost twice that of the general population. However, care coordination moderated each of these effects.	This study suggests that health care coordination can reduce in patient utilization and costs.
NA	1. Length of hospital stay 2. Costs of hospitalizations	From the review they conclude that those patients receiving care coordination had shorter hospital stays and lower health care costs.	Highlights the potential benefits of health care coordination
NA	The effect of "outliers" on overall effect (methodological concern)	The authors of the original paper respond by stating that the outliers had not been removed from their analysis but that both the median and the mode had been calculated.	This paper highlights the need to consider both the median and the mode when undertaking analysis of data concerning case management. There is also a need to make contextual factors explicit.

2. What contribution does case management make to the care of people with I/DD who also have mental illness?

Papers addressing the above question (see Table 10-2) include three reports of randomized trials (Coelho, Kelley, Deatsman-Kelley, & Eaton-Ingham,1993; Hassiotis et al., 2001; Tyrer, Hassiotis, Ukoumunne, Piachaud, & Harvey, 1999), one multi-center study (Hassiotis et al., 2001), and research from both the United States and the United Kingdom. This suggests that perhaps greater confidence can be placed in the findings of such studies. Nonetheless, the authors note limitations to their findings in terms of sample size, sample characteristics, and restriction to defined geographic areas, suggesting the need for some caution when seeking to generalize from the findings of these studies. These latter two studies, however, report upon different stages of the same study.

STUDY INFORMATION	RESEARCH DESIGN	LEVEL OF EVIDENCE	POPULATION STUDIED	TOTAL NUMBER OF SUBJECTS	AGES OF SUBJECTS	INTERVENTION
Coelho et al., 1993 (USA)	Experimental— Randomized trial	Level I Group research	Adults with developmental disabilities and mental illness	46 23 intervention and 23 control group	20–67 (mean 34)	Active treatment— case management of increased frequency and intensity of contact, individualized treatment, and access to 24-hour crisis support
Patterson et al., 1995 (USA)	Retrospective review of hospital admission data	Level IV— Group research	People with developmental disabilities and mental illness	Not stated	Not stated	Inter-agency consortium that included a joint funded liaison post, after hours and respite service, proactive inter-agency treatment planning

CONTROL GROUP INTERVENTION	OUTCOMES OF INTEREST	MEASURES USED	RESULTS	CLINICAL IMPORTANCE
Traditional case management	1. Adaptive functioning 2. Maladaptive functioning 3. Use of day/residential service 4. Psychiatric in-patient usage	1. Intake questionnaire 2. AAMD Adaptive Behavior Scale 3. Michigan Maladaptive Behavior Scale	Maladaptive behaviors decreased in the active treatment group but remained constant in the traditional treatment group. Adaptive behaviors significantly increased in the active treatment group but dropped in the traditional treatment group. Active treatment facilitated movement towards less staff-intensive day and residential services. Those in active treatment made more use of acute inpatient facilities but none were admitted to State inpatient facilities.	The study notes limitations in respect of sample size, the fact that the sample comprised those most likely to require institutionalization, and the fact that it is confined to one geographical area. Nonetheless, it does suggest that active treatment in the form of intensive case management may offer benefits in respect of client outcomes and service usage.
NA	1. Number of admissions 2. Appropriateness of admissions 3. Length of stay 4. Number of days awaiting discharge pending community placement	Data from agency records	Admissions did not reduce significantly but frequency of appropriate admissions significantly increased. Mean and median length of hospital stays decreased but not significantly. There was a significant decrease in the length of time awaiting placement at discharge.	Limitations: lack of baseline data, only state hospital admissions; number of clients diverted to community unknown; no randomization. Suggests collaborative care systems may improve utilization of health care and increase inter-agency collaboration.

(continued)

TABLE 10-2 *Continued*

STUDY INFORMATION	RESEARCH DESIGN	LEVEL OF EVIDENCE	POPULATION STUDIED	TOTAL NUMBER OF SUBJECTS	AGES OF SUBJECTS	INTERVENTION
Tyrer et al., 1999 (UK)	Randomized trial	Level I Group research	Patients with psychosis who had normal or borderline intelligence	562 Intervention group: borderline intelligence $N = 47$, normal intelligence $N = 227$ Control group: borderline intelligence $N = 53$, normal intelligence $N = 235$	Not stated	Intensive case management
Polgar et al., 2000 (USA)	Survey	Level II Outcomes research (analytic survey)	Program leaders within mental health, developmental disabilities, and substance misuse services	100	NA	NA

Some findings, however, appear consistent between studies and may, therefore, be worthy of further exploration. Intensive case management, defined in terms of smaller caseloads for case managers, additional forms of service provision, and more assertive outreach, is reported as having positive benefits in terms of reduced more appropriate hospitalizations, and improved client outcomes. An increase in client satisfaction has also been noted (Hassiotis et al., 2001). However, definitions of "intensive" case management do not appear consistent between studies and this should be addressed in future research.

The studies reviewed in relation to this question tended to focus on those with

CONTROL GROUP INTERVENTION	OUTCOMES OF INTEREST	MEASURES USED	RESULTS	CLINICAL IMPORTANCE
Standard case management	1. Days in hospital 2. Number of admissions over a 2-yr period	1. National Adult Reading Test 2. Mean number of days spent in hospital 3. Mean number of admissions	Patients with borderline intelligence and psychosis were similar to those of normal intelligence in mean days in hospital and number of admissions. Intensive case management significantly reduced days in hospital/admissions for those with borderline intelligence.	While "standard" case management has improved, benefits do not extend to those with borderline intelligence and psychosis who may require assertive outreach and intensive care management.
NA	1. Organizational setting 2. Social network relationships—intra-organizational, variety of services provided, inter-organizational relationships	Survey instrument derived from earlier studies of organizational issues in mental health settings	Variety of services used was greater in developmental disabilities services. Developmental disabilities service leaders had the most external relationships.	The authors identify a number of indicators of best practice from their survey findings and from field observations. These are a single portal of entry into services, inter-agency councils, special linkages between services for people with developmental disabilities and those for people with mental health or substance misuse problems, strong leadership and consistency of mission.

(continued)

mild I/DD and those with borderline intelligence. The potential impact on those with more severe I/DD thus requires further investigation.

3. What contribution can case management make to the health and well-being of people with I/DD and their families/caregivers?

The studies reviewed in relation to this question (see Table 10-3) were diverse both in terms of country of origin and the client group who forms the focus of the studies. The provision of case management services to both young children and

TABLE 10-2 *Continued*

STUDY INFORMATION	RESEARCH DESIGN	LEVEL OF EVIDENCE	POPULATION STUDIED	TOTAL NUMBER OF SUBJECTS	AGES OF SUBJECTS	INTERVENTION
Hassiotis et al. 2001 (UK)	Randomized controlled trial (part of larger, multisite study)	Level I Group research	Patients with severe psychotic illness including a subgroup of those with borderline intelligence	586 Intervention group: borderline intelligence $N = 50$, normal intelligence $N = 237$ Control group: borderline intelligence $N = 54$, normal intelligence $N = 245$	Not stated	Intensive case management (defined as a caseload of 10–15 clients) as opposed to a caseload of 30–35 for standard case management which the control group received)
Hassiotis, 2002 (UK)	Review of research literature	Level V Non-empirical	People with intellectual disabilities/developmental disabilities who also have mental health problems	NA	NA	Concerned with service models of which one is the study immediately above

NA, Not applicable.

older people with I/DD is considered, as are different family configurations (e.g., parents and grandparents). This highlights the need to consider the contribution that case management makes to a variety of subgroups rather than considering people with I/DD as a homogeneous group.

The studies tended to be relatively small in scale, used different measures, and focused on different outcomes of interest. This makes comparison difficult and limits the potential to generalize. Nonetheless, some key themes emerged that could have implications for both practice and research:

CONTROL GROUP INTERVENTION	OUTCOMES OF INTEREST	MEASURES USED	RESULTS	CLINICAL IMPORTANCE
Standard case management (defined as a caseload of 30–35 clients)	1. Days in hospital for psychiatric reasons 2. Costs of care 3. Clinical outcomes 4. Satisfaction	1. Prospective analysis of resource use data over a 2-yr period 2. Range of validated clinical assessment tools 3. Satisfaction with mental health services assessment tools	Intensive case management was significantly more beneficial for those with borderline intelligence and psychosis than for those with normal intelligence in terms of the number of days spent in hospital, number of hospital admissions, and total costs, and needs. There were also significantly higher levels of satisfaction among this subgroup. No significant differences were found in relation to clinical outcomes.	Limitations: local service arrangements may limit generalization; further research needed to increase sample size. Conclude that patients with borderline intelligence respond better to intensive case management than do those with normal intelligence. Suggest improvements in outcome and lower total costs demonstrated in this study indicate that intensive case management is more cost-effective than standard case management for people with borderline intelligence and psychosis.
NA	As above	NA	NA	See above.

► Case management services generally appear to be valued by families, although the satisfaction of people with I/DD themselves is not assessed in these studies.

► Case management does appear to play a role in both providing information and in enabling access to other services. The need to consider informal supports is also important.

► Case managers require particular knowledge and skills if they are to provide an effective service.

TABLE 10-3 *Studies Related to the Contribution of Case Management to the Health*

STUDY INFORMATION	RESEARCH DESIGN	LEVEL OF EVIDENCE	POPULATION STUDIED	TOTAL NUMBER OF SUBJECTS	AGES OF SUBJECTS	INTERVENTION
Marcenko and Smith, 1992 (USA)	Pre–post/test design	Level IV Group research	Families of children with developmental disabilities and significant health problems	32 families	Children aged 0–26 (70% under age 9)	Family-centered case management system
Levy et al., 1996 (USA)	Survey—interviews	Level II—outcomes research	Families with children with mental retardation/ developmental disabilities	132 families	2–51 yrs	NA
Ardito et al., 1997 (USA)	Survey	Level II—outcome research	Mothers of children with mental retardation/ developmental disabilities	70	Mothers 21–75 yrs Children Under age 41	NA

4. Can effective and acceptable case management systems be developed?

The papers reviewed are outlined in Table 10-4. They are primarily opinion/review papers with only one paper involving empirical research. Nonetheless some key themes emerge that may warrant further research:

and Well-Being of Persons with I/DD

CONTROL GROUP INTERVENTION	OUTCOMES OF INTEREST	MEASURES USED	RESULTS	CLINICAL IMPORTANCE
NA	1. Service needs and usage 2. Satisfaction (at follow up) 3. Family stress and coping 4. Maternal life satisfaction	Semi-structured interviews gathering both qualitative and quantitative data. Likert scales—maternal life satisfaction and sibling coping	Family-centered case management led to increased frequency of service usage. The need for a range of support identified including family and child recreational activities. Maternal life satisfaction significantly increased at follow up.	Case management services appear to increase access to other services. This was, however, limited by those services which were available in the area.
NA	Types and helpfulness of supports	Modified version of the Family Supports Scale	Mothers relied more heavily upon professional supports rather than upon family and friends. The two most available forms of informal support were non-disabled children and friends.	Suggests that those families using case management may be those with fewer informal supports and/or that case managers tend to recommend use of professional supports. Suggests case managers should monitor interventions and promote empowerment rather than encouraging dependency.
NA	Family resources —basic, money, time, and child-related	Family Resources Scale	Families reported inadequate resources in all four areas. Key deficits included inadequate time for sleep/rest and inadequate levels of money to buy equipment for child.	

(continued)

➤ The needs for partnership with families and for a client-focused approach are identified. In the future, researchers could usefully investigate approaches that best facilitate such a partnership emphasizing person-centered care.

➤ The need for case managers to be skilled and knowledgeable is noted. Researchers could usefully explore these aspects in more detail, specifically in relation to the

TABLE 10-3 *Continued*

STUDY INFORMATION	RESEARCH DESIGN	LEVEL OF EVIDENCE	POPULATION STUDIED	TOTAL NUMBER OF SUBJECTS	AGES OF SUBJECTS	INTERVENTION
Bigby, 1998 (Australia)	Survey	Level II—outcomes research	Adults with mental retardation/ developmental disability	62	55–87 yrs	NA
McCallion et al., 2000 (USA)	Evaluation of a demonstration project	Level II—outcomes research	Grandparent caregivers of children with developmental disabilities	97 grand-parents 171 children	Grand-parents 40–82 yrs of age Children 2–25 yrs of age	NA
Freedman and Boyer, 2000 (USA)	Exploratory qualitative study	Level II—outcomes research	Families of children with developmental disabilities	31 (21 mothers and 8 fathers representing 26 families)	Children aged 3–37	NA

CONTROL GROUP INTERVENTION	OUTCOMES OF INTEREST	MEASURES USED	RESULTS	CLINICAL IMPORTANCE
NA	Aspects of subjects' lives and their formal and informal supports since leaving parental care	Data were gathered via semi-structured interviews.	Only six people were in receipt of case management. Functions of case management varied from service planning to irregular monitoring. Disability care managers were inexperienced in relation to needs of older people with mental retardation/ developmental disabilities.	Author suggests that among key sub groups of people with mental retardation/ developmental disabilities there may be differing needs. Older people are one such sub group.
NA	Processes involved in the project	Intake data, semi-structured interviews with staff, minutes of agency meetings	Interview themes— grandparent problems, unresponsive services, falling between the cracks, mutual support and the need for long term planning. Some children not registered as having developmental disabilities thus could not access services. Grandparents and children required a range of services.	Findings suggest there is a need to recognize the particular needs of grandparent caregivers. There is also a need for better coordination of services.
NA	Family perceptions of their experiences of, and the effects of, family supports.	NA—data gathered via focus groups	13 families used case management services. Recognized as a 'critical' form of support by some participants, both in terms of direct support and in accessing other services.	

(*continued*)

TABLE 10-3 *Continued*

STUDY INFORMATION	RESEARCH DESIGN	LEVEL OF EVIDENCE	POPULATION STUDIED	TOTAL NUMBER OF SUBJECTS	AGES OF SUBJECTS	INTERVENTION
Vogler et al., 2002 (USA)	Randomized trial	Level I—group research	Families with children with developmental disabilities	159 Families (treatment group $N = 88$, control group $N = 71$)	Children were under the age of 6 yrs	Intensive case management delivered by para-professionals (caseload of 30 visiting once every 1–2 wks)
Bigby et al., 2002 (Australia)	Process outcome evaluation	Level II—outcomes research	Older parents of adults with mental retardation/developmental disabilities	44 Clients (parent + child = one client)	Parents 50–90 yrs of age Children 18–54 yrs of age	Two pilot projects were established targeted specifically at older people with mental retardation/developmental disabilities and their families. Services included intensive case management + access to discretionary funds.

NA, Not applicable

CONTROL GROUP INTERVENTION	OUTCOMES OF INTEREST	MEASURES USED	RESULTS	CLINICAL IMPORTANCE
Basic case management delivered by nurse (caseload of 70 visiting once every 1–2 mos	1. Completion rate and time to acquisition of developmental assessment or service plan 2. Number, initiation rate, and time to recommend early intervention services 3. Number of kept and missed sessions for each completed early intervention service 4. Compliance rate	Documentation used by study staff Attendance rates from 30+ early intervention sites	Intensive case management reduced time taken to complete developmental assessments and increased recommendations and initiation of needed services. Compliance rates were equal but net effect was to increase early intervention services for the intensive case management group within 1 yr of referral.	The findings suggest that specific efforts are required in order to improve outcomes in relation to early intervention services.
NA	Outcomes of special program and whether aims had been met in terms of program design, client views of the process, and the place of the program in the wider service system.	Data were gathered via semi-structured interviews with key stakeholders (people with mental retardation/developmental disabilities, their families, case managers, and service providers)	Elements of case management: dual focus (person and parents), use of relationships to effect change, long-term episodes of varying intensity, focused support, multiple levels of intervention, working though existing networks. Preparation for leaving the parental home was significant outcome.	

TABLE 10-4 *Studies Related to the Development of Effective and Acceptable Case*

STUDY INFORMATION	RESEARCH DESIGN	LEVEL OF EVIDENCE	POPULATION STUDIED	TOTAL NUMBER OF SUBJECTS	AGES OF SUBJECTS
Wehmeyer, 1993 (USA)	Opinion paper	Level V Nonempirical	NA	NA	NA
Saunders, 1995 (USA)	Opinion paper	Level V Nonempirical	NA	NA	NA
Wetzel et al., 1996 (USA)	Evaluation—multi methods	Level II—outcomes research	Case management supervisors, people served, families, case managers, and service providers.	90 ISPP meetings were evaluated (86% response rate); 124 responses to the quality survey (34% response rate)	NA

254

OUTCOMES OF INTEREST	MEASURES USED	RESULTS		CLINICAL IMPORTANCE
NA	NA	NA		Author argues that case managers need to support and encourage choice and decision making among clients regardless of the level or severity of disability. The author also argues that the principles of normalization and integration need to be embraced, and empowerment promoted.
NA	NA	NA		The author argues that in the context of IDEA Part H the case manager can come from a variety of backgrounds but will usually be the person most involved with the family. Case management requires a partnership with the family. The differing roles played by case management are noted and it is argued that in this context it needs to operate in a medical–social model.
Inclusion of consumers Team agreements and collaborative planning	Documentation associated with plan meetings and a quality survey	Person receiving services is present at 86% of ISPP meetings. 93% of teams reported clarity in working toward long-term goal. There was no significant difference in relation to the number of objectives and outcomes identified, but significant differences in relation to service plan components and team agreements/assignments. The process was deemed to be effective in terms of quality by 75% of respondents. There were no significant differences in terms of overall time estimates but time taken after meeting was significantly shorter.		The authors argue that this study demonstrates the importance of identifying the person and family-centered approaches that will support the service recipient, and then designing the necessary documentation procedures.

(*continued*)

TABLE 10-4 *Continued*

STUDY INFORMATION	RESEARCH DESIGN	LEVEL OF EVIDENCE	POPULATION STUDIED	TOTAL NUMBER OF SUBJECTS	AGES OF SUBJECTS
Cambridge, 1999 (UK)	Opinion/ review paper	Level V Nonempirical	NA	NA	NA
Koenig et al., 2002 (USA)	Single case study design	Level V Nonempirical	One child with Smith-Lemli-Opitz Syndrome	1	12 yrs of age

NA, Not applicable.

knowledge and skills required to provide effective support for people with I/DD and their families/caregivers in future studies.

5. What impact does managed care have on the health and well-being of people with I/DD?

The papers reviewed are set out in Table 10-5. Each falls within the Level V (nonempirical) level of evidence; hence only the study reference, level of evidence, country of origin, and clinical importance are included.

Goel and Keefe (2003) note that, at the time of writing their paper, there had been no empirical studies investigating the impact of Medicaid managed care on people with I/DD. The papers reviewed here thus draw upon the wider literature regarding managed care and health care policy along with some emerging models of managed care systems for people with I/DD.

OUTCOMES OF INTEREST	MEASURES USED	RESULTS	CLINICAL IMPORTANCE
NA	NA	NA	The paper argues that case management needs to be inclusive of all people with intellectual disabilities/developmental disabilities. It notes that evidence suggests that small caseloads (20–30 clients) are more effective. It argues that case management time needs to be prioritized and that case managers need to be able to interpret and understand the needs and life of the person. Financial systems also need to be in place to support case management decisions. The skills and competencies of case managers need to be carefully considered.
NA	NA	This study highlights a lack of knowledge on the part of care-givers and primary care providers, a lack of access to specialized psychiatric services, and a smooth interface between services.	The need for a nurse with clinical expertise and health care providers with knowledge of the range of available services is highlighted.

It is not possible, from this review, to draw conclusions regarding the impact of managed care on the health and well-being of people with I/DD because of this lack of empirical evidence. It is possible, however, to identify the following emerging issues:

➤ That managed care would appear to offer both potential benefits and possible drawbacks in relation to providing effective and equitable health care for people with I/DD.

➤ That, if the potential benefits are to be realized, there is a need to ensure that effective systems are in place; that specialist knowledge and skills are used appropriately; that primary, secondary, and community services are coordinated; and that the additional support needs of people with I/DD and their families are both recognized and met.

➤ That research is required to determine the impact of managed care on the health and well-being of people with I/DD.

TABLE 10-5 *Studies Related to the Impact of Managed Care on the Health and Well-Being of People with I/DD*

STUDY INFORMATION	LEVEL OF EVIDENCE	CLINICAL IMPORTANCE
Hall, 1996 (USA)	Level V Nonempirical	The author discusses a model of service delivery for people with developmental disabilities that combines community-centered boards and a managed care structure. The example offered by community-centered boards in Colorado is presented as a basis for the implementation of such a model. The need to move from a service to a support orientation is discussed. It is argued that there is a need to develop models of managed care that combine the benefits of both outcomes-based management and systems that involve service users, and that are thus informed by their views and preferences.
Kastner et al., 1997a (USA)	Level V Nonempirical	The authors discuss the nature and development of managed care along with its perceived advantages and disadvantages for people with developmental disabilities. Significant issues are identified as being the need for disability-specific interventions, care coordination, quality, individual and family support, and interdisciplinary assessment. It is concluded that the success of managed care in meeting the needs of people with developmental disabilities and their families will be dependent on how carefully it is planned and the extent to which it addresses the coordination of care along with the provision of support for both the individual and their family.
Kastner et al., 1997b (USA)	Level V Nonempirical	The authors argue that demonstration projects have shown promising results but that practical knowledge is limited, particularly in relation to long-term care. Experience suggests that there may be gains from redirecting inpatient and hospital specialty resources toward improved care coordination and primary and enhanced administrative support. There is a need to explore managed care models that encompass long-term care needs while retaining sensitivity to the needs of clients with developmental disabilities. It is noted, however, that this may require a shift in both the culture and values of service providers.
Birenbaum & Cohen, 1998 (USA)	Level V Nonempirical	This paper is concerned with the impact that managed care may have on university affiliated programs (UAPs). The authors argue that, because of the nature of staffing within UAPs, and the experience they have in developing interdisciplinary models of care, they may be well placed to provide specialized services for clients with developmental disabilities within managed care systems. The key contributions are identified as diagnosis and assessment, case management, training, development and testing of new program approaches, research and dissemination.

258

Walsh & Kastner, 1999 (USA)	Level V Nonempirical	The authors identify the need for health-related quality indicators and performance measures specific to the needs of people with developmental disabilities. They argue that there is a need to develop functional health measures that encompass the full range of functioning among this client group along with specialized patient satisfaction measures. There is also a need to develop supports within the health care system to integrate people with developmental disabilities into existing managed care systems while recognizing their special health needs. Other problems that, it is argued, require addressing include the development of case-mix-based risk adjustment models for setting capitation rates, workable case management and care coordination systems, appropriate clinical guidelines, the development of training for health professionals concerning developmental disabilities, a workable and equitable ombudsman system, provider support and referral systems, improved management information systems, and provider networks that have the capacity to handle the clinical components of health care.
Ronder et al., 1999 (USA)	Level V Nonempirical	The authors argue that managed care can be a useful tool in overcoming some of the difficulties experienced in providing comprehensive health care for people with developmental disabilities. Some examples of demonstration projects are provided. It is argued, however, that for managed care to achieve this potential it will be necessary for people with developmental disabilities, advocacy organizations, public health organizations, and managed care organizations to work together to develop community efforts focused on preventing disease and promoting health. It is also argued that disease management programs currently utilized in relation to people with chronic illness may offer potential benefits if developed for use in relation to health care for people with developmental disabilities.
Goel & Keefe, 2003 (USA)	Level V Nonempirical	The authors explore the potential impact of Medicaid's managed care on people with developmental disabilities. The philosophy that underpins services for people with developmental disabilities, and that of managed care, are examined. Some potential models of managed care are discussed and the issues for policy analysis and research are identified. Key questions proposed for research are: How will Medicaid managed care affect the accessibility of services for both specialized and primary care? How will rationing of services for people with developmental disabilities affect the quality of those services? Will the shift to Medicaid managed care for acute health care services be followed by the inclusion of long-term care services as well, practically none of which are medical in nature?

Conclusions

In reviewing the papers for this chapter it was difficult to assign some studies to the levels of evidence used as a guide for this book (see Table A in the Preface). Some studies also provided a great deal of detail that is difficult to summarize within tables. Readers are thus advised to use this chapter as a guide and to follow up by reading the original studies where appropriate.

Limitations have been noted in respect to the studies reviewed, namely:

➤ There are few randomized trials and only one multisite study.

➤ The experimental studies tend to focus on "standard" versus "intensive" case management, but definitions of these two levels of intervention are not consistent across studies and settings.

➤ The studies tend to be small in scale and to use different outcome measures. This makes comparison between studies difficult.

Each of these factors limits the extent to which it is possible to generalize from the studies reviewed. Further limitations are:

➤ The outcomes of interest tend to relate to the usage of health care facilities and the impact on cost rather than to changes in health status.

➤ Where studies focus on the process of case management, the perceptions sought tend to be those of service providers and families rather than those of persons with I/DD.

➤ The effectiveness of case management/care coordination in relation to primary health promotion does not seem to have been investigated.

These limitations are important in the context of the definition of case management offered at the beginning of this chapter. If these aspects are not researched then it is difficult to determine the impact on quality of life from the perspective of individuals who experience case management or to determine the effectiveness of care management in identifying and meeting health care needs.

The papers do, however, provide some information in relation to both the process and outcomes of case management:

➤ Health care coordination/case management does appear to have a positive impact on usage of health care facilities and the costs incurred from such use. These findings are important when the cost containment element of care management and managed care are considered.

➤ Nurse practitioners who combine clinical and care coordination aspects within their roles appear to have a positive impact on outcomes.

➤ Case management does appear to be generally valued by families and, in one study (Hassiotis et al., 2001), to have a positive impact on client satisfaction.

Directions for Future Practice and Research

In view of the limitations noted, it would seem premature to recommend the development of clinical guidelines in relation to care management/care coordination/managed care. However, the research reviewed suggests that case management/care coordination is an effective method of care planning and delivery that is valued by families. Services should thus aim to ensure that they provide care that is coordinated across the lifespan and between agencies. The studies reviewed here suggest elements that need to be in place if this is to be achieved.

Further research is indicated focusing in the following areas:

➤ The impact of case management on client health outcomes

➤ The impact of case management on key subgroups. Studies here have included children and older people. However, adults with complex health care needs are a group whose needs for coordinated packages of care are increasingly challenging services.

➤ The views of people with I/DD concerning their experience of case management/care coordination/managed care

➤ The replication of some existing studies to strengthen the evidence base

➤ The development of multi-center and possibly multinational studies to strengthen the evidence base. This would require, however, that work be undertaken to clarify and agree upon the meaning of concepts such as "basic" and "intensive" case management.

➤ The impact of managed care on health care services for people with I/DD

REFERENCES

American Nurses Association. (1986). *Standards of community health nursing practice*. Kansas City, MO: American Nurses Association.

Anon. (1997). Coordinated care model for developmentally disabled improves care, saves money. *Cost Reengineering Report, July,* 100–103.

Ardito, M., Botuck, S., Freeman, S. E., & Levy, J. M. (1997). Delivering home-based case management to families with children with mental retardation and developmental disabilities. *Journal of Case Management, 6*(2), 56–61.

Bigby, C. (1998). Shifting responsibilities: The patterns of formal service use by older people with intellectual disabilities in Victoria. *Journal of Intellectual and Developmental Disability, 23,* 229–243.

Bigby, C., Ozanne, E., & Gordon, M. (2002). Facilitating transition: Elements of successful case management practice for older parents of adults with intellectual disability. *Journal of Gerontological Social Work, 37*(3/4), 25–43.

Birenbaum, A., & Cohen, H. J. (1998). Managed care and quality health services for people with developmental disabilities: Is there a future for UAPs? *Mental Retardation, 36,* 325–329.

Cambridge, P. (1999). Building care management competence in services for people with learning disabilities. *British Journal of Social Work, 29,* 393–415.

Coelho, R. J., Kelley, P. S., Deatsman-Kelley, C., & Eaton-Ingham, C. (1993) An experimental investigation of an innovative community treatment model for persons with a dual diagnosis (DD/MI). *Journal of Rehabilitation, 59*(2), 37–42.

Criscione, T., Kastner, T. A., O'Brien, D., & Nathanson, R. (1994). Replication of a managed health care initiative for people with mental retardation living in the community. *Mental Retardation, 32,* 43–52.

Criscione, T., Kastner, T. A., Walsh, K. K., & Nathanson, R. (1993). Managed health care services for people with mental retardation: Impact on inpatient utilization. *Mental Retardation, 31,* 297–306.

Criscione, T., Walsh, K. K., & Kastner, T. A. (1995). An evaluation of care coordination in controlling inpatient hospital utilization of people with developmental disabilities. *Mental Retardation, 33,* 364–373.

Department of Health Social Services Inspectorate. (1991). *Care management and assessment: Managers' guide.* London: HMSO.

Freedman, R. I., & Boyer, N. C. (2000). The power to choose: Supports for families caring for individuals with developmental disabilities. *Health and Social Work, 25*(1), 59–68.

Goel, N. L., & Keefe, R. H. (2003). Medicaid managed care meets developmental disabilities: Proceed with caution. *Journal of Health and Social Policy, 16*(3), 75–89.

Hall, S. R. (1996). The community-centered board model of managed care for people with developmental disabilities. *Health and Social Work, 21,* 225–229.

Hassiotis, A. (2002). Community mental health services for individuals with intellectual disabilities. Issues and approaches to optimizing outcomes. *Disease Management and Health Outcomes, 10,* 409–417.

Hassiotis, A., Ukoumunne, O., Byford, S., Tyrer, P., Harvey, K., Piachaud, J., et al. (2001). Intellectual functioning and outcome of patients with severe psychotic illness randomised to intensive case management. *British Journal of Psychiatry, 178,* 168–171.

Huber, D. (1996) *Leadership and nursing care management.* Philadelphia: Saunders.

Jackson, B., Finkler, D., & Robinson, C. (1995). A cost analysis of a case management system for infants with chronic illness and developmental disabilities. *Journal of Pediatric Nursing, 10,* 304–310.

Kastner, T. A., & Walsh, K. K. (1999). Cost of care coordination for children with special health care needs. *Archives of Pediatric and Adolescent Medicine, 153,* 1003–1004.

Kastner, T. A., Walsh, K. K., & Criscione, T. (1997a). Overview and implications of Medicaid managed care for people with developmental disabilities. *Mental Retardation, 35,* 257–269.

Kastner, T. A., Walsh, K. K., & Criscione, T. (1997b). Technical elements, demonstration projects, and fiscal models in Medicaid managed care for people with developmental disabilities. *Mental Retardation, 35,* 270–285.

Koenig, K., Scahill, L., & Teague, B. (2002). The challenge of providing continuity in the care of a disabled child: Smith-Lemli-Opitz syndrome. *Issues in Mental Health Nursing, 23,* 641–648.

Levy, J. M., Rimmerman, A., Botuck, S., Ardito, M., Freeman, S. E., & Levy, P. H. (1996). The support network of mothers of younger and adult children with mental retardation and developmental disabilities receiving case management. *The British Journal of Developmental Disabilities, 42*(1), 24–31.

Marcenko, M. O., & Smith, L. K. (1992). The impact of a family-centered case management approach. *Social Work in Health Care, 17*(1), 87–100.

McCallion, P., Janicki, M. P., Grant-Griffin, P., & Kolomer, S. (2000). Grandparent carers II: Service needs and service provision issues. *Journal of Gerontological Social Work, 33*(3), 57–84.

Nehring, W. M., Roth, S. P., Natvig, D., Morse, J. S., Savage, T., & Krajicek, M. (1998). *Statement on the scope and standards for the nurse who specializes in developmental disabilities and/or mental retardation.* Washington, DC: American Nurses Publishing.

Patterson, T., Higgins, M., & Dyck, D. G. (1995). A collaborative approach to reduce hospitalization of developmentally disabled clients with mental illness. *Psychiatric Services, 46,* 243–247.

Polgar, M. F., Johnsen, M. C., Starrett, B. E., Fried, B. J., & Morrisey, J. P. (2000). New patterns of community care: Coordinated services for dually diagnosed adults in North Carolina. *JHSA, Summer,* 50–64.

Ronder, R. W., Kastner, T., Parker, S. J., & Walsh, K. (1999). Serving people with developmental disabilities in Medicaid managed care. *Managed Care Quarterly, 7*(2), 23–30.

Saunders, E. J. (1995). Services for infants and toddlers with disabilities: IDEA, Part H. *Health and Social Work, 20*(1), 39–45.

Tyrer, P., Hassiotis, A., Ukoumunne, O., Piachaud, J., & Harvey, K. (1999). Intensive case management for psychotic patients with borderline intelligence. *The Lancet, 354,* 999–1000.

Vogler, S. D., Davidson, A. J., Crane, L. A., Steiner, J. F., & Brown, J. M. (2002). Can paraprofessional home visitation enhance early intervention service delivery? *Developmental and Behavioural Pediatrics, 23,* 208–216.

Walsh, K. K., & Kastner, T. A. (1999). Quality of health care for people with developmental disabilities: The challenge of managed care. *Mental Retardation, 37,* 1–15.

Walsh, K. K., Kastner, T., & Criscione, T. (1997). Characteristics of hospitalizations for people with developmental disabilities: Utilization, costs, and impact of care coordination. *American Journal of Mental Retardation, 101,* 505–520.

Wehmeyer, M. L. (1993). Sounding a certain trumpet. Case management as a catalyst for the empowerment of people with developmental disabilities. *Journal of Case Management, 2*(1), 14–18.

Wetzel, M. C., Sheets, C. L., & McNaboe, K. A. (1996). Reforming personal planning: The Arizona Division of Developmental Disabilities case management project. *Journal of Rehabilitation Administration, 20,* 231–245.

11

COMPLEMENTARY AND ALTERNATIVE MEDICINE

Edward A. Hurvitz, MD

Complementary and alternative medicine (CAM) has become an increasingly widespread and acceptable health care option. CAM is exceptionally hard to define and classify, as many of the traditional CAM modalities slowly enter into the general medical community as acceptable treatment options even without significant supportive evidence of efficacy. The National Center for Complementary and Alternative Medicine (NCCAM, the National Institutes of Health home for CAM study) defines CAM as "a group of diverse medical and health care systems, practices, and products that are not presently considered to be part of conventional medicine" (http://www.nccam.nih.gov). Complementary medicine refers to medical practices that are used in conjunction with "standard" medical techniques. Alternative medicine indicates the use of the CAM modality instead of conventional treatment. More than 80 million Americans use CAM, and spend more than 34 billion dollars a year out of pocket for the treatment (Eisenberg et al., 1993, 1998). Astin (1998) found a prevalence of 40% use of CAM among adults, generally associated with chronic health problems.

CAM is fairly popular for children as well. In the general pediatric population, estimates of CAM use vary from 1.8% to 21%, depending on how CAM is defined. If visiting a CAM practitioner is used, lower numbers are obtained (Davis & Darden, 2003; Spigelblatt, Laine-Ammara, Pless, & Guyver, 1994). Ottolini et al. (2001) found that 21% of children in the Washington, DC area had used CAM, but only about one third of those had actually gone to a CAM practitioner. The rest had used home remedies such as vitamins and herbal preparations. In children with chronic diseases, syndromes, and disabilities, however, the prevalence of use is much higher. Families of children with cerebral palsy elected CAM methods 56% of the time, especially massage and aquatherapy (Hurvitz, Leonard, Ayyangar, & Nelson, 2003). Similar high rates of usage were observed for children with chronic problems such as attention deficit–hyperactivity disorder (Baumgaertel, 1999), asthma (Kemper, 1996), cancer (Friedman, 1997), cystic fibrosis (Stern, Canada, & Doershuk, 1992), and juvenile rheumatoid arthritis (Southwood, Nalleson, & Roberts-Thompson, 1990).

CAM users tend to be highly educated and prone toward a holistic view of health care. They generally like CAM modalities as adjuncts to standard health care, particularly in chronic diseases and syndromes for which standard health care does not offer a great deal. They like the fact that CAM modalities are often focused on improving quality of life, and that there are fewer side effects (Astin, 1998; Hurvitz et al., 2003). Since intellectual and developmental disability (I/DD) is a chronic problem without a remedial treatment, and since individuals with I/DD tend to have a number of difficult problems such as sleep disorders, aggressive behaviors, and poor social adaptation, one would expect that individuals with I/DD would be prime candidates for CAM use. Indeed, a plethora of research articles and case reports in the literature document the use of CAM interventions with individuals with I/DD. There are an even greater number of Web sites and chat rooms that describe treatment techniques and provide anecdotal reports of success. While, generally speaking, CAM modalities have a very low rate of adverse events, there are still good reasons to carefully weigh the pros and cons of using one of these methods. First, any method of treatment has costs both in money and in time. CAM in particular often requires much of both. Second, the pursuit of CAM can interfere with having the time and resources to pursue more proven, helpful interventions.

RESEARCH QUESTIONS

The goal of this chapter is to review the published, peer-reviewed literature on CAM for individuals with I/DD, and to evaluate and summarize the findings in those reports. This review was conducted with these research questions in mind:

1. What methods of CAM seem to have the most and best evidence of efficacy?

2. Which common symptoms were responsive to CAM modalities?

3. Where would be the most fruitful areas for future study, based on the current literature?

4. Are there aspects of CAM that should be incorporated into the more "standard" care of individuals with I/DD to improve their overall quality of life?

DEFINITION OF CAM

Any review of CAM must start out with a definition of CAM. Aside from the general definition mentioned above, the NCCAM defines five major domains of CAM. These include:

1. Alternative medical systems, such as Chinese medicine and homeopathy

2. Mind–body interventions such as meditation, hypnosis, and prayer

3. Biological-based therapies such as herbal medicines, shark cartilage, and mega-vitamins

4. Manipulative and body-based therapies such as chiropractic manipulation and massage

5. Energy therapies such as magnetic therapy, therapeutic touch, and light therapies

Despite the definitions and categorization, it is still challenging to determine what modalities and treatment methods should be included in a survey on the use of CAM. For example, acupuncture seems to be a certain candidate for the list, but it is taught in many medical schools and commonly practiced by physicians who are not identified as alternative or Chinese medicine practitioners. There is even a group of physicians (the American Academy of Medical Acupuncture) that promotes the use and study of acupuncture (http://www.medicalacupuncture.org). On the other hand, counseling and self-help groups are listed under mind–body interactions, but many studies of alternative medicine do not include interventions such as these on their lists. Prayer also presents a unique problem—about 80% of Americans attend religious services, or at least feel that religion is an important part of their lives (Sheler, 2002). Indeed, studies that include prayer, as well as diet and exercise, report markedly higher rates of CAM use in their study groups. Rhee, Garg, and Hershey (2004), for example, reported a usage rate of 85% when these interventions were included as CAM. This review attempted to include most methods listed by the NCCAM as CAM modalities in its search for publications.

Methods

An information specialist was hired to identify all relevant research articles about CAM for individuals with I/DD from any available source. The following databases were searched: Medline, CINAHL, SocioFile, Health Star, PsychInfo, Pharmaceutical Abstracts, Web Science, Academic Search Premiere, Ingenta, and GPO Access. The following search terms were used besides the topic: *mental retardation, developmental disabilities,* and *Down syndrome.* Forty-nine studies were identified. On further examination, eight of these studies did not meet inclusion criteria, either because they were not about CAM, were not patient trials, or were not published as full manuscripts.

Also, additional computer-based literature reviews were performed using many CAM modalities as key words, such as *chiropractic, massage, orthokinetic, acupuncture,* and others. When review articles were obtained (Cook & Botting, 1997; Lancioni, Cuvo, & O'Reilly, 2002), the articles reviewed within them that met criteria for this review were analyzed and included. These investigations added an additional 14 studies.

The 55 articles that met criteria for the review are summarized here in four tables. Table 11-1 describes the intervention used, the sample studied, and the setting for

TABLE 11-1 *Interventions, Samples, and Settings in CAM Studies Including Persons with I/DD*

STUDY INFORMATION	INTERVENTION	CONTROL GROUP INTERVENTION IF DIFFERENT	SAMPLE STUDIED	TOTAL NUMBER OF SUBJECTS	AGES OF SUBJECTS YRS	SETTING (HOME/FAMILY, CONGREGATION, INSTITUTION)
Alternative Medical Systems						
Svedberg et al., 2001	Electro- and regular acupuncture	NA	Nonambulatory I/DD children	6	4–16	Home/family
Wong et al. 2001	Tongue acupuncture	NA	Children with I/DD (CP/Angleman's)	10	2–18, mean 7.3	Home/family
Moore & Adler, 2000	Ayurveda	NA	I/DD child	1	5	Home/family
Xinsheng et al., 1999	Electroacupuncture	Nao Fu Kang, 75 mg/day	Children with Down syndrome	36	6–16	Home/family
Oswal, 1996	Ayurveda, G therapy	NA	Children with I/DD and cerebral palsy	707	Not specified, except 479 were over 6	Home/family
Lingdi et al., 1995	Combination acupuncture	No treatment	I/DD children	192	8–14	Home/family
Dave et al., 1993	Ayurveda, mentat, an herbal preparation (BR-16A)	NA	Children with I/DD and with epilepsy	59	1–18	Home/family
Xu, 1985	Herbal medicine	NA	I/DD children	19	"School age"	Home/family
Hubbard, 1965	Homeopathy	NA	I/DD children	4	8–19	Home/family
Mind–Body Interventions						
Singh et al., 2003	Mind–body (MB): meditation	NA	Young adult with developmental disabilities	1	27	Institution
Altabet et al., 2002	Light therapy	NA	Profoundly I/DD Adults	3	42–68	Institution
Flitton & Buckroyd, 2002	Art therapy	NA	Children with moderate LD	4	6–12	Home/family
Hooper, 2002	Music therapy vs. "other" therapy	NA	Adults with I/DD	2	34–50	Institution
Huang & Dodder, 2002	Creative (art, music) Therapy	No creative therapy	Individuals with DD living in facilities	519	Unspecified	Institution

Study	Intervention	Other environments	Population	N	Age	Setting
Cuvo et al., 2001	Snoezelen	Other environments	Adults with I/DD	4	44–65	Institution
Duffy & Fuller, 2000	Music therapy, emphasis on social skills	Nonmusical social skills program	Children with moderate I/DD	32	5–10	Home/family
To & Chan, 2000	MB: abbreviated progressive relaxation	NA	IQ 40–70 with aggressive behavior	10	16–47	Institution
MacDonald et al., 1999	Music therapy	No intervention or nonmusical communal activity	Teens/adults with mild to moderate I/DD	59	17–58	Home/family
Alvares, 1998	Music therapy	NA	Children with pervasive developmental disorder (PDD)	2	5–6	Home/family
Braithwaite & Sigafoos, 1998	Music therapy vs. Social antecedent	NA	I/DD children	5	6 or younger	Institution
Cooke & Thompson, 1998	Light therapy	NA	I/DD individuals with SAD	2	9–44	Home/family
Houghton et al., 1998	Snoezelen	NA	I/DD children, some with visual impairment (VI) or heavy impairment (HI)	17	5–18	Home/family
Silliman-French et al., 1998	Music therapy	NA	Young I/DD adults	7	25–34	Institution
Lancioni et al., 1997	Biofeedback (auditory)	NA	Adults with I/DD	2	24, 60	Institution
Lindsay et al., 1997	Snoezelen, hand massage/aromatherapy, relaxation, active therapy	NA	Adults with I/DD	8	23–62	Institution
Screws & Surburg, 1997	MB: mental imagery	Physical intervention, no intervention	Children with mild I/DD	30	11–13	Home/family
Shapiro et al., 1997	Snoezelen	NA	I/DD children and stereotypic behaviors	20	5–10	Institution
Lindsay & Morrison, 1996	MB: Relaxation	Quiet reading	Adults with severe I/DD	20	Adults	Institution
Ashby et al., 1995	Snoezlen	NA	Adults with I/DD	8	23–62	Institution
Lindsay et al., 1994	MB: cue control retardation	NA	Adults with I/DD	5	29–48	Institution
Banks et al., 1993	Art therapy, directed vs. nondirected	NA	Children with development disabilities	3	4–6	Home/family

(continued)

TABLE 11-1 *Continued*

STUDY INFORMATION	INTERVENTION	CONTROL GROUP INTERVENTION IF DIFFERENT	SAMPLE STUDIED	TOTAL NUMBER OF SUBJECTS	AGES OF SUBJECTS YRS	SETTING (HOME/FAMILY, CONGREGATION, INSTITUTION)
Guilleminault et al., 1993	Light therapy	NA	I/DD children with sleep disturbance	14	9 mos to 4 yrs	Home/family
Heal & O'Hara, 1993	Music therapy	NA	Woman with Down syndrome and anorexia	1	28	Home/family
Long & Haig, 1992	Snoezelen	NA	Adults with I/DD	4	Adults	Institution
Silliman et al., 1992	Music therapy	NA	I/DD, blind child	1	10	Institution
Marriott & White, 1991	Art therapy	NA	Adult with I/DD	1	52	Institution
Calamari et al., 1987	MB: relaxation and biofeedback	Listening to classical music	Adults with I/DD	32	Adults	Institution
Biologically Based Therapies						
Francis & Dempster, 2002	Valerian	NA	I/DD children with sleep disorder	5	7–14	Home/family
Singh et al., 2002	Coenzyme Q	NA	I/DD child with tuberous sclerosis	1	5	Home/family
Jan, 2000	Melatonin	NA	I/DD children with sleep disorder	10	1–11	Home/family
Pace & Toyer, 2000	Vitamin supplement	NA	I/DD child with pica	1	9	Home/family
Bidder et al., 1989	Megavitamins and minerals	Placebo	Children with Down syndrome	19	8 mos to 5 yrs	Home/family
Menolascino et al., 1989	Megavitamins and minerals, thyroid supplementation	Placebo	I/DD children	24	5–15	Home/family
Coleman et al., 1985	Vitamin B_6	Placebo	Children with Down syndrome	19	Infants less than 8 wks	Home/family
Ellman et al., 1984	Megavitamins and minerals	Placebo	I/DD adolescents and adults	20	16–23	Institution
Bennett et al., 1983	Megavitamins and minerals	Placebo	Children with Down syndrome	20	5–13	Home/family

270

Study	Intervention	Control	Population	N	Age	Setting
Coburn et al., 1983	Megavitamin, mega B	Placebo, regular vitamin	Children with I/DD, Down syndrome	48	16–30	Institution
Ellis & Tomporowski, 1983	Megavitamins and minerals	Placebo	I/DD adults	40	21–40	Institution
Weathers, 1983	Megavitamins and minerals	Placebo	Children with Down syndrome	47	6–17	Home/family
Harrell et al., 1981	Megavitamins and minerals, thyroid supplementation	Placebo	I/DD Children	16	5–15	Home/family
Pueschel et al., 1980	5-Hydroxytryptamine (serotonin) and/or pyridoxine (three groups)	Placebo	Children with Down syndrome	89	First 3 yrs of life	Home/family
Manipulative and Body-Based Methods—See Lindsay et al. 1997 (Mind–Body/Snoezelen)						
Energy Fields						
Green & Nicoll, 2001	Therapeutic touch	NA	I/DD man	1	25	Institution
Hegarty & Gale, 1996	Therapeutic touch	NA	I/DD woman	1	23	Institution
Sigafoos & Pennell, 1995	Therapeutic touch	NA	Child with I/DD	1	10	Home/family

NA, not applicable

the study. Table 11-2 describes the study design including the length of treatment and the number of subjects in each group (if applicable), and the level of evidence of the study based on the classification system designed by Sackett, Richardson, Rosenberg, and Haynes (1997). Any study that was given a Level I or II rating is described in the text to help the reader evaluate the quality of the study. Table 11-3 focuses on the outcomes of interest, the results, and the method of analysis. Table 11-4 includes only the five studies that had any adverse events, and describes those. The other 50 studies gave no indication of adverse events. Within each table, the studies are organized by the NCCAM classification of CAM modalities noted previously. Within each of the five sections, the studies are organized by CAM method, and then by year of publication for each method.

Results

ALTERNATIVE MEDICAL SYSTEMS

There were four studies that investigated the use of acupuncture in individuals with I/DD. Xinsheng, Shulan, Rui, and Jiawei (1999) performed a randomized controlled trial (RCT) comparing electroacupuncture to a non-acupuncture traditional Chinese therapy. The outcome, however, was a neurophysiologic test (P3 latencies) that is of questionable clinical significance. Lingdi, Shijuan, Enrong, Hui, and Zhilan (1995) performed an RCT using combination acupuncture, and demonstrated improvement in cognitive performance on the Chinese version of the WISC-R, especially among the most involved children. The control group, however, received no therapy, raising the question of a placebo effect of an intervention vs. no intervention. A case series by Wong, Sun, and Wong (2001) of tongue acupuncture demonstrated an intriguing improvement in drooling, a difficult problem otherwise managed by medications or surgery. There were minor side effects (fear of the needles, some pain), but families found it helpful even months after the treatment. Other studies of Ayurveda (a medical system from India involving extensive herb use), herbal medicine, and homeopathy were case series with questionable measurement techniques.

MIND–BODY INTERVENTIONS

This category of CAM produced the greatest number of articles relating to individuals with I/DD. Creative therapies such as art and music therapy are popular treatments with this population, and a number of investigators attempted to demonstrate their efficacy. Although a few case presentations suggested that art therapy led to general improvements (Banks, Davis, Howard, & McLaughlin, 1993; Flitton & Buckroyd, 2002; Marriott & White, 1991), Huang and Dodder's large case control study (2002) could find no difference in the amount of initiation of activities between institutionalized individuals who received art therapy versus those who did not. MacDonald, O'Donnell, and Davies (1999) performed a non-blinded RCT on music therapy versus a nonmusical activity or no therapy, and noted an improvement in musical attainment and in communication skills (based on the *Communication Assessment Profile for Adults with a Mental Handicap* [CASP]; see Table 11-3) in the treatment group.

TABLE 11-2 *Designs and Level of Evidence in CAM Studies Including Persons with I/DD*

STUDY INFORMATION	RESEARCH DESIGN	LEVELS OF EVIDENCE	TREATMENT DURATION	NUMBER OF SUBJECTS IN TREATMENT GROUP	NUMBER OF SUBJECTS IN CONTROL GROUP
Alternative Medical Systems					
Wong et al., 2001	Case series	V	30 sessions over 6 wks	10	NA
Svedberg et al., 2001	Single subject design	II	6–8 sessions over several weeks	6	NA
Moore & Adler, 2000	Case presentation	V	4 yrs	1	NA
Xinsheng et al., 1999	RCT, not blinded	II	Daily for 4 mos	20	16
Oswal, 1996	Case series	V	Unspecified	707	NA
Lingdi et al., 1995	RCT, not blinded	II	6 wks	128	64
Dave et al., 1993	Case series	V	Unspecified	59	NA
Xu, 1985	Case series	V	3 mos	19	NA
Hubbard, 1965	Case series	V	Weeks to months	4	NA
Mind–Body Interventions					
Singh et al., 2003	Case presentation	V	12 mos	1	NA
Altabet et al., 2002	Case series	IV	12 wks	3	NA
Flitton & Buckroyd, 2002	Case series	V	14 wks	4	NA
Hooper, 2002	Case series	V	10 sessions	2	NA
Huang & Dodder, 2002	Case/control	III	1 yr	168	351
Cuvo et al., 2001	Case series	V	3 wks	4	NA
Martin et al., 2001	RCT, not blinded	II	5 sessions	3	3
Duffy & Fuller, 2000	Non-randomized controlled trials	II	8 wks	16	16
To & Chan, 2000	Case series	V	4 wks	10	NA
MacDonald et al., 1999	RCT, not blinded	II	10 wks	19	16, 24
Alvares, 1998	Case series	V	5 mos	2	NA
Braithwaite & Sigafoos, 1998	Single-subject design	II	27 sessions	5	NA
Cooke & Thompson, 1998	Case series	V	More than 3 yrs	2	NA
Houghton et al., 1998	Case series	V	4 wks	17	NA
Silliman-French et al., 1998	Case series	V	45 sessions in 15 days	7	NA
Lancioni et al., 1997	Single-subject design	II	7 mos	2	NA
Lindsay et al., 1997	Case series	V	Several sessions of each therapy	8	NA
Screws & Surburg, 1997	RCT, not blinded	II	5/wk sessions, unspecified no. of weeks	10	10 physical intervention, 10 no intervention

(continued)

TABLE 11-2 *Continued*

STUDY INFORMATION	RESEARCH DESIGN	LEVELS OF EVIDENCE	TREATMENT DURATION	NUMBER OF SUBJECTS IN TREATMENT GROUP	NUMBER OF SUBJECTS IN CONTROL GROUP
Shapiro et al., 1997	Case series	V	2 wks	20	NA
Heal & O'Hara, 1993	Case presentation	V	9 mos	1	NA
Lindsay & Morrison, 1996	RCT, not blinded	II	Unspecified	10	10
Ashby et al., 1995	Case series	V	20 wks	8	NA
Lindsay et al., 1994	Case series	V	30 sessions	5	NA
Banks et al., 1993	Case series	V	A few weeks	3	NA
Guilleminault et al., 1993	Case series	V	Up to 2 yrs	14	NA
Long & Haig, 1992	Case series	V	6 mos	4	NA
Silliman et al., 1992	Single-subject design	V		1	NA
Marriott & White, 1991	Case presentation	V	3 yrs	1	NA
Calamari et al., 1987	RCT, not blinded	II	9 days, 6 sessions	16	16
Biologically Based Therapies					
Francis & Dempster, 2002	"N of 1" RCT	I	8 wks	5	NA
Singh et al., 2002	Case presentation	V	4 wks	1	NA
Jan, 2000	Case series	V	4–12 mos	10	NA
Pace & Toyer, 2000	Single-subject design	III	3 wks	1	NA
Bidder et al., 1989	Double-blind crossover	II	3 mos	19	The same 19, crossover
Menolascino et al., 1989	Double-blind RCT	II	8 mos	11	13
Coleman et al., 1985	Double-blind RCT	II	3 yrs	10	9
Ellman et al., 1984	Double-blind RCT	II	6 mos	10	10
Bennett et al., 1983	Double-blind RCT	II	8 mos	10	10
Coburn et al., 1983	Double-blind RCT	II	20 wks	18	30
Ellis & Tomporowski, 1983	Double-blind RCT	II	7 mos	19	21
Weathers, 1983	Double-blind RCT	II	4 mos	24	23
Harrell et al., 1981	Double-blind RCT	II	8 mos	5	11
Pueschel et al., 1980	Double-blind RCT	II	3 yrs	23,22,24*	20
Manipulative and Body-Based Methods—See Lindsay et al. 1997 (Mind–Body/Snoezelen)					
Energy Fields					
Green & Nicoll, 2001	Case presentation	V	10 wks	1	NA
Hegarty & Gale, 1996	Case presentation	V	12 sessions	1	NA
Sigafoos & Pennell, 1995	Single-subject design	II	Several 5-min sessions in one day	1	NA

* Three study groups.

TABLE 11-3 *Outcome, Results, and Clinical Importance of CAM Studies Involving Persons with I/DD*

STUDY INFORMATION	OUTCOME OF INTEREST	MEASURES USED	RESULTS	CLINICAL IMPORTANCE	STATISTICS
Alternative Medical Systems					
Svedberg et al., 2001	Increased skin temperature	Multiple skin measurements	Some increase in three children	Questionable result	ABAB analysis with *t*-test comparisons
Wong et al., 2001	Decreased drooling	Visual analog scale; drooling quotient; drooling severity and frequency	Improvement in all measures	Mean F/U at 6 mos, families felt drooling still improved (no formal measures)	Wilcoxon matched-pairs signed-rank analysis
Moore & Adler, 2000	Improved cognition	Observation	Lead poisoning	Not all CAM methods are safe!	Observation
Xinsheng et al., 1999	P3 latency and amplitude (neuro-physiologic cerebral test)	Measurement of P3	Improved latency in treatment group compared to controls, signigicant	Clinical significance of P3 is not clear	*t*-test
Oswal, 1996	Improved overall performance	Observations, observational rating scales	Many improvements, notably in speech, less effective in microcephaly	Questionable significance due to reporting method	Qualitative, a few tables of frequencies
Lingdi et al., 1995	IQ and social adaptation behavior	WISC-R, Chinese Version Social Viability Chart for Infants and Junior Middle School Students	Significant improvement on tests compared to controls	More involved children had greater improvements	*t*-test
Dave et al., 1993	Behavior	Children's Behavior Index	Improvement noted after treatment in measure and in behaviors	Limited significance due to measurement technique	Frequencies
Xu, 1985	Improved learning ability	Teacher and parent report	5 marked, 10 some, 4 none	"Enhancement of neuronal function"	Frequencies
Hubbard, 1965	Multiple	Observation	Mild improvements	Limited significance	Observation

(continued)

TABLE 11-3 *Continued*

STUDY INFORMATION	OUTCOME OF INTEREST	MEASURES USED	RESULTS	CLINICAL IMPORTANCE	STATISTICS
Mind–Body Interventions					
Singh et al., 2003	Decreased aggression	Number of incidents	Decreased incidents	Single case	Observation
Altabet et al., 2002	Improvement in sleep pattern, depression, irritability	DASH Depression Scale, ABC Irritability Scale, Lethargy Scale	All three improved	Improvement in sleep pattern maintained at 8-wk follow-up	Absolute scores
Flitton & Buckroyd, 2002	Improved self-concept	Observation	Improvements noted	Small group	Observation
Hooper, 2002	Improved behavior	Frequencies	Decreased aggression, improved social interactions	Music therapy led to more improvements than other therapy	Frequencies
Huang & Dodder, 2002	Amount of initiation	Developmental Disabilities Quality Assurance Questionnaire; hours of therapy	No significant difference between groups	Creative therapy not supported	t-test and Chi square
Cuvo et al., 2001	Increased engagement, decreased stereotypic behavior	Observation	Positive results in room, back to baseline out of room	Snoezelen only effective in the room, no carryover	Observation
Martin et al., 2001	Alpha brain wave activity	EEG measures	Statistically significant increase in treatment group	Unclear what increased alpha does for the subject	t-test
Duffy & Fuller, 2000	Social skills	Social skills survey, non-standardized	Minimal significant difference between groups	Music did not add significantly to social skill attainment	Two-way ANOVA
To & Chan, 2000	Decreased aggressive behaviors	Checklist of aggressive behavior	14.7% decrease of score, nonsignificant	Some behaviors had 100% reduction	Wilcoxon signed rank test
MacDonald et al., 1999	Musical skills, communication	Elmes Test of Musical Attainment, Communication Assessment Profile for Adults with a Mental Handicap (CASP)	Test group had significant gains on the Elmes and the CASP not seen in controls	Documents improvement in music skills with intervention, limited communication improvement	3X2 ANOVA

276

Study	Variable	Measure	Results	Comments	Design/Analysis
Alvares, 1998	Increased involvement	Observation	Involvement Increased	Small group	Observation
Braithwaite and Sigafoos, 1998	Appropriate communication	Frequencies	Improved communication with musical antecedent	Small group	ABAB reversal design
Cooke & Thompson, 1998	Decreased depression	Observation	Happier, sleep improvement (in one), other changes	Small group, but interesting combined with other studies	Observation
Houghton et al., 1998	Acquisition of new skills	Functional Outcome Statement skills	New skills were noted	Some evidence of carryover	ANOVA
Silliman-French et al., 1998	Improved posture	Postural feedback device	Improved with music more so than aversive tone	Small group	Randomized multiple treatment design
Lancioni et al., 1997	Reduction in loudness	Frequency of episodes (determined by the biofeedback device)	Decreased episodes when device was used	Small group, but good design	ABABABAB design
Lindsay et al., 1997	Increased enjoyment and concentration	Video assessments of performance of a task	Positive results with Snoezelen and relaxation	Small series, no major changes	Multiple intervention crossover design, ANOVA
Screws & Surburg, 1997	Improved motor performance	Peg Board and Pursuit Rotor	Both physical practice and mental imagery produced improved performance	Mental imagery can be used to help motor performance	ANOVA
Shapiro et al., 1997	Changes in behavior and heart rate	Behavior checklist, Holter Monitor	Significant changes with Snoezelen in behaviors and to some degree with heart rate	Snoezelen only effective in the room, no carryover	MANOVA, ANCOVA, ANOVA
Lindsay & Morrison, 1996	Memory, learning	Digit span test, general knowledge test, incidental learning test	Short term memory and incidental learning improved	Relaxation can help some skills	ANOVA
Ashby et al., 1995	Concentration, responsiveness	Performance of a task, reviewer rating	Some improvement in 7/8 subjects	Some effect noted immediately after therapy	Frequencies
Lindsay et al., 1994	Increased relaxation	Behavioral anxiety scales	Decreased anxiety, improved concentration	Small group	Visual analysis of results
Banks et al., 1993	Decreasing target behaviors	Observation of aggressive behaviors, social initiation, eye contact	Two improved in social behavior with directed therapy	Directed therapy may have more benefit than non-directed	Visual analysis of results

(continued)

TABLE 11-3 *Continued*

STUDY INFORMATION	OUTCOME OF INTEREST	MEASURES USED	RESULTS	CLINICAL IMPORTANCE	STATISTICS
Guilleminault et al., 1993	Improving sleep patterns	Sleep time, nocturnal sleep time	5/14 responded	Some non-responders had clinical deterioration	Sleep logs, measurement of hours
Heal & O'Hara, 1993	Decrease anorexia	Observation	Anorexia decreased	Single case	Observation
Long & Haig, 1992	Behavior	Observation	Some improvement seen	Small series, no carryover	Frequencies
Silliman et al., 1992	Improved motor skills	Scoring activities	Skills improved	Single case	AB design, visual inspection
Marriott & White, 1991	General improvement	Description	Various improved expression	Single case	Observation
Calamari et al., 1987	Increased relaxation	Physiologic measures (skin temp, EMG muscle activity, Relaxation Training Rating Scale)	Less EMG, higher scale score. No change in skin temp	Differences not dependent on level of function	Standard parametric statistics
Biologically Based Therapies					
Francis & Dempster, 2002	Sleep pattern	Sleep latency, hours of sleep, awakenings, quality of sleep	Significant changes with valerian, not seen with placebo	Appeared effective for problem with no adverse effects	Repeated measures ANOVA
Singh et al., 2002	Decreasing seizures, improving cognition	Observation	Seizures controlled, better cognitive and physical performance	Single case	Observation
Jan, 2000	Sleep pattern	Increased hours of sleep, decreased awakenings, nights with delayed onset or early arousal	Minor improvement of hours, more so of other categories, no significance noted	Effectively treated the problem with no adverse effects	Frequencies
Pace & Toyer, 2000	Decreased pica	Number of episodes	Pica decreased	Single case	BAB design
Bidder et al., 1989	Cognitive performance, appearance	Griffiths Developmental Scales, photos	No significant changes	No effect of treatment	t-test
Menolascino et al., 1989	IQ, social adaptive behavior, neuro-psychologic development	Wechsler, Vineland, Nebraska Neuropsychological Test	No significant changes	Replicated and improved Harrell study w/o findings	ANOVA

Study	Outcome	Tools/Measures	Results	Conclusion	Statistical test
Coleman et al., 1985	Improved over all	Cognitive testing, health outcomes, tongue protrusion	No significant difference noted	No evidence that B6 Rx is helpful	Chi square, t-test
Ellman et al., 1984	IQ and adaptive behavior	Stanford-Binet or Leiter, Adaptive Behavior Scale	No differences between groups	No effect	t-test
Bennett, 1983	IQ scores, physical features	Stanford-Binet, Peabody individual achievement test, others	No difference between groups	Argued against previous study by Harrell	ANOVA
Coburn et al., 1983	IQ scores	Stanford-Binet	No changes, no difference between groups	Argued against previous study by Harrell	ANOVA
Ellis & Tomporowski, 1983	IQ, educability	Leiter, Likert scale for educability	No difference between groups	No effect	t-test
Weathers, 1983	IQ, vision, visual–motor integration	Stanford-Binet, ophthalmologic examination	No effect	Not an effective treatment	Hotteling's T-Square technique
Harrel et al., 1981	IQ scores	Stanford-Binet	Improved scores compared to placebo	Physical improvements noted as well	t-test
Pueschel et al., 1980	Muscle tone, cognitive function	Muscle tone by exam, Bayley Scale, Vineland Social Maturity Scale, Receptive-Expressive Emergent Language Scale	No effect from treatment	Not an effective treatment	Tests for interactions using the F statistic

Manipulative and Body-based Methods—See Lindsay et al. 1997 (Mind–Body/Snoezleen)
Energy Fields

Study	Outcome	Tools/Measures	Results	Conclusion	Statistical test
Green & Nicoll, 2001	General improved quality of life	Observation	Improved appetite, relaxation, others	Appeared beneficial	Observation
Hegarty & Gale, 1996	Improved behaviors	Observation	Decreased episodes of behavior	Appeared beneficial	Frequencies
Sigafoos & Pennell, 1995	Decreased self-injurious behavior	Frequency of episodes	Decreased episodes based on pattern of touch	Appeared beneficial	Single subject ABAC design with visual inspection

TABLE 11-4 *Adverse Effects (Condensed to Show Only Positive Findings) in CAM Studies Including Persons with I/DD*

STUDY INFORMATION	TYPE OF ADVERSE EFFECTS	NUMBER OF CASES TO EXPERIENCE EACH TYPE OF ADVERSE EFFECT
Alternative Medical Systems		
Wong et al., 2001	Fear, "minor pain"	Unclear
Moore & Adler, 2000	Lead poisoning	1
Dave et al., 1993	Change in stools	2
Mind–Body Interventions		
No adverse effects were found in any study.		
Biologically Based Therapies		
Bidder et al., 1989	Flushing, vomiting, tightness of the skin	"High frequency"
Xu, 1985	Nausea	2
Manipulative and Body-based Methods		
Energy Fields		
No adverse effects were found in any study.		

Case series and case reports on music therapy demonstrated apparent improvements in motor skills, posture, communication, and in other areas. Several articles looked at the use of Snoezelen, a method of providing a pleasurable multisensory environment by placing the subject in a room that offers a variety of sensory experiences. The investigators found positive changes in behavior, concentration, and other factors but generally only in the Snoezelen room or immediately after, with little carryover. There were three non-blinded, RCTs into the use of relaxation techniques and mental imagery (Calamari, Geist, & Shahbazian, 1987; Lindsay & Morrison, 1996; Screws & Surburg, 1997). These studies demonstrated improvements in motor performance and concentration, with decreased anxiety. Calamari et al. (1987) demonstrated less electromyographic (EMG) muscle activity even in individuals with a low level of function after a program involving relaxation and biofeedback, compared to another group that only listened to classical music. Another very small (six patients) non-blinded RCT of biofeedback (Martin, Melnyk, & Taylor, 2001) demonstrated changes in alpha brain wave activity, but it was unclear as to what practical difference this made to the subjects. A few case series on light therapy (using exposure to bright lights to influence brain circadian rhythms) suggested improvements in sleep pattern in a number of subjects.

BIOLOGICALLY BASED THERAPIES

The most significant and well-studied intervention in this category involved nutritional supplements, particularly orthokinetic therapy for Down syndrome. In a series of double-blind RCTs published mostly during the 1980s, the question of megavitamins as a treatment for Down syndrome and I/DD in general was explored. Harrell, Capp, Davis, Peerless, and Ravitz (1981) were the first to suggest that a collection of high-dose vitamins and minerals given over a course of 8 months could increase IQ in a group of children with I/DD. They also suggested that physical improvements occurred as well. In addition to the megavitamins and minerals, thyroid supplementation was given to several of the children based on body temperature (the Barnes method). In the decade that followed, a number of investigators sought to either repeat Harrell et al.'s findings by either conducting a study that repeated and improved on their methodology, or by changing the study in some way (i.e., adult populations or different time periods of administration). Menolascino et al. (1989) included thyroid supplementation in an attempt to match methodologies more closely, while others left this aspect out. In summary, no group has been able to show any effect of the treatment on any IQ score, behavioral scale, or any other measure. Most authors point to flaws in Harrell's design that appear to have led to inaccurate results. It is worth noting that despite the extensive series of Level I studies suggesting that this is not an effective therapy, it remains popular with about 30% of families, who stated in a recent survey that they use nutritional supplements of some kind (Hornyak, Hurvitz, Klipp, & Rommeny, in preparation).

Of perhaps greater interest in this area are two small case series using valerian (Francis and Dempster, 2002) and melatonin (Jan, 2000) in children with I/DD who had a sleep disturbance. The valerian study was designed as an "N of 1" RCT. Both studies demonstrated improvement in sleep, including number of hours of sleep and decreased awakenings. Combined with the trials of light therapy noted earlier (mind–body interventions), sleep disturbance appeared to be one of the more effectively treated symptoms through CAM for individuals with I/DD.

MANIPULATIVE AND BODY-BASED METHODS

This area of CAM involves such treatments as chiropractic therapy, massage, and craniosacral manipulation. Only one study was identified that mentions massage (Lindsay et al., 1997) and included hand massage combined with aromatherapy on one of four groups, while the others received Snoezelen, relaxation, and "active therapy." Video assessments were done to assess for enjoyment and concentration on task, and only Snoezelen and relaxation therapy appeared to help. While it is certain that these types of intervention are commonly used in individuals with I/DD (about one quarter of families with children with cerebral palsy [Hurvitz et al, 2003] and Down syndrome [Hornyak et al., in preparation] use massage therapy), there does not seem to have been much interest in studying the techniques to determine their true efficacy.

ENERGY FIELDS

There were three case reports of using therapeutic touch in individuals with I/DD. One (Sigafoos & Pennell, 1995) used a single subject design. All three reported improvements in such problems as poor appetite, self-injurious behavior, and others. Other common energy field modalities such as Reiki and magnet therapy did not appear in the literature search.

ADVERSE EFFECTS

One of the most important considerations of CAM, and truly one of its most attractive aspects to consumers, is the lack of adverse effects associated with the modalities almost throughout the spectrum. In this review of CAM modalities for individuals with I/DD, only five studies noted adverse effects from the treatment investigated (Table 11-4). Only one study of acupuncture (Wong et al., 2001) noted that there was pain with the treatment, as well as some fear of having acupuncture needles placed in the tongue. Moore and Adler (2000) reported a case of a child who became ill with lead poisoning after exposure to Ayurveda treatment as a result of a high lead content in the treatment agents, demonstrating that not all CAM is safe and requires the same vigilance against bodily harm that is practiced in "standard" medicine. Of all of the studies of megavitamins and minerals, only Bidder et al. (1989) noted significant complications, but they noted them with a relatively high frequency. The authors were curious as to why this was not more generally reported, and expressed concern about under-reporting of complications from this treatment.

Summary and Future Directions

As can be seen from this review, numerous CAM modalities have been tried to alleviate a variety of symptoms in individuals with I/DD, including attempts to increase IQ, improve poor behavioral patterns, and increase societal participation. None of the modalities investigated in the papers covered in this review are supported by strong evidence of efficacy. Some of the mind–body techniques, such as relaxation therapy, were tested with non-blinded RCTs and found to have some positive effects. These techniques are certainly harmless to the subject, and are supported by a "common sense" approach to the problems at which they are aimed. The studies support the time and effort that goes into them. CAM treatment for sleep seemed somewhat promising, although the literature was sparse. Melatonin has been promoted for children with a variety of disabilities (e.g., Ross et al., 2002), and was effective in the cases reviewed here. Valerian and light therapy also seemed to help, and suggest that this may be an area for further investigation. Tongue acupuncture as a treatment for drooling was also interesting, if only because the study was done on a limited symptom with fairly good measures, albeit in a small group with no control.

Is CAM good for individuals with I/DD? There is a great call for well designed, double-blinded RCTs of CAM throughout the field of medicine, and a will to support such studies through the NCCAM. This chapter reveals that the need to study CAM use in individuals with I/DD is definitely great. As a population with a chronic condition and a number of symptoms that are not responsive to "standard" medical treatments, individuals with I/DD are at "high risk" for exposure to CAM by families and caregivers who are not finding answers elsewhere. Although the risk of adverse effects is low, it is present. There is certainly a risk of investing time, energy, and resources into a treatment that is not effective, or no more effective than a similar, less expensive and less time-consuming intervention. Although the numerous case reports and case series reviewed here provide a low level of evidence, they can provide directions for research if they are carefully performed and carefully noted. It is of great importance for practitioners of CAM to start recording their results, putting them out into the medical literature, and either beginning the pathway toward controlled studies or creating liaisons with academic centers that can partner with them for these studies.

The other side of this coin is that despite the very low level of evidence presented in this review, the use of CAM is widespread, as noted in the introduction, and shows no sign of slowing. Health care professionals and caregivers should strongly consider what factors attract individuals to CAM. Several characteristics make CAM attractive to families who are dealing with chronic disability, including greater control over their loved one's care, practitioners who take time to listen as part of their therapy, a focus on quality of life, hands-on treatment, and other aspects that make a visit to a CAM practitioner or the use of a CAM modality a pleasant, positive experience that is not always found in the office of a "standard" health care practitioner. An important direction for future research and action is to determine which of these factors are most important to families, and to discover the best way to bring them into "standard" medical care for the benefit of the individuals with I/DD and their families.

REFERENCES

Altabet, S., Neumann, J. K., & Watson-Johnston, S. (2002). Light therapy as a treatment of sleep cycle problems and depression. *Mental Health Aspects of Developmental Disabilities, 5*(1), 1–5.

Alvares, T. S. (1998). Healing through imagery: Gabriel's and Maria's journeys. *The Arts in Psychotherapy, 25,* 313–322.

American Academy of Medical Acupuncture Web site: http://www.medicalacupuncture.org

Ashby, M., Lindsay, W. R., Pitcaithy, D., Broxholme, S., & Geelen, N. (1995). Snoezelen: Its effects on concentration and responsiveness in people with profound mental handicaps. *British Journal of Occupational Therapy, 58,* 303–307.

Astin, J. A. (1998). Why patients use alternative medicine: Results of a national survey. *Journal of the American Medical Association, 279,* 1548–1553.

Banks, S., Davis, P., Howard, V. F., & McLaughlin, T. F. (1993). The effects of directed art activities on the behavior of young children with disabilities: A multi-element baseline analysis. *Art Therapy: Journal of the American Art Therapy Association, 10,* 235–240.

Baumgaertel. A. (1999). Alternative and controversial treatments for attention deficit/hyperactivity disorder. *Pediatric Clinics of North America, 46,* 977–992.

Bennett, F. C., McClelland, S., Kriegsmann, E. A., Andrus, L. B., & Sells, C. J. (1983). Vitamin and mineral supplementation in Down syndrome. *Pediatrics, 72,* 707–713.

Bidder, R., Gray, P., Newcombe, R. G., Evans, B. K., and Hughes, M. (1989). The effects of multivitamins and minerals on children with Down syndrome. *Developmental Medicine & Child Neurology, 31,* 532–537.

Braithwaite, M., & Sigafoos, J. (1998). Effects of social versus musical antecedents on communication responsiveness in five children with developmental disabilities. *Journal of Music Therapy, 35,* 88–104.

Calamari, J. E., Geist, G. O., & Shahbazian, M. J. (1987). Evaluation of multiple component relaxation training with developmentally disabled persons. *Research in Developmental Disabilities, 8,* 55–70.

Coburn, S. P., Schaltenbrand, W. E., Mahureen, J. D., Clausman, R. J., & Townsend, D. (1983). Effect of megavitamin treatment on mental performance and plasma vitamin B6 concentrations in mentally retarded young adults. *American Journal of Clinical Nutrition, 38,* 352–355.

Coleman, M., Sobel, S., Bhayagan, H. N., Coursin, D., Marquardt, A., Guay, M., et al. (1985). A double blind study of vitamin B6 in Down syndrome infants. Part I—Clinical and biochemical results. *Journal of Mental Deficiency, 29,* 233–240.

Cook, R., & Botting, D. (1997). Use of orthomolecular therapy for those with behavioural problems and mental handicap: A review. *Complementary Therapies in Medicine, 5,* 228–232.

Cooke, L. B., & Thompson, C. (1998). Seasonal affective disorder and response to light in two patients with learning disability. *Journal of Affective Disorders, 48,* 145–148.

Cuvo, A. J., May, M. E., & Post, T. M. (2001). Effects of living room, Snoezelen room, and outdoor activities on stereotypic behavior and engagement by adults with profound mental retardation. *Research in Developmental Disabilities, 22,* 183–204.

Dave, U. P., Chauvan, V., & Dalvi, J. (1993). Evaluation of BR-16 A (Mentat) in cognitive and behavioural dysfunction of mentally retarded children—A placebo-controlled study. *Indian Journal of Pediatrics, 60,* 423–428.

Davis, M. P., & Darden, P. M. (2003). Use of complementary and alternative medicine by children in the United States. *Archives of Pediatrics & Adolescent Medicine, 157,* 393–396.

Duffy, B., & Fuller, R. (2000). Role of music therapy in social skills development in children with moderate intellectual disability. *Journal of Applied Research in Intellectual Disabilities, 13,* 77–89.

Eisenberg, D. M., Davis, R. B., Ettner, S. L., Appel, S., Wilkey, S., Van Rompay, M., et al. (1998). Trends in alternative medicine in the United States, 1990–1997: Results of a follow-up national survey. *Journal of the American Medical Association, 280,* 1569–1575.

Eisenberg, D. M., Kessler, R. C., Foster, C., Norlock, F. E., Calkins, D. R., & Deblanco, T. L. (1993). Unconventional medicine in the United States: Prevalence, costs and patterns of use. *New England Journal of Medicine, 328,* 246–252.

Ellis, N. R., & Tomporowski, P. D. (1983). Vitamin/mineral supplements and intelligence of institutionalized mentally retarded adults. *American Journal of Mental Deficiency, 88,* 211–214.

Ellman, G., Silverstein, C. I., Zingarelli, G., Schafer, E. W. P., & Silverstein, L. (1984). Vitamin-mineral supplement fails to improve IQ of mentally retarded young adults. *American Journal of Mental Deficiency, 88,* 688–691.

Flitton, B., & Buckroyd, J. (2002). Exploring the effects of a 14-week person-centered counseling intervention with learning disabled children. *Emotional and Behavioural Difficulties, 7,* 164–177.

Francis, A. J. P., & Dempster, R. J. W. (2002). Effect of valerian, *Valeriana edulis,* on sleep difficulties in children with intellectual deficits: Randomized trial. *Phytomedicine, 9,* 273–279.

Friedman, T., Slayton, W., Allen, L., Pollack, B. H., Dumont-Driscoll, M., Mehta, P., et al. (1997). Use of alternative therapies for children with cancer. *Pediatrics, 100,* E1.

Green, C., & Nicoll, L. (2001). Therapeutic caring: A learning disability experience. *Complementary Therapies in Nursing & Midwifery, 7,* 180–187.

Guilleminault, C., McCann, C. C., Quera-Salva, M., & Cetel, M. (1993). Light therapy as treatment of dyschronosis in brain impaired children. *European Journal of Pediatrics, 152,* 754–759.

Harrell, R. F., Capp, R. H., Davis, D. R., Peerless, J., & Ravitz, L. R. (1981). Can nutritional supplements help mentally retarded children? An exploratory study. *Proceedings of the National Academy of Science, 78,* 574–578.

Heal, M., & O'Hara, J. (1993). The music therapy of an anorectic mentally handicapped adult. *British Journal of Medical Psychology, 66,* 33–41.

Hegarty, J. R., & Gale, E. (1996). Touch as a therapeutic medium for people with challenging behaviours. *British Journal of Learning Disabilities, 24,* 26–32.

Hooper, J. (2002). Using music to develop peer interaction: An examination of the response of two subjects with a learning disability. *British Journal of Learning Disabilities, 30,* 166–170.

Hornyak, J., Hurvitz, E. A., Klipp, D. A., & Rommeny, M. (in preparation). The use of complementary and alternative medicine for children with Down syndrome.

Houghton, S., Douglas, G., Brigg, J., Langsford, S., Powell, L., West, J., et al. (1998). An empirical evaluation of an interactive multi-sensory environment for children with disability. *Journal of Intellectual and Developmental Disabilities, 23,* 267–278.

Huang, Q., & Dodder, R. A. (2002). Creative therapy and initiative activities among people with developmental disabilities in public facilities. *Journal of Disability Policy Studies, 13,* 138–143.

Hubbard, E. W. (1965). Results with the Potentized Simillimum in retarded children. *Journal of the American Institute of Homeopathy, 5,* 338–342.

Hurvitz, E. A., Leonard, C., Ayyangar, R. N., & Nelson, V. S. (2003). Complementary and alternative medicine use in families of children with cerebral palsy. *Developmental Medicine & Child Neurology, 45,* 364–370.

Jan, M. M. S. (2000). Melatonin for the treatment of handicapped children with severe sleep disorders. *Pediatric Neurology, 23,* 229–232.

Kemper, K. J. (1996) *The holistic pediatrician.* New York: HarperCollins.

Lancioni, G. E., Cuvo, A. J., & O'Reilly, M. F. (2002). Snoezelen: An overview of research with people with developmental disabilities and dementia. *Disability and Rehabilitation, 24,* 175–184.

Lancioni, G. E., Van Houten, K., & Ten Hoopen, G. (1997). Reducing excessive vocal loudness in persons with mental retardation through the use of a portable auditory-feedback device. *Journal of Behavioral Therapy and Exploratory Psychiatry, 28,* 123–128.

Lindsay, W. R., Fee, M., Michie, A., & Heap, I. (1994). The effects of cue control relaxation on adults with severe mental retardation. *Research in Developmental Disabilities, 15,* 425–437.

Lindsay, W. R., & Morrison, F. M. (1996). The effects of behavioural relaxation on cognitive performance in adults with severe mental retardation. *Journal of Intellectual Disability Research, 40,* 285–290.

Lindsay, W. R., Pitchaithly, D., Geelen, N., Buntin, L., Broxholme, S., & Ashby, M. (1997). A comparison of the effects of four therapy procedures on concentration and responsiveness in people with profound learning disabilities. *Journal of Intellectual Disability Research, 41,* 201–207.

Lingdi, T., Shijuan, Y., Enrong, B., Hui, C., & Zhilan, Z. (1995). Composite acupuncture treatment of mental retardation in children. *Journal of Traditional Chinese Medicine, 15*(1), 34–37.

Long, A. P., & Haig, L. (1992). How do clients benefit from Snoezelen? An exploratory study. *British Journal of Occupational Therapy, 55*(3), 103–106.

MacDonald, R. A. R., O'Donnell, P. J., & Davies, J. B. (1999). An empirical investigation into the effects of structured music workshops for individuals with intellectual disabilities. *Journal of Applied Research in Intellectual Disabilities, 12,* 225–240.

Marriott, B., & White, M. P. (1991). The impact of art therapy on the life of a woman who was mentally retarded. *The American Journal of Art Therapy, 30,* 10–16.

Martin, W., Melnyk, W. T., & Taylor, I. A. (2001). Alpha biofeedback conditioning and retarded subjects. *Education, 101,* 389–394.

Menolascino, F. J., Donaldson, J. Y., Gallagher, T. F., Golden, C. J., Wilson, J. E., Huth, J. A., et al. (1989). Vitamin supplements and purported learning enhancement in mentally retarded children. *Journal of Nutrition Science and Vitaminology, 35,* 181–192.

Moore, C., & Adler, R. (2000). Herbal vitamins: Lead toxicity and developmental delay. *Pediatrics, 106,* 600-602.

National Center for Complementary and Alternative Medicine (NCCAM) Web site: *www.nccam.nih.gov*

Oswal, G. D. (1996). New homeopathic medication in rehabilitation of cerebral palsy and mental retardation. *The Nursing Journal of India, 87,* 242–264.

Ottolini, M. C., Hamburger, E. K., Loprieato, J. O., Coleman, R. H., Sachs, H. C., Madden, R., et al. (2001). Complementary and alternative medicine use among children in the Washington DC area. *Ambulatory Pediatrics, 2,* 122–125.

Pace, G. M., & Toyer, E. A. (2000). The effects of a vitamin supplement on the pica of a child with severe mental retardation. *Journal of Applied Behavior Analysis, 33,* 619–622.

Pueschel, S. R., Reed, T., Cronk, C. E., & Goldstein, B. I. (1980). 5-Hydroxytryptophan and pyrixodine: Their effects in young children with Down Syndrome. *American Journal of Diseases in Children, 134,* 838–844.

Rhee, S. M., Garg, V. K., & Hershey, C. O. (2004). Use of complementary and alternative medicines by ambulatory patients. *Archives of Internal Medicine 164,* 1004–1009.

Ross, C., Davies, P., & Whitehouse, W. (2002). Melatonin treatment for sleep disorders in children with neurodevelopmental disorders: An observational study. *Developmental Medicine & Child Neurology, 44,* 339–344.

Sackett, D. L., Richardson, W. S., Rosenberg, W., & Haynes, R. B. (1997). *Evidence-based medicine: How to practice and teach EBM.* New York: Churchill Livingstone.

Screws, D. P., & Surburg, P. R. (1997). Motor performance of children with mild mental disabilities after using mental imagery. *Adapted Physical Activity Quarterly, 14,* 119–130.

Shapiro, M., Parush, S., Green, M., & Roth, D. (1997). The efficacy of the "Snoezelen" in the management of children with mental retardation who exhibit maladaptive behaviors. *British Journal of Developmental Disabilities, 43,* 140–155.

Sheler, J. L. (May 6, 2002). Faith in America. *U.S. News and World Reports,132,* 40–49.

Sigafoos, J., & Pennell, D. (1995). Noncontingent application versus contingent removal of tactile stimulation: Effects on self-injury in a young boy with multiple disabilities. *Behavioural Change, 12,* 139–143.

Silliman, L. M., French, R., & Tynan, D. (1992). Use of sensory reinforcement to increase compliant behavior of a child who is blind and profoundly mentally retarded. *Clinical Kinesiology, 5,* 3–9.

Silliman-French, L., French, R., Sherrill, C., & Gench, B. (1998). Auditory feedback and time-on-task of postural alignment of individuals with profound mental retardation. *Adapted Physical Activity Quarterly, 15,* 51–63.

Singh, N. N., Wahler, R. G., Adkins, A. D., Myers, R. E., & The Mindfulness Research Group. (2003). Soles of the feet: A mindfulness-based self-control intervention for aggression by an individual with mild mental retardation and mental illness. *Research in Developmental Disabilities, 24,* 158–169.

Singh, R. B., Kartikey, K., & Moshiri, M. (2002). Effect of omega $Qgel_T$ (coenzyme Q10 and fish oil) in a patient with tuberous sclerosis. *Journal of Nutritional & Environmental Medicine, 12,* 295–299.

Southwood, T. R., Nalleson, P. N., & Roberts-Thompson, P. J. (1990). Unconventional remedies used for patients with juvenile arthritis. *Pediatrics, 85,* 150–154.

Spigelblatt, L., Laine-Ammara, G., Pless, I. B., & Guyver, A. (1994). The use of alternative medicine by children. *Pediatrics, 96,* 811–814.

Stern, R. C., Canada, E. R., & Doershuk, C. F. (1992). Use of nonmedical treatment for cystic fibrosis patients. *Journal of Adolescent Health, 13,* 612–615.

Svedberg, L. E., Nordahl, U. E. G., & Lundeberg, T. C. M. (2001). Effects of acupuncture on skin temperature in children with neurologic disorders and cold feet: An exploratory study. *Complementary Therapies in Medicine, 9,* 89–97.

To, M. Y. F., & Chan, S. (2000). Evaluating the effectiveness of progressive muscle relaxation in reducing the aggressive behaviors of mentally handicapped patients. *Archives of Psychiatric Nursing, 14*(1), 39–46.

Weathers, C. (1983). Effects of nutritional supplementation on IQ and certain other variables associated with Down syndrome. *American Journal of Mental Deficiency, 88,* 214–217.

Wong, V., Sun, J. G., & Wong, W. (2001). Traditional Chinese medicine (tongue acupuncture) in children with drooling problems. *Pediatric Neurology, 25*(1), 47–54.

Xinsheng, L., Shulan, F., Rui, J., & Jiawei, Z. (1999). The effect of electroacupuncture on auditory P300 potential in mongolism cases. *Journal of Traditional Chinese Medicine, 19,* 259–263.

Xu, J. (1985). The treatment of mental retardation in children by tonifying the kidney. *Journal of Traditional Chinese Medicine, 5,* 185–186.

12

SUBSTANCE ABUSE AND TOBACCO USE

Paula M. Minihan, PhD, MPH

ealthy People 2010, the federal government's action plan for improving the health status of the American people, lists substance abuse and tobacco use among the nation's major health problems (Department of Health and Human Services [DHHS], 2000b). Cigarette smoking is the single most preventable cause of disease and death in the United States, and more than 430,000 adult deaths per year are tobacco related (DHHS, 2000b). Alcohol abuse and illicit drug use are linked with life-threatening health problems, including heart disease, cancer, motor vehicle injuries, and HIV/AIDS, and cause turmoil that affects families and communities (DHHS, 2000a; McGinnis & Foege, 1993; Mokdad, Marks, Stroup, & Gerberding, 2004).

The aim of this chapter is to provide current information about how alcohol abuse, illicit drug use, and smoking affect people with intellectual/developmental disabilities (I/DD). Revolutionary changes in how people with I/DD are supported, including the centrality of community integration and consumer choice, and growing awareness of the relationship between personal behaviors and health, require new ways of viewing the health of people with I/DD that go beyond monitoring the individual's receipt of medical and other clinical services. A new and broader approach is required that also takes into account health promotion and wellness issues, such as healthy eating, physical activity, and drinking in moderation. This effort to synthesize baseline information about how people with I/DD are affected by substance abuse is an important step in that direction.

The chapter begins with national data describing the prevalence of substance abuse in the general population, as a backdrop for considering these issues among people with I/DD. This is followed by an evaluation of the strengths and limitations of the evidence on this issue. The mid-portion of the chapter is divided into two sections: (1) alcohol abuse and illicit drug use and (2) smoking. Each section includes prevalence estimates, as well as information about use patterns, risk factors, consequences of abuse, and issues related to treatment and prevention. The chapter concludes with a summary of the findings, a discussion of current gaps in information, and recommendations for research and practice.

PREVALENCE OF SUBSTANCE ABUSE IN THE GENERAL POPULATION

Table 12-1 presents current information about the prevalence of substance use and abuse among Americans, as measured in national surveys conducted by the federal government.

Methods

LITERATURE SEARCH

The literature was searched initially using the MEDLINE, PsychINFO, and National Guideline Clearinghouse search engines to identify references to substance abuse among people with I/DD from 1980 to the present. The search was conducted using the key words *mental retardation (MR), developmental disabilities, intellectual disabilities, substance use, substance abuse, drug use, drug abuse, alcoholism, addiction, smoking,* and *tobacco.* Additional papers were subsequently identified from the reference lists in the initial papers. Thirty-two papers were identified with information about alcohol or illicit drug use and 16 with information about smoking; many papers contained information about multiple substances.

METHODOLOGY FOR EVIDENCE CLASSIFICATION

The strength of the information presented in each paper was evaluated using a modification of the U.S. Preventive Service Task Force (USPSTF) *Guide to Clinical Preventive Services,* 2nd edition (USPSTF, 1996) and the *AACPDM Methodology for Developing Evidence Tables and Reviewing Treatment Outcome Research* (Butler & Campbell, 2000) (see Table A in Preface). These methodologies were focused largely on analytic studies and did not always apply to the papers reviewed in this chapter, which included many descriptive studies (Hennekens & Buring, 1987). Based on this schematic, studies classified as Levels I and II were judged to provide strong evidence; Level III and IV studies were judged to provide moderate evidence; and Level V studies were judged to provide weak to nonexistent evidence.

TABLE 12-1 *Prevalence of Substance Use and Abuse in the General Population*

SOURCE	AGE GROUP, YRS	MEASURES	PREVALENCE (%)
Alcohol			
2001 National Health Interview Survey (NHIS) (CDC, 2003a,b)	18 and older	Current drinkers[a]	62.7
		Lifetime abstainers	22.5
		Former drinkers	14.8
2001–2002 National Epidemiologic Survey on Alcohol & Related Conditions (NESARC) (NIAAA) in Grant et al. (2004)	18 and older	DSM-IV criteria for alcohol abuse[b]	4.6
		DSM-IV criteria for alcohol dependence[c]	3.8
2003 National Youth Risk Behavior Survey (YRBS) (CDC, n.d.)	High school	Current alcohol use[d]	44.9
		Lifetime alcohol use[e]	74.9
		Binge drinking[f]	28.3
Illicit Drug Use			
2001 National Household Survey on Drug Abuse (SAMHSA, 2001)	12 and older	Illicit drug use in preceding month	7.1
		Illicit drug use at least once in lifetime	41.7
Smoking			
2001 National Health Interview Survey (NHIS) (CDC, 2002)	18 and older	Current smoker[g]	22.8
2001 National Youth Risk Behavior Survey (YRBS) (CDC, n.d.)	High school	Current smoker[h]	28.5
		Lifetime smoker[i]	63.9

Note: The measures for substance use and abuse are defined below

[a]Current drinkers (NHIS): had 12 drinks in lifetime and at least one drink in past year

[b]DSM-IV criteria for alcohol abuse: individual meets at least one of the following criteria during preceding 12 months and doesn't currently meet DSM-IV alcohol dependence criteria: recurrent drinking resulting in failure to fulfill major role obligations; recurrent drinking in hazardous situations; recurrent drinking-related legal problems; continued drinking despite recurrent social or interpersonal problems caused or exacerbated by drinking (Grant et al., 2004)

[c]DSM-IV criteria for alcohol dependence: individual meets at least three of the following criteria during preceding 12 months: tolerance; withdrawal syndrome or drinking to relieve or avoid withdrawal symptoms; drinking larger amounts or for longer periods than intended; persistent desire or unsuccessful attempts to cut down on drinking; spending a great deal of time obtaining alcohol, drinking, or recovering from its effects; giving up important social, occupational, or recreational activities in favor of drinking; continued drinking despite physical or psychological problems caused or exacerbated by drinking (Grant et al., 2004)

[d]Current alcohol use (YRBS): at least one drink of alcohol on one or more of the past 30 days

[e]Lifetime alcohol use (YRBS): at least one drink of alcohol on one or more days during life

[f]Binge drinking (YRBS): five or more alcohol drinks in a couple of hours, on one or more of past 30 days

[g]Current smoker (NHIS): ever smoked 100 cigarettes in lifetime and smoking now on every or some days

[h]Current smoker (YRBS): smoked on one or more of 30 days preceding the survey

[i]Lifetime smoker (YRBS): ever smoked cigarettes, even one or two puffs

TABLE 12-2 *Papers with Information on Alcohol and Illicit Drug Use by Content and Level of Evidence (N = 32)*

CONTENT	NUMBER	LEVEL OF EVIDENCE (NO., %)
Magnitude of problem	17	III: 9 (53%) IV: 5 (29%) V: 3 (18%)
Treatment issues	17	III: 3 (18%) IV: 2 (12%) V: 12 (71%)
Prevention/education	2	I: 1 (50%) V: 1 (50%)

Results and Discussion

OVERVIEW OF THE QUALITY OF EVIDENCE

Tables 12-2 and 12-3 provide an overview of the level of evidence provided by the 39 papers reviewed in this chapter. A full summary of all of the papers reviewed in this chapter is included in Table 12-4.

Overall, the evidence about substance abuse among people with I/DD was moderate to weak. Among the papers containing information about alcohol and illicit drug use, the strongest evidence involved the magnitude of the problem, but even this information provided only moderate evidence at best. Of 17 papers with information on treatment issues, 12 were review articles or provided expert opinions, not evidence. Of the two papers dealing with prevention and education, one was a well-designed RCT that provided strong evidence about the effectiveness of a program specially designed for people with I/DD. Among the papers with information about smoking, the strongest evidence involved the magnitude of the problem, but, again, this evidence was moderate at best. Only three papers addressed smoking cessation, and just one, the RCT trial referenced previously, addressed smoking prevention and education.

A number of other limitations characterized these studies and may compromise their validity. First, every study was based on a convenience sample, and many had small sample sizes; these factors reduce the likelihood that the results represent the wider population of people with I/DD. Furthermore, alcohol use, abuse, and illicit drug use were measured inconsistently across studies, and the measures used typically did not reflect standard public health measures. In addition, the information about substance use was generally self-reported or reported by key informants, and lacked validation. Simpson (1998) raised a more philosophical objection to estimates of the prevalence of substance use among people with I/DD. He contended that such estimates are inherently flawed because most individuals with I/DD live in supervised settings where they are denied the opportunity to use substances.

TABLE 12-3 *Papers with Information on Smoking by Content and Level of Evidence (N = 16)*

CONTENT	NUMBER	LEVEL OF EVIDENCE (NO., %)
Magnitude of problem	16	III: 10 (63%) IV: 6 (37%)
Treatment issues/smoking cessation initiatives	3	III: 1 (33%) IV: 1 (33%) V: 1 (33%)
Prevention/education	1	I: 1 (100%)

Note: Many papers covered multiple substances and content areas

This means that prevalence calculations that include individuals who are not allowed to use substances in the denominator underestimate true prevalence.

In an effort to acknowledge the validity of Simpson's (1998) concerns and other limitations, the information highlighted in this chapter was taken primarily from studies in which the majority of subjects lived in community settings and in which sample sizes appeared adequate. Nonetheless, it is probable that many subjects lived with families or supervisors who restricted their access to alcohol or drugs, thus underestimating true prevalence, and perhaps masking actual experiences. It is important to note that 10 papers were authored by researchers from the United Kingdom or Canada. Inclusion of these papers introduces cultural and systemic differences into the analysis, but a number of these authors offered perspectives that were unlike those of American authors and warrant being heard.

Summary of the Evidence: Alcohol Abuse and Illicit Drug Use

MAGNITUDE OF THE PROBLEM

Adults

There were no population-based estimates of the prevalence of alcohol use and alcohol and illicit drug abuse among people with I/DD. Studies based on convenience samples that were drawn from individuals known to public service systems suggested that the prevalence among adults was lower than in the general population. In a seminal ethnographic study, Edgerton (1986) reported that the majority of adults with I/DD were abstinent and drank and used drugs at significantly lower rates than in the general population. This was despite ready access, according to the research team. Other investigators reported higher estimates of alcohol and drug use than Edgerton, but these estimates were still lower than in the general population. Krishef (1986) found that 52% of people with MR, ages 18 and older, who lived in the community were "ever" alcohol users, 13% were current users, and 5% drank daily.

TABLE 12-4 *Summary Table of Research Articles Related to Substance Abuse and Tobacco Use Among People with I/DD*

STUDY INFORMATION AND LEVEL OF EVIDENCE	RESEARCH DESIGN	POPULATION STUDIED	NUMBER OF SUBJECTS	SUBJECT CHARACTERISTICS	SETTING	MEASURES	MAIN FINDINGS (P-VALUES)
Beange et al., 1995 Level IV	Cross-sectional study of characteristics of randomly selected individuals Data collection: clinical examinations and medical record abstraction Compared with data from National Heart Foundation Risk Factor Prevalence Study/ Australia	Adults with MR associated with public system in Australia	202	M: 49% Ages: 20–29: 47% 30–39: 34% 40–49: 19% Level of MR: Mild: 35% Moderate: 40% Severe: 14% Profound: 11%	Family/ independent: 40% Group home: 31% Institution: 29%	"Drinker" "Non-drinker" "Smoker" "Non-smoker" (not defined)	Drinkers: 25% Non-drinkers: 75% (Non-drinkers in general population comparison group: 13%; $p < .0005$) Smokers: 6% Non-smokers: 94% (Non-smokers in general population comparison group: 53%; $p < .0005$)
Burgard et al., 2000 Level V	Review article, expert opinion, and anecdote	"Mentally retarded persons"	NA	NA	NA	NA	Conc.: "Mentally retarded persons appear to use/abuse alcohol at about the same rate as their non-cognitively impaired counterparts, and illicit drugs at moderately lower rates." "Little is known regarding which assessments and interventions are most effective in this population …" "Anecdotal data suggests that

Study/Level	Design	Population	N	Demographics	Setting	Definitions	Findings
							treatment for these individuals requires modifications of existing empirically-derived substance abuse interventions to accommodate their unique needs."
Burtner et al., 1995 Level IV	Cross-sectional study of individuals. Data collection: clinical dental observations verified by structured staff interviews	Youth and adults with developmental disabilities	749	M: 64% Av. age: 38 Level of MR: Mild: 7.5% Moderate: 8.8% Severe: 11.5% Profound: 72.2%	Institution 100%	Smoked occasionally: (< 3×/day); Smoked frequently: (> or = 3×/day)	Smoking prevalence overall: 2.1% % smoking occasionally: 0.13% % smoking frequently: 2.0% % mild/moderate MR who smoked: 9.8% % severe/profound MR who smoked: 0.64%
Campbell et al., 1994 Level IV	Cross-sectional study of programs. Data collection: mail survey of key informants from DD and substance abuse treatment programs. Presents statistical comparisons of programs by type (DD vs. SA)	People with "learning differences," including MR/DD, receiving services in Minnesota	74 programs SA programs: 42 DD programs: 32	NA	NA	Treatment needs of people with MR/DD; treatment barriers	Definition of treatment success, all respondents: Greater awareness of impact of drinking: 77% Completing program: 69% Regular AA attendance: 61% Total abstinence: 59% Reduction of drinking: 51% Barriers to SA treatment—all respondents: Clients' poorer comprehension: 78% Need more one-on-one time: 54% Lack of social skills: 50% Lack of treatment group experience: 31% Staff lack training: 90% Staff lack experience: 78%

(continued)

TABLE 12-4 *Continued*

STUDY INFORMATION AND LEVEL OF EVIDENCE	RESEARCH DESIGN	POPULATION STUDIED	NUMBER OF SUBJECTS	SUBJECT CHARACTERISTICS	SETTING	MEASURES	MAIN FINDINGS (P-VALUES)
							Comparison of barriers—DD vs SA staff: Poorer comprehension: 88% vs. 71% ($p < .05$) Need more one-on-one time: 66% vs. 45% ($p < .05$) Lack of social skills: 69% vs. 36% ($p < .05$) Lack of treatment group experience: 44% vs. 21% ($p < .05$)
Christian and Poling, 1997 Level V	Review article and expert opinion	People with MR	NA	NA	NA	NA	Conc.: "There are no empirically validated 'best practices' for detecting, treating, or preventing drug abuse among people with mental retardation."
Clarke and Wilson, 1999 Level V	Case reports	Adults with intellectual disability and alcohol-related problems (Great Britain)	4	M: 75% Av. age: 36	Family: 50% Residential setting: 25% Independent: 25%	Alcohol problems	Conc.: Treatment for people with ID and SA would benefit from ID and addiction service staff both receiving cross-training, having closer liaisons, and working together more.
Degenhardt, 2000 Level V	Review article and expert opinion	Adults with an intellectual disability and an alcohol use disorder (Australia)	NA	NA	NA	NA	Focus: Outlines various interventions that may be appropriate for adults with ID and alcohol use disorder, including pharmacologic treatments, such as disulfiram, and skills training;

Delaney and Poling, 1990 Level V	Review article and expert opinion	People with MR	NA	NA	NA	Treatment experiences and needs of clients with MR and SA problems	Conc.: People with MR who inappropriately use alcohol or other drugs are an overlooked subgroup. Lauds treatment model designed by Maine DMH and MR (effectiveness unknown); had three components: assessment, treatment (AA and short-term reinforcement for appropriate behavior); after-care. Notes finding AA group for MR abusers may be hard. uses social and political considerations to frame discussion; calls for research to evaluate efficacy of interventions with this group.
Draheim et al., 2002 Level III	Cross-sectional study of individuals Data collection: source of smoking data not clear Presents statistical comparisons by diagnosis	Adults with mild MR	Total: 145 Down syndrome: 75 Other MR: 70	DS: M: 45% Other MR: M: 57%	% living in group home: DS/M: 47% DS/F: 49% MR/M: 53% MR/F: 30%	"Cigarette smoking" (not defined)	Smoking prevalence by diagnosis and gender: DS/M: 3% vs. MR/M: 23% (p < .01) DS/F: 2% vs. MR/F: 10% (NS)

(continued)

TABLE 12-4 *Continued*

STUDY INFORMATION AND LEVEL OF EVIDENCE	RESEARCH DESIGN	POPULATION STUDIED	NUMBER OF SUBJECTS	SUBJECT CHARACTERISTICS	SETTING	MEASURES	MAIN FINDINGS (*P-VALUES*)
Edgerton, 1986 Level IV	Case series based on convenience samples Data collection: ethnographic interviews and observations	Adults with mild MR	Total: 181 (four subgroups)	Group I: *N* = 48 M: 46% Av. age: 27; % white: 100% Group II: *N* = 40 M: 50% Av. age: 31 % white: NA Group III: *N* = 45 M: 47% Av. age: 25 % white: 0 Group IV: *N* = 48 M: 42% Av. age: NA % white: NA	Group I: "white middle class;" lived with parents or in group home Group II: independent Group III: "black, poor," inner city Group IV: former state hospital clients	Alcohol and drug use: Abstinence: (no known use); Infrequent: no > than 2 beers, wine or 1 joint up to twice/wk; Moderate: use of beer, wine, marijuana once or twice/wk; Heavy or abusive: alcohol or drug intoxication several times/wk	Comparisons by group (hand-calculated): Group 1: % abstinence: 83.3% % infrequent use: 6.3% % moderate use: 0 % heavy or abusive use: 10.4% Group 2: % abstinence: 82.5% % infrequent use: 12.5% % moderate use: 0 % heavy or abusive use: 5% Group 3: % abstinence: 66.7% % infrequent use: 13.3% % moderate use: 15.5% % heavy or abusive use: 4.4% Group 4: % abstinence: 68.8% % infrequent use: 14.6% % moderate use: 8.3% % heavy or abusive use: 8.3% Conc.: use low, despite ready access

Study / Level	Design & data collection	n	Demographics	Living situation	Measures	Results
Hymowitz et al., 1997 Level III	Cross-sectional study of individuals Data collection: Subjects completed health form with help of research assistant and accompanying person; Smoking information verified by accompanying person Presents statistical comparisons by smoking status	136	Adults with MR and mental illness treated at university Behavioral Health Care Center M: 57% Av. age: 35 White: 54%	Lived in "residences made available through NJ Div. Of DD." 73%	"Currently smoking" (not defined) Av. age at smoking initiation	Smoking prevalence: Overall: 18.4% Severe/moderate MR: $p < 10\%$ Mild MR: 30% Borderline MR: 37% Av. age initiation: about 15 Smoked $p > 11$ cigarettes/day: 48% Characteristics of smokers vs. nonsmokers: Smokers more likely to: Live in supervised apt. rather than with family (NS) Have mild or borderline MR: ($p = .001$) Report using alcohol ($p < .001$) Report using drugs ($p < .001$) Have schizophrenia diagnosis ($p < .002$)
Krishef, 1986 Level III	Cross-sectional study of individuals Data collection: structured interviews with subjects Presents statistical comparisons by drinking status (drinking vs. non-drinking)	214	Adults with mild MR Total: M: 54% White: 70% 18–45: 86% Current drinkers (28): M: 62% White: 73% "younger" than group overall	Lived in community: 100% Family: 53% Group home: 9% Independent: 5% Foster care: 3%	Patterns and consequences of alcohol use and abuse; lifetime use: had ever consumed an alcoholic beverage; current use: drinking at time of study	Drinking patterns overall: Lifetime alcohol use: 52% (111) Current alcohol use: 13% (28) Among current drinkers: Use frequency: <1/mo: 61%; 1/wk: 30%; daily: 9% % with family discord, 13%; law violations, 7%; medical problems, 7%; drinking alone, 71%; consuming 7 or more drinks/occasion, 20% Comparison of drinkers vs. non-drinkers: Living arrangements: NS Leisure patterns: NS

(continued)

297

TABLE 12-4 *Continued*

STUDY INFORMATION AND LEVEL OF EVIDENCE	RESEARCH DESIGN	POPULATION STUDIED	NUMBER OF SUBJECTS	SUBJECT CHARACTERISTICS	SETTING	MEASURES	MAIN FINDINGS (*P*-VALUES)
Krishef and DiNitto, 1981 Level III	Cross-sectional study of individuals Data collection: mail survey of randomly selected administrators of ATP and ARC programs Presents statistical comparisons by program type (ATP vs. ARC)	Mainly adults (handful <18) with MR identified as "experiencing alcohol problems"	Total : 414 ATPs: 275 ARCs: 139	ATPs: M: 81% (224) <18: 6% 18–45: 74% ARCs: M: 83% (115) <18: 0 18–45: 92%	Group care: 29% Alone: 27% Parents: 22% Spouse: 12% Other: 10%	"Experiencing alcohol problems" (not defined); patterns and consequences of alcohol abuse; key informants' opinions about SA treatment for people with MR	Overall: % with alcohol-related job problems: 63% % with alcohol-related arrests: 44% (hand-calculated) More abusers lived alone than in group care ($p < .01$) Comparison of ATP vs. ARC clients: Problem duration similar for males/females (NS) Problem duration > ATP (< .001) % with job problems: 67% vs. 59% (NS) % with arrests: 55% vs. 23% (NA) Treatment issues: SA informants using different treatment techniques for MR clients: 68%. Techniques described as helpful to MR clients: Extending treatment length; Using more support and less confrontation; Using more one-on-one and less groups; Being more directive; Emphasizing education about alcohol; Offering more simplified education and repetition of concepts; Using more behavioral therapy

	Design	Population	n	Characteristics	Living situation	Research question	Findings
Lawrenson et al., 1995 Level IV	Cross-sectional study of individuals Data collection: Alcohol questionnaire read to subjects by interviewer Compared with regional health data	Adolescents and adults with learning difficulties (Scotland)	55	M: 55% (30) Level of MR: all mild to moderate Age range: 16–60 Av. age: 31.6 yrs	All lived at home.	Do you drink alcohol? Yes or No Av. alcohol consumption; where drinking occurs and with whom	Comparisons with general population: Fewer men and women with LD consume alcohol: 68% of F/MR drink (vs. 93% all women); 83% of M/MR drink (vs. all 98% men). People with MR consume less alcohol per week than general population (but men and women with MR consume about same). Drinking patterns of people with MR: most drink with others: (12% of M vs. 0 F drink alone) Many drink in pubs (64% of M/MR and 30% of F/MR)
Lindsay et al., 1991 Level V	Case reports, expert opinion, and anecdotes	People with "learning difficulties" ("mild mental handicap") (Scotland)	2	M: 100% Ages: 23 and 44	Independent with supervision	Treatment experiences and needs of clients with MR who abuse alcohol	Describes Alcohol Education Services, a program for people who abuse alcohol following a move into more independent living situations; notes a lack of leisure activities alternative to pubs may be one motivation for drinking.
Lottman, 1993 Level IV	Cross-sectional study of programs Data collection: structured telephone interviews with key informants from substance abuse	People with MR who were clients of SA treatment programs	19 SA programs	NA	NA	MR clients' access to SA treatment; treatment needs of people with MR; barriers to effective treatment;	% SA programs routinely accepting MR clients: 63% (12/19) % SA programs not routinely accepting MR clients: 37% (7/19) All respondents reported little or no training/experience with MR clients. Comparison of SA programs

299

(continued)

TABLE 12-4 *Continued*

STUDY INFORMATION AND LEVEL OF EVIDENCE	RESEARCH DESIGN	POPULATION STUDIED	NUMBER OF SUBJECTS	SUBJECT CHARACTERISTICS	SETTING	MEASURES	MAIN FINDINGS (*P*-VALUES)
	treatment programs Presents statistical comparisons of programs accepting and not accepting clients with MR.					merits of mainstream vs. specialized treatment	accepting or not accepting MR clients: No differences re: organizational structure, clientele, service availability, staff training in MR. % accepting Medicaid: 58% vs. 0 ($p < .05$) Mean rating of difficulty of integrating MR clients: 2.1 vs. 4.7 ($p < .001$) Rating of treatment barriers/MR clients (note: table hard to interpret): No. 1: Staff lack training in MR No. 2: Aftercare follow-up for MR clients No. 3: MR clients take more time. Conc.: inadequate SA case detection capacity with MR service systems
McDermott et al., 1997 Level III	Cross-sectional study of individuals Data collection: medical record abstraction	Adult patients in a primary care practice Cases: patients with primary MR diagnosis	Total: 1539 Cases: 366 Controls: Medicaid: 427	Cases: M: 38% Av. age: 40.2 White: 66%	Community settings supported by state agency	"Substance abuse" "Chronic smoker" (not defined)	Comparison of cases vs. controls on Medicaid and controls with other insurance: Prevalence of substance abuse: 0.5% vs. 12.6% vs. 6.8% ($p = .05$) Prevalence of chronic smoking: 3.3% vs. 13.1% vs. 8.8%; ($p = .05$)

Study	Design / Method	Population	Sample	Demographics	Setting	Measures	Results
	Statistical comparisons by MR status	Controls: patients without MR	On other Insurance: 746				
McGillicuddy and Blane, 1999 Level I ("Study 2") (also Level III; see below)	Randomized controlled trial\n\nIntervention: 10-wk behavioral repertoire group program tailored to special needs	Individuals with mild and moderate MR	Total: 84\n\nBehavioral intervention:\nAssertivness group: 21\nModeling group: 21\nControl group: 42	NA	"Recruited from local community agencies"	Refusal and assertiveness skills; model discrimination; knowledge and attitudes about substance use and misuse	Results of intervention by groups:\nAlcohol misuse: no differences\nCigarette use: no differences\nAssertiveness group showed more assertiveness ($p < .10$) and better refusal skills ($p < .05$); Modeling group showed more substance knowledge ($p < .05$).
McGillicuddy and Blane, 1999 Level III ("Study 1")	Cross-sectional study of individuals\n\nData collection: structured interviews with people with MR using standardized instruments tailored to special needs\n\nPresents statistical comparisons by use status (non-users, users, misusers)	Individuals with mild and moderate MR	122	M: 49%\nAv. age: 27\nWhite: 81%\nEmployed: 91%	"Recruited from local community agencies"	Use quantity and frequency; misuse measure based on 10 criteria: (user: drank but achieved 0 or 1 criteria; misuser: achieved 2 or more criteria)	Past month use overall:\nAlcohol: 39%\nNicotine: 23%\nIllicit drugs: 4%\nPast month alcohol use overall:\nNon-users: 61%\nUsers: 21%\nMisusers: 18% ("nearly 50% of people with MR using alcohol, misused it.")\nMisuser characteristics: higher IQs; smoked most cigarettes; higher % used marijuana; fewer skills to avoid SA.\nComparison of alcohol misusers vs. users vs. non-users:\nNo. of cigarettes/wk: 108.5 vs. 24.3 vs. 9.4 ($p < .001$)\n% marijuana users: .04 vs. 00 vs. 00 ($p < .01$)\nRefusal skills: 2.6 vs. 2.9 vs. 2.8 ($p < .01$)

301

(continued)

TABLE 12-4 *Continued*

STUDY INFORMATION AND LEVEL OF EVIDENCE	RESEARCH DESIGN	POPULATION STUDIED	NUMBER OF SUBJECTS	SUBJECT CHARACTERISTICS	SETTING	MEASURES	MAIN FINDINGS (P-VALUES)
McGillivray and Moore, 2001 Level III	Case-control study Data collection: structured interviews with subjects Presents statistical comparisons by offender status	Adults with mild intellectual disability (Australia) Cases: people with MR in criminal justice system Controls: non-offenders with MR from local agencies (matched on SES, functional level, residential hx)	Total: 60 Cases: 30 Controls: 30	Cases: M: 90% Av. age: 30 Controls: M: 90% Av. age: 31	Cases: Community settings: 33% Secure units: 67% Controls: Community settings: 100%	Knowledge and patterns of substance use and abuse; associations between substance abuse and criminal activity	Comparison of offenders vs. non-offenders: (all correlations $p < .05$, one-tailed) Beer consumption: At least 1/mo: 17% vs. 13% ≥ 1/wk: 33% vs. 27% Usually daily: 27% vs. 3% Wine consumption: At least 1/mo: 10% vs. 13% ≥ 1/wk: 7% vs. 7% Usually daily: 30% vs. 0 Spirits consumption: At least 1/mo: 20% vs. 13% ≥ 1/wk: 17% vs. 13% Usually daily: 23% vs. 0 Used cocaine: 3% vs. 0 Used amphetamines: 13% vs. 3% Marijuana consumption (NS): Never: 47% vs. 77% < 1/mo: 20% vs. 10% At least 1/mo: 3% vs. 3% At least 1/wk: 7% vs. 10% Usually every day: 23% vs. 0 Alcohol and drug knowledge: Offenders generally more knowledgeable about laws and health effects of drug use than non-offenders.

				Independent	Describes intervention, including use of videotapes	Goal: to help clients moderate consumption, not abstinence. Intervention session topics:
McMurran and Lismore, 1993 Level V	Case reports	People with learning dis-abilities (Great Britain)	2	M: 50% Ages: 35 and 44 Mild MR: 100%		1: Listing pros and cons of drinking 2: Rate control strategies 3: Alternative activities 4: Videotape exercise Client is shown videotape of drinker describing problems and asked to advise drinker on ways to reduce her drinking. Conc.: Videotape intervention is brief, simple, has visually pre-sented material, helps clients identify specific strategies that will be potentially helpful to them too.
Minihan, 1999 Level IV	Cross-sectional study of residen-tial supervisors' opinions and beliefs Data collection: Mail survey completed by residential supervisors Presents statistical comparisons by residential type	Adults with MR in state-supported system	3897	Gender: NA Age range: adults (NA)	Vendor-op community: 63% State-op community: 8% Institution: 28%	"Among consumers covered by this questionnaire, approximately how many would you say smoke?"	Smoking prevalence overall: 12.7% Smoking prevalence by residential type ($p < .01$): Vendor-op residences: 15.3% State-op residences: 9.7% State-op institution: 6.8% Residential supervisors' assessments: Frequency of clients' smoking cessation attempts: Almost never: 47% Sometimes: 44% Often: 5% Very often: 4%

(continued)

TABLE 12-4 *Continued*

STUDY INFORMATION AND LEVEL OF EVIDENCE	RESEARCH DESIGN	POPULATION STUDIED	NUMBER OF SUBJECTS	SUBJECT CHARACTERISTICS	SETTING	MEASURES	MAIN FINDINGS (P-VALUES)
							% citing factor as associated with clients' smoking cessation attempts: MD/nurse asks them to quit: 59% Own desire for good health: 48% Family/staff asks them to quit: 45% Cigarette price increased: 33% Friends/peers are nonsmokers: 31% % rating smoking cessation technique as "highly" useful: Group program just for people with MR: 55% One-on-one counseling program: 36% Nicotine patch: 26% Free public group cessation program: 22% Nicotine gum: 10%
Moore and Polsgrove, 1989 Level V	Review article and expert opinion	"Disabled individuals, including those with developmental handicaps"	NA	NA	NA	NA	No conclusions are specific to people with I/DD. Authors summarize research problems contributing to limited information on this topic, and list variables for which data are sorely needed, e.g., age at onset, concurrent use of prescribed and OTC medications, prevention approaches.

Source/Level	Design	Sample	N	Demographics		Purpose/Measures	Results
Pack et al., 1998 Level IV	Cross-sectional study of individuals Data collection: Study 1: confidential interview at home; Study 2: anonymous school-based questionnaire Compared with national and state data on African-American youth from CDC YRBS (Youth Risk Behavior Survey)	African-American adolescents with mild MR	Confidential interview: 138 Anonymous school-based survey: 56	Interview: M: 54% Ages: 14–16 Questionnaire: M: 65% Ages: 14–17	All lived with families	Patterns of substance use and abuse; used measured from the CDC YRBS	Comparison of anonymous questionnaire data (authors deemed more valid) vs. state and national YRBS data: Lifetime alcohol use: 51% vs. 76% vs. 80% 30-day alcohol use: 43% vs. 44% vs. 43% Alcohol binge: 31% vs. 24% vs. 19% Lifetime marijuana use: 29% vs. 31% vs. 34% 30-day marijuana use: 18% vs. 18% vs. 19% Lifetime cocaine use: 3% (sic) vs. 2% vs. 2% 30-day cocaine use: 5% vs. 1% vs. 1% Cigarette use/past 30 days: 22% vs. 20% vs. 15% > 20 cigarettes/day: 2% vs. 2% vs. 5% (Note: African-American youth smoke at lower rates than youth overall)
Paxon, 1995 Level V	Case reports and expert opinion	Adults with developmental disabilities	2	M: 100% Ages: 29 and 24	NA	Treatment experiences and needs of MR clients who abuse substances	Conc.: Adults with DD can benefit from relapse prevention programs (prevent return to alcohol/drug use after abstinence by preventing reestablishment of contact with drug-centered people, places, and things).

(continued)

TABLE 12-4 *Continued*

STUDY INFORMATION AND LEVEL OF EVIDENCE	RESEARCH DESIGN	POPULATION STUDIED	NUMBER OF SUBJECTS	SUBJECT CHARACTERISTICS	SETTING	MEASURES	MAIN FINDINGS (P-VALUES)
Peine et al., 1998 Level V	Case report	Adults with MR and maladaptive behaviors	2	M: 100% Av. age: 47 Mild MR: 50% Mod MR: 50%	Institution	Reduction in no. of cigarettes obtained	Behavioral program: Both subjects decreased no. of cigarettes they obtained and smoked, without altering frequency of maladaptive behaviors.
Rimmer et al, 1994 Level III	Cross-sectional study of individuals Data collection: health form completed by parent or staff Compares data by residence and with Framingham Offspring Study	Adults with MR (mild to severe)	329	Institution: M: 57% Av. age/M: 37 Group home: M: 62% Av. age/M: 37 With family: M: 55%; Av. age: 33	Institution: 56% (184) Group home: 12% (39) With family: 32% (106)	Cigarettes/day; smokes more than 10 cigarettes/day	Comparison by residence: % smoking > 10 cigarettes/day: Overall: NA Institution: M: 3.8%; F: 0 ($p < .001$) Group home: M: 20.8%; F: 6.7% (NA) With family: M: 6.9%; F: 2.1% ($p < .001$) Framingham Offspring Study: M: 27.5%; F: 27.0%
Rimmer et al, 1995 Level III	Cross-sectional study of individuals Data collection: health behavior form completed by parent or staff Presents statistical comparisons by residence	Adults with MR (mild to severe)	329 Note: same subjects as in Rimmer et al., 1994	Institution: M: 57% Av. age/M: 37 Group home: M: 62% Age/M: 37 With family: M: 55%; Av. age: 33	Institution: 56% (184) Group home: 12% (39) Family: 32% (106)	Cigarettes/day; alcoholic drinks/day	No. of cigarettes/day Institution: M: 1.4; F: 0.19 Group home: M: 8.5; F: 2.7 With family: M: 2.2; F: 0.42 Group home residents smoked and drank the most ($p < .001$). Males smoked > than females ($p < .001$). No. of alcoholic drinks/day Institution: M: 0.0; F: 0.0 Group home: M: 0.57; F: 0.36 With family: M: 0.16; F: 0.0

Rivinus, 1988 Level V	Review article and expert opinion	Individuals with MR	NA	NA	NA	NA	Attempt to alert readers to potential for substance abuse disorders among people with MR by outlining risk factors, listing symptoms to aid in case-finding and diagnosis, and noting potential for effective treatment.
Robertson et al., 2000 Level III	Cross-sectional study of individuals Data collection: Structured interviews with randomly selected staff Presents statistical comparisons by living arrangement	People with intellectual disabilities (Great Britain)	500	Across three living arrange- ments (villages, NHS campuses, dispersed housing): M: 62%, 59%, 60% (NS) Av. age: 40.1, 47.5, 45.5 ($p<0.001$) White: 100%, 96%, 96% (NS)	Village communities (86), NHS campuses (133), dispersed housing (281)	Patterns of alcohol use and abuse; smoking	Drinking overall: "No drinking exceeded recommendations." People living in dispersed housing most likely to drink, but still drank less than general population. Comparisons by living arrangement: Male alcohol use ($p<.01$): Non-drinkers: 45%, 73%, 49% Low: 55%, 27%, 50% Moderate: 0, 0, 1% High: 0, 0, 0 Female alcohol use ($<.01$): Non-drinkers: 82%, 96%, 76% Low: 18%, 4%, 24% Moderate/high: 0, 0, 0 Smoking (NS): % non-smoking: 98%, 92%, 88% % smokes 1–20/wk: 2%, 5%, 8% % smokes 20+/wk: 0, 3%, 4%

TABLE 12-4 *Continued*

STUDY INFORMATION AND LEVEL OF EVIDENCE	RESEARCH DESIGN	POPULATION STUDIED	NUMBER OF SUBJECTS	SUBJECT CHARACTERISTICS	SETTING	MEASURES	MAIN FINDINGS (*P*-VALUES)
Simpson, 1998 Level V	Expert opinion	People with learning difficulties (UK)	NA	NA	NA	NA	Conc.: Existing research base does not support current emphasis on potential dangers of alcohol consumption. Questions abstinence data because it ignores fact that most people with LD have no opportunity to drink. Alcohol may have social benefits for people with LD and should not be denied them without valid justification.
Small, 1981 Level V	Expert opinion and case report	People with MR	NA	NA	NA	NA	Describes Emotions Anonymous, a 12-step program specifically designed for people with MR.
Tracy and Hosken, 1997 Level III (smoking education program) (also Level IV; see below)	Evaluation of group smoking education program for smokers (involved substantial modification of mainstream "Fresh Start" program) Data collection: "Questionnaires were administered at the beginning	Adults with developmental disabilities (Australia)	11	M: 73% <25: 100%	Institution	At course end: % Stopped smoking % Decreased amount smoked % Interest in quitting % Increased concern and knowledge about health effects	Smokers wanting to quit: 46% (100% recalled being advised to do so) Smokers with unsuccessful quit attempts: 69% Program initially offered in convenient community location but elicited little interest; subsequently offered in institution (captured subjects). Outcomes at course end: Stopped smoking: 27% (3/11) Significantly cut down amount smoked: 27% (3/11)

and end of the course."						Expressed interest in quitting: 82% (9/11) Expressed increased concern and knowledge about health effects: 100% (11/11)
Tracy and Hosken, 1997 Level IV (smoking prevalence survey)	Cross-sectional study of individuals Data collection: structured interviews with clients	Adults with intellectual disabilities (Australia)	36	M: 50% <35: 69% >Age 55: 8%	Independent living supported by public ID system	Current smokers (not defined); ex-smokers; age at smoking initiation; reasons for starting to smoke	Current smoking prevalence: Overall: 36% (13) M: 39% F: 33% Ex-smokers: 25% Never smokers: 39% (hand-calculated) Knowledge of health effects: % who thought they could die from smoking: 94% % able to name a smoking-related disease: 97% Among current smokers: Amount smoked: < 10 cigarettes/day: 54% > 40 cigarettes/day: 1 (% NA) Age initiation: < 18: 85% Reasons for starting to smoke: Peer group influences: 54% Stress/tension relief: 15% Note: Only study to report people with MR smoke more than general population.

(continued)

TABLE 12-4 *Continued*

STUDY INFORMATION AND LEVEL OF EVIDENCE	RESEARCH DESIGN	POPULATION STUDIED	NUMBER OF SUBJECTS	SUBJECT CHARACTERISTICS	SETTING	MEASURES	MAIN FINDINGS (*P*-VALUES)
Tyas and Rush, 1993 Level III	Cross-sectional study of individuals Data collection: interviews with program administrators from every Ontario SA treatment program (Supplement to 1989 triennial survey of all SA programs in Ontario) Presents statistical comparisons by program type	Clients of SA treatment programs with "developmental handicaps" (DH) in 1988–1989 (Ontario)	949	NA	NA	Presence and treatment needs of clients with DH in SA treatment programs	% of Ontario SA caseload with DH: Overall: 2.3% Detox programs: 1.4% Short-term residential programs: 1.8% Long-term residential programs: 2.6% Nonresidential programs: 1.9% Assessment/referral programs: 3.5% SA programs tailored to clients with DH: Overall: 8.2% Detox programs: 0 Short-term residential programs: 11.6% Long-term residential programs: 1.9% Nonresidential programs: 10.9% Assessment/referral programs: 15.1% Ratings: Level of difficulty of DH clients: (1, much less difficult, to 7, much more difficult): Detoxification: 4.9 Short-term residential: 5.6 Long-term residential: 5.5 Nonresidential: 5.5 Assessment/referral: 5.4 % believing staff needed additional training to deal with DH clients: 75%

Citation, Level	Study Design/Data Collection	N	Sample	Demographics	Setting	Definitions	Results
Tyler and Bourquet, 1997 Level IV	Cross-sectional study of individuals. Data collection: medical record abstraction	21	Adults with MR in primary care setting	M: 95%; Age range: 27–67; White: 86%; Severe/profound MR: 77%	Small community residences supported by state DD system	"Cigarette smokers" (not defined); health effects	Smoking prevalence: 14.3% (3/21); Health effects seen among smokers: Severe chronic obstructive pulmonary disease (COPD); Peptic ulcer disease; Underweight
Walkup et al., 1999 Level IV	Cross-sectional study of individuals. Data collection: data file created by matching NJ HIV and AIDS Registry and NJ Medicaid file. Presents descriptive comparisons of HIV/AIDS Medicaid beneficiaries with and without MR (no p-values)	Cases (MR): 119 (1.4%); Controls (without MR): 8175	Cases: Medicaid recipients with MR (ICD-9-CM Codes 317, 318, 319) and HIV/AIDS; Controls: Adults in data file without MR	Cases (MR): M: 46% (52/114); White: 22% (25/113); People with MR more likely to be female and/or Black	Community-dwelling people with MR	Injection drug use: noted in registry data base; Substance abuse: having 1 or more claims with diagnosis of alcoholic psychoses, drug psychoses, alcoholic dependence, drug dependence, or nondependent abuse	Comparisons of HIV/AIDS Medicaid beneficiaries with and without MR: (no p-values) % with substance abuse claims: Mild MR: 79%; Unspecified MR: 75%; Severe: 52%; without MR: 52%; For Registry-based group, levels of injection drug use: Mild MR: 71%; Unspecified MR: 63%; Severe MR: 20%; Without MR: 58%; Authors claim injection drug levels are similar for those with and without MR but appear higher. Authors' note: "Data probably represent a conservative estimate of the number of HIV-infected persons with MR in NJ. Substance abuse appears to be important route of HIV transmission among people with MR."

(continued)

311

TABLE 12-4 *Continued*

STUDY INFORMATION AND LEVEL OF EVIDENCE	RESEARCH DESIGN	POPULATION STUDIED	NUMBER OF SUBJECTS	SUBJECT CHARACTERISTICS	SETTING	MEASURES	MAIN FINDINGS (*P-VALUES*)
Wenc, 1981 Level V	Review article and expert opinion	People with developmental disabilities	NA	NA	NA	NA	Focus: Recommends modifications to mainstream treatment programs to accommodate needs of people with DD; advocates closer working relationships between mental health, alcohol and other drug, and DD fields.
Westermeyer, 1990 Level V	Expert opinion	"Special populations in need of substance abuse treatment," including people with MR	NA	NA	NA	Treatment experiences and needs of clients with MR who abuse alcohol and illicit drugs	Conc.: Mainstream SA programs are able to serve special needs clients but this requires staff and programmatic modifications; specialized treatment is less important during detox, crisis intervention, and assessment stages. Social network reconstruction is essential, albeit challenging, for MR people.

312

| Westermeyer et al., 1996 Level III | Cross-sectional study of individuals

Data collection: patient interviews, extensive clinical examinations, including scales measuring SA severity, [Michigan Alcohol/Drug Screening Test (MADST) and Substance Abuse Problem Scale (SAPS)]

Presents statistical comparisons of people with and without MR | Cases: Adults with mild MR admitted to SA treatment programs

Controls: Adults without MR admitted to SA treatment programs | Total: 348

SA and MR: 40

SA/no MR: 308 | SA and MR: M: 68% Av. age: 32.2

SA/no MR: M: 64% Av. age: 31.2 | NA | Patterns of substance abuse (% lifetime use; age at first use; use frequency) treatment experiences and needs of clients with MR in SA treatment programs | Comparison of SA and MR vs. SA/no MR:
% with SA fathers: 68% vs. 42% ($p < .002$)

% lifetime use:
Alcohol: 100% vs. 98% (NS)
Illicit drug: 63% vs. 91% ($p < .0001$)
Marijuana: 60% vs. 82% ($p < .001$)
Cocaine: 20% vs. 57% ($p < .0001$)
Tobacco: 83% vs. 87% (NS)

Av. age at first use:
Alcohol: 17.5 vs. 15.1 ($p < .01$)
Illicit drug: 20.7 vs. 16.5 ($p < .01$)
Tobacco: 17 vs. 15.2 (NS)

Av. use frequency/ # days past yr:
Alcohol: 88 vs. 133 ($p < .03$)
Illicit drug: 41 vs. 157 ($p < .0001$)
Tobacco: 226 vs. 306 ($p < .0001$)

SA severity: 14.1 vs. 27.4 ($p < .0001$)
SAPS scale: 26.7 vs. 25.6 (NS)

Treatment options deemed effective with clients with MR and SA:
Residential placements in familiar facilities
Contingency contracting
Involvement of family and others
Close supervision, long-term
Day and evening programs
Supervised disulfiram treatment (with careful monitoring)
Long-term attention to supporting rewarding lifestyle |

(continued)

313

TABLE 12-4 *Continued*

STUDY INFORMATION AND LEVEL OF EVIDENCE	RESEARCH DESIGN	POPULATION STUDIED	NUMBER OF SUBJECTS	SUBJECT CHARACTERISTICS	SETTING	MEASURES	MAIN FINDINGS (*P*-VALUES)
Westermeyer et al., 1988 Level III	Case-control study Data collection: interviews with subjects and someone else who knew them Presents statistical comparisons of cases and controls	Adults with mild MR: Cases: DSM III SA diagnosis Controls: no SA diagnosis	Total: 80 Cases: 40 Controls: 40	Cases: M: 68% Av. age: 32.2 Controls: M: 65% Av. age: 30.6	NA	Patterns and consequences of substance abuse; personal, family and social complications	Comparison of cases vs. controls: % lifetime use: (hand-calculated) Alcohol: 100% vs. 85% ($p < .01$) Tobacco: 83% vs. 35% ($p < .001$) Marijuana: 60% vs. 5% ($p < .001$) Cocaine: 20% vs. 3% ($p < .05$) % using alone: 75% vs. 17% ($p < .001$) % most friends with alcohol/drug problems: 65% vs. .05% ($p < .001$) % decreased time at work: 53% vs. 0 ($p < .001$) % with physical fights: 48% vs. 0 ($p < .001$) % decreased work productivity or school grades: 48% vs. 0 ($p < .001$) % conviction for driving while intoxicated: 15% vs. 0 ($p < .01$)

ARC, Association for Retarded Citizens; ATP, alcohol treatment program; MR, mental retardation; SA, substance abuse

McGillicuddy and Blane (1999) reported that 39% of adults "recruited from local community agencies" had used alcohol and 4% had used illicit drugs during the previous month; 18% were identified as alcohol "misusers," based on an alcohol misuse measure. Other studies reporting lower rates of substance use and abuse among adults with I/DD than in the general population included Beange, McElduff, and Baker (1995); Lawrenson, Lindsay, and Walker (1995); McDermott, Platt, and Krishnaswami (1997); and Robertson et al. (2000).

A handful of studies were based on convenience samples that were drawn from individuals with known support needs, in addition to I/DD, and these studies reported prevalence estimates that approximated or exceeded those in the general population. When Westermeyer, Kemp, and Nugent (1996) compared the experiences of adults with and without I/DD in substance abuse (SA) treatment programs, adults with I/DD were less likely to report lifetime substance use than adults without I/DD. Nonetheless, adults with I/DD were using substances—100% reported lifetime use of alcohol, 63% reported lifetime use of illicit drugs, and 20% reported lifetime use of cocaine. In an earlier study, Westermeyer, Phaobtong, and Neider (1988) found that 60% of people with I/DD in SA treatment programs reported lifetime use of marijuana, 33% lifetime use of amphetamines, and 20% lifetime use of cocaine. Walkup, Sambamoorthi, and Crystal (1999) investigated substance abuse and injection drug use among Medicaid beneficiaries with HIV/AIDS, including 119 with I/DD. Within this sample, 79% of beneficiaries with mild I/DD, 75% with unspecified I/DD, and 52% with severe I/DD had a substance abuse claim, compared with 52% of beneficiaries without I/DD. Seventy-one percent of beneficiaries with mild I/DD, 63% with unspecified I/DD, and 20% with severe I/DD were injection drug users, compared with 58% of beneficiaries without I/DD.

Adolescents

Pack, Wallander, and Browne (1998) compared the prevalence of substance use and abuse among African-American youth with mild I/DD with public health data for African-American youth in the state and nationally. Fifty-one percent of youth with I/DD reported lifetime alcohol use (compared with 76% of African-American youth in the state, and 80% nationally); 43% reported alcohol use within the previous 30 days (compared with 44% in the state and 43% nationally); 31% reported binge drinking (compared with 24% in state and 19% nationally); 29% reported lifetime marijuana use (compared with 31% in the state and 34% nationally); and 18% reported marijuana use during the previous 30 days (compared with 18% in the state, and 19% nationally).

PATTERNS OF USE

Compared with the general population, people with I/DD appeared to initiate substance use at older ages (Westermeyer et al., 1996), to use at lower doses (Krishef, 1986; Lawrenson et al., 1995), and to use less frequently (Krishef, 1986; Lawrenson et al., 1995; Westermeyer et al., 1996). People with I/DD in the United States were more likely to drink alone (Krishef, 1986; Westermeyer et al., 1988), although this finding was contradicted by Lawrenson et al. (1995), who reported that most subjects with I/DD in Scotland drank in pubs, not alone. People with I/DD had the same tendency as the general population to use and abuse multiple substances (Hymowitz, Jaffe, Gupta, & Feuerman, 1997; McGillicuddy & Blane, 1999; McGillivray & Moore, 2001; Westermeyer et al., 1988; Westermeyer et al., 1996).

RISK FACTORS

People with I/DD shared many risk factors with the general population. These included male gender (challenged only by Westermeyer et al., 1996); having a father or siblings with substance abuse histories (Westermeyer et al., 1988, 1996); having friends with alcohol or drug problems (Westermeyer et al., 1988, 1996); and having coexisting mental illness (Hymowitz et al., 1997). Other risk factors, specific to people with I/DD, included having a higher level of functioning (McGillicuddy & Blane, 1999) and living in a less restrictive setting (cited universally).

QUESTION OF SPECIAL SUSCEPTIBILITY

Several studies suggested that people with I/DD were more susceptible to developing substance abuse problems than the general population. In 1981, Krishef and DiNitto hypothesized that people with I/DD were less able to foresee the consequences of excessive alcohol use because of cognitive impairments, and more susceptible to alcohol and drug abuse problems. More recently, McGillicuddy and Blane (1999) reported that people with I/DD faced a higher risk of converting from alcohol "user" to "misuser" status than other individuals; nearly 50% of alcohol users in their study misused it. Westermeyer's research involving people in SA treatment programs (Westermeyer et al., 1988, 1996), led to the conclusion that people with I/DD have "remarkably low tolerances," resulting in blackouts and negative social, legal, and work problems at lower doses and with less frequent use than for other individuals.

CONSEQUENCES

Studies suggested that substance abusers with I/DD experienced the same or even worse consequences than other substance abusers. Krishef and DiNitto (1981), for example, reported that 63% of clients with MR and alcohol problems had alcohol-related job problems, and many had alcohol-related criminal offenses. In Krishef's later study (1986), 13% of current drinkers reported drinking-related family discord and 7% reported violations of the law. Fifty-three percent of adults with I/DD in SA treatment (Westermeyer et al., 1988) reported decreased time at work, 47% being involved in physical fights, 48% decreased work productivity or school grades, and 15% a conviction for driving while intoxicated. Substance abuse may also exacerbate preexisting medical conditions (Krishef, 1986); interact negatively with medications (Burgard, Donohue, Azrin, & Teichner, 2000; Krishef, 1986); and increase the risk that people with I/DD will be victimized, particularly in drinking and drug-taking environments (Westermeyer et al., 1988, 1996).

SUBSTANCE ABUSE TREATMENT

Several authors highlighted the difficulties of diagnosing SA in people with I/DD, and identified lack of coordination and communication between the I/DD and SA fields as a major barrier to timely diagnosis, referral, and treatment (Christian & Poling, 1997; Clarke & Wilson, 1999; Degenhardt, 2000; Rivinus, 1988; Westermeyer et al., 1988, 1996). Differences of opinion also existed about the appropriate response when people with I/DD were identified as problem drinkers or substance abusers. Colleagues from the United Kingdom focused on helping people with I/DD moderate their consumption, not abstain (Lindsay, Allen, Walker, Lawrenson, & Smith, 1991; McMurran & Lismore, 1993; Simpson, 1998). In the United States, Campbell, Essex, and Held (1994) also reported variation in how key informants in SA and DD programs defined treatment success. In this study, treatment was deemed successful when clients with I/DD showed a greater awareness of the impact of drinking, according to 77% of respondents; completed the program, for 69%; attended AA regularly, for 61%; achieved total abstinence, for 59%; and reduced their drinking, for 51%.

Mainstream SA Treatment Programs

There were no outcomes-based data on the effectiveness of SA treatment for people with I/DD. In an early study, 50% of SA staff expressed the opinion that clients with I/DD were as successful as other clients in overcoming alcohol problems (Krishef & DiNitto, 1981). Most studies, however, gave the impression that the rate of participation of people with I/DD in mainstream SA programs was low (Krishef, 1986; Krishef & DiNitto, 1981; Lottman, 1993; McGillivray & Moore, 2001; Tyas & Rush, 1993). Entry to treatment was also said to occur later than for other individuals and at a point at which problems were more severe (Krishef & DiNitto, 1981; Lottman, 1993; Westermeyer et al., 1996).

An important issue was whether mainstream SA treatment models met the needs of people with I/DD. Although most studies suggested that people with I/DD encountered barriers to treatment, most felt these barriers could be overcome with special modifications. Substance abuse program staff who were asked to rate the level of difficulty of working with clients with I/DD, on a scale of 1 (easy) to 7 (difficult), viewed these clients as difficult to work with (Tyas & Rush, 1993). Clients in short-term residential programs were rated as presenting the highest level of difficulty (5.6), while clients in detoxification were rated as presenting the lowest (4.9).

In Campbell et al. (1994), 90% of SA staff cited lack of staff training as a major barrier to treating people with I/DD. Other barriers cited by staff included lack of experience with people with I/DD (noted by 78%); I/DD clients' diminished comprehension (noted by 78%); and I/DD clients need for more one-on-one time (noted by 54%). The need for additional time was also identified as a treatment barrier by Krishef & DiNitto (1981) and Lottman (1993). Other barriers noted in the literature included prohibitions on psychotropic medication use in some programs (Campbell et al., 1994); finances (Lottman, 1993); and discrimination against people with I/DD (Krishef & DiNitto, 1981; Lottman, 1993).

The following modifications were suggested to improve the accessibility of SA treatment programs for people with I/DD: extended lengths of stay, use of less confrontation and more support, reduced use of groups and more use of one-on-one interactions, substitution of oral and visual materials for written materials, and use of simple contingencies or reinforcements (Campbell et al., 1994; Krishef & DiNitto, 1981; Tyas & Rush, 1993).

There was no empirical information about the optimal treatment model for people with I/DD, although 80% of SA staff respondents in Campbell et al. (1994) recommended a program that combined mainstream and specialized elements.

PREVENTION/EDUCATION

The one study with evidence about substance abuse prevention and education (McGillicuddy & Blane, 1999) involved a well-designed RCT of a group SA program tailored to the needs of people with I/DD. Although the intervention groups demonstrated improved substance knowledge and skills, there were no differences between the intervention and control groups relative to changes in alcohol misuse, cigarette use, or attitudes about substance use.

Summary of the Evidence: Smoking

MAGNITUDE OF THE PROBLEM

It is a curious historical fact that people with I/DD were typically encouraged to smoke in state institutions, despite constraints on most areas of their lives, and some have suggested that individuals who became addicted to smoking in institutions continued to smoke when they moved to the community (Hymowitz et al., 1997; Minihan, 1999). Nonetheless, there were no population-based estimates of the prevalence of smoking among people with I/DD.

Adults

Convenience samples suggested that the prevalence of smoking among adults was lower than in the general population, although some adults, including those with dual diagnoses and those who previously lived in institutions, appeared to smoke at higher rates. Estimates of prevalence ranged from 2% among people living in an institution (Burtner, Wakham, McNeal, & Garvey, 1995) and 3% among patients in a primary care practice, many of whom had severe I/DD (McDermott et al., 1997), to 18% among adults with I/DD and mental illness served in a behavioral health care clinic (Hymowitz et al., 1997).

Adolescents

The prevalence of smoking among adolescents more closely approximated the experiences of other youth. Twenty-two percent of African-American youth with mild I/DD (Pack et al., 1998) reported cigarette use in the past 30 days, compared with 22% of African-American youth in the state and 15% nationally.

RISK FACTORS

People with I/DD shared many risk factors with the general population. These included male gender (all papers), the presence of coexisting psychiatric conditions (Hymowitz et al., 1997), misuse of other substances (Hymowitz et al., 1997; McGillicuddy & Blane, 1999; Westermeyer et al., 1988, 1996), and peer group influences (Tracy & Hosken, 1997). Other risk factors appeared specific to people with I/DD. These included living in less restrictive settings (Hymowitz et al., 1997; Rimmer, Braddock, & Fujiura, 1994; Robertson et al., 2000), and having a higher functional level (Hymowitz et al., 1997).

SMOKING CESSATION

Effectiveness and Related Issue

In one uncontrolled trial of a smoking cessation program, specifically designed for people with I/DD but enrolling only 11 subjects, three of the 11 had stopped smoking and another three had significantly cut down by the end of the program; all eleven expressed increased concern and knowledge about the health effects of smoking (Tracy & Hosken, 1997).

Minihan (1999) queried supervisors in a statewide residential system about the frequency with which they observed clients who smoked attempting to quit: 47% replied "almost never," while 44% said "sometimes," 5% "often," and 4% "very often." Residential supervisors were also asked to cite factors that, in their experience, were associated with clients' attempts to quit. The factor cited by the highest proportion of respondents (59%) was "doctor or nurse asks them to quit," followed by the clients' own desire for good health (cited by 48%); family/staff ask them to quit (cited by 45%); and an increase in the price of cigarettes (cited by 33%). When asked to rate the usefulness of various smoking cessation techniques specific to people with I/DD, 55% rated a group program especially designed for people with I/DD as highly useful. The following proportions of supervisors also rated other techniques as useful: one-on-one counseling program (noted by 36%), nicotine transdermal patch (noted by 26%), and nicotine gum noted by (9%).

PREVENTION AND EDUCATION

The one RCT that tested the effectiveness of a program designed to meet the needs of people with I/DD (McGillicuddy & Blane, 1999) found no differences in smoking rates between the intervention and control groups.

Conclusions

Because the evidence about how alcohol abuse, illicit drug use, and smoking affect people with I/DD is only moderate to weak, one should approach the information in this chapter primarily as evidence that people with I/DD are not immune to problems related to substance abuse—an important finding, in and of itself—and acknowledge that the true magnitude of these behaviors is currently unknown.

Within the wider world of public health, alcohol abuse and illicit drug and tobacco use are considered indicators of the overall health status of the general population, although they are not viewed this way within the I/DD field, and this may be one reason why data are so limited. The evidence that does exist suggests that the number of adults with I/DD who use and abuse substances is small, particularly relative to the general population. These low prevalence estimates might reflect low usage, but they might also reflect Simpson's contention (1998) that any estimate of the prevalence of substance use among people with I/DD is inherently an underestimate because so many individuals are prevented from engaging in these behaviors by external supervisors.

Some adults may be abusing substances at higher rates than others with I/DD. The few studies that investigated substance abuse among people with special needs in addition to I/DD, including substance abuse diagnoses, provided prevalence estimates that approximated or exceeded those in the general population. These studies may reflect more closely the experiences of individuals with I/DD who have the opportunity to drink and use drugs, and thus provide more realistic estimates of what the true prevalence might be, if the majority of people with I/DD had this option. Of special concern were data indicating that adolescents with I/DD were using substances at rates similar to or even higher than youth in the general population. It may be that adolescents with I/DD, who have grown up in communities where they were exposed to contemporary social pressures, are at heightened risk for substance abuse.

Even if the number of people with I/DD who abuse alcohol and other substances is eventually determined to be small, these individuals still deserve our attention and support. Although data are very limited, there is some evidence that people with I/DD who use substances are more likely to abuse them. When people with I/DD abuse substances, they experience the same or even harsher consequences as other substance abusers, including work problems and problems involving the criminal justice system.

It is particularly worrisome that people with I/DD appear to have less access than other individuals to treatment programs prepared to meet their needs. It is also of concern that I/DD service systems in the United States may be ignoring this problem. Many of the papers cited in this chapter were authored by researchers from either the SA field or I/DD systems in other countries.

For all these reasons, it is essential that service and support systems for people with I/DD in the United States improve their capacity to address substance abuse issues. The growing popularity of supportive living models, so positive in many respects, could result in an increase in the prevalence of SA among people with I/DD, particularly if community support systems remain deprived of adequate funding. People with I/DD with limited life experience with alcohol and drugs, coupled with new exposures to peers who use substances and media messages that promote substance use—in the absence of education and support—make for a potent and potentially problematic situation. "Best practice" recommendations are sorely needed with respect to substance abuse prevention and education, case-finding, treatment, maintenance of recovery, abstinence, and smoking cessation, but they cannot be developed without a sound research base that is built upon much more comprehensive information than exists at present.

I/DD service and support systems need not confront these issues on their own. This review of the literature suggested that there are individuals associated with the SA field who have both the expertise and interest to work in partnership with I/DD professionals to better address the problem of SA among people with I/DD. Seeking out these partnerships should be the first step in addressing this issue.

REFERENCES

Beange, H., McElduff, A., & Baker, W. (1995). Medical disorders of adults with mental retardation: A population study. *American Journal on Mental Retardation, 99,* 595–604.

Burgard, J. F., Donohue, B., Azrin, N. H., & Teichner, G. (2000). Prevalence and treatment of substance abuse in the mentally retarded population: An empirical review. *Journal of Psychoactive Drugs, 32,* 293–298.

Burtner, A. P., Wakham, M. D., McNeal, D. R., & Garvey, T. P. (1995). Tobacco and the institutionalized mentally retarded: Usage choices and ethical considerations. *Special Care in Dentistry, 15*(2), 56–60.

Butler, C., & Campbell, S. (2000). Evidence of the effects of intrathecal baclofen for spastic and dystonic cerebral palsy. *Developmental Medicine & Child Neurology, 42,* 634–645.

Campbell, J. A., Essex, E. L., & Held, G. (1994). Issues in chemical dependency treatment and aftercare for people with learning differences. *Health & Social Work, 19*(1), 63–70.

Centers for Disease Control and Prevention. (2002). Trends in cigarette smoking among high school students—United States, 1991–2001. *MMWR Morbidity and Mortality Weekly Report, 51*(19), 409–412.

Centers for Disease Control and Prevention. (2003a). Alcohol consumption by persons 18 years of age and over, according to selected characteristics: United States, selected years 1997–2001. In *Health, United States, 2003.* Retrieved July 19, 2004, from: http://www.cdc.gov/nchs/products/pubs/pubd/hus/trendtables.htm

Centers for Disease Control and Prevention. (2003b). Cigarette smoking among adults—United States, 2001. *MMWR Morbidity and Mortality Weekly Report, 52*(40), 953–956.

Centers for Disease Control and Prevention. (n.d.) Trends in the prevalence of alcohol use. In *National Youth Risk Behavior Survey: 1991–2003.* Retrieved June 4, 2004, from: http://www.cdc.gov/HealthyYouth/yrbs/pdfs/trends-alcohol.pdf

Christian, L. A., & Poling, A. (1997). Drug abuse in persons with mental retardation: A review. *American Journal on Mental Retardation, 102,* 126–136.

Clarke, J. J., & Wilson, D. N. (1999). Case report—Alcohol problems and intellectual disability. *Journal of Intellectual Disability Research, 43,* 135–139.

Degenhardt, L. (2000). Interventions for people with alcohol use disorders and an intellectual disability: A review of the literature. *Journal of Intellectual & Developmental Disability, 25,* 135–146.

Delaney, D., & Poling, A. (1990). Drug abuse among mentally retarded people: An overlooked problem? *Journal of Alcohol and Drug Education, 35*(2), 48–54.

Department of Health and Human Services (2000a). Substance abuse. In *Healthy people 2010* (2nd ed.): *with understanding and improving health and objectives for improving health.* 2 vols. Retrieved May 11, 2004, from: http://www.healthypeople.gov/document/HTML/Volume2/26 Substance.htm.

Department of Health and Human Services (2000b). Leading health indicators. In *Healthy people 2010* (2nd ed.): *with understanding and improving health and objectives for improving health.*

2 vols. Retrieved January 6, 2004, from: http://www.healthypeople.gov/document/html/uih/uih_bw/uih_4.htm

Draheim, C. C., McCubbin, J. A., & Williams, D. P. (2002). Differences in cardiovascular disease risk between nondiabetic adults with mental retardation with and without Down syndrome. *American Journal on Mental Retardation, 107,* 201–211.

Edgerton, R. B. (1986). Alcohol and drug use by mentally retarded adults. *American Journal of Mental Deficiency, 90,* 602–609.

Grant, B. F., Dawson, D. A., Stinson, F. S., Chou, S. P., Dufour, M. C., & Pickering, R. P. (2004). The 12-month prevalence and trends in DSM-IV alcohol abuse and dependence: United States, 1991–1992 and 2001–2002. *Drug and Alcohol Dependence, 74,* 223–234.

Hennekens, C. H., & Buring, J. E. (1987). *Epidemiology in medicine.* Boston: Little, Brown.

Hymowitz, N., Jaffe, F. E., Gupta, A., & Feuerman, M. (1997). Cigarette smoking among patients with mental retardation and mental illness. *Psychiatric Services, 48*(1), 100–102.

Krishef, C. H. (1986). Do the mentally retarded drink? A study of their alcohol usage. *Journal of Alcohol and Drug Education, 31,* 64–70.

Krishef, C. H., & DiNitto, D. M. (1981). Alcohol abuse among mentally retarded individuals. *Mental Retardation, 19*(4), 151–155.

Lawrenson, H., Lindsay, W. R., & Walker, P. (1995). The pattern of alcohol consumption within a sample of mentally handicapped people in Tayside. *Mental Handicap Research, 8*(1), 54–59.

Lindsay, W. R., Allen, R., Walker, P., Lawrenson, H., & Smith, A. H. W. (1991). An alcohol education service for people with learning difficulties. *Mental Handicap, 19,* 96–100.

Lottman, T. J. (1993). Access to generic substance abuse services for persons with mental retardation. *Journal of Alcohol and Drug Education, 39,* 41–55.

McDermott, S., Platt, T., & Krishnaswami, S. (1997). Are individuals with mental retardation at high risk for chronic disease? *Family Medicine, 29,* 429–434.

McGillicuddy, N. B., & Blane, H. T. (1999). Substance use in individuals with mental retardation. *Addictive Behaviors, 24,* 869–878.

McGillivray, J. A., & Moore, M. R. (2001). Substance use by offenders with mild intellectual disability. *Journal of Intellectual & Developmental Disability, 26*(4), 297–310.

McGinnis, J. M., & Foege, W. H. (1993). Actual causes of death in the United States. *Journal of the American Medical Association, 270,* 2207–2212.

McMurran, M. & Lismore, K. (1993). Using video-tapes in alcohol interventions for people with learning disabilities—An exploratory study. *Mental Handicap, 21,* 29–31.

Minihan, P. M. (1999). Smoking policies and practices in a state-supported residential system for people with mental retardation. *American Journal on Mental Retardation, 104,* 131–142.

Mokdad, A. H., Marks, J. S., Stroup, D. F., & Gerberding, J. L. (2004). Actual causes of death in the United States, 2000. *Journal of the American Medical Association, 291,* 1238–1245.

Moore, D., & Polsgrove, L. (1989). Disabilities, developmental handicaps and substance misuse: A review. *Social Pharmacology, 3,* 375–408.

Pack, R. P., Wallander, J. L., & Browne, D. (1998). Health risk behaviors of African-American adolescents with mild retardation: Prevalence depends on measurement method. *American Journal on Mental Retardation, 102,* 409–420.

Paxon, J. E. (1995). Relapse prevention for individuals with developmental disabilities, borderline intellectual functioning, or illiteracy. *Journal of Psychoactive Drugs, 27,* 167–172.

Peine, H. A., Darvish, R., Blakelock, H., Osborne, J. G., & Jenson, W. R. (1998). Non-aversive reduction of cigarette smoking in two adult men in a residential setting. *Journal of Behavior Therapy and Experimental Psychiatry, 29,* 55–65.

Rimmer, J. H., Braddock, D., & Fujiura, G. (1994). Cardiovascular risk factor levels in adults with mental retardation. *American Journal on Mental Retardation, 98,* 510–518.

Rimmer, J. H., Braddock, D., & Marks, B. (1995). Health characteristics and behaviors of adults with mental retardation residing in three living arrangements. *Research in Developmental Disabilities, 16*(6), 489–499.

Rivinus, T. (1988). Alcohol use disorder in mentally retarded persons. *Psychiatric Aspects of Mental Retardation Reviews, 7*(4), 19–25.

Robertson, J., Emerson, E., Gregory, N., Hatton, C., Turner, S., Kessissoglou, S., & Hallam, A. (2000). Lifestyle related risk factors for poor health in residential settings for people with intellectual disabilities. *Research in Developmental Disabilities, 21,* 469–486.

Simpson, M. K. (1998). Just say 'no'? Alcohol and people with learning difficulties. *Disability & Society, 13*(4), 541–555.

Small, J. (1981). Emotions Anonymous: Counseling the mentally retarded substance abuser. *Alcohol Health and Research World, 5,* 46.

Substance Abuse and Mental Health Services Administration (SAMHSA). (2001). *SAMHSA factsheet: National Household Survey on Drug Abuse, 2001.* Retrieved July 28, 2004, from: http://www.whitehousedrugpolicy.gov/drugfact/nhsda01.html.

Tracy, J., & Hosken, R. (1997). The importance of smoking education and preventative health strategies for people with intellectual disability. *Journal of Intellectual Disability Research, 41,* 416–421.

Tyas, S., & Rush, B. (1993). The treatment of disabled persons with alcohol and drug problems: Results of a survey of addiction services. *Journal of Studies on Alcohol, 54,* 275–282.

Tyler, C. V., & Bourquet, C. (1997). Primary care of adults with mental retardation. *Journal of Family Practice, 44,* 487–494.

U.S. Preventive Services Task Force. (1996). *Guide to clinical preventive services* (2nd ed.). Baltimore, MD: Williams & Wilkins.

Walkup, J., Sambamoorthi, U. & Crystal, S. (1999). Characteristics of persons with mental retardation and HIV/AIDS infection in a statewide Medicaid population. *American Journal on Mental Retardation, 104*(4), 356–363.

Wenc, F. (1981). The developmentally disabled substance abuser. *Alcohol Health and Research World, 5,* 42–46.

Westermeyer, J. (1990). Treatment for psychoactive substance use disorder in special populations: Issues in strategic planning. *Advances in Alcohol & Substance Abuse, 8*(3/4), 1–8.

Westermeyer, J., Kemp, K., & Nugent, S. (1996). Substance disorder among persons with mild mental retardation—A comparative study. *The American Journal on Addictions, 5*(1), 23–31.

Westermeyer, J., Phaobtong, T., & Neider, J. (1988). Substance use and abuse among mentally retarded persons: A comparison of patients and a survey population. *American Journal of Drug and Alcohol Abuse, 14*(1), 109–123.

13

SECONDARY CONDITIONS RISK APPRAISAL FOR ADULTS

Tom Seekins, PhD, Meg Ann Traci, PhD,
Donna Bainbridge, PT, EdD, ATC,
and Kathleen Humphries, PD

There has been an explosion of interest in the health and wellness of people with intellectual and developmental disabilities (I/DD) (Brandt & Pope, 1997; Pope & Tarlov, 1991; U.S. Department of Health and Human Services [DHHS], 2000). People with I/DD represent about 17% of the population, but account for as much as 47% of medical care expenditures (Rice & Turpin, 1996). Yet, people with I/DD often are not included in programs to promote healthy lifestyles or other efforts to manage health care costs. As such, efforts to promote the health and wellness of individuals with I/DD have a great potential to both improve their health and independence and to reduce medical care costs accordingly.

Health risk appraisal (HRA) is a popular health promotion method. In general, HRA focuses on mortality as the dependent variable (Foxman & Edington, 1987; Gazmararian, Foxman, Yen, Morgenstern, & Edington, 1991). Independent or risk variables (e.g., smoking) are used to predict mortality and achievable age (Yen, McDonald, Hirschland, & Edington, 2003). In an HRA, an individual answers a series

---

The opinions expressed represent those of the authors but do not necessarily represent those of the federal government.

of questions about personal factors and health behavior demonstrated to be predictive of mortality. His or her responses are used to create a health risk profile that highlights lifestyle variables that put the individual at increased risk. Based on the profile, information about health practices to reduce risk is provided to individuals, along with estimates of the years of life that might be gained if those specific changes are made.

Health care professionals who use HRA also help motivate the person to make the necessary behavioral changes (Doerr & Hutchins, 1981; Foxman & Edington, 1987; Gazmararian et al., 1991).

HRA has been applied to the general population, and to several distinct subgroups, including employees of large corporations and organizations (Ozminkowski, 2004; Musich, Adams, DeWolf, & Edington, 2001). HRA has also been applied to predict medical service utilization and costs (e.g., Ozminkowski et al., 2004), and morbidity (e.g., Doerr & Hutchins, 1981; Musich et al., 2001; Yen et al., 2003).

There are few reported applications of HRA to groups characterized by specific impairments that lead to I/DD, however. Historically, longevity among the population of people with I/DD has been significantly lower than in the general population but appears to be increasing (Seelman & Sweeney, 1995). Unfortunately, specific conditions (e.g., Down syndrome) or disability, in general, are seldom used as demographic identifiers in major data sets that can be related to mortality. This presents serious obstacles to developing HRA for this population.

At the same time, researchers, service providers, and policy makers have begun to focus interest in the health of people with I/DD, specifically examining secondary conditions or morbidity. For example, researchers and service providers are focusing on limitation in community participation (i.e., quality of life) due to secondary conditions (Brandt & Pope, 1997; Lollar, 1994; Marge, 1988; Pope, 1992; Pope & Tarlov, 1991).

Secondary conditions are preventable health problems that are experienced by an individual after he or she has a primary impairment (Marge, 1988; Pope & Tarlov, 1991; Traci, Seekins, Szalda-Petree, & Ravesloot, 2002). Secondary conditions range from medical complications such as pressure sores and urinary tract infection to problems of psychosocial adjustment such as depression, to environmental issues such as access problems. Disability is viewed as increasing one's risk for a variety of these problems that can limit health, functional capacity, participation in life activities, and independence.

Accordingly, an additional approach to HRA in the population of adults with I/DD might involve developing secondary condition risk appraisal. Risk factors might be understood to include physiologic, environmental, and behavioral variables. By definition, the physiologic impairments are related to secondary conditions. Traci and her colleagues (2002) report that environmental variables, such as stressful life changes, are directly related to reported limitations due to secondary conditions. Presumably, various behavioral practices can influence limitation due to secondary conditions, both in the way they affect the general population, and in the unique ways they may affect those with particular impairments.

Figure 13-1 outlines a basic model of risk variables, the role they play in risk for secondary conditions, and their relation to limitation due to secondary conditions.

FIGURE 13-1 *A basic model of the interaction of environmental, physiologic, and behavioral variables that lead to limitations due to secondary conditions is presented. Selected variables that fall into each category are included.*

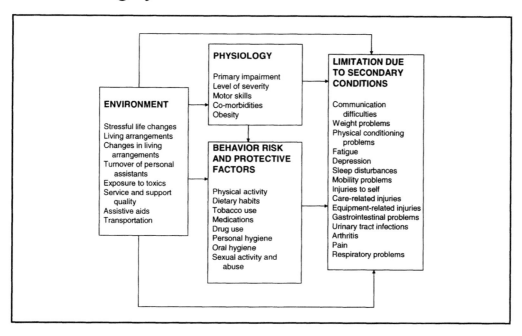

In this model, physiologic variables include the impairments that contribute to I/DD, the level of severity of impairment, overall health, and similar other issues. Environmental variables include supports for leading a healthy lifestyle, types and quality of living and work arrangements, and various program policies and practices. Behavioral variables include the frequency and levels of physical activity, dietary practices, and social participation. These variables contribute to the limitation in participation due to secondary conditions.

LITERATURE ON THE HEALTH STATUS OF ADULTS WITH I/DD

Surprisingly little appears to have been published about the health status or risk factors experienced by those with I/DD (Hayden & Kim, 2002; Horowitz, Kerker, Owens, & Zigler, 2000; Robertson et al., 2000). Where risk assessments have been completed, they tend to focus on one or a few variables reported by relatively narrow convenience samples. Further, the risk and protective factors are rarely connected directly to either limitation due to secondary conditions or health status. For example, researchers at the Center of Residential Service and Community Living at the University of Minnesota (Hayden & Kim, 2002) reviewed a broad set of literature on health status and service utilization of adults with I/DD published from 1989 to 2001. They found only 18 studies that met any of the following criteria: (1) described health status, health care access, utilization, patterns, and levels of care needed by groups of individuals with I/DD; (2) compared those same variables between groups of people in or out of institutional settings; (3) identified barriers to community-based medical care; or (4) made recommendations for improving community medical services. The studies were all based on convenience samples. The number of subjects ranged from 15 to 1073. While several of the studies reported on one or more risk factors (e.g., type of residence, change in residence, obesity, etc.), none reported on a comprehensive assessment of health risks.

Frey, Szalda-Petree, Traci, and Seekins (2001) conducted a literature review focused on prevention strategies that addressed 20 of the most pervasive secondary conditions that severely limit participation. They found only 25 studies that met both prevention and empirical criteria reported in the 5 years from 1994 to 1999. The prevention criteria were based on accepted definitions that included primary, secondary, and tertiary prevention efforts. The minimum empirical criteria for inclusion were the use of a comparison group or pre–post measures.

Robertson and her colleagues (2000) assessed the weight, amount of physical activity, diet, and tobacco use among 500 adults with I/DD living in supported arrangements. They examined the relationship between living arrangement and risk factors. They found that those living in less restrictive residential settings had poorer diet, were more likely to smoke, and experienced greater obesity.

Pack, Wallander, and Browne (1998) conducted assessments of 194 African-American adolescents with mild mental retardation using two data collection methods, an interview and an anonymous group survey. They found that respondents were at substantially elevated risk for binge drinking and carrying guns. They also found that those completing the anonymous survey reported engaging in risk behaviors at a higher rate.

Their comparison of data collection procedures underscores the difficulty of collecting information about behavioral patterns from a population of adults who experience both I/DD and communication difficulties. In many instances, proxies are used to report on behavior and health status. Todorov and Kirchner (2000) report that proxies responding to the National Health Inventory Survey-Disabilities (NHIS-D) often under-reported disabilities for adults younger than 65 years of age and over-reported for those older than 65 years. In a validation study of Census disability items, Andresen, Fitch, McLendon, and Meyers (2000) found low agreement between respondents with I/DD and proxies, where proxies underestimated impairment severity relative to respondents with I/DD. As such, while proxy reporting is often the only method for assessing health status, those ratings need to be weighed with caution.

Havercamp, Scandlin, and Roth (2004) adapted items from the North Carolina Behavior Risk Factor Surveillance System (BRFSS) and used them to collect data on health risk and status from 946 randomly selected individuals served by the North Carolina Developmental Disability Services system and living in the community. They used a mixed method of responding, including record reviews, face-to-face interviews, and proxy reports to collect the information. Because they adapted items from the BRFSS, they were able to compare results from their respondents to the general population and others with I/DD. They found that adults with I/DD were more likely to lead sedentary lifestyles, and seven times as likely to report inadequate emotional support compared with adults without I/DD. They also found that their respondents were at risk from low utilization of breast and cervical cancer screening.

Horowitz and her colleagues (2000) conducted a comprehensive review of the literature on the health status and needs of individuals with mental retardation for Special Olympics International. A portion of their review on health behaviors involved obesity, physical activity, smoking, and oral hygiene. They found studies that showed that the prevalence of obesity varied with living arrangement and the etiology of impairment, with those living in more independent arrangements and those with Down syndrome more likely to be obese. They found few studies reporting on physical activity levels but those available suggested sedentary patterns. Their review also suggested that tobacco smoking varied by living condition and severity of impairment; again, the literature suggests that those with more severe impairments and living under more supervised arrangements were less likely to smoke (see Chapter 12).

Finally, Horowitz and her colleagues (2000) also assessed the status of the literature on dental health (see Chapter 7). Their review shows that adults with mental retardation (MR) have poorer overall oral health and hygiene than the general population. Both dental health and oral hygiene practices may be related to level of impairment, living situation, age, and medications. They report that oral health practices have been shown to be consistently poor among individuals with MR. Surprisingly, they report that those with moderate to severe MR tend to brush their teeth more regularly then those with mild MR. Their level of impairment often requires support for such routine tasks. Again, however, the authors point to the problem of convenience samples and other methodologic issues that make interpretation of the data difficult.

Preliminary Finding for One Secondary Conditions Risk Appraisal Study

Given the paucity of comprehensive, systematic assessments of risk for adults with I/DD, there was a need to begin to understand the distribution of these factors across this population. In response, we developed the Health and Secondary Conditions Instrument for Adults with Developmental Disabilities (HSCIADD) to assess limitation in participation due to secondary conditions, life changes experienced, behavioral and environmental risk factors, and medical service utilization (Traci et al., 2002). The HSCIADD collects information on 7 physiological variables, 39 life event variables, 8 medical service utilization variables, 18 environmental and 34 behavioral risk variables, and 45 secondary conditions.

We have conducted a series of studies using the HSCSIADD with Montana adults with I/DD living in supported living arrangements. The following sections report on the rates of behavioral and environmental risk factors derived from the largest of these studies. Preliminary analyses leading toward the development of risk appraisal are also presented. These data offer another step in understanding both methods and variables in conducting secondary conditions risk assessment with this population.

TABLE 13-1 *Types and Lengths of Relationships Between Proxies and Consumer Respondents*

PROXY RELATIONSHIP TO CONSUMER RESPONDENT	PERCENTAGE OF SURVEYS REPORTED	MEDIAN MONTHS OF RELATIONSHIP REPORTED
Personal assistant provider	73	43
Work supervisor	21	42
Case manager	4	55
Parent	2	208
Guardian	1	361

DEMOGRAPHY OF RESPONDENTS

Montana is a sparsely populated, rural state with a population of 917,621. In 1999, the Montana Developmental Disabilities Program provided services and supports to a total of 2230 adults. We sent surveys to all 1920 adult consumers living in supported living arrangements operated by private service corporations under contract to the state. A total of 749 responses were collected through proxy ratings. Table 13-1 presents the types of relationship the proxy rater had with the consumers for whom they were reporting. The majority of proxy respondents were direct care personal assistants (73%) or work supervisors (21%). The average duration of the relationship between the proxy and the consumer was 48 months.

Table 13-2 lists the primary impairments reported by respondents. In addition to these impairments, 12.6% were diagnosed as also having a mental illness and 0.4% were reported to have Prader-Willi syndrome. The average age of respondents was 43.5 years, ranging from 16 to 93 years. Fifty-five percent of respondents were males and 45% were females.

TABLE 13-2 *Percentages of Primary Impairments Reported by Respondents (N = 739)*

Mental retardation	92.8	Macrocephalus	1.1
Epilepsy or seizure disorder	17.2	Hydrocephalus	.9
Down syndrome	12.4	Fetal alcohol syndrome	.8
Cerebral palsy	10.3	Spina bifida	.5
Autism	3.9	Muscular dystrophy	.5

TABLE 13-3 *Percentage Overall Level of Severity of Disability Reported*

Mild	46
Moderate	34
Severe	20

Table 13-3 reports the distribution of severity of disability. Respondents rated their overall health as 1.87 (Good) on a four-point scale, where "0" equaled poor and "3" equaled excellent. They reported their overall independence as 1.98 (Good) on a similar scale.

BEHAVIORAL AND LIFESTYLE VARIABLES

A wide variety of behavioral practices and lifestyle variables have been identified as influencing health outcomes in this population (e.g., Horowitz et al., 2000). Few have been linked to limitations due to secondary conditions. Behavioral and lifestyle factors include such variables as physical activity, nutrition, oral hygiene, personal hygiene and appearance, drug use and medications, and sexual activity and abuse.

Physical Activity

Physical activity is widely recognized as a protective factor. The Surgeon General Report on Physical Activity and Health (U.S. Department of Health and Human Services, 1996) calls for members of the general population to engage in a minimum of 30 minutes of moderate-intensity physical activity on most, if not all days of each week. Appropriate levels of physical activity might reduce limitations experienced by people with I/DD due to lack of fitness or stamina, fatigue, depression, pain, respiratory problems, sleep disturbances, weight problems, and other issues. Respondents in our sample reported significantly raising their heart rate on an average of 2.95 days per week, including any work or exercise. The duration of this activity lasted an average of 12.3 minutes. Some respondents appeared to be very active, with 29.7% of respondents engaged in significant physical activity on 5 or more days per week and 18.2% reporting that they engaged in such activity for 25 or more minutes at a time. The overall rating of the daily activity level fell at the mid-point, however—between very sedentary and very active—but 33.8% reported being quite sedentary.

For many adults with I/DD, practicing routine, active range-of-motion exercises is an important element in maintaining function. While such exercises may not be necessary for all adults with I/DD, only 21% of respondents reported doing range-of-motion routines to maintain flexibility (see also Chapter 6).

Nutrition

Nutrition has been implicated in a range of health outcomes. This includes evidence that it may affect certain secondary conditions as they are experienced in the general population (e.g., weight, fatigue, etc.). We collected a limited amount of information about dietary intake. Respondents reported eating an average of 3.21 servings of fruits or vegetables each day. Only 23.3% of respondents reported eating the recommended five to nine servings of fruits and vegetables each day, with only 1.8% eating as many as eight servings per day and none reporting more. On a scale of "0" (does not eat junk food) to "7" (only eats junk food), respondents reported an average of 2.29 for a typical day. Twenty-one respondents reported primarily eating junk food for their entire diet, however.

Respondents (i.e., proxy raters) also rated their impression of the consumer's weight on a scale ranging from very underweight to very overweight. While nearly 90% were reported to be in the range of somewhat underweight to somewhat overweight, Traci (2000) found that these self-ratings tended to underestimate obesity when compared to body mass index (see also Chapter 2).

Respondents reported consuming an average of 2.6 caffeinated beverages (e.g., coffee, tea, soda, etc.), 4.5 noncaffeinated liquids, and 1.9 cups of milk on most days.

Oral Hygiene

Researchers and service providers have found that the oral health habits such as regular brushing and oral health status (e.g., untreated caries, gingivitis, loss of natural teeth, etc.) of adults with I/DD is poor (Cumella, Ransford, Lyons, & Burnham, 2000; Feldman et al. 1997; Gabre & Gahnberg, 1997). Presumably, poor oral hygiene might contribute to limitation due to social isolation, pain, depression, and nutritional deficits and gastrointestinal dysfunction from inability to eat properly. Oral health, in turn, is influenced by an array of factors, including health behavior practices. In our sample, 82.2% of respondents reported having their own teeth. Of those who did not have their own teeth, 5.4% had partial dentures, 8% had full dentures, and 5.4% had no teeth at all. Further, we found that 79.2% of respondents visited a dentist in the past year and that 44.3% had their teeth cleaned. On average, respondents reported brushing their teeth or dentures 2.52 times per day but 23.9% reported difficulty in cleaning their teeth or dentures.

The quality and duration of brushing is related to its effectiveness. For this population, the type of brush used and the social consequences of brushing may affect both the quality and duration of brushing (e.g., Bainbridge, Traci, Seekins, Peterson, Huckebe, & Millar, 2004). Thus, the environmental contingencies of reinforcement, related to the organization of the living environment, may play a significant role in maintaining oral health and managing limitation due to oral health problems.

Personal Hygiene and Appearance

Personal hygiene has a broad influence on both health and social limitation. Some aspects of personal hygiene may be directly related to secondary conditions. Others may lead to social limitation because poor hygiene can drive others away. Personal hygiene can include a wide range of practices as well as appearance issues.

Respondents rated the condition of toenails and fingernails on a seven-point scale, where "0" was poor condition and "7" was well cared for. On average, respondents rated the condition of fingernails as 5.7 and toenails as 5.8. While this is quite good, 13% and 14% of respondents reported a rating of three or less (poor) for the care of their fingernails and toenails, respectively.

Respondents reported that 58.4% of consumers bathed once or more per day but that 8.8% bathed two or fewer times per week. Similarly, 51.4% of consumers were reported to wash their hair at least once per day but 5.4% washed it 1 day per week or less. Eighty-seven percent of consumers reported being neatly dressed on at least 5 days each week.

Tobacco and Alcohol Use

Drug use has been shown to have a wide range of health effects for the general population (e.g., DHHS, 2001) but has not been linked to secondary conditions for the population of adults with I/DD. Presumably, tobacco use could increase limitation due to respiratory problems, lack of physical fitness, fatigue, and cancer, among others. Respondents in our sample reported smoking an average of 1.2 cigarettes per day—91.6% did not smoke at all but 3.8% smoked 20 or more cigarettes per day. Only 2.3% of respondents reported chewing tobacco.

Overall, the rate of alcohol consumption was very low, with only 4% reporting drinking any alcohol at all. The issue of exposure and access to alcohol and drugs is discussed under the section on environmental variables later in this chapter (see also Chapter 12).

Medications

Medications are generally thought of as treatment for various conditions. Their use may have both side effects, and short- and long-term negative consequences that limit participation, however. Some medications may increase limitation due to fatigue. Others (e.g., antibiotics, antiarrhythmics, barbiturates, and anticonvulsants) may make tooth brushing painful and contribute to oral health problems. As many as 400 medications can cause dry mouth, a risk factor for increased dental caries, periodontal inflammation, and oral infections (Ciancio, 2004). Respondents reported taking an average of 2.76 prescribed medications on a regular basis. Only 21.7% took no medications but 43.3% reported taking three or more prescribed medications on a regular basis.

Sexual Activity and Abuse

Sexual activity can affect a broad array of health conditions, as well as social and emotional functioning. Only 9.3% of respondents to our survey were reported as being sexually active, while 13.5% of proxy respondents indicated they did not know for sure whether the consumer was sexually active or not (see also Chapter 8).

Respondents reported that 16.3% of consumers had been abused at some time in the past, although, again, 33% of respondents indicated that they did not know for sure (see also Chapter 9).

ENVIRONMENTAL RISK VARIABLES

The New Paradigm of Disability argues that the environment is a major contributor to disability (e.g., Steinfeld & Danford, 1999). Several researchers are exploring the role of environmental variables in secondary conditions (e.g., Whiteneck, Gerhart, & Cusick, 2004). Some of these relationships can be complex. For example, Robertson and her colleagues (2000) found that individuals living in less restrictive environments reported higher rates of obesity and poorer diet, but higher levels of physical activity. Similarly, LaPlante, Kaye, Kang, and Harrington (2004) found adverse health effects associated with inadequate hours of personal assistance. Still, there is no consistent theory of how the environment affects secondary conditions that suggest either a comprehensive set of variables, their relationship to secondary conditions, or methods to assess these.

We collected data about stressful life changes that we reported elsewhere (Traci, 2000). Overall, consumers reported experiencing an average of 4.48 stressful life changes over the course of a year. Thirty-two percent reported experiencing six or more stressful life changes, however. We also collected data on a range of environmental issues, including changes in living arrangements, toxic exposure, service and support quality, assistive aids, and transportation.

Changes in Living Environments

Table 13-4 presents the distribution of respondents across the types of living situations. Such arrangements can have subtle but direct influences on the experience of limitations due to secondary conditions. For example, several researchers have found that weight increases (e.g., Robertson et al., 2000) and oral hygiene practices decline (Horowitz et. al., 2000) as individuals with I/DD move from more to less restrictive arrangements. Service providers and advocates have also been concerned about increases in isolation and possible depression in such moves.

Change, in and of itself, can be a risk factor for deleterious health consequences. Eighty-two percent of respondents reported no change in living arrangement over the previous year but 14% reported a move to a less restrictive environment. While moving to a less restrictive environment may enhance a wide range of values (e.g., independence), without adequate supports, such a move may negatively affect the individual's health and participation. These issues deserve more attention. Specifically, strategies for mitigating the harmful effects need to be designed and implemented to ensure success.

Exposure to Toxic Agents

While the rate of smoking appears to be quite low in this population, 22% of respondents reported that consumers were exposed to second-hand smoke in 20% or more

TABLE 13-4 *Percentage Distribution of Respondents Across Living Situations (N = 635)*

Group home	26.3
Supported living arrangement	22.8
Family home	18.2
Independent residence	14.0
Intensive group home	13.3
Institution	5.5
Foster home	2.1

of their daily living environments. Alcohol was also easily available to the consumer. Moreover, 10% of respondents reported that one or more of a consumer's peers abused alcohol or drugs (see also Chapter 12).

Service and Support Quality

One way to assess treatment quality related to secondary conditions is to assess the number of formal individualized habilitation plans (IHP) to address secondary conditions that are in place. These may either manage existing conditions or prevent limitations due to secondary conditions. Respondents reported an average of 3.2 IHPs addressing secondary conditions. Thirty-five percent reported having no IHP to address existing secondary conditions, however.

Another measure of the quality of service programs is the degree to which personal assistants are familiar with various signs and symptoms of problems. Urinary tract infections (UTI) can be common treatable secondary conditions. Nineteen percent of respondents indicated that they were not sure of the signs of a UTI, however.

Assistive Aids

For many people with I/DD, assistive technology can be one of the most important facilitators available. Sixty-five percent of respondents reported that assistive technology was not needed. Of the rest, 7% reported that consumers did not have access to the equipment they needed—this in a system organized specifically to provide support to this population. Further, respondents indicated that 50% of the equipment was very appropriate to meeting the consumers' needs but that 8% was inappropriate. Finally, 48% of respondents reported using memory-enhancing environmental supports.

Transportation

The lack of transportation is consistently one of the most significant problems reported by people with I/DD and those who serve them (e.g., Bernier & Seekins, 1999). Transportation is often critical to securing medical services and is also often the key to a broad range of opportunities to participate in community life. Seventy-four percent of respondents were able to get where they needed to go 80% or more of the time. Five percent were unable to get where they needed to go 80% or more of the time.

EXAMINATION OF RELATIONSHIPS BETWEEN RISK FACTORS AND SECONDARY CONDITIONS

Using this same data set of 749 respondents, we examined the correlations between six risk factors hypothesized to affect limitations due to the two secondary conditions of weight and physical conditioning problems. The risk factors included age, daily consumption of fruits and vegetables, consumption of junk food, days per week engaging in activities that substantially raised heart rate, rating of daily activity level (ranging from very active to very sedentary), and number of medications. Table 13-5 presents the Pearson correlation indices describing the strength and direction of relationships.

As can be seen from this table, the number of hours of limitation associated with the secondary conditions of weight and physical conditioning problems are significantly associated with one another. In general, individuals who reported eating more junk food, raising their heart rate fewer days during the week, engaging in more sedentary behavior, and taking more medication reported greater limitations due to weight and due to physical conditioning problems. In addition, older individuals tended to report greater limitations due to physical conditioning problems.

Table 13-5 also shows relationships among the risk factors. For example, as the amount of junk food consumed increased, the daily consumption of fruits and vegetables declined. Similarly, as the level of reported daily activity became more sedentary, the number of days with heart-raising physical activity declined.

We also examined the potential effects of changes in personal assistants and changes in living arrangement on secondary conditions and related health variables. We found positive and significant correlations among turnover of personal assistants, limitation due to secondary conditions, and medical service utilization (Seekins, Traci, & Szalda-Petree, 1999). Further, those who moved to a less restrictive living arrangement in the past year (14.1%) experienced more hours of limitation associated with injury-related secondary conditions, depression, and weight and conditioning problems than those in the sample who had not changed living arrangements.

These preliminary results suggest the types of analyses that might be conducted to establish a science of secondary conditions risk appraisal. Further data collection should emphasize both larger and more diverse samples, as well as longitudinal measures. In addition, conceptually, research might be expected to construct estimates of gains in achievable participation to parallel HRA's achievable age predictions.

TABLE 13-5 *Correlation Matrix for Six Risk and Protective Factors and the Secondary Conditions of Weight and Conditioning Problems*

	WEIGHT PROBLEMS	PHYSICAL CONDITIONING PROBLEMS	AGE	DAILY FRUITS AND VEGETABLES	JUNK FOOD EATEN	DAYS PER WEEK RAISING HEART RATE	AVERAGE DAILY ACTIVITY LEVEL	NUMBER OF MEDICATIONS
Weight problems	1.000							
Physical conditioning problems	.606**	1.000						
Age	−.015	.174**	1.000					
Daily fruits and vegetables	.012	−.035	−.077	1.000				
Junk food eaten	.118**	.111**	−.216**	−.370**	1.000			
Days per week raising heart rate	−.014**	−.144**	−.128**	.031	.041	1.000		
Average daily activity level	.285**	.417**	.149**	.010	.005	−.485**	1.000	
Number of medications	.154**	.263**	.230**	.228**	−.146**	−.124**	.252**	1.000

**Significant at *p* < .01.

Discussion and Recommendations

In general, it appears that the overall health of adults with I/DD living in supported living arrangements is good. Moreover, their years of healthy and productive life appear to have been increasing. At the same time, there appears to be room for improvement, as risk factors appear at increased levels when compared to population guidelines or the practice of the general population.

The literature on the health status and risk factors experienced by adults with I/DD, and our own research reported here, point to a wide range of behavioral variables affecting health outcomes. In particular, physical activity, diet and weight, and oral hygiene appear to be three behavior risk factors of potential significance reported across most studies. Service providers might work to bring dietary intake more in line with recommended patterns, increase the frequency and duration of physical activity, and improve oral hygiene.

Similarly, the type of living situation or change in living situation is an environmental variable that may pose risks to some individuals. Given the finding that some risks appear to increase with moves to less restrictive environments, advocates and program planners should develop systems to support healthy lifestyles in increasingly independent settings. Some may view this objective to be in conflict with the values of independence and choice implied in moving to a less restrictive situation. Nonetheless, by virtue of their participation in the structured service system, the participants acknowledge that they are in need of some level of support provided by society. At the very minimum, service providers should provide enough education and training to ensure that consumers can make informed choices about their health and lifestyle.

Several steps could be taken to improve health education and health promotion in ways that are consistent with the philosophy of informed choice. First, a structured system of secondary conditions risk appraisal would be a very useful adjunct to the annual individual habilitation planning process. Traci and her colleagues (2002) describe the role risk and secondary conditions appraisal might play in both individual habilitation planning and inservice system development. Figure 13-2 outlines the components of the model that would be involved in a behavioral health-monitoring and promotion system. The model illustrates a method for systematically addressing the prevention and management of secondary conditions among adult consumers of developmental disabilities service programs. Such a model would be anchored on one end with a site-based (i.e., local services) individual risk assessment and management system and, on the other end, by a state's developmental disabilities and health agencies. These agencies would monitor population health and risks, and would develop system wide interventions to target selected conditions of high prevalence or cost.

Such a system could also contribute to or fit within critical incident reporting systems that the Centers for Medicare and Medicaid Services (2003) are encouraging states to develop. These systems are needed to balance the goals of autonomy with the needs for safety and security as individuals move from institutional to self-directed supports.

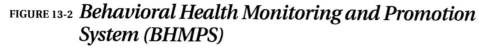

FIGURE 13-2 *Behavioral Health Monitoring and Promotion System (BHMPS)*

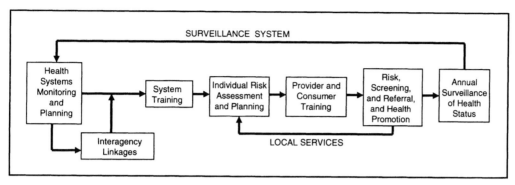

There is a need to understand the range of risk factors affecting the morbidity of this population. To do so, researchers will need to collect data from more representative samples and to do so over time. Researchers might first collect data on a broad range of risk and protective factors from samples that reflect the population of people with I/DD. Particular attention might be given to understanding the interaction between the type of living environment (i.e., degree of supervision, structure, etc.), risk factors, and health outcomes.

Not all of the environmental and risk variables may prove to be important or predictive. More data and analysis are needed to link risk and protective variables to limitations due to secondary conditions. Further, cost-effectiveness analyses should be conducted to determine whether interventions designed to improve secondary risk assessment scores can be justified economically, from both individual preference and societal perspectives.

Not all individuals with I/DD live or work within structured community services systems. The majority live at home and many with mild limitations live quite comfortably and effectively on their own. Still, researchers should explore secondary conditions risk appraisal for each group under the presumption that living arrangement and impairment interact to present different risk profiles. Further, the effectiveness of any interventions is likely to be affected dramatically by the differences in contexts.

Researchers will also need to examine the variation in risk profiles and outcomes across impairment groups. Individuals with some specific conditions (e.g., Down syndrome) may be more or less sensitive to specific risk factors. Researchers and service providers developing interventions to promote health will have to tailor programs to these variations in profiles, as well as the variation in impairments.

Most of the local agencies that provide community services and supports participate in one or more accreditation systems. These accreditation bodies should develop health and wellness standards to include in their accreditation reviews. Such standards could set clear expectations for practice and provide common, easily available tools for meeting those standards.

The existing community-based service system for adults with I/DD is not the only formal system that has responsibilities for promoting the health of this population.

The Americans with Disabilities Act (1990) makes it clear that all public programs must make their services and products available to people with I/DD. Those responsible for developing health education programs (e.g., federal agencies, national nonprofit health organizations, state departments of public health, etc.) need to include accommodations for the unique needs of this population (e.g., literacy, assistance in reading and interpreting, etc.) as they develop and deliver their programs.

People with I/DD are an important part of every American community today. Many live and work within structured systems of supports. While these systems have been designed to maximize choice and independence, they have not typically put health education and wellness high on their agenda. Researchers, service providers, policy makers, advocates, and consumers need to ensure that health and the various pathways to achieving health are available as choices, as well. The purpose is not to improve the health status of the population, in and of itself. Rather, it is to recognize that health is a foundation for participation in community life.

ACKNOWLEDGMENTS

Preparation of this manuscript was supported, in part, by grants from the Centers for Disease Control and from the National Institute on Disability and Rehabilitation Research. The authors wish to thank the staff of the many service corporations who took time from their busy and important work to help complete the survey instruments. We thank the many consumers and agency staff who gave of their time to the project described here. We are particularly indebted to the administrators of the community service agencies for their support and trust.

REFERENCES

Americans with Disabilities Act of 1990, P. L. 101-336, 104 Stat. 328 (1991).

Andresen, E. M., Fitch, C. A., McLendon, P. M., & Meyers, A. R. (2000). Reliability and validity of disability questions for US Census 2000. *American Journal of Public Health, 90,* 1297–1299.

Bainbridge, D. B., Traci, M. A., Seekins, T., Peterson, S., Huckebe, R., & Millar, S. (2004). *Oral health program for adults with intellectual and/or developmental disabilities: Results of a pilot study.* Missoula, MT: Rural Institute on Disabilities, The University of Montana.

Bernier, B., & Seekins, T. (1999). Rural transportation voucher program for people with disabilities: Three case studies. *Journal of Transportation and Statistics, 2*(1), 61–70.

Brandt, E. N., & Pope, A. M. (1997). Disability and the environment. In *Enabling America: Assessing the role of rehabilitation science and engineering* (pp. 147–169). Washington, DC: National Academy Press.

Ciancio, S. G. (2004). Medications' impact on oral health. *Journal of American Dental Association, 135,* 1440–1448.

Centers for Medicare and Medicaid Services (2003). *Home and community-based services: From institutional care to self-directed supports & services.* Retrieved January 11, 2005, from: http://www.cms.hhs.gov/newfreedom/528hill.pdf

Cumella, S., Ransford, N., Lyons, J., & Burnham, H. (2000). Needs for oral care among people with intellectual disability not in contact with community dental services. *Journal of Intellectual Disability Research, 44,* 45–52.

Doerr, B. T., & Hutchins, E. (1981). Health risk appraisal: Process, problems, and prospects for nursing practice and research. *Nursing Research, 30,* 299–306.

Feldman, C., Giniger, M., Sanders, M., Saporito, R., Zohn, H. K., & Perlman, S. P. (1997). Special smiles: Assessing the feasibility of epidemiologic data collection. *Journal of the American Dental Association, 128*, 1687–1696.

Foxman, B., & Edington, D. W. (1987). The accuracy of health risk appraisal in predicting mortality. *American Journal of Public Health, 77*, 971–974.

Frey, L., Szalda-Petree, A., Traci, M. A., & Seekins, T. (2001). Prevention of secondary health conditions in adults with developmental disabilities: A review of the literature. *Disability and Rehabilitation, 23*, 361–369.

Gabre, P., & Gahnberg, L. (1997). Inter-relationships among degree of mental retardation, living arrangements, and dental health in adults with mental retardation. *Special Care Dentistry, 17*, 7–12.

Gazmararian, J. A., Foxman, B., Yen, L. T., Morgenstern, H., & Eddington, D. W. (1991). Comparing the predictive accuracy of health risk appraisal: The Centers for Disease Control versus Carter Center program. *American Journal of Public Health, 81*, 1296–1301.

Havercamp, S. M., Scandlin, D., & Roth, M. (2004). Health disparities among adults with developmental disabilities, adults with other disabilities, and adults not reporting disability in North Carolina. *Public Health Reports, 119*, 418–426.

Hayden, M. G., & Kim, S. H. (2002). *Health status, health care utilization patterns, and health care outcomes of persons with intellectual disabilities: A review of the literature.* Policy Research Brief. Minneapolis, MN: University of Minnesota, Institute on Community Integration.

Horowitz, S. M., Kerker, B. D., Owens, P. L., & Zigler, E. (2000). *The health status and needs of individuals with mental retardation.* New Haven, CT: Department of Epidemiology and Public Health, Yale University School of Medicine and Department of Psychology. Retrieved January 4, 2005, from: http://www.specialolympics.org/NR/rdonlyres/e5lq5czkjv5vwulp5lx5tmny4mcwh yj5vq6euizrooqcaekeuvmkg75fd6wnj62nhlsprlb7tg4gwqtu4xffauxzsge/healthstatus_needs.pdf

LaPlante, M. P., Kaye, H. S., Kang, T., & Harrington, C. (2004). Unmet needs for personal assistance services: Estimating the shortfall in hours of help and adverse consequences. *Journal of Gerontology: Series B: Psychological Science and Social Sciences, 59B*(2): S98–S108.

Lollar, D. J. (Ed). (1994, February). *Preventing secondary conditions associated with spina bifida or cerebral palsy: Proceedings and recommendations of a symposium.* Washington, DC: Spina Bifida Association of America.

Marge, M. (1988). Health promotion for persons with disabilities: Moving beyond rehabilitation. *American Journal of Health Promotion, 2*, 29–44.

Musich, S., Adams, L., DeWolf, G., & Edington, D. W. (2001). A case study of 10-year health risk appraisal participation patterns in a comprehensive health promotion program. *American Journal of Health Promotion, 15*, 237–240.

Ozminkowski, R. J., Goetzel, R. Z., Santoro, J., Saenz, B., Eley, C., & Gorsky, B. (2004). Estimating risk reduction required to break even in a health promotion program. *American Journal of Health Promotion, 18*, 316–325.

Pack, R. P., Wallander, J. L., & Browne, D. (1998). Health risk behaviors of African American adolescents with mild mental retardation: Prevalence depends on measurement method. *American Journal of Mental Retardation, 102*, 409–420.

Pope, A. M. (1992). Preventing secondary conditions. *Mental Retardation, 30*, 347–354.

Pope, A. M., & Tarlov, A. R. (1991). *Disability in America: Toward a national agenda for prevention.* Washington, DC: National Academy Press.

Rice, M. W., & Turpin, L. (1996). Medical expenditures for people with disabilities. *Disability Statistics Abstract, 12*, 1–4.

Robertson, J., Emerson, E., Gregary, N., Hatton, C., Rutner, S., Kessissoglou, S., & Hallam, A. (2000). Lifestyle related risk factors for poor health in residential settings for people with intellectual disabilities. *Research in Developmental Disabilities, 21*, 469–486.

Seekins, T., Traci, M. A., & Szalda-Petree, A. (1999). Preventing and managing secondary conditions experienced by people with disabilities: Roles for personal assistants providers. *Journal of Health and Human Services Administration, 22,* 259–269.

Seelman, K., & Sweeney, S. (1995). The changing universe of disability. *American Rehabilitation, Autumn-Winter,* 2–13.

Steinfeld, E., & Danford, G. S. (1999). *Enabling environments: Measuring the impact of environment on disability and rehabilitation.* New York: Kluwer Academic/Plenum.

Todorov, A., & Kirchner, C. (2000). Bias in proxies' report of disability: Data from the National Health Interview Survey on Disability. *American Journal of Public Health, 90,* 1248–1253.

Traci, M. A. (2000). Life events as potential predictors of secondary conditions. *Dissertation Abstracts International.*

Traci, M. A., Seekins, T., Szalda-Petree, A. C., & Ravesloot, C. H. (2002). Assessing secondary conditions among adults with developmental disabilities: A preliminary study. *Mental Retardation, 40,* 119–131.

U.S. Department of Health and Human Services. (1996). *Physical activity and health: A report to the Surgeon General.* Atlanta, GA: Centers for Disease Control and Prevention, National Center for Chronic Disease Prevention and Health Promotion.

U.S. Department of Health and Human Services. (2000). *Healthy people 2010: Understanding and improving health* (2nd ed.). Washington, DC: U.S. Government Printing Office.

U.S. Department of Health and Human Services. (2001). *Treating tobacco use and dependency: A public health service sponsored clinical guideline.* Retrieved January 6, 2005, from: *http:// www.ncbi,nim.gov/books/bv.fcgi)*

Whiteneck, G., Gerhart, K. A., & Cusick, C. P. (2004). Identifying environmental factors that influence the outcomes of people with traumatic brain injury. *Journal of Health Trauma Rehabilitation, 19,* 191–204.

Yen, L., McDonald, T., Hirschland, D., & Edington, D. W. (2003). Association between wellness score from a health risk appraisal and prospective medical claims costs. *Journal of Occupational and Environmental Medicine, 45,* 1049–1057.

14

CAN YOU REALLY BE HEALTHY AS A PERSON WITH A DISABILITY?

Teresa Moore and Juliana Huereña

D isability and health promotion may seem like they don't go together. So can you *really* be healthy as a person **with** a disability?

When I talk to most of my friends, they say that their doctors and family members often blame all illnesses and injuries on their disability and they feel that some of their basic health issues are overlooked. So, how much is related? In reality, just like for a person without a disability, many items come into play; this is the wonderful part of being human.

I am going to try to relate my personal life and my friends' lives to what my fellow presenters have informed us about throughout this conference. It is by no means a replacement for statistics or studies, clinical data, or clinical case studies, but I seek to complement data with the real life of a person with a disability. This is natural for me, being a self-advocate, as I want to use self-determination to gain more control over my health.

I will highlight some general themes as I review the topics that were presented today. The first presentation was on hypertension. I learned that people of color are more at-risk of getting hypertension. Adding a disability and the likelihood of living in poverty adds greatly to the implications of having this chronic illness, and this fact is often not mentioned in educational materials, on TV, or in research. Dr. Draheim spoke of the daily need for exercise.

It is important to note that for people with disabilities living in residential settings, staff preparation of healthy food is not a priority beyond those special diets that have been ordered by a physician. Not having the right diet or eating the right quantity and quality of food plays into the person with disability's lifestyle as compared to the general public. This also applies to someone with a disability who is not living in a residential setting, but is living in poverty. This individual often doesn't have the money to acquire the right food.

Many of my friends have said that their family and staff had discouraged them from cooking because of safety concerns. They have said that they would eat only what they can make, but they do not have that choice. "Mom said I could not use the stove, but that I could use the microwave," one friend said. Many commercially prepared microwave foods are high in sodium and other chemicals and are the only options for many people with disabilities.

There are also issues with medications used for hypertension. The first relates to the side effects of the medication, such as fatigue and dry mouth. The second are the consistent levels of chemicals in your body and unknown side effects. Persons with disabilities need to be aware of these side effects and interactions with other drugs they may be taking.

The second presentation by Dr. Bandini was on obesity. Being overweight is a subject that many of us hear about as affecting the general population. We don't often have the opportunity to learn what it means to those of us who have disabilities. We don't know if our conditions that cause disability affect our weight and if they do, in what way.

Our weight is also affected by our environment, for example, our living situation. This can mean what food is available to us, our knowledge of proper nutrition, our financial ability to purchase healthy food, and how much exercise we get or are encouraged to get. Support staff is not allowed to transport me to the grocery store so I don't think about it. I don't know what is available for me to purchase and I don't often think of the right foods when I do purchase food. Food is a comfort; food makes me feel better, especially junk food. If you share a place with folks in a group home, you have a tendency to buy in volume and cheaply. Staff may not know how to prepare food, and will often buy what is easy to make, with low cost being a priority. For me, staff are inexperienced in preparing healthy meals or suggesting new things and providing a healthy variety of foods. Many staff members are also in the same situation, living in poverty, being obese, and having cultural and language barriers.

Furthermore, people with disabilities often have slower metabolisms (e.g., as in Down syndrome). Many who experience obesity tell me that they do not receive positive support to be more active or to care more about what they eat in order to assist them when weight is an issue.

The third and fourth presentations had to do with respiratory health and swallowing disorders in adults and children. Dr. Sheppard spoke about dysphagia and how refusing to eat may be a sign of this disorder. I know that I do not enjoy eating anymore. I have found that the things that I like to eat result in consequences for me. Dr. Lefton-Grief spoke about many of the same things as they relate to children.

Dr. Coulter presented the fifth topic which was on epilepsy. He emphasized the need to know triggers for seizures and about auras, which are the signs that indicate that you are getting closer to having a seizure.

Dr. Benson spoke about mental health. She spoke about medications, therapies, and interpersonal skills that can be helpful.

Dr. Rimmer talked about the importance of physical activity. He spoke about the evidence on falls, balance, and need for community education to change exercise habits.

Dr. Larson was the eighth presenter and spoke about access to health care. She spoke about general health and dental needs, communication, attitudes of health care professionals, caregiver reporting, specialty doctors, unmet needs, specialty physicians, and reimbursement needs. One item that she mentioned was the need for exam tables and equipment to be accessible for people with a variety of physical problems.

Reproductive health was Dr. White-Scott's presentation topic. She emphasized that people with disabilities were often not seen as sexual beings by health care professionals. I know that consent is a major issue for people with disabilities regarding their reproductive health. Often, exams are done without the consent of people with disabilities and most times are done without the person with disabilities understanding why they need to be done.

The next three presentations dealt with violence (Dr. Sobsey), case management/care coordination (Dr. Northway), and alternative and complementary medicine (Dr. Hurvitz). Dr. Hurvitz mentioned that alternative and complementary medicine is not considered conventional medicine and that often persons with disabilities do not have these services available to them as Medicaid does not have this option among those for which reimbursement is available. The final presentations were on substance abuse/tobacco use (Dr. Minihan) and conceptual health promotion models (Dr. Cerrito).

After listening to these presentations and thinking of my own and my friends' lives, I know that people with disabilities need to learn: (1) to understand their diagnoses and health care needs, including secondary conditions and normal aging changes; (2) how to work with different health care professionals; (3) how to work with staff and caregivers to be more healthy; (4) how to take care of themselves; (5) how to cope with new and current diagnoses; (6) about their bodies and when something is wrong with them and how to seek help; (7) about their medications and why they need to take them; and (8) how to prevent secondary conditions from occurring or getting worse.

All people, regardless of age, race, or disability, desire to be healthy and to know how to care for themselves so that they may remain healthy or become healthier. This is not an unusual request. It is tiresome to hear from a health professional that "don't you know, you are disabled" so why would you want to participate in health-promoting behaviors? This is the time for all people with disabilities to be proactive and positive about their health. It is also a time for health professionals to become knowledgeable about disabilities and sensitive to all of our health care needs across the lifespan.

Individuals with disabilities WANT to be healthy! What they need is the skill to be successful self-advocates for their health needs, among other needs, and to receive ongoing support to achieve this goal. This involves first, a change in attitude and better communication. Educational materials must also be available, in understandable language, to inform persons with disabilities about: (1) healthy development across the lifespan, what to expect and how to respond (e.g., when to know when menopause is beginning and what types of symptoms they might expect to experience, or that changes in their eyesight and hearing may be due to aging, not their disability); (2) what health prevention measures are appropriate for their age, such as blood work to check for high cholesterol; (3) how to ask questions of family members to learn about family health problems; (4) how to begin an exercise program and what types of exercise are good for you; (5) how to find a doctor and other health professionals who will know how to take care of you; (6) how to get transportation to and from your home to a health care agency or hospital, or other places for eating, exercising, or having fun; (7) signs and symptoms of depression or other mental health problems; (8) how to deal with a fire, bad weather, or other types of emergencies; and (9) the need not to smoke or use drugs. Health professionals should also be available to discuss, in detail, any of these items, probably more than once, so that persons with disabilities are able to learn how to be more healthy and knowledgeable about their own health.

I have found that health professionals often don't take the time to consider what our health promotion needs are; what we need to do to be HEALTHY! It is important that health professionals do not look at our disability as an ILLNESS; it is not! Instead, we are individuals who need well care and ways to maintain or increase our level of health. We need health professionals to be educated first in the importance of health promotion, not just illness management. Then, we need them to understand that everyone is a person first and everyone should be treated the same! You really can be healthy as a person with a disability!

I appreciated listening to the presenters talk about the current state of research concerning health promotion in persons with intellectual and developmental disabilities. We have a long way to go, but I was happy that so much had been done. In the future, we must involve more people with disabilities in the research process in addition to asking them to participate. Federal agencies must see that supporting and funding such research will help us to be healthier. There are many people with disabilities who would be willing to serve on advisory committees to ensure that appropriate research is being done. I hope that we can continue to discuss these important topics and that these findings and future research will lead to better health care practice.

HEALTH PROMOTION FOR PERSONS WITH INTELLECTUAL/ DEVELOPMENTAL DISABILITIES

The State of Scientific Evidence

PHILADELPHIA MARRIOTT HOTEL, PHILADELPHIA, PA, JUNE 1, 2004

AGENDA

7:30 a.m.–8:00 a.m.	**REGISTRATION**
8:00 a.m.–8:40 a.m.	WELCOME AND INTRODUCTIONS

DOREEN CROSER, MS, Executive Director, American Association on Mental Retardation

LEILA BARKS, MS, ARNP, PhD(c), Chair, Health Promotion and Prevention Committee, American Association on Mental Retardation

JOSE CORDERO, M.D, MPH, Director, National Center on Birth Defects and Developmental Disabilities, Centers for Disease Control and Prevention

WENDY NEHRING, RN, PhD, FAAN, Board Member, American Association on Mental Retardation

BODY FUNCTIONS AND STRUCTURE

8:40 a.m.–9:00 a.m.	*Hypertension,* CHRISTOPHER C. DRAHEIM, PhD
9:00 a.m.–9:20 a.m.	*Obesity,* LINDA BANDINI, PhD, RD
9:20 a.m.–9:40 a.m.	*Respiratory Health, Nutrition, and Associated Swallowing Behaviors in Adults,* JUSTINE JOAN SHEPPARD, PhD, CCC/SLP
9:40 a.m.–10:00 a.m.	*Feeding/Swallowing Disorders in Children,* MAUREEN A. LEFTON-GREIF, PhD., CCC-SLP, BRS-S
10:00 a.m.–10:20 a.m.	*Epilepsy,* DAVID L. COULTER, MD
10:20 a.m.–10:40 a.m.	*Mental Health,* BETSEY A. BENSON, PhD
10:40 a.m.–11:00 a.m.	**MORNING BREAK**

11:00 a.m.–11:20 a.m.	**QUESTIONS**
	ACTIVITIES LIMITATION/ PARTICIPATION
11:20 a.m.–11:40 a.m.	*Physical Activity,* JAMES H. RIMMER, PhD
11:40 a.m.–12:00 noon	*Access to Health Care,* SHERYL A. LARSON, PhD
12:00 noon–12:20 p.m.	**QUESTIONS**
12:20 p.m.–1:20 p.m.	**LUNCH ON OWN**
	ENVIRONMENTAL FACTORS
1:20 p.m.–1:40 p.m.	*Reproductive Health,* SHERYL WHITE-SCOTT, MD, FACP
1:40 p.m.–2:00 p.m.	*Violence,* RICHARD SOBSEY, EdD
2:00 p.m.–2:20 p.m.	*Case Management/Care Coordination,* RUTH NORTHWAY, RNMH, ENB 805, Cert Ed, PhD
2:20 p.m.–2:40 p.m.	*Alternative and Complementary Medicine,* EDWARD A. HURVITZ, MD
2:40 p.m.–3:00 p.m.	**QUESTIONS**
3:00 p.m.–3:20 p.m.	**AFTERNOON BREAK**
	HEALTH RISKS
3:20 p.m.–3:40 p.m.	*Substance Abuse/Tobacco Use,* PAULA M. MINIHAN, PhD, MPH
3:40 p.m.–4:00 p.m.	*Health Risk Assessment Tools,* TOM SEEKINS, PhD
4:00 p.m.–4:20 p.m.	*Conceptual Health Promotion Models,* MARY CERRETO, PhD
4:20 p.m.–4:40 p.m.	*Response and Comments,* TERESA MOORE
4:40 p.m.–5:00 p.m.	**QUESTIONS AND COMMENTS**
5:00 p.m.–5:30 p.m.	**CONCLUSIONS**

CPSIA information can be obtained at www.ICGtesting.com
Printed in the USA
243624LV00001B/8/P

9 780940 898912